Hakumei & I

D0924788

🌿 Takuto Kashik

Translation: **TAYLOR ENGEL** ♣ Lettering: **ABIGAIL BLACKMAN**

This book is a work of fiction. Names, characters, places, and incidents are the product of the author's imagination or are used fictitiously. Any resemblance to actual events, locales, or persons, living or dead, is coincidental.

HAKUMEI TO MIKOCHI Volume 5
© Takuto Kashiki 2017
First published in Japan in 2017 by KADOKAWA CORPORATION, Tokyo.
English translation rights arranged with KADOKAWA CORPORATION, Tokyo through TUTTLE-MORI AGENCY, Inc., Tokyo.

English translation © 2019 by Yen Press, LLC

Yen Press, LLC supports the right to free expression and the value of copyright. The purpose of copyright is to encourage writers and artists to produce the creative works that enrich our culture.

The scanning, uploading, and distribution of this book without permission is a theft of the author's intellectual property. If you would like permission to use material from the book (other than for review purposes), please contact the publisher. Thank you for your support of the author's rights.

Yen Press
1290 Avenue of the Americas
New York, NY 10104

Visit us at yenpress.com
facebook.com/yenpress
twitter.com/yenpress
yenpress.tumblr.com
instagram.com/yenpress

First Yen Press Edition: April 2019

Yen Press is an imprint of Yen Press, LLC.
The Yen Press name and logo are trademarks of Yen Press, LLC.

The publisher is not responsible for websites (or their content) that are not owned by the publisher.

Library of Congress Control Number: 2018941284

ISBN: 978-1-9753-0295-5

10 9 8 7 6 5 4 3 2 1

WOR

Printed in the United States of America

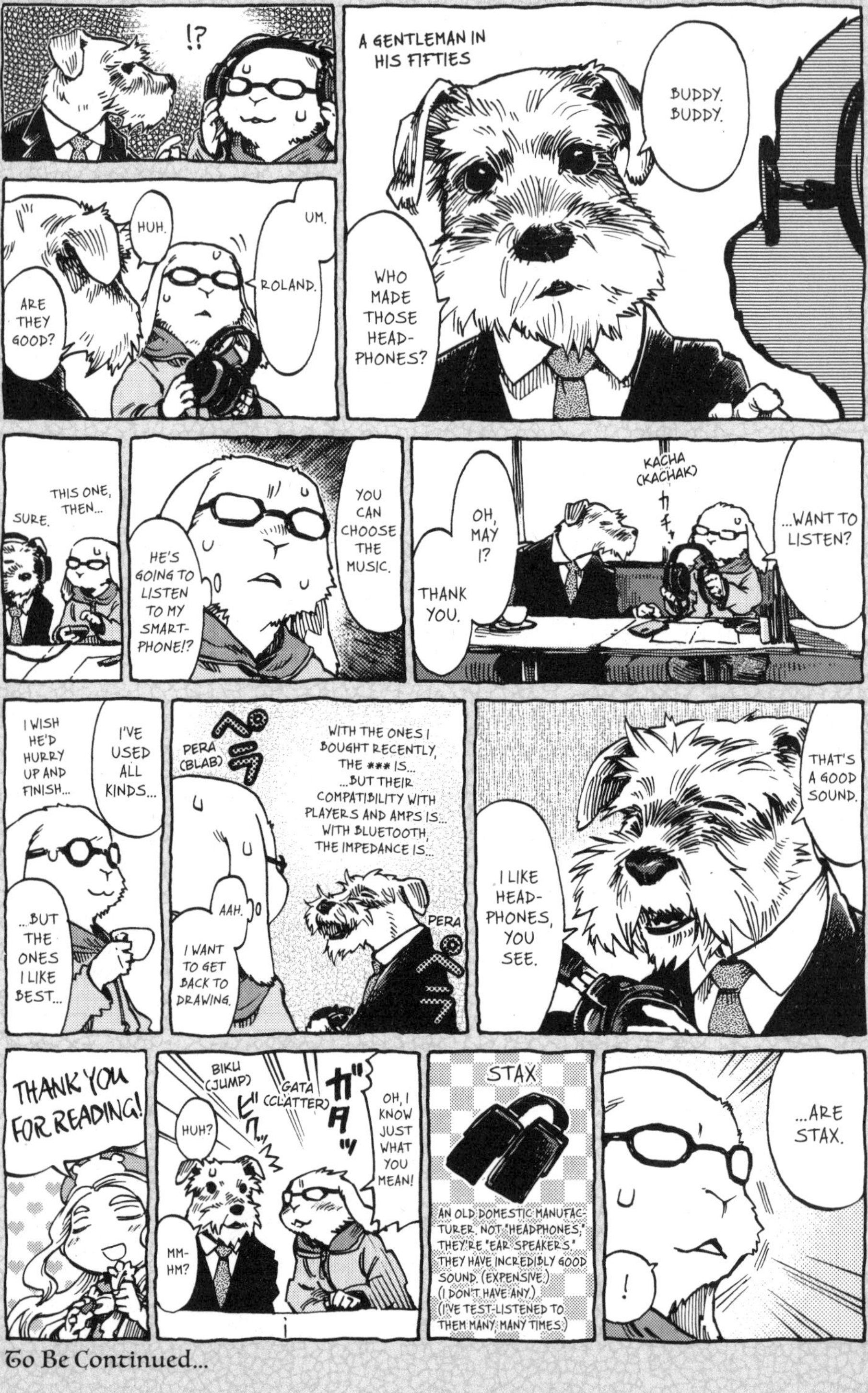
A GENTLEMAN IN HIS FIFTIES
BUDDY. BUDDY.
WHO MADE THOSE HEAD-PHONES?
!?
UM. ROLAND.
HUH.
ARE THEY GOOD?
...WANT TO LISTEN?
KACHA (KACHAK)
OH, MAY I?
THANK YOU.
YOU CAN CHOOSE THE MUSIC.
HE'S GOING TO LISTEN TO MY SMART-PHONE!?
THIS ONE, THEN...
SURE.
THAT'S A GOOD SOUND.
I LIKE HEAD-PHONES, YOU SEE.
WITH THE ONES I BOUGHT RECENTLY, THE *** IS... ...BUT THEIR COMPATIBILITY WITH PLAYERS AND AMPS IS... WITH BLUETOOTH, THE IMPEDANCE IS...
PERA (BLAB)
PERA
AAH.
I WANT TO GET BACK TO DRAWING.
I'VE USED ALL KINDS...
I WISH HE'D HURRY UP AND FINISH...
...BUT THE ONES I LIKE BEST...
...ARE STAX.
!
STAX
AN OLD DOMESTIC MANUFACTURER. NOT "HEADPHONES," THEY'RE "EAR SPEAKERS." THEY HAVE INCREDIBLY GOOD SOUND. (EXPENSIVE.) (I DON'T HAVE ANY.) (I'VE TEST-LISTENED TO THEM MANY, MANY TIMES.)
OH, I KNOW JUST WHAT YOU MEAN!
GATA (CLATTER)
BIKU (JUMP)
HUH?
MM-HM?
THANK YOU FOR READING!

To Be Continued...

SEP – – 2022

Hakumei & Mikochi 5
Tiny Little Life in the Woods

NO LONGER PROPERTY OF
SEATTLE PUBLIC LIBRARY

Takuto Kashiki

Contents

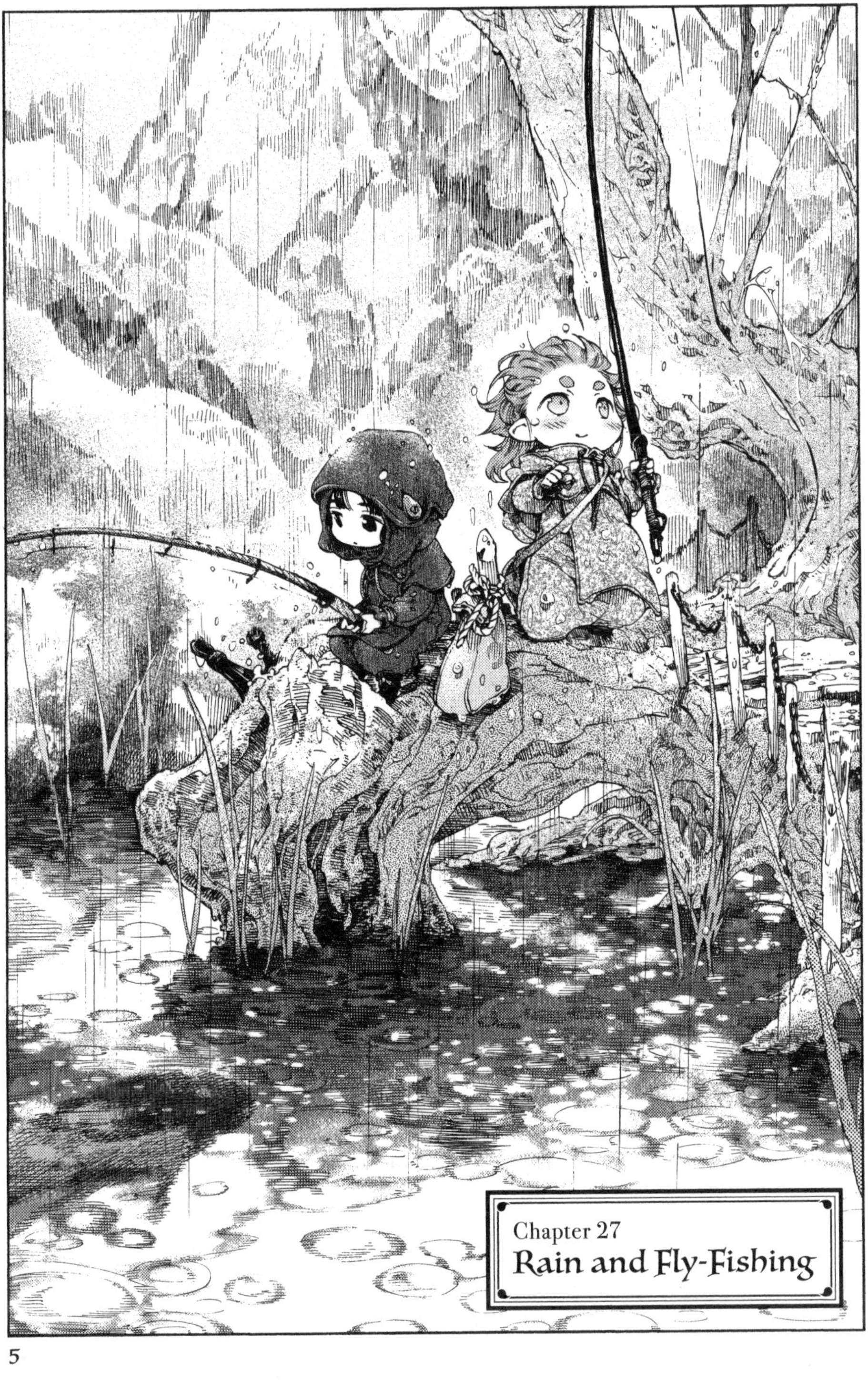
Chapter 27
Rain and Fly-Fishing

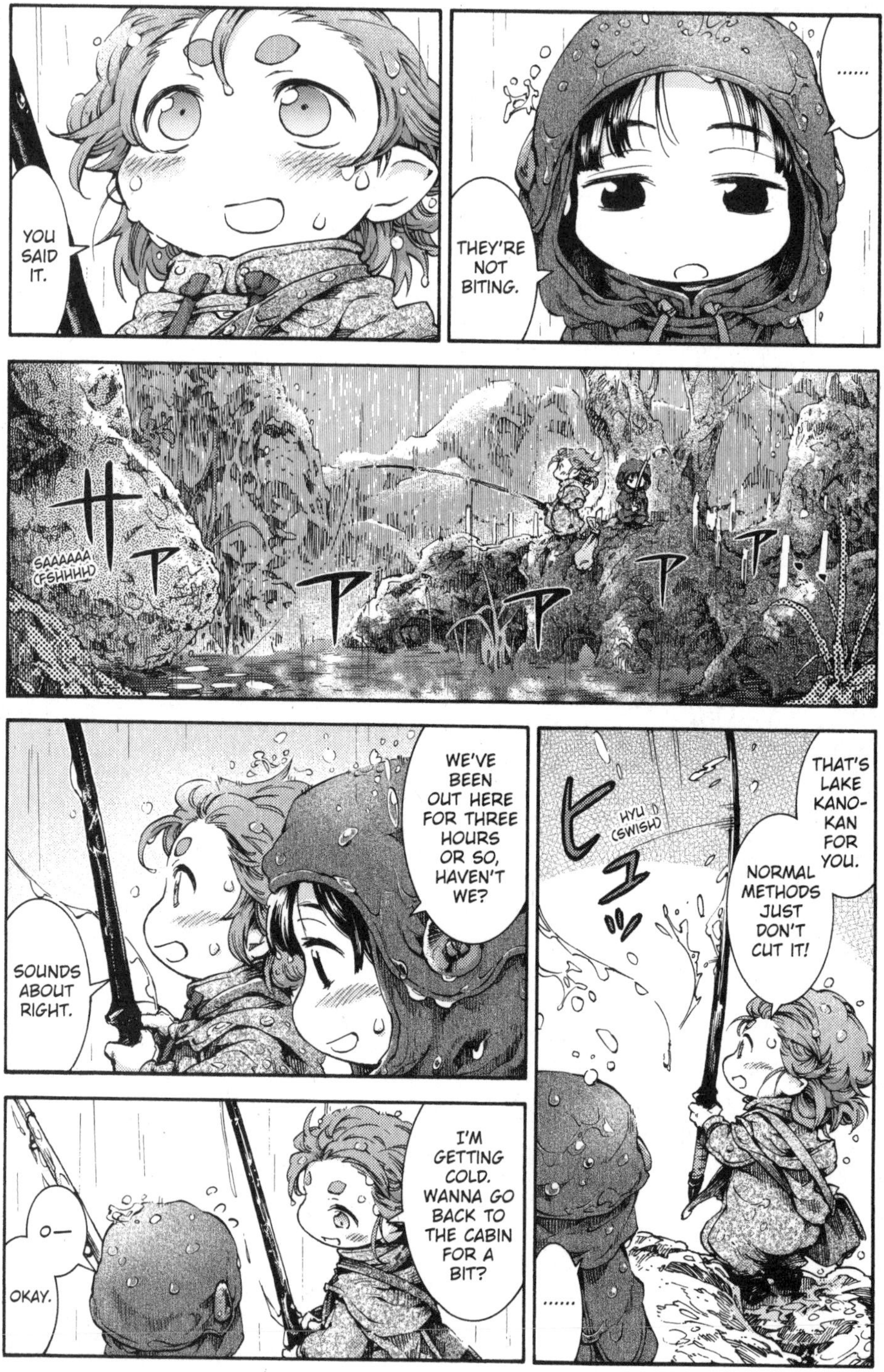
......
THEY'RE NOT BITING.
YOU SAID IT.
SAAAAAA (FSHHHH)
HYU (SWISH)
THAT'S LAKE KANO-KAN FOR YOU.
NORMAL METHODS JUST DON'T CUT IT!
......
WE'VE BEEN OUT HERE FOR THREE HOURS OR SO, HAVEN'T WE?
SOUNDS ABOUT RIGHT.
I'M GETTING COLD. WANNA GO BACK TO THE CABIN FOR A BIT?
O—
OKAY.

SIGN: KANOKAN FISHING CABIN

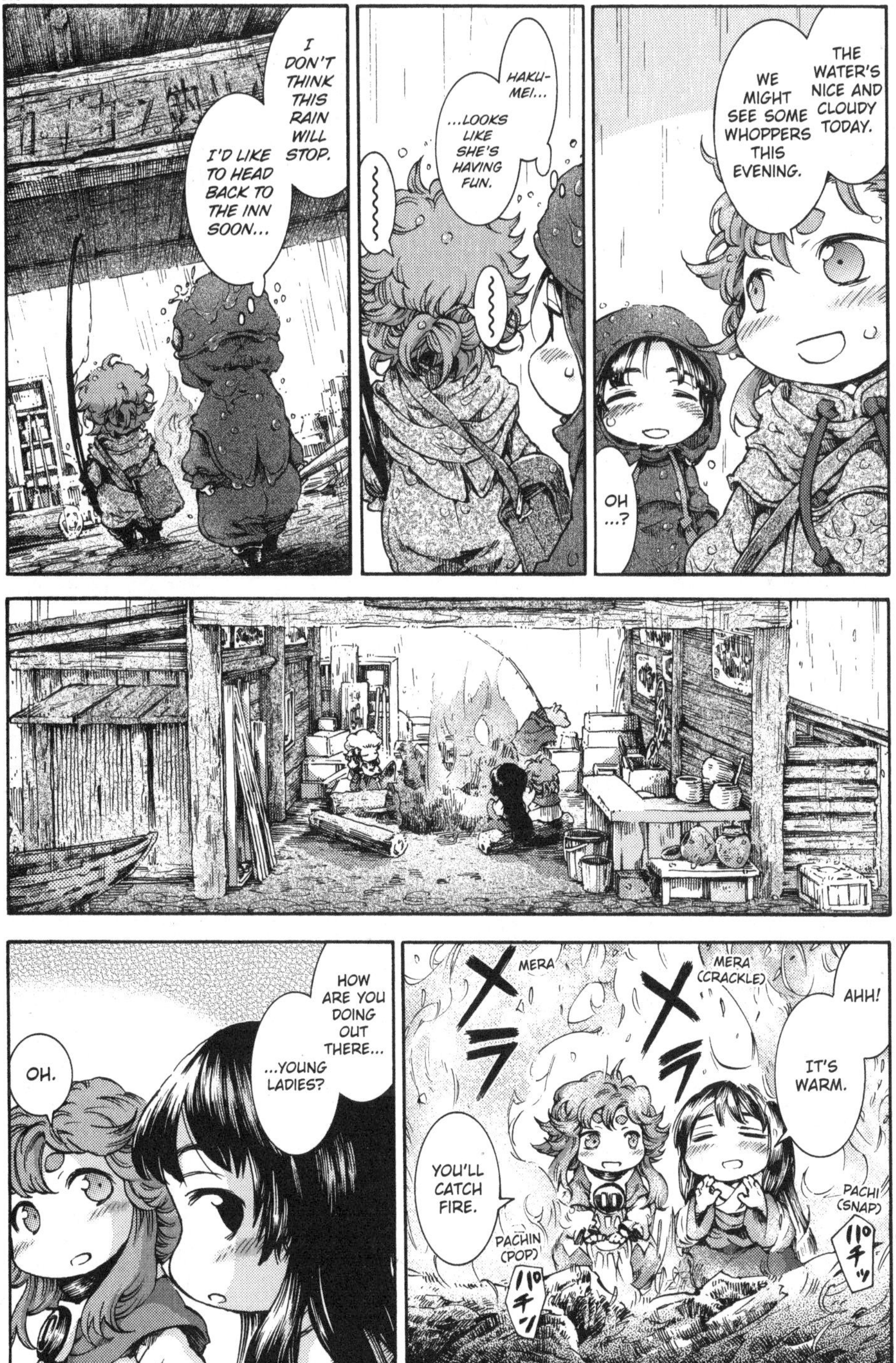
THE WATER'S NICE AND CLOUDY TODAY.
WE MIGHT SEE SOME WHOPPERS THIS EVENING.
OH ...?
HAKU-MEI...
...LOOKS LIKE SHE'S HAVING FUN.
I DON'T THINK THIS RAIN WILL STOP.
I'D LIKE TO HEAD BACK TO THE INN SOON...
AHH!
IT'S WARM.
MERA (CRACKLE)
メラ
MERA
メラ
YOU'LL CATCH FIRE.
PACHI (SNAP)
パチッ
PACHIN (POP)
パチン
HOW ARE YOU DOING OUT THERE...
...YOUNG LADIES?
OH.

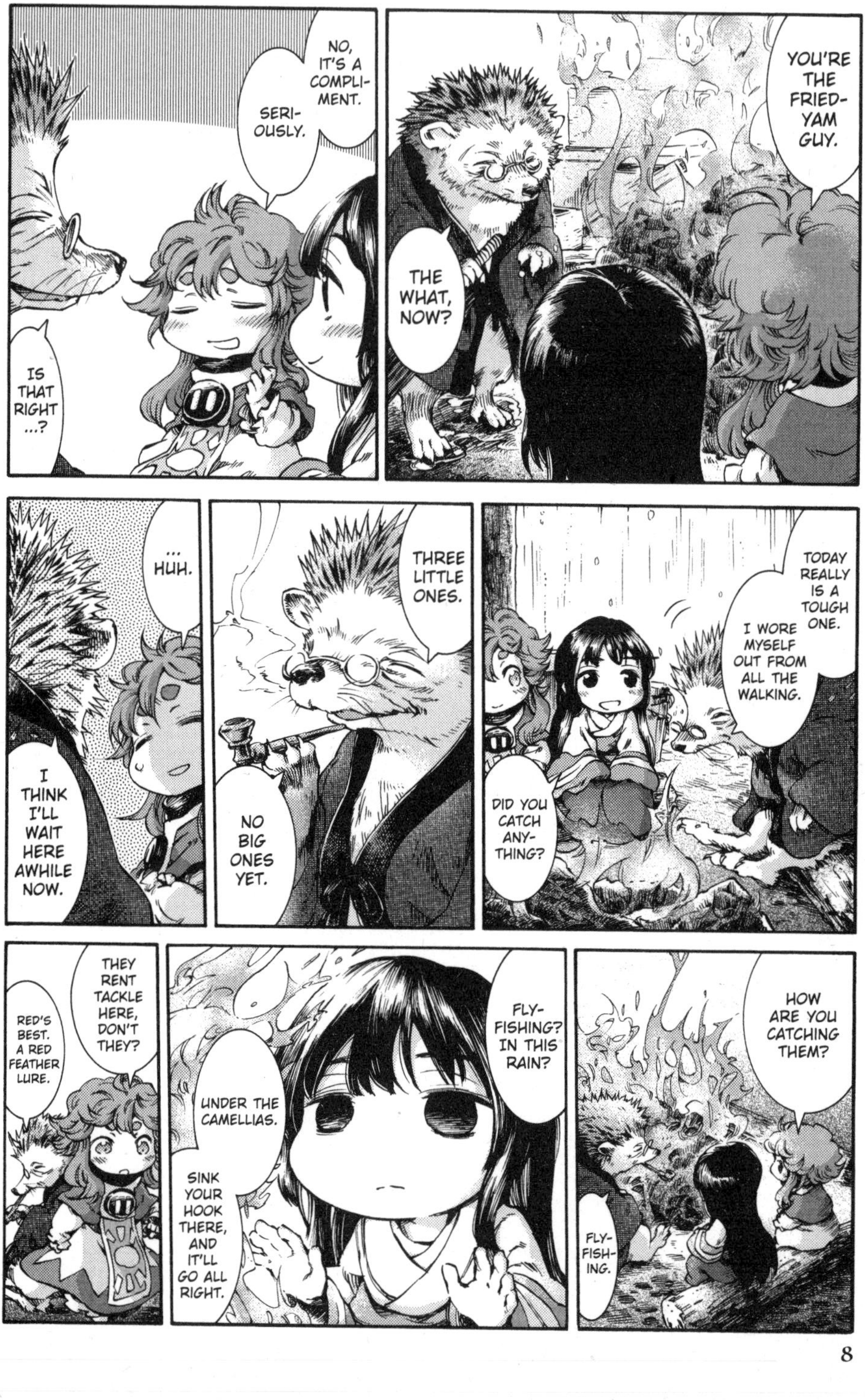
YOU'RE THE FRIED-YAM GUY.
THE WHAT, NOW?
NO, IT'S A COMPLIMENT.
SERIOUSLY.
IS THAT RIGHT ...?
TODAY REALLY IS A TOUGH ONE.
I WORE MYSELF OUT FROM ALL THE WALKING.
DID YOU CATCH ANYTHING?
THREE LITTLE ONES.
NO BIG ONES YET.
... HUH.
I THINK I'LL WAIT HERE AWHILE NOW.
HOW ARE YOU CATCHING THEM?
FLY-FISHING.
FLY-FISHING? IN THIS RAIN?
UNDER THE CAMELLIAS.
SINK YOUR HOOK THERE, AND IT'LL GO ALL RIGHT.
THEY RENT TACKLE HERE, DON'T THEY?
RED'S BEST. A RED FEATHER LURE.

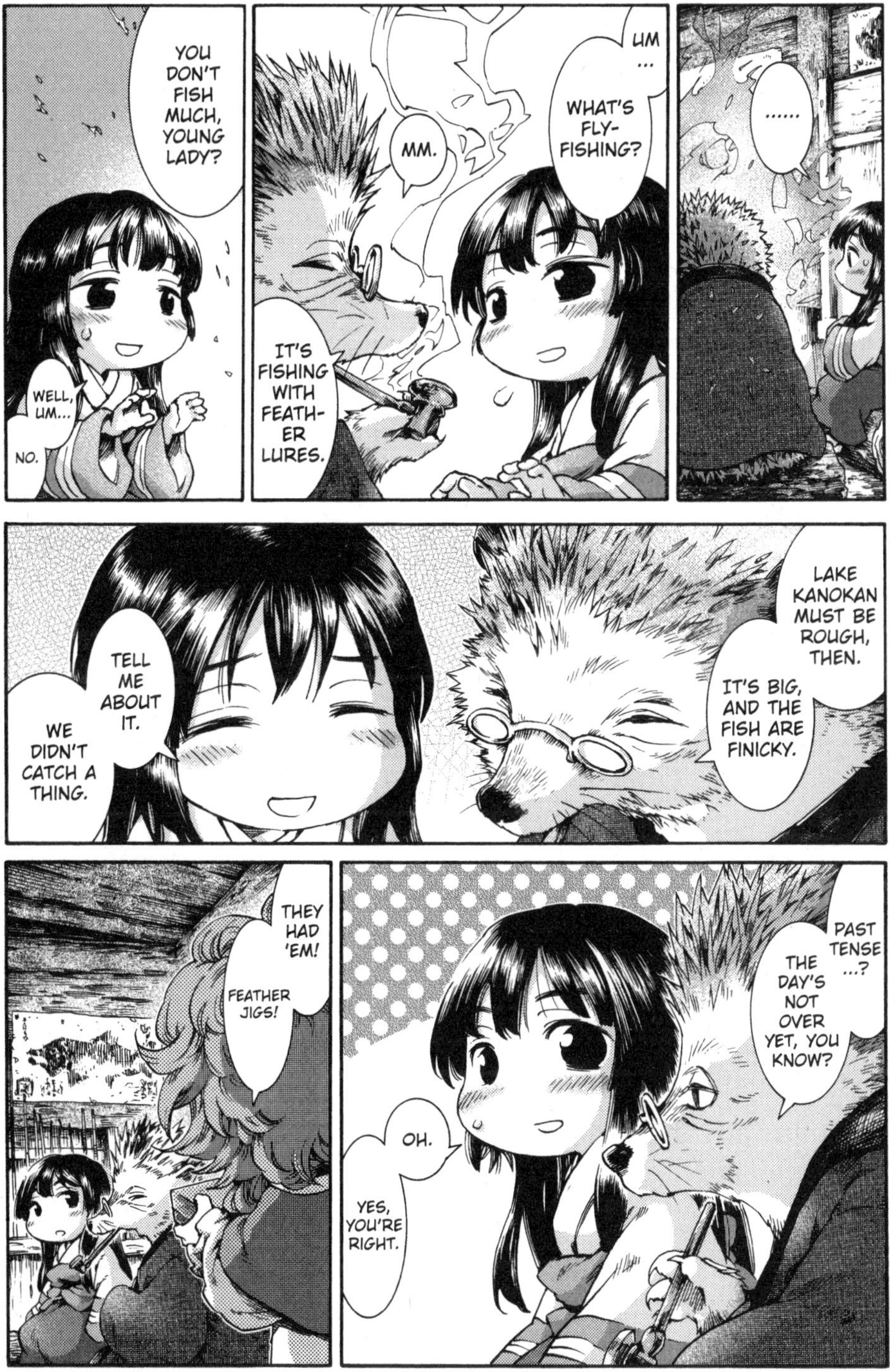
......
UM ...
WHAT'S FLY-FISHING?
MM.
IT'S FISHING WITH FEATHER LURES.
YOU DON'T FISH MUCH, YOUNG LADY?
WELL, UM...
NO.
LAKE KANOKAN MUST BE ROUGH, THEN.
IT'S BIG, AND THE FISH ARE FINICKY.
TELL ME ABOUT IT.
WE DIDN'T CATCH A THING.
PAST TENSE ...?
THE DAY'S NOT OVER YET, YOU KNOW?
OH.
YES, YOU'RE RIGHT.
THEY HAD 'EM!
FEATHER JIGS!

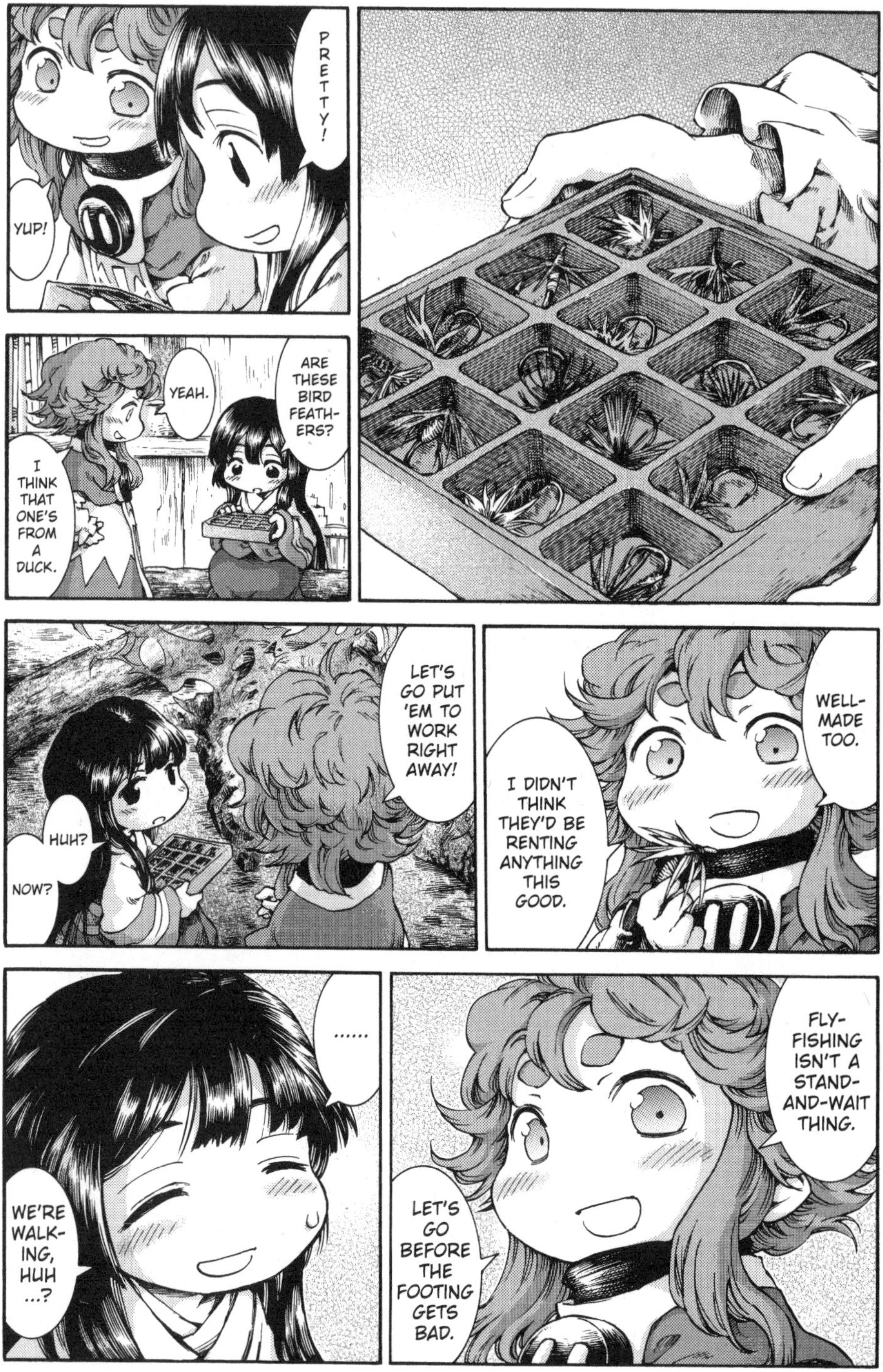
PRETTY!
YUP!
ARE THESE BIRD FEATHERS?
YEAH.
I THINK THAT ONE'S FROM A DUCK.
WELL-MADE TOO.
I DIDN'T THINK THEY'D BE RENTING ANYTHING THIS GOOD.
LET'S GO PUT 'EM TO WORK RIGHT AWAY!
HUH?
NOW?
FLY-FISHING ISN'T A STAND-AND-WAIT THING.
LET'S GO BEFORE THE FOOTING GETS BAD.
......
WE'RE WALKING, HUH ...?

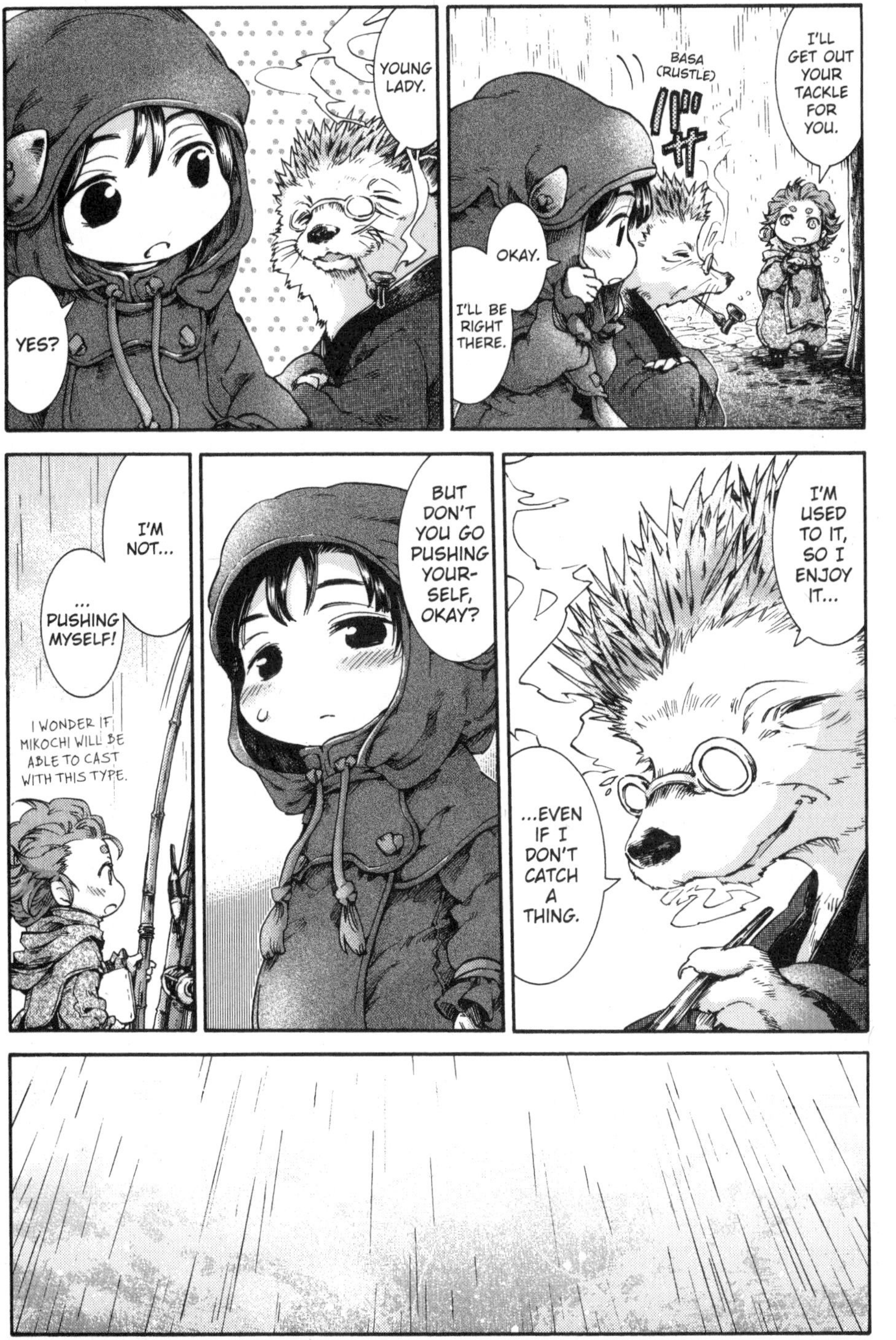
I'LL GET OUT YOUR TACKLE FOR YOU.
BASA (RUSTLE)
OKAY.
I'LL BE RIGHT THERE.
YOUNG LADY.
YES?
I'M USED TO IT, SO I ENJOY IT...
...EVEN IF I DON'T CATCH A THING.
BUT DON'T YOU GO PUSHING YOUR-SELF, OKAY?
I'M NOT...
... PUSHING MYSELF!
I WONDER IF MIKOCHI WILL BE ABLE TO CAST WITH THIS TYPE.

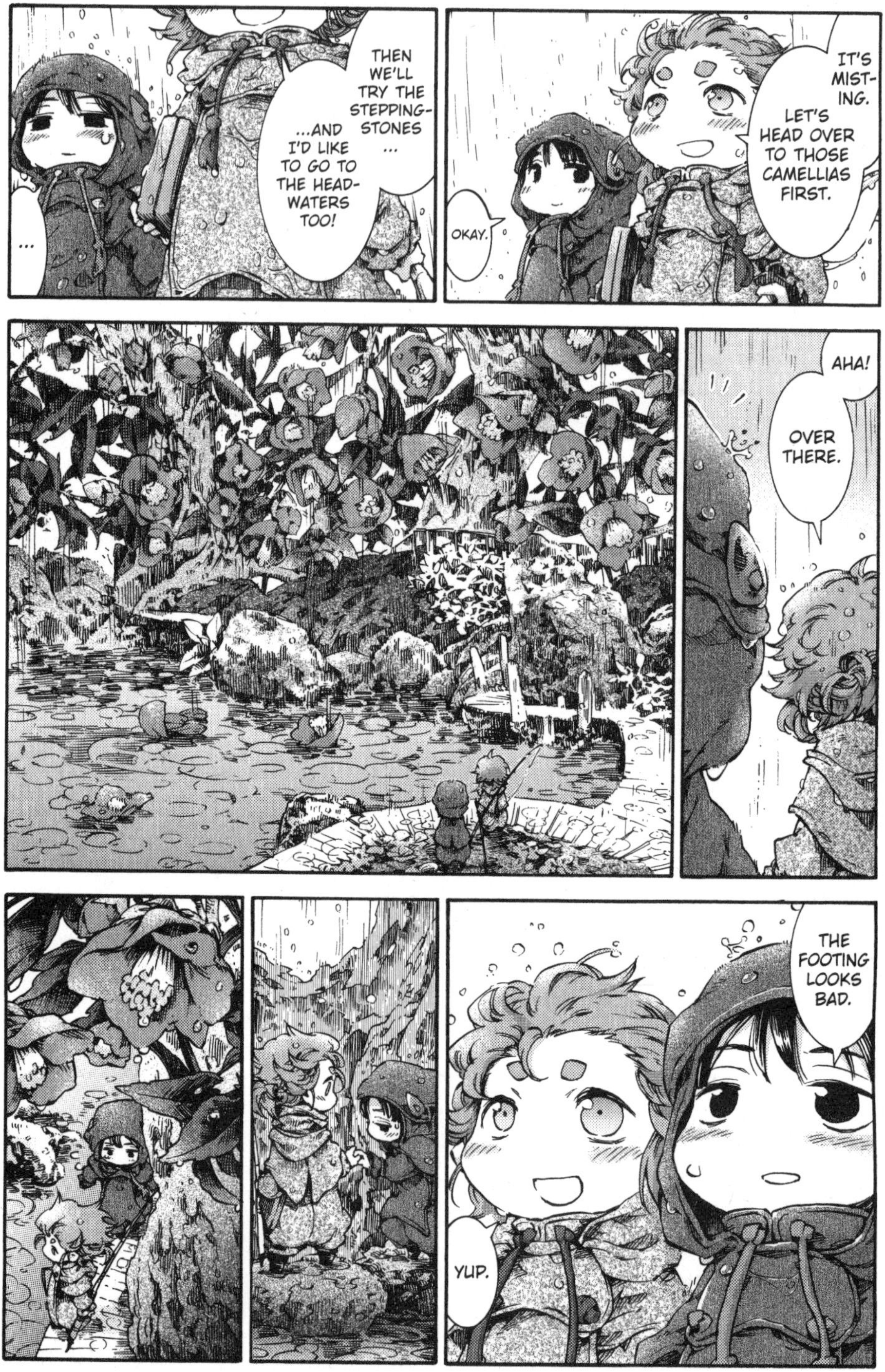
IT'S MISTING. LET'S HEAD OVER TO THOSE CAMELLIAS FIRST.
OKAY.
THEN WE'LL TRY THE STEPPING-STONES ...
...AND I'D LIKE TO GO TO THE HEAD-WATERS TOO!
...
AHA! OVER THERE.
THE FOOTING LOOKS BAD.
YUP.

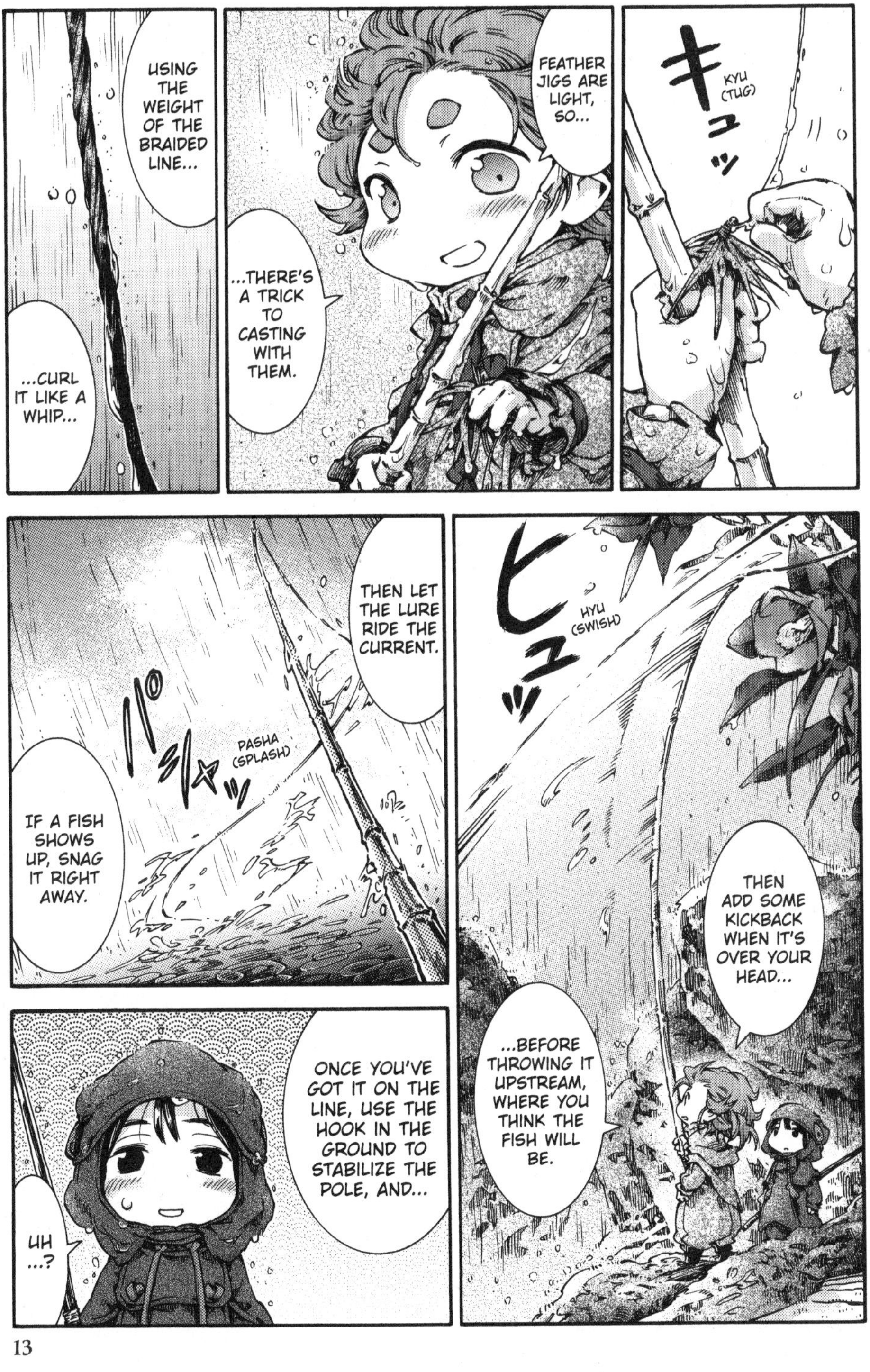
キュッ
KYU (TUG)
FEATHER JIGS ARE LIGHT, SO...
...THERE'S A TRICK TO CASTING WITH THEM.
USING THE WEIGHT OF THE BRAIDED LINE...
...CURL IT LIKE A WHIP...
ヒュッ
HYU (SWISH)
THEN ADD SOME KICKBACK WHEN IT'S OVER YOUR HEAD...
...BEFORE THROWING IT UPSTREAM, WHERE YOU THINK THE FISH WILL BE.
THEN LET THE LURE RIDE THE CURRENT.
パシャッ
PASHA (SPLASH)
IF A FISH SHOWS UP, SNAG IT RIGHT AWAY.
ONCE YOU'VE GOT IT ON THE LINE, USE THE HOOK IN THE GROUND TO STABILIZE THE POLE, AND...
UH ...?

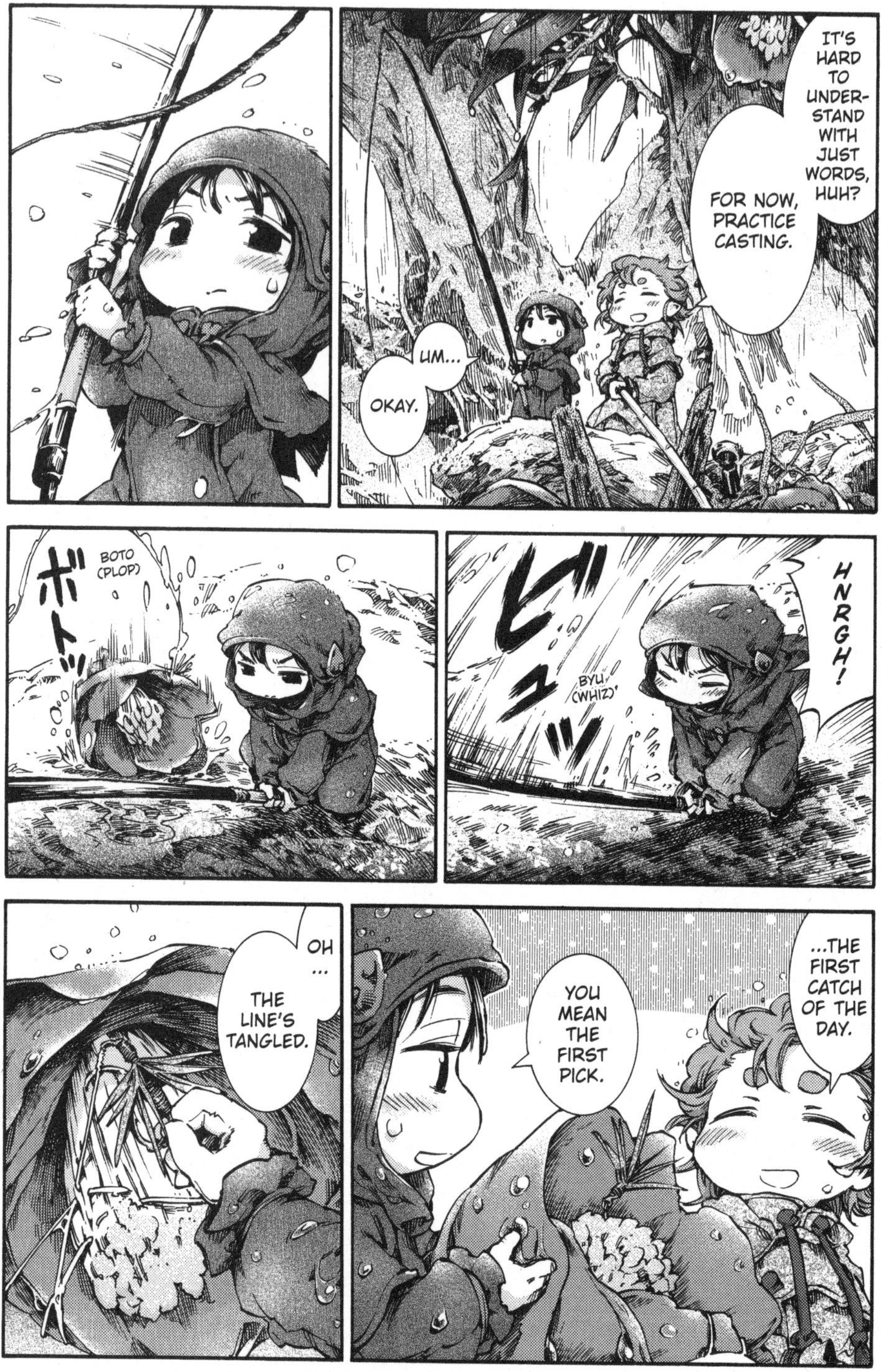
IT'S HARD TO UNDER-STAND WITH JUST WORDS, HUH?
FOR NOW, PRACTICE CASTING.
UM...
OKAY.
HNRGH!
ビュッ
BYU (WHIZ)
ボトッ
BOTO (PLOP)
...THE FIRST CATCH OF THE DAY.
YOU MEAN THE FIRST PICK.
OH ...
THE LINE'S TANGLED.

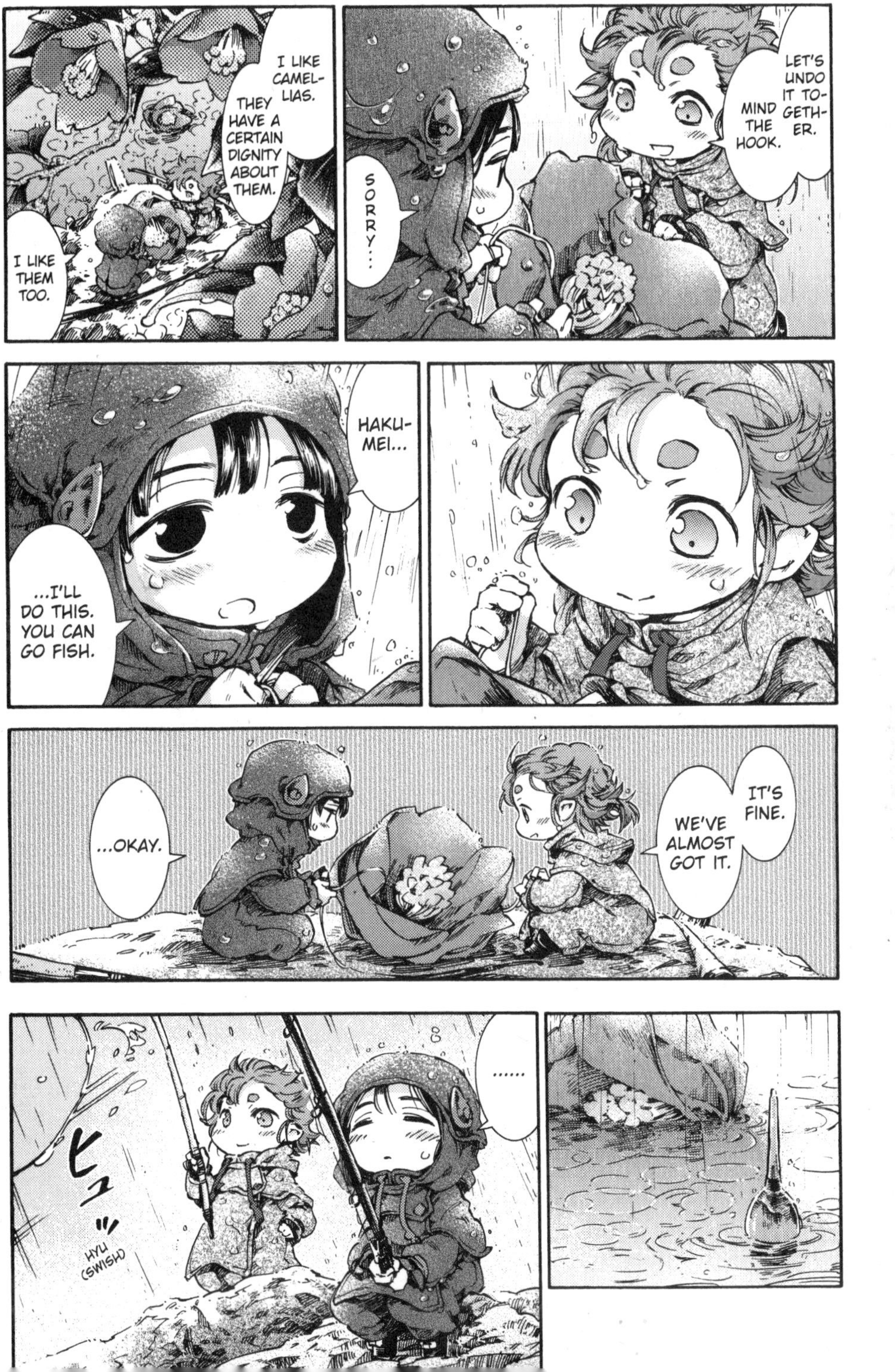
LET'S UNDO IT TO-GETH-ER.
MIND THE HOOK.
SORRY...
I LIKE CAMEL-LIAS.
THEY HAVE A CERTAIN DIGNITY ABOUT THEM.
I LIKE THEM TOO.
HAKU-MEI...
...I'LL DO THIS. YOU CAN GO FISH.
IT'S FINE.
WE'VE ALMOST GOT IT.
...OKAY.
......
ヒュッ
HYU (SWISH)

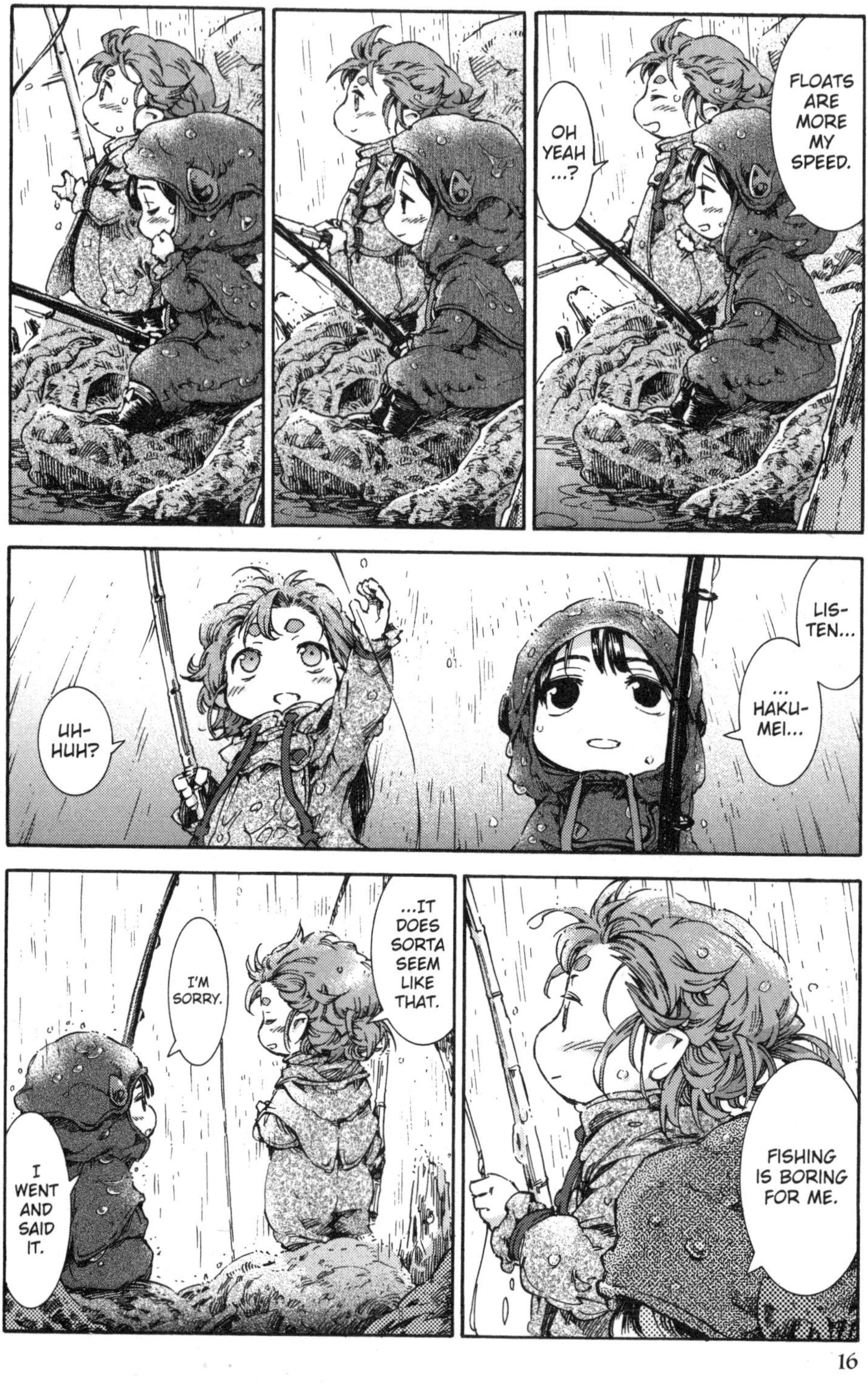
FLOATS ARE MORE MY SPEED.
OH YEAH ...?
LIS-TEN...
... HAKU-MEI...
UH-HUH?
FISHING IS BORING FOR ME.
...IT DOES SORTA SEEM LIKE THAT.
I'M SORRY.
I WENT AND SAID IT.

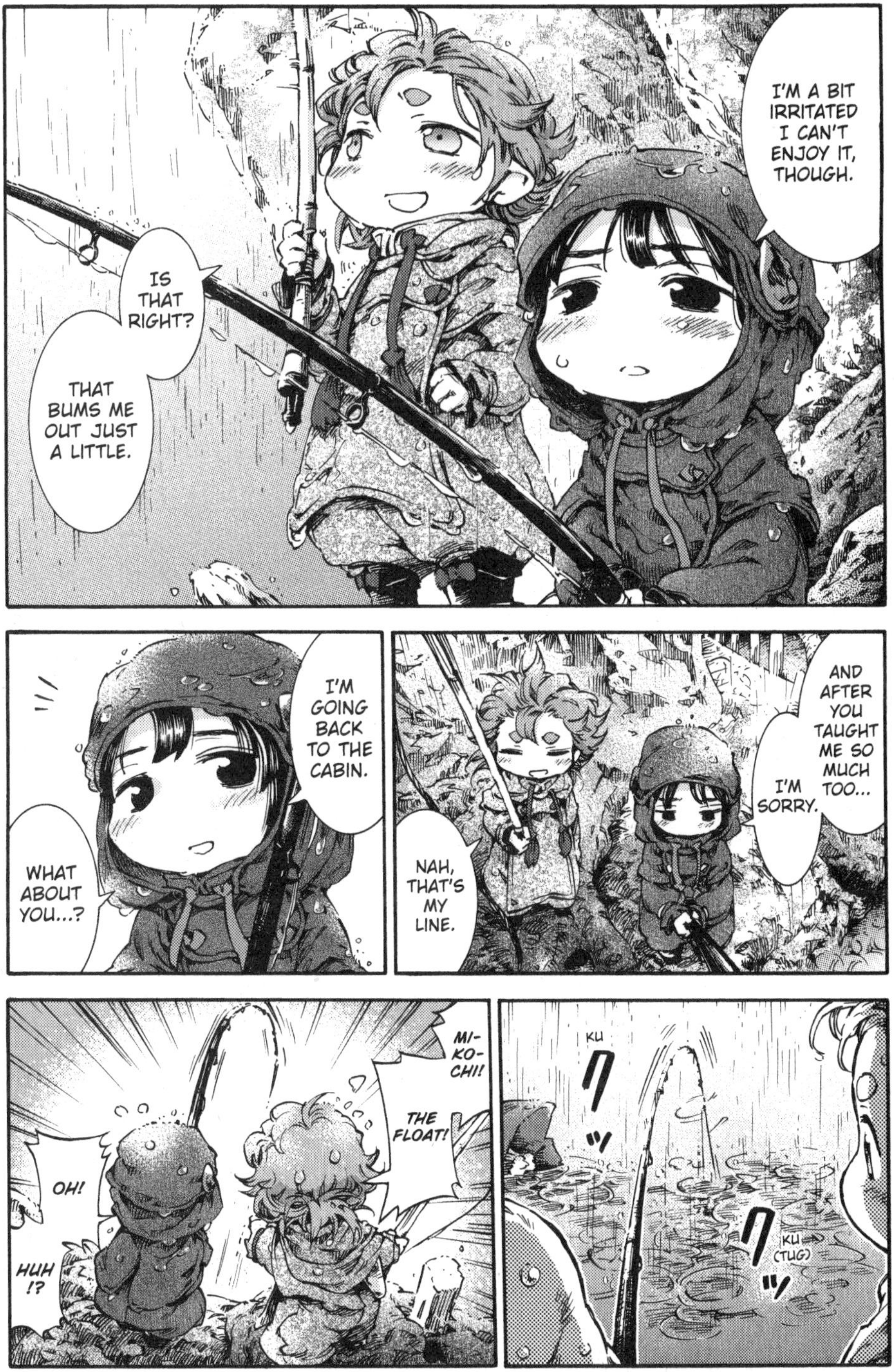
I'M A BIT IRRITATED I CAN'T ENJOY IT, THOUGH.
IS THAT RIGHT?
THAT BUMS ME OUT JUST A LITTLE.
AND AFTER YOU TAUGHT ME SO MUCH TOO...
I'M SORRY.
NAH, THAT'S MY LINE.
I'M GOING BACK TO THE CABIN.
WHAT ABOUT YOU...?
KU
クッ
クッ
KU (TUG)
MI-KOCHI!
THE FLOAT!
OH!
HUH!?

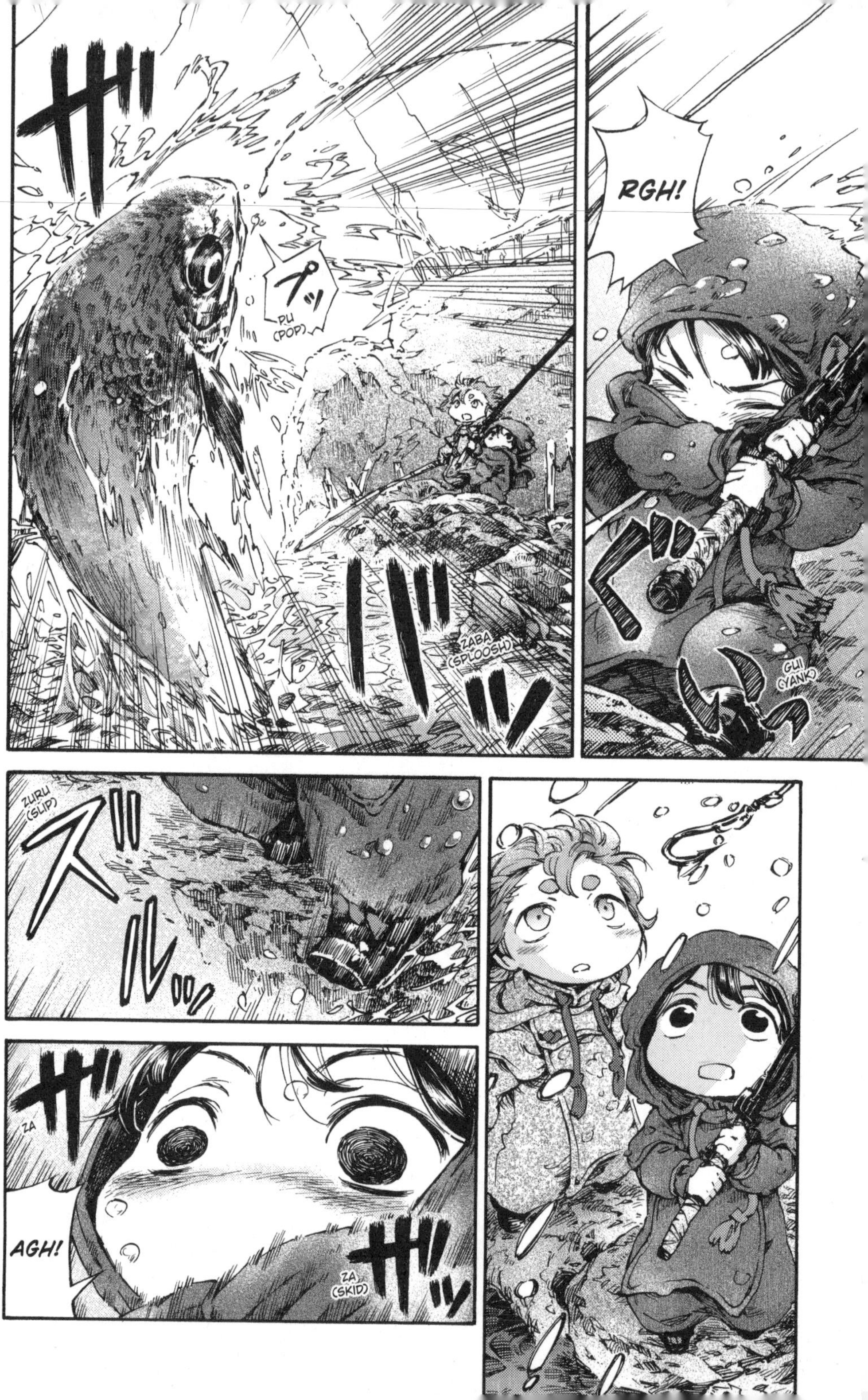
RGH!
グイッ
GUI (YANK)
ザッ
プッ
PU (POP)
ザバッ
ZABA (SPLOOSH)
ズル…
ZURU (SLIP)
ザッ
ZA
AGH!
ザッ
ZA (SKID)

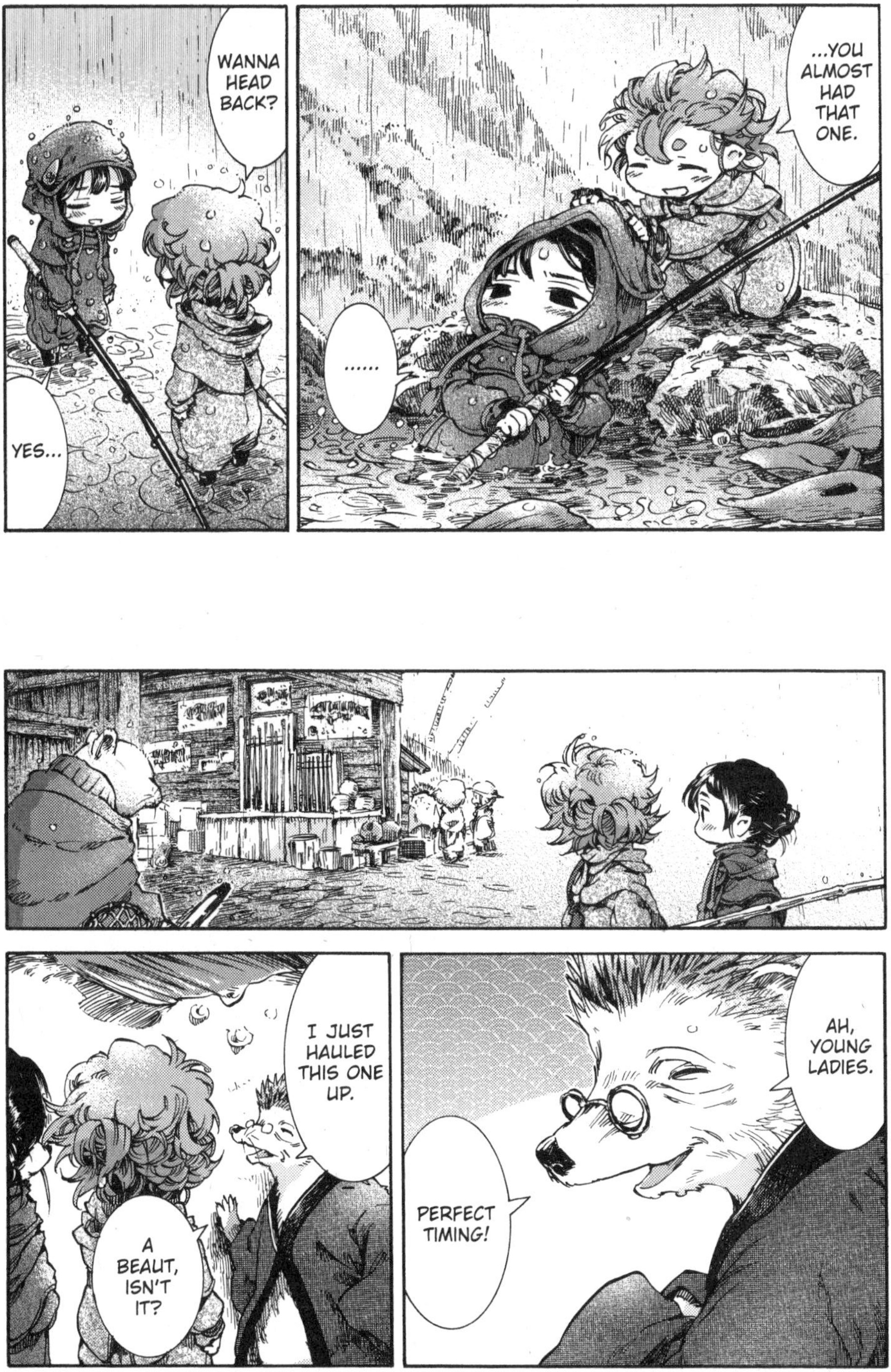
...YOU ALMOST HAD THAT ONE.
......
WANNA HEAD BACK?
YES...
AH, YOUNG LADIES.
PERFECT TIMING!
I JUST HAULED THIS ONE UP.
A BEAUT, ISN'T IT?

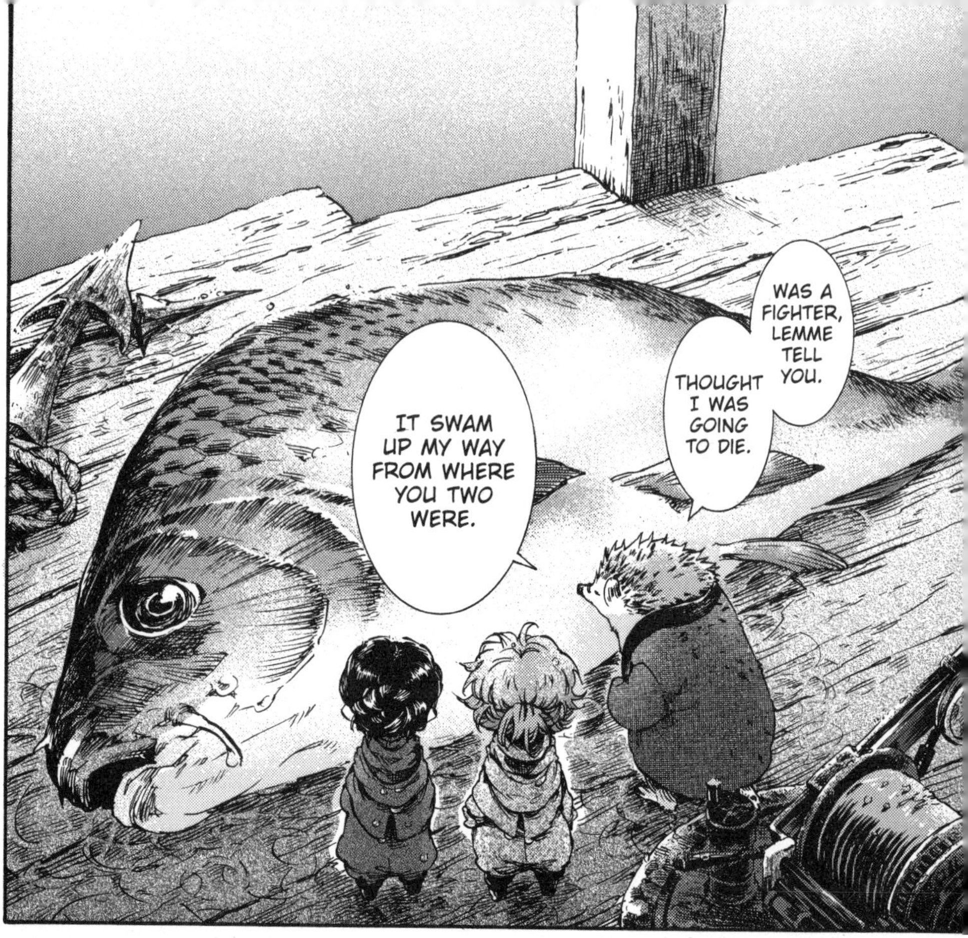
WAS A FIGHTER, LEMME TELL YOU.
THOUGHT I WAS GOING TO DIE.
IT SWAM UP MY WAY FROM WHERE YOU TWO WERE.

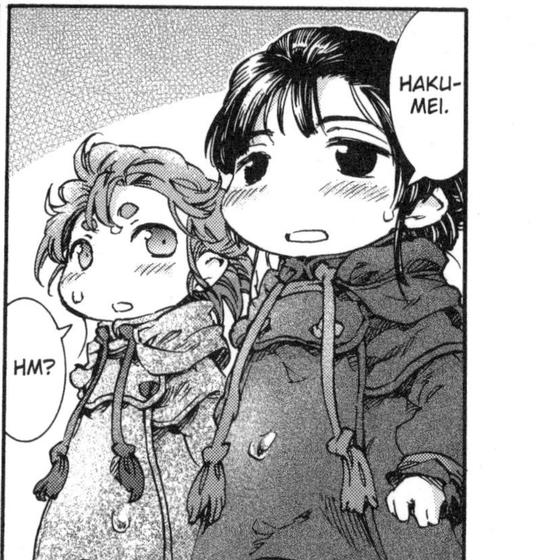
HAKU-MEI.
HM?

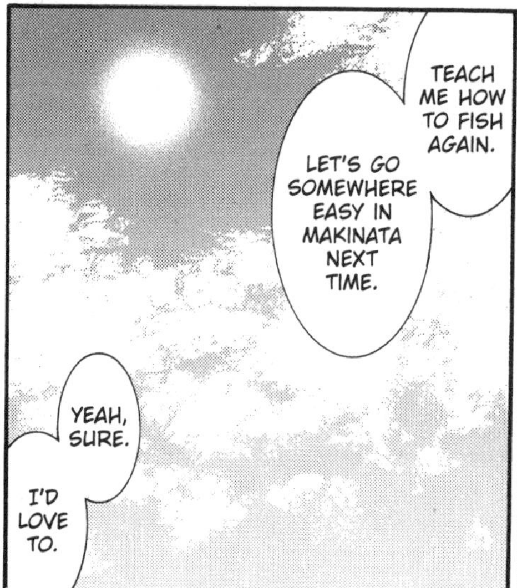
TEACH ME HOW TO FISH AGAIN.
LET'S GO SOMEWHERE EASY IN MAKINATA NEXT TIME.
YEAH, SURE.
I'D LOVE TO.

Chapter 27 • End

Here's the rain gear Mikochi made using oilcloth.
In Makinata, raincoats are typically made from oilpaper, which is what Mikochi used for her initial attempts. However, since Hakumei kept ripping hers, Mikochi started making them out of cloth instead. Because she prioritized ease of movement, they aren't as water-resistant.

The pattern is the same for both coats, but Mikochi's is dark brown, while Hakumei's is spring green.

Chapter 28
Neighbor's Breakfast

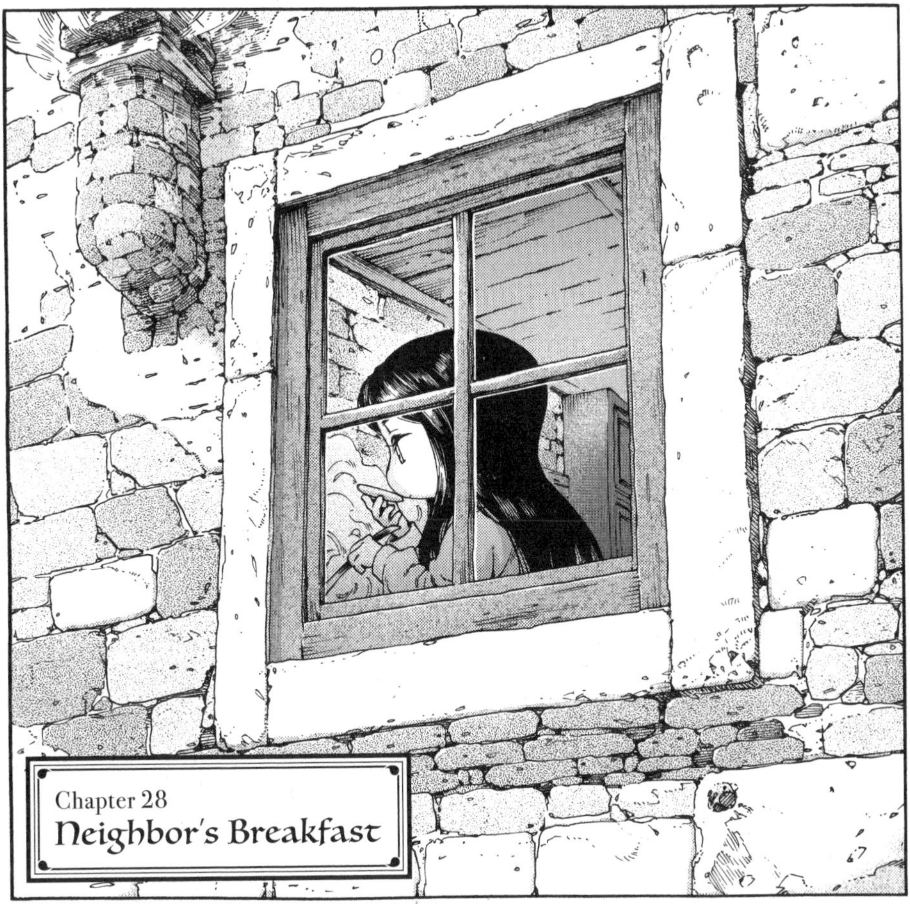

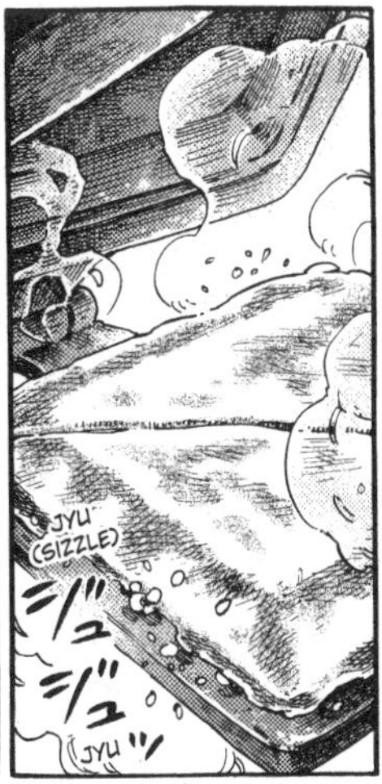
JYU (SIZZLE)
ジュ
ジュ
JYU ッ

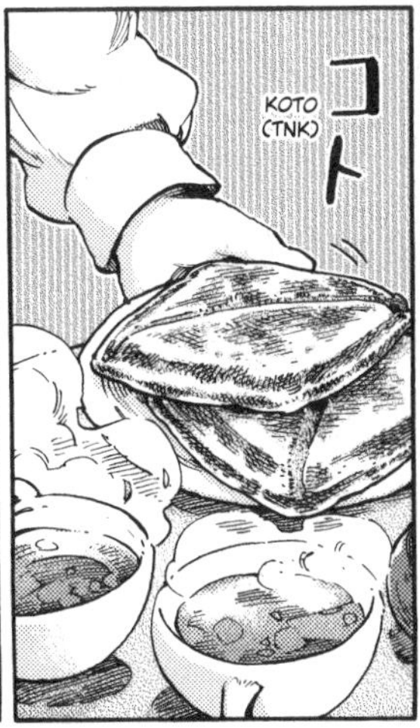
KOTO (TNK)
コト

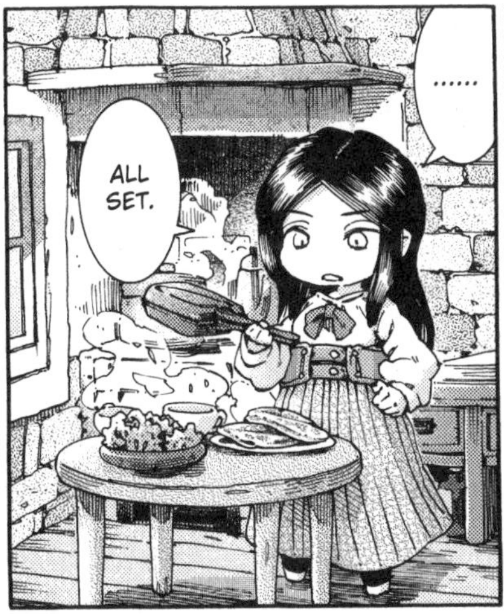
......
ALL SET.

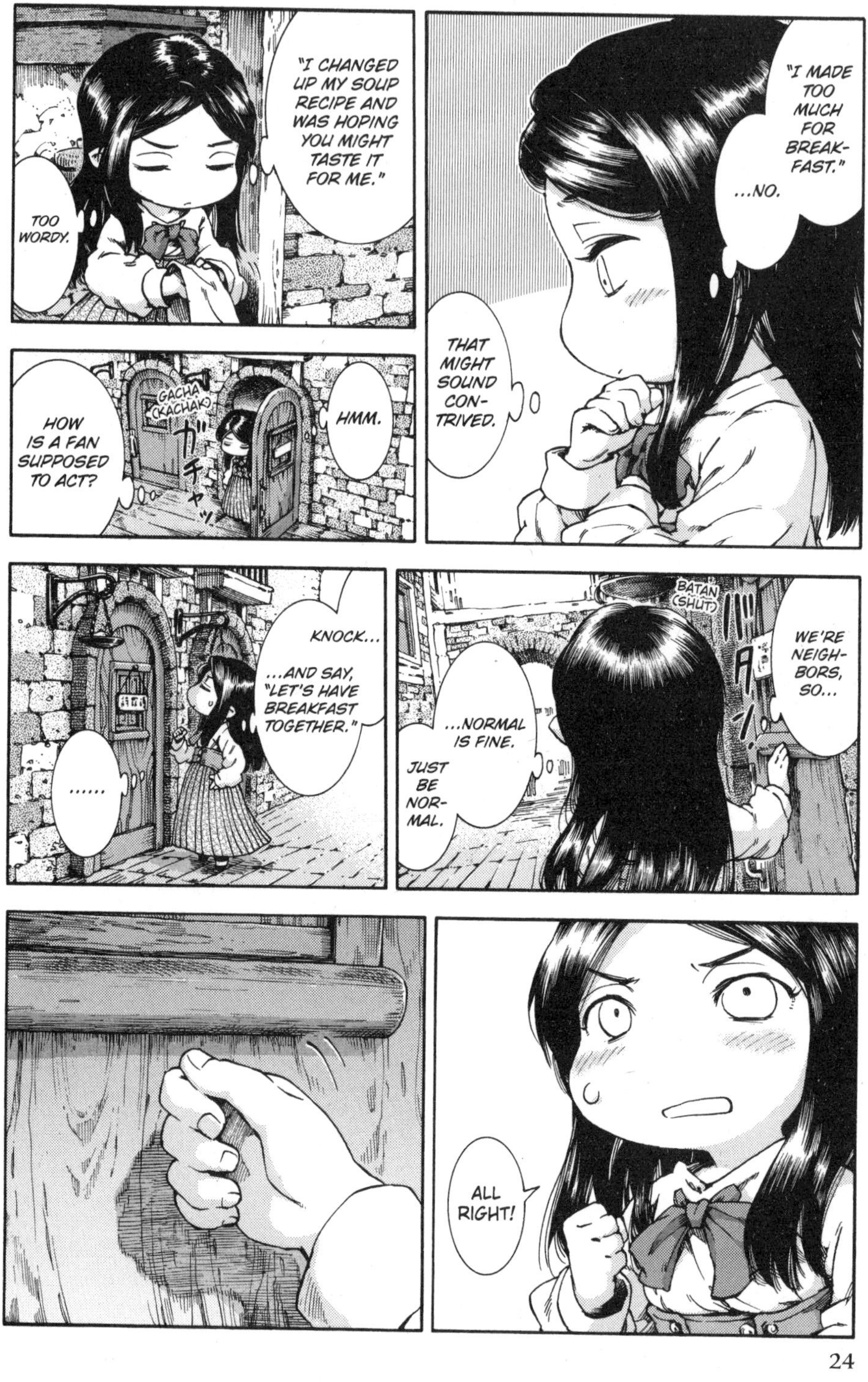
"I MADE TOO MUCH FOR BREAKFAST."
...NO.
THAT MIGHT SOUND CONTRIVED.
"I CHANGED UP MY SOUP RECIPE AND WAS HOPING YOU MIGHT TASTE IT FOR ME."
TOO WORDY.
HMM.
GACHA (KACHAK)
ガチャッ
HOW IS A FAN SUPPOSED TO ACT?
BATAN (SHUT)
バタン
WE'RE NEIGHBORS, SO...
...NORMAL IS FINE.
JUST BE NORMAL.
KNOCK...
...AND SAY, "LET'S HAVE BREAKFAST TOGETHER."
......
ALL RIGHT!

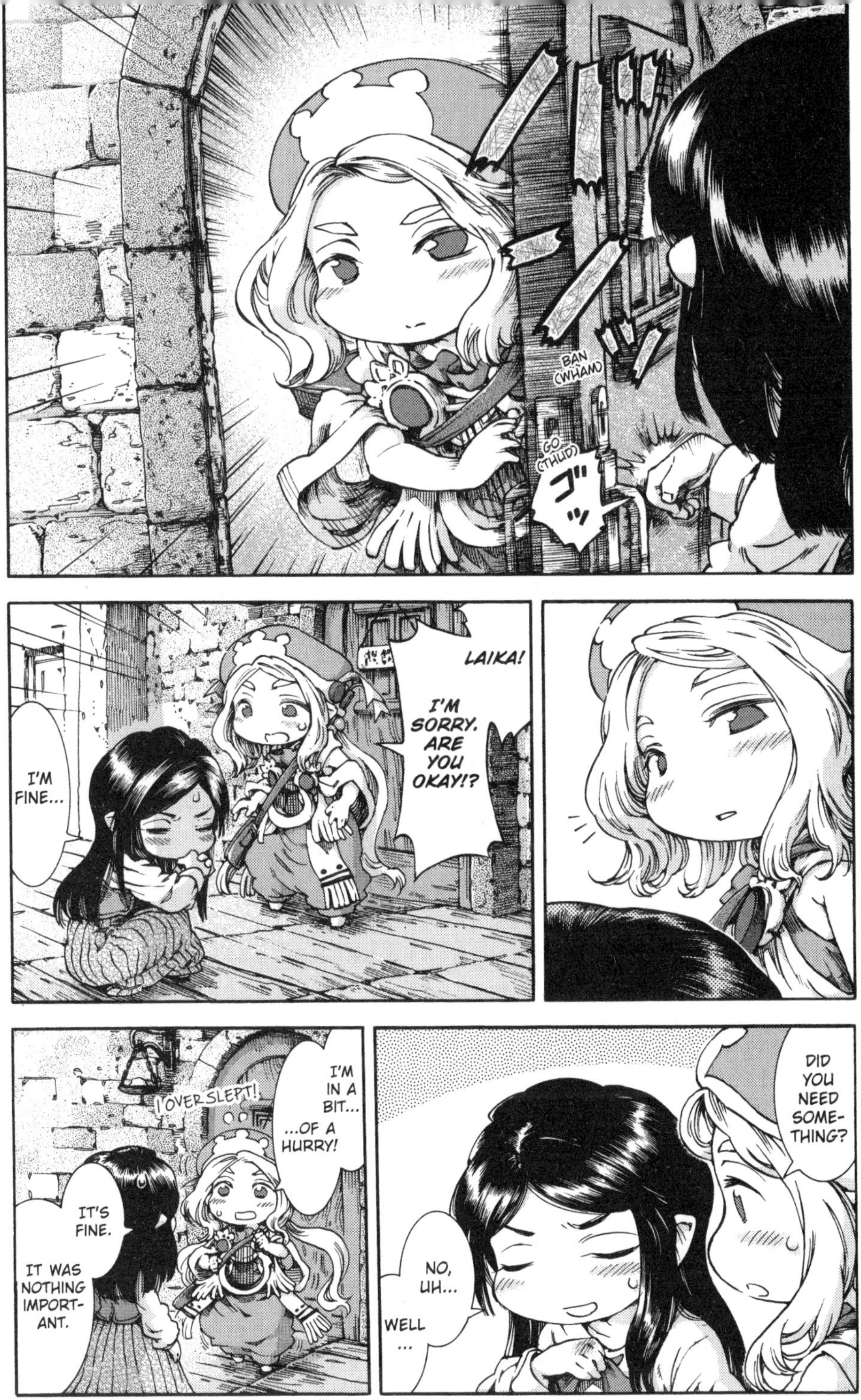
BAN (WHAM)
GO (THUD)
ゴッ
LAIKA!
I'M SORRY. ARE YOU OKAY!?
I'M FINE...
DID YOU NEED SOMETHING?
NO, UH...
WELL ...
I'M IN A BIT... ...OF A HURRY!
I OVERSLEPT!
IT'S FINE.
IT WAS NOTHING IMPORTANT.

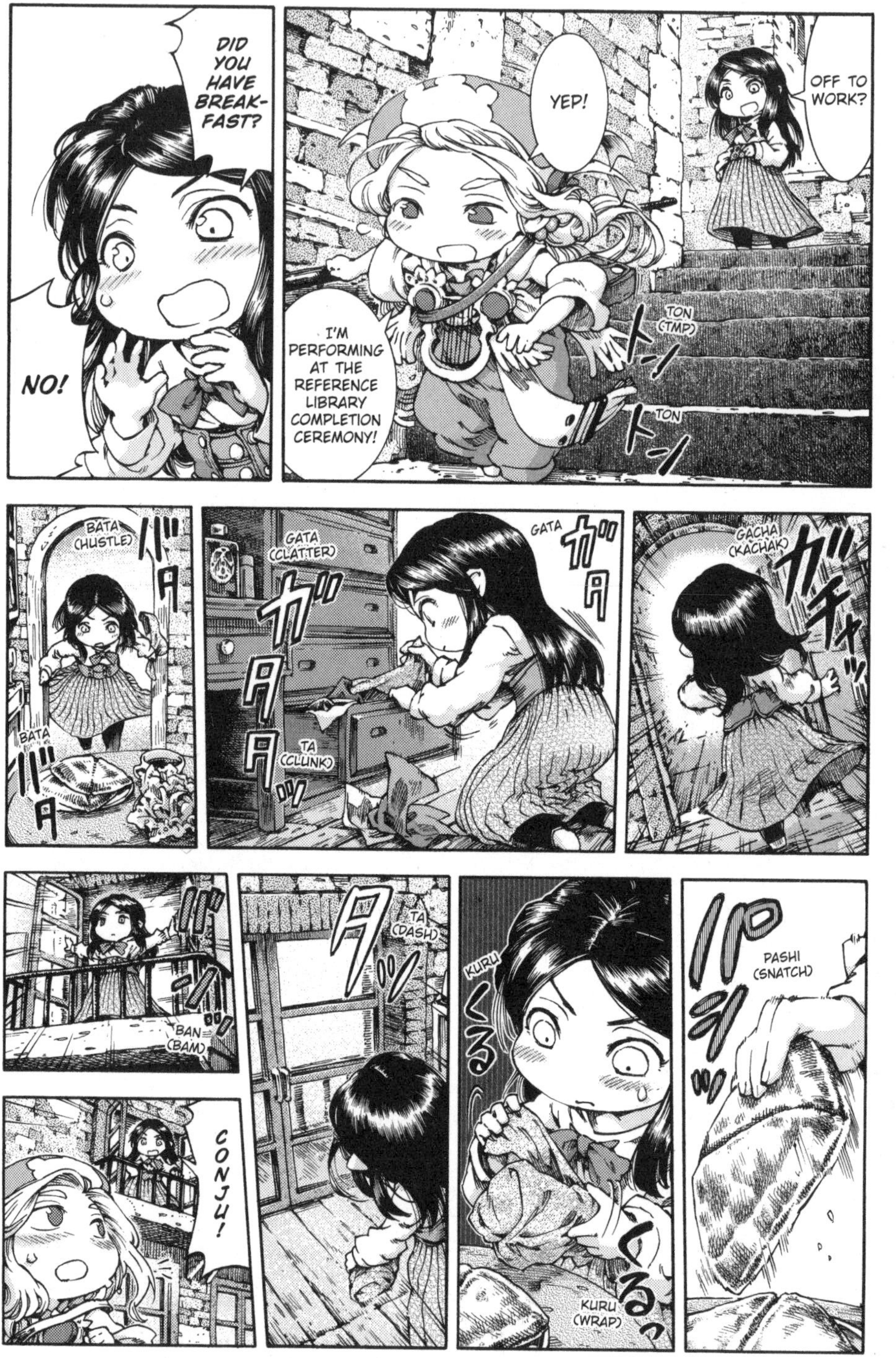

OFF TO WORK?
YEP!
I'M PERFORMING AT THE REFERENCE LIBRARY COMPLETION CEREMONY!
TON (TMP)
TON
DID YOU HAVE BREAK-FAST?
NO!
GACHA (KACHAK)
GATA
GATA (CLATTER)
TA (CLUNK)
BATA (HUSTLE)
BATA
PASHI (SNATCH)
KURU
KURU (WRAP)
TA (DASH)
BAN (BAM)
CONJU!

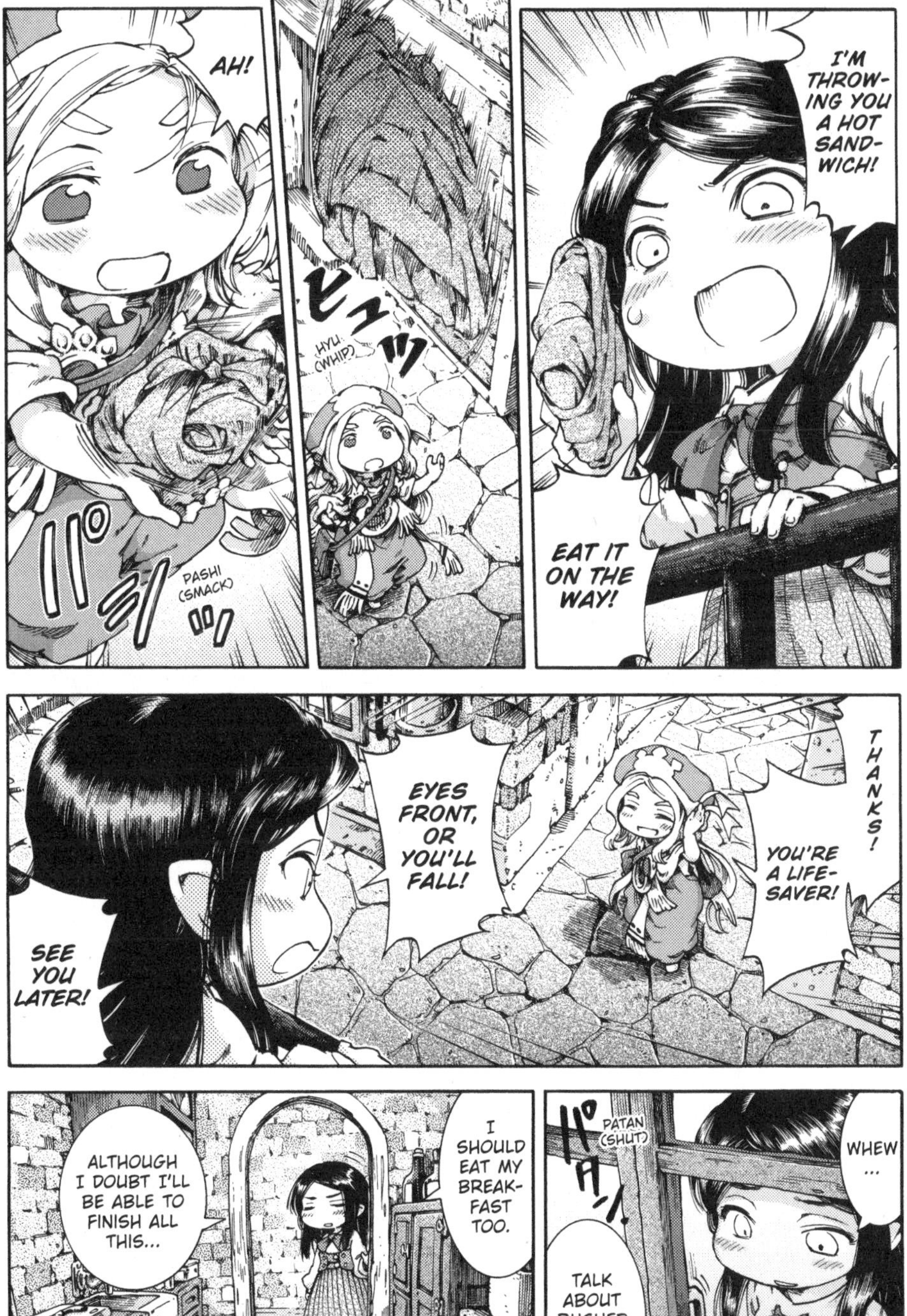
I'M THROWING YOU A HOT SANDWICH!
EAT IT ON THE WAY!
ヒュッ
HYU (WHIP)
AH!
パシッ
PASHI (SMACK)
THANKS!
YOU'RE A LIFE-SAVER!
EYES FRONT, OR YOU'LL FALL!
SEE YOU LATER!
パタン
PATAN (SHUT)
WHEW ...
TALK ABOUT RUSHED ...
I SHOULD EAT MY BREAKFAST TOO.
ALTHOUGH I DOUBT I'LL BE ABLE TO FINISH ALL THIS...

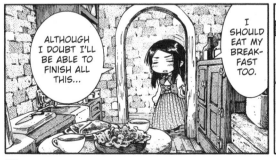

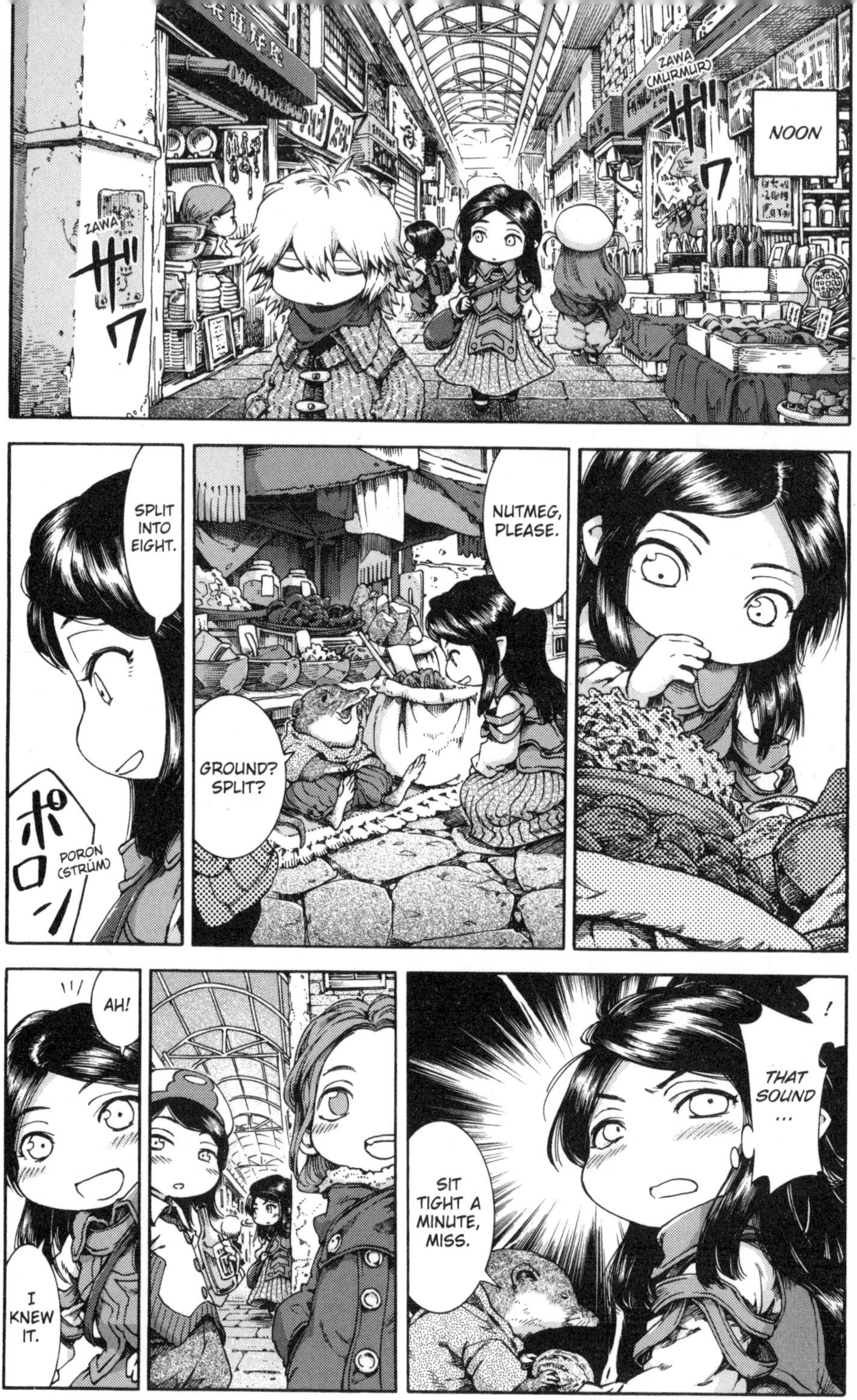
NOON
ザワ
ZAWA (MURMUR)
ザワ
ZAWA
NUTMEG, PLEASE.
GROUND? SPLIT?
SPLIT INTO EIGHT.
ポロン
PORON (STRÚM)
!
THAT SOUND ...
SIT TIGHT A MINUTE, MISS.
AH!
I KNEW IT.

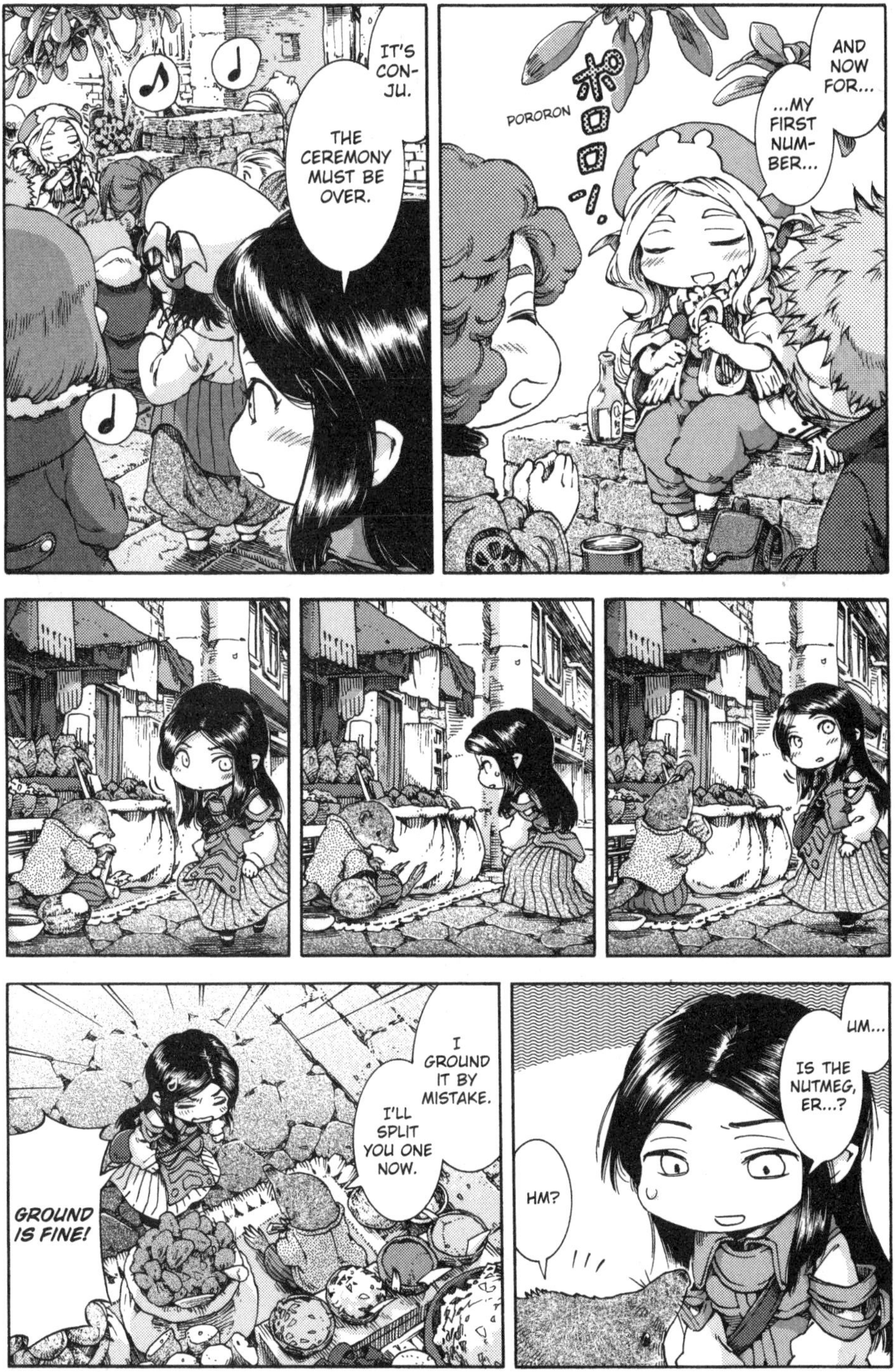
PORORON
AND NOW FOR...
...MY FIRST NUMBER...
IT'S CONJU.
THE CEREMONY MUST BE OVER.
UM...
IS THE NUTMEG, ER...?
HM?
I GROUND IT BY MISTAKE.
I'LL SPLIT YOU ONE NOW.
GROUND IS FINE!

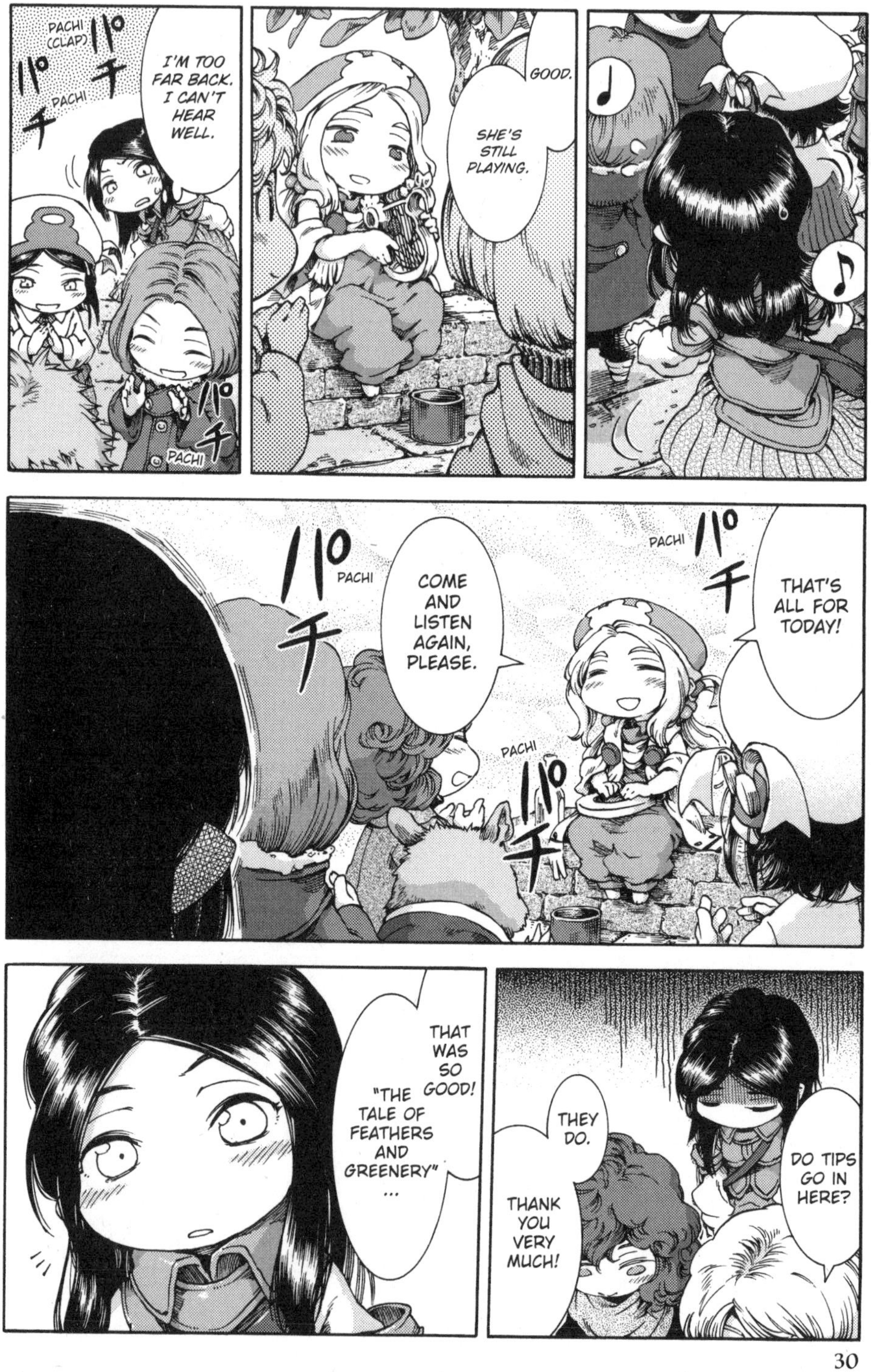
GOOD.
SHE'S STILL PLAYING.
PACHI (CLAP) パチ
PACHI パチ
I'M TOO FAR BACK. I CAN'T HEAR WELL.
PACHI パチ
PACHI パチ
THAT'S ALL FOR TODAY!
PACHI パチ
COME AND LISTEN AGAIN, PLEASE.
PACHI パチ
DO TIPS GO IN HERE?
THEY DO.
THANK YOU VERY MUCH!
THAT WAS SO GOOD! "THE TALE OF FEATHERS AND GREENERY"...

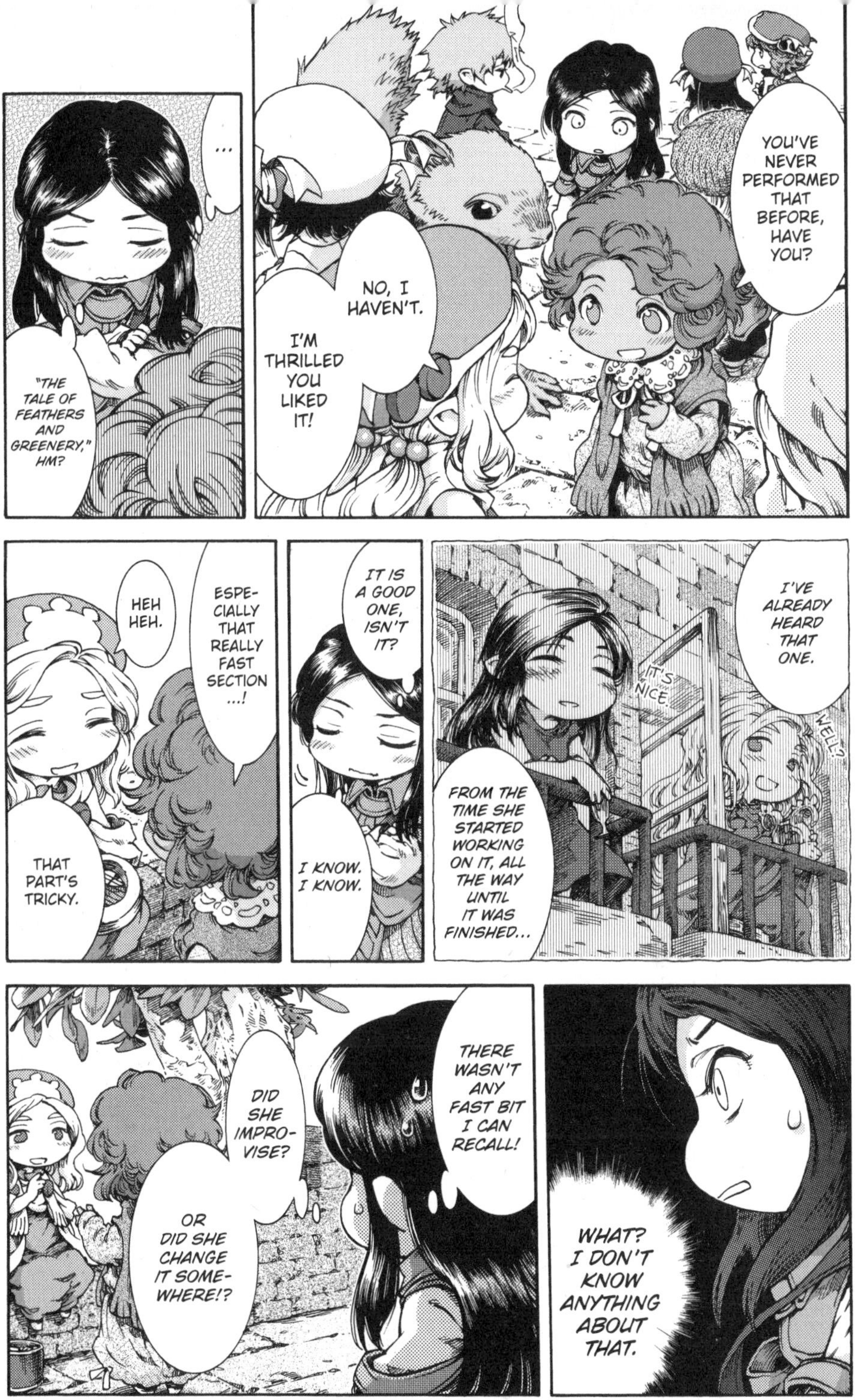
YOU'VE NEVER PERFORMED THAT BEFORE, HAVE YOU?
NO, I HAVEN'T.
I'M THRILLED YOU LIKED IT!
...
"THE TALE OF FEATHERS AND GREENERY," HM?
I'VE ALREADY HEARD THAT ONE.
WELL?
IT'S NICE.
FROM THE TIME SHE STARTED WORKING ON IT, ALL THE WAY UNTIL IT WAS FINISHED...
IT IS A GOOD ONE, ISN'T IT?
I KNOW. I KNOW.
ESPE-CIALLY THAT REALLY FAST SECTION ...!
HEH HEH.
THAT PART'S TRICKY.
WHAT? I DON'T KNOW ANYTHING ABOUT THAT.
THERE WASN'T ANY FAST BIT I CAN RECALL!
DID SHE IMPROV-VISE?
OR DID SHE CHANGE IT SOME-WHERE!?

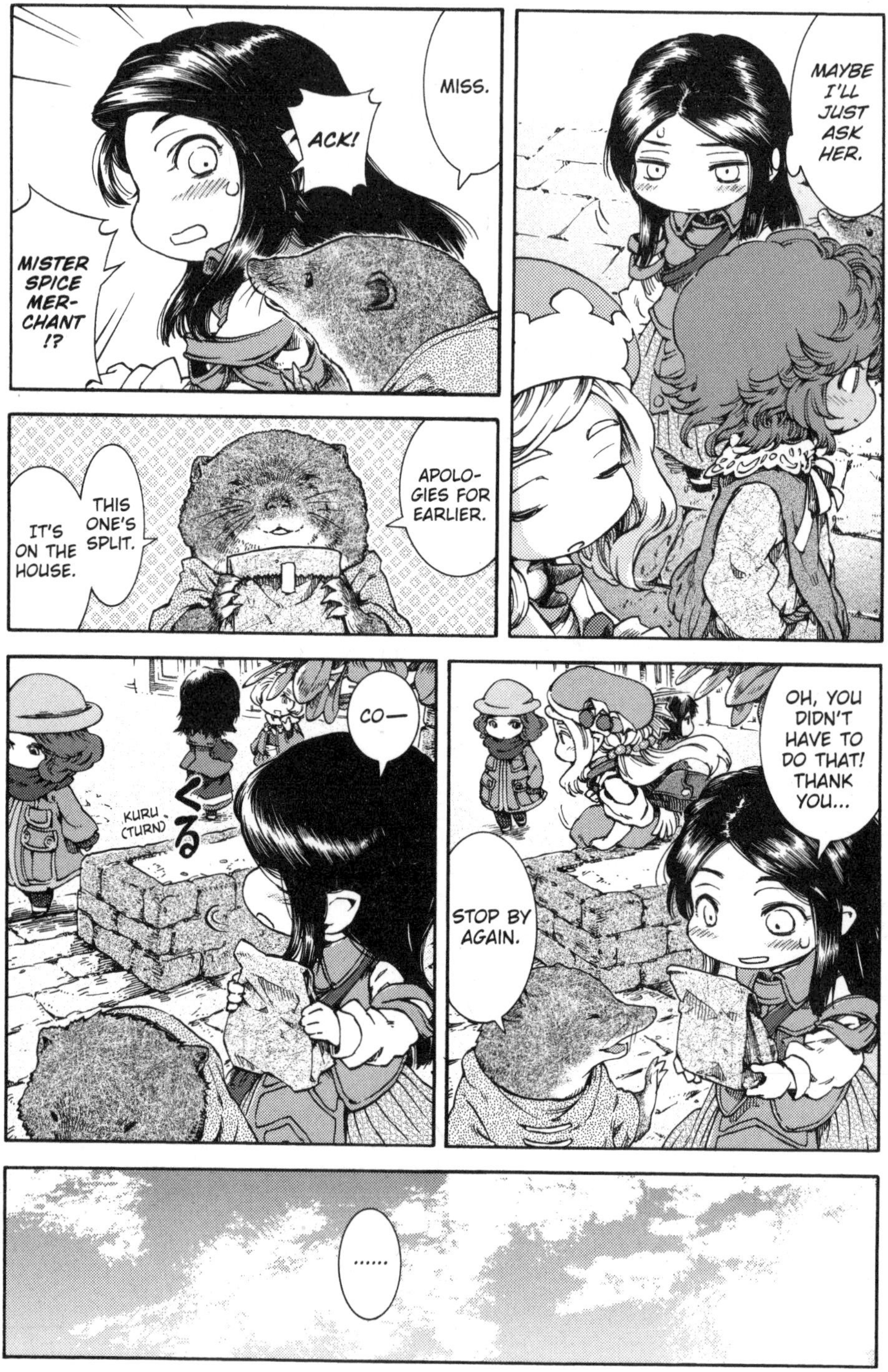
MAYBE I'LL JUST ASK HER.
MISS.
ACK!
MISTER SPICE MERCHANT!?
APOLOGIES FOR EARLIER.
THIS ONE'S SPLIT.
IT'S ON THE HOUSE.
OH, YOU DIDN'T HAVE TO DO THAT! THANK YOU...
STOP BY AGAIN.
CO—
くる
KURU (TURN)
......

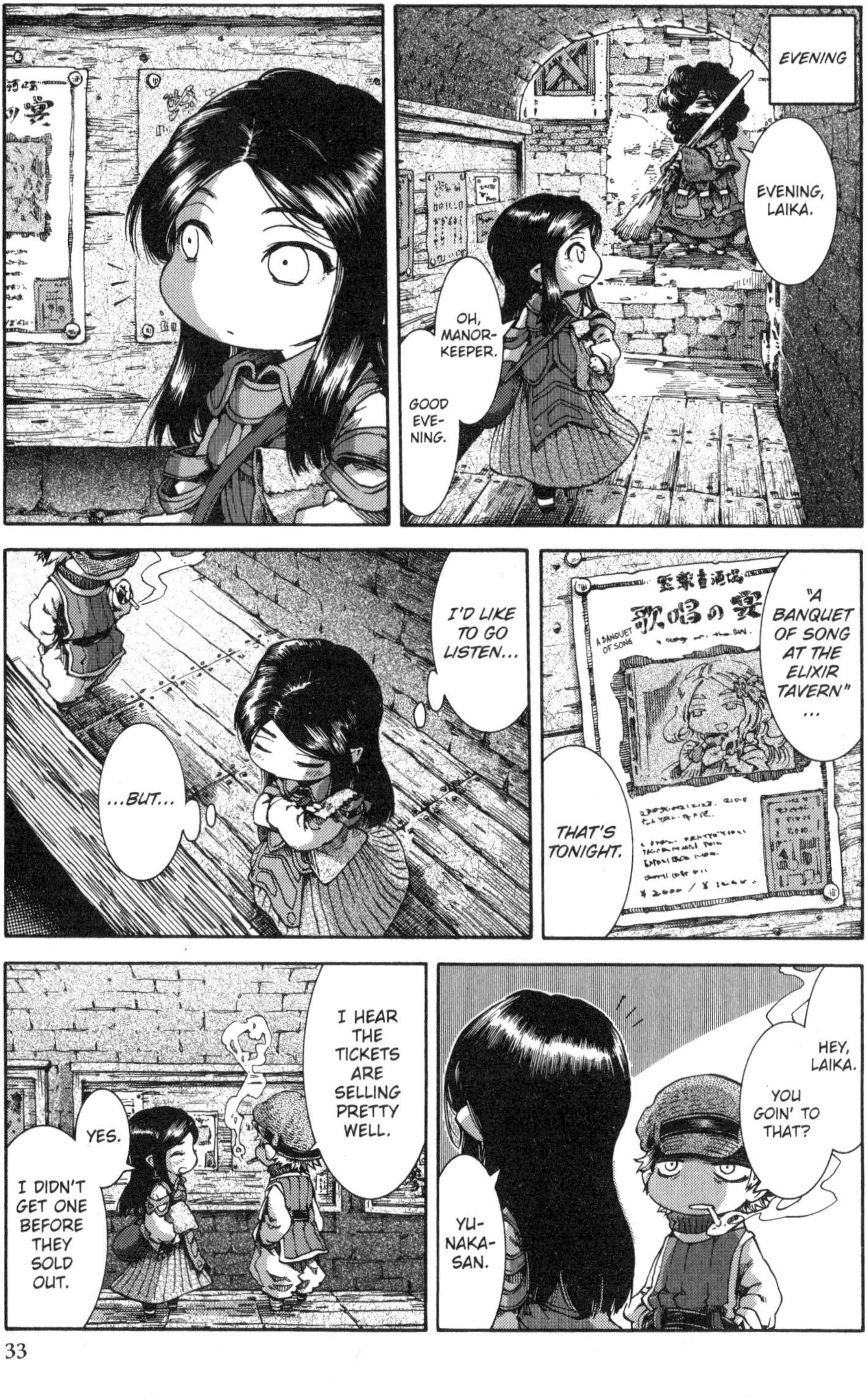
EVENING
EVENING, LAIKA.
OH, MANOR-KEEPER.
GOOD EVE-NING.
歌唱の宴
A BANQUET OF SONG
"A BANQUET OF SONG AT THE ELIXIR TAVERN"...
THAT'S TONIGHT.
I'D LIKE TO GO LISTEN...
...BUT...
HEY, LAIKA.
YOU GOIN' TO THAT?
YU-NAKA-SAN.
I HEAR THE TICKETS ARE SELLING PRETTY WELL.
YES.
I DIDN'T GET ONE BEFORE THEY SOLD OUT.

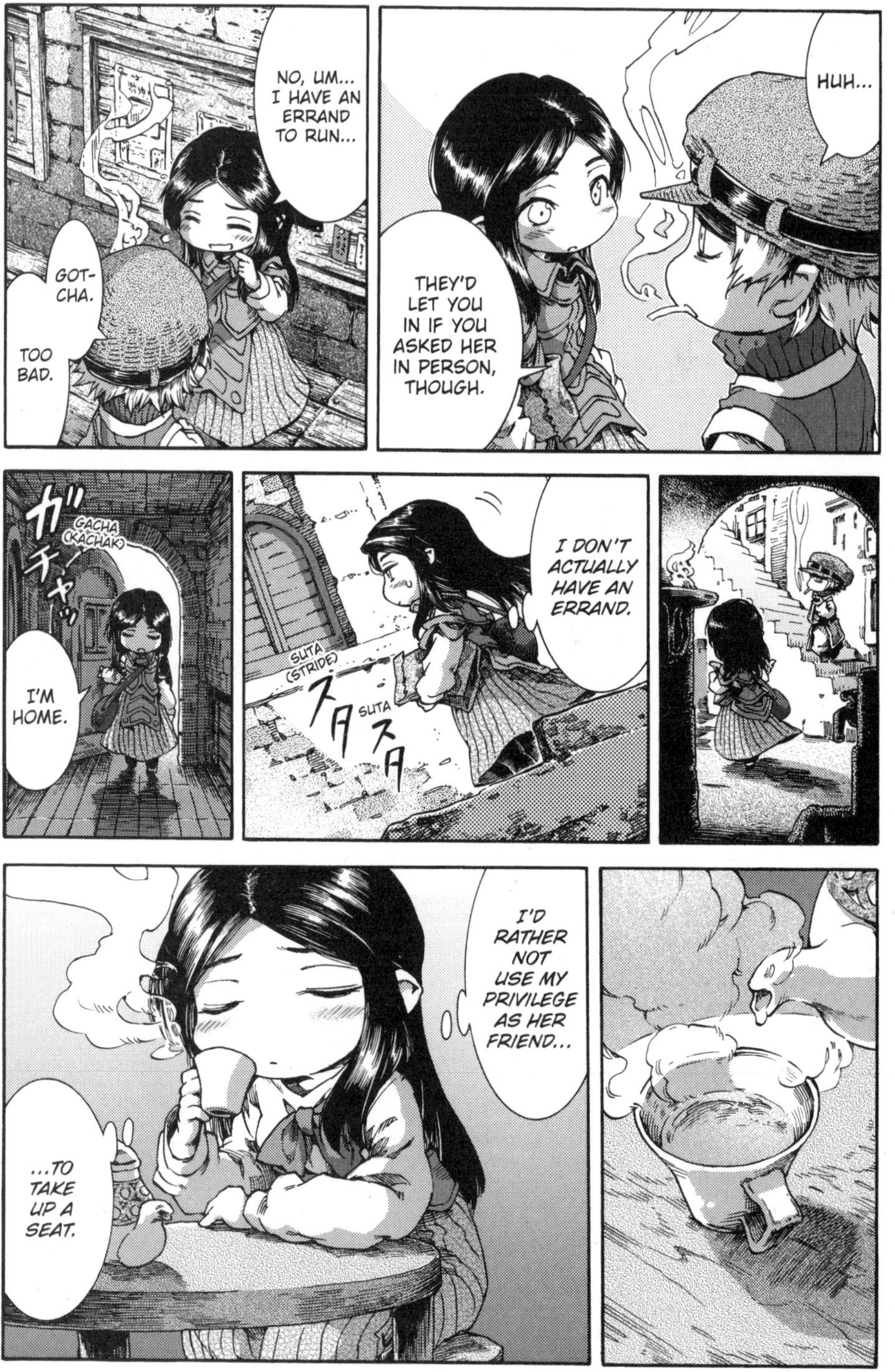
HUH...
THEY'D LET YOU IN IF YOU ASKED HER IN PERSON, THOUGH.
NO, UM... I HAVE AN ERRAND TO RUN...
GOT-CHA.
TOO BAD.
I DON'T ACTUALLY HAVE AN ERRAND.
スタ SUTA (STRIDE)
スタ SUTA
ガチャッ GACHA (KACHAK)
I'M HOME.
I'D RATHER NOT USE MY PRIVILEGE AS HER FRIEND...
...TO TAKE UP A SEAT.

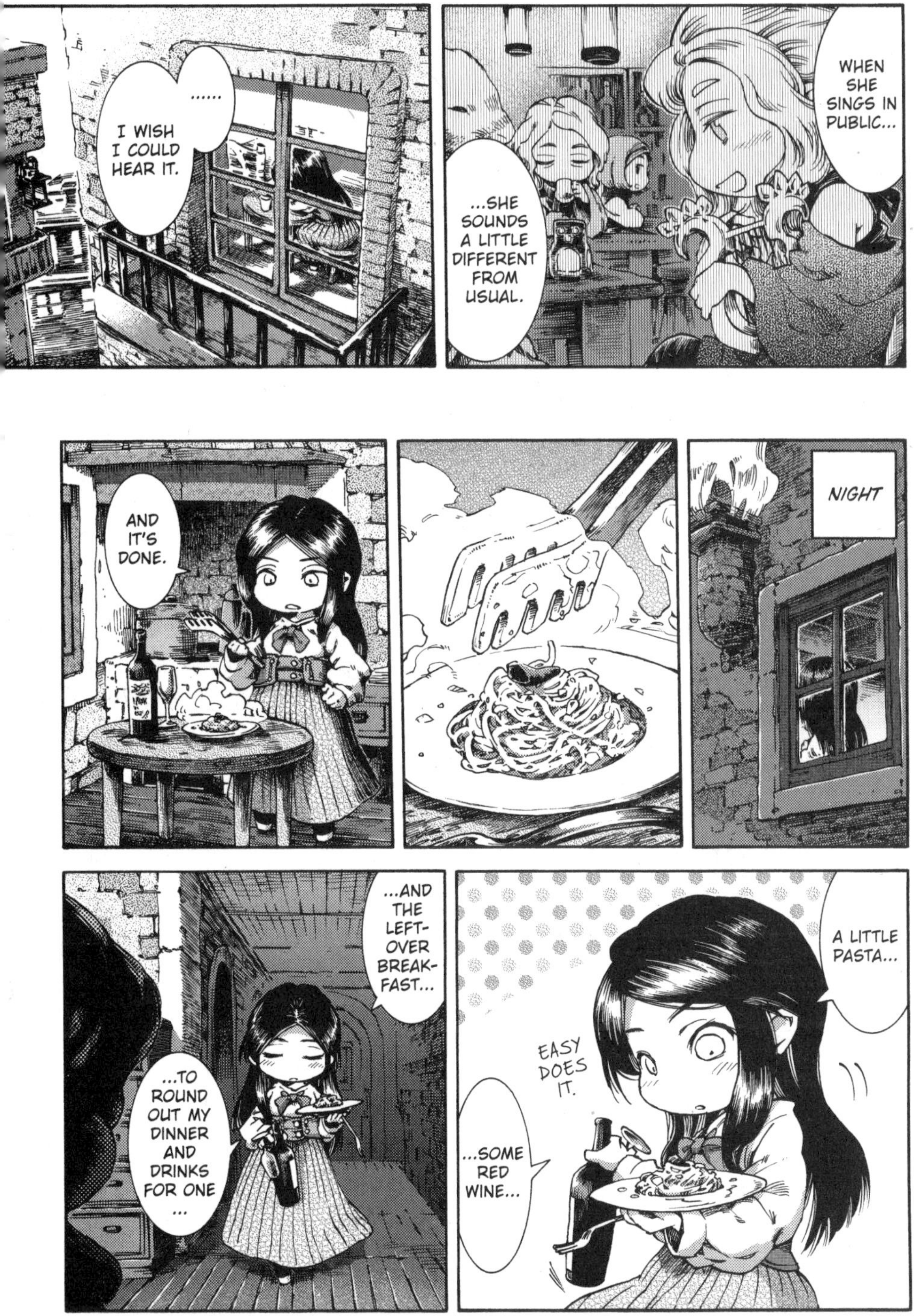
WHEN SHE SINGS IN PUBLIC...
...SHE SOUNDS A LITTLE DIFFERENT FROM USUAL.
......
I WISH I COULD HEAR IT.
NIGHT
AND IT'S DONE.
A LITTLE PASTA...
EASY DOES IT.
...SOME RED WINE...
...AND THE LEFT-OVER BREAK-FAST...
...TO ROUND OUT MY DINNER AND DRINKS FOR ONE ...

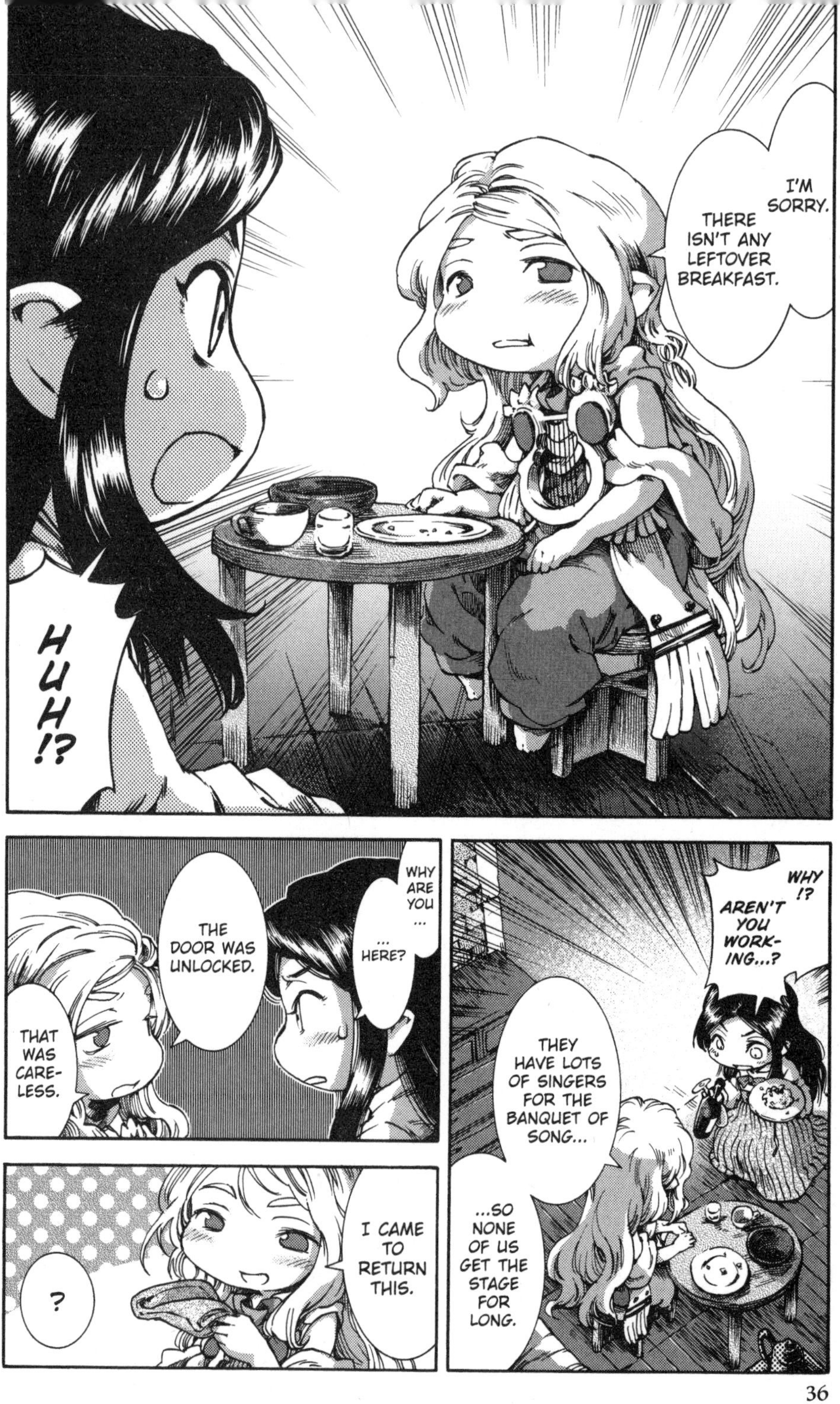
I'M SORRY. THERE ISN'T ANY LEFTOVER BREAKFAST.
HUH!?
WHY ARE YOU ... ... HERE?
THE DOOR WAS UNLOCKED.
THAT WAS CARELESS.
I CAME TO RETURN THIS.
?
WHY!? AREN'T YOU WORKING...?
THEY HAVE LOTS OF SINGERS FOR THE BANQUET OF SONG...
...SO NONE OF US GET THE STAGE FOR LONG.

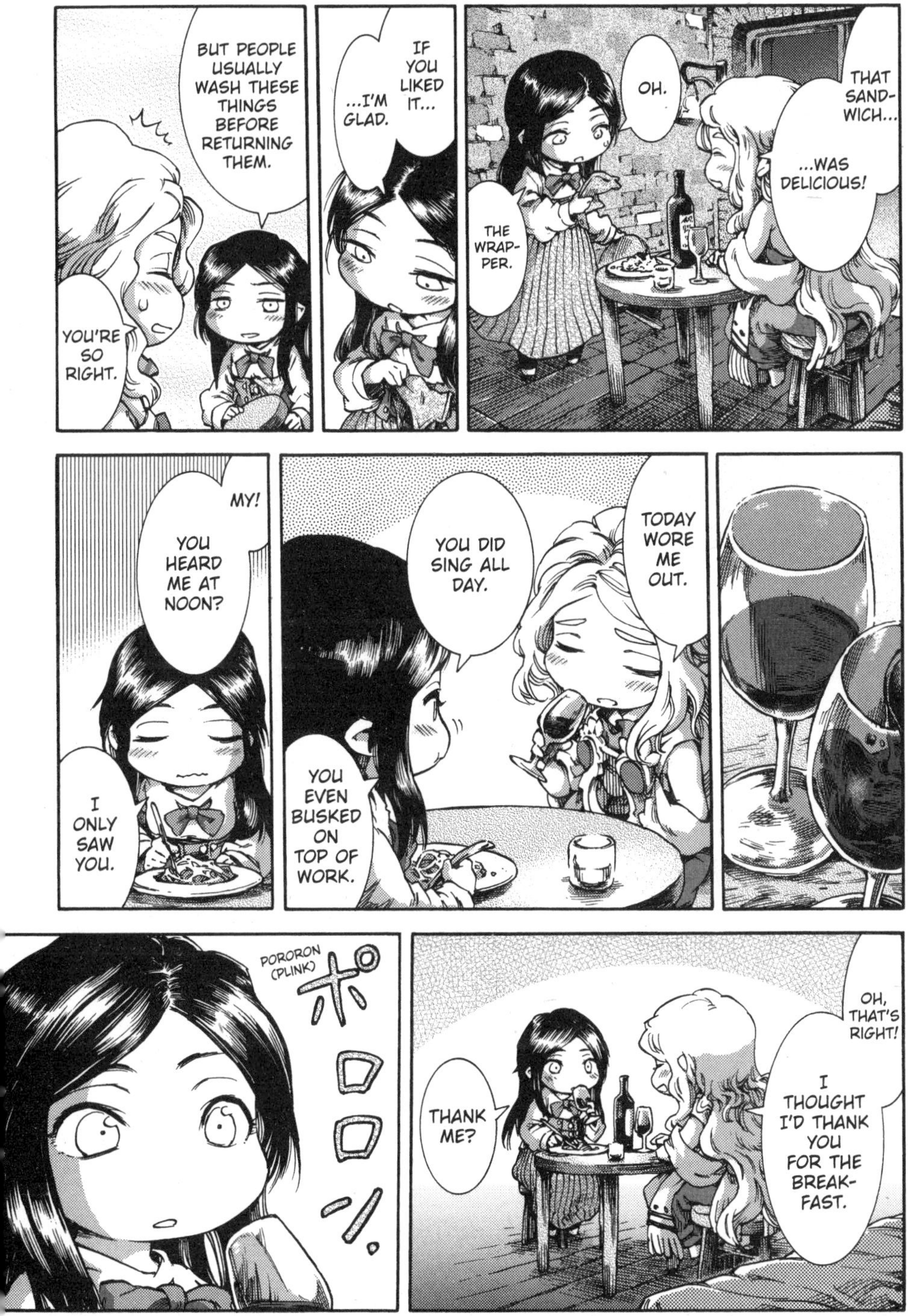
THAT SANDWICH...
...WAS DELICIOUS!
OH.
THE WRAPPER.
IF YOU LIKED IT...
...I'M GLAD.
BUT PEOPLE USUALLY WASH THESE THINGS BEFORE RETURNING THEM.
YOU'RE SO RIGHT.
TODAY WORE ME OUT.
YOU DID SING ALL DAY.
YOU EVEN BUSKED ON TOP OF WORK.
MY!
YOU HEARD ME AT NOON?
I ONLY SAW YOU.
OH, THAT'S RIGHT!
I THOUGHT I'D THANK YOU FOR THE BREAKFAST.
THANK ME?
POROROON (PLINK)

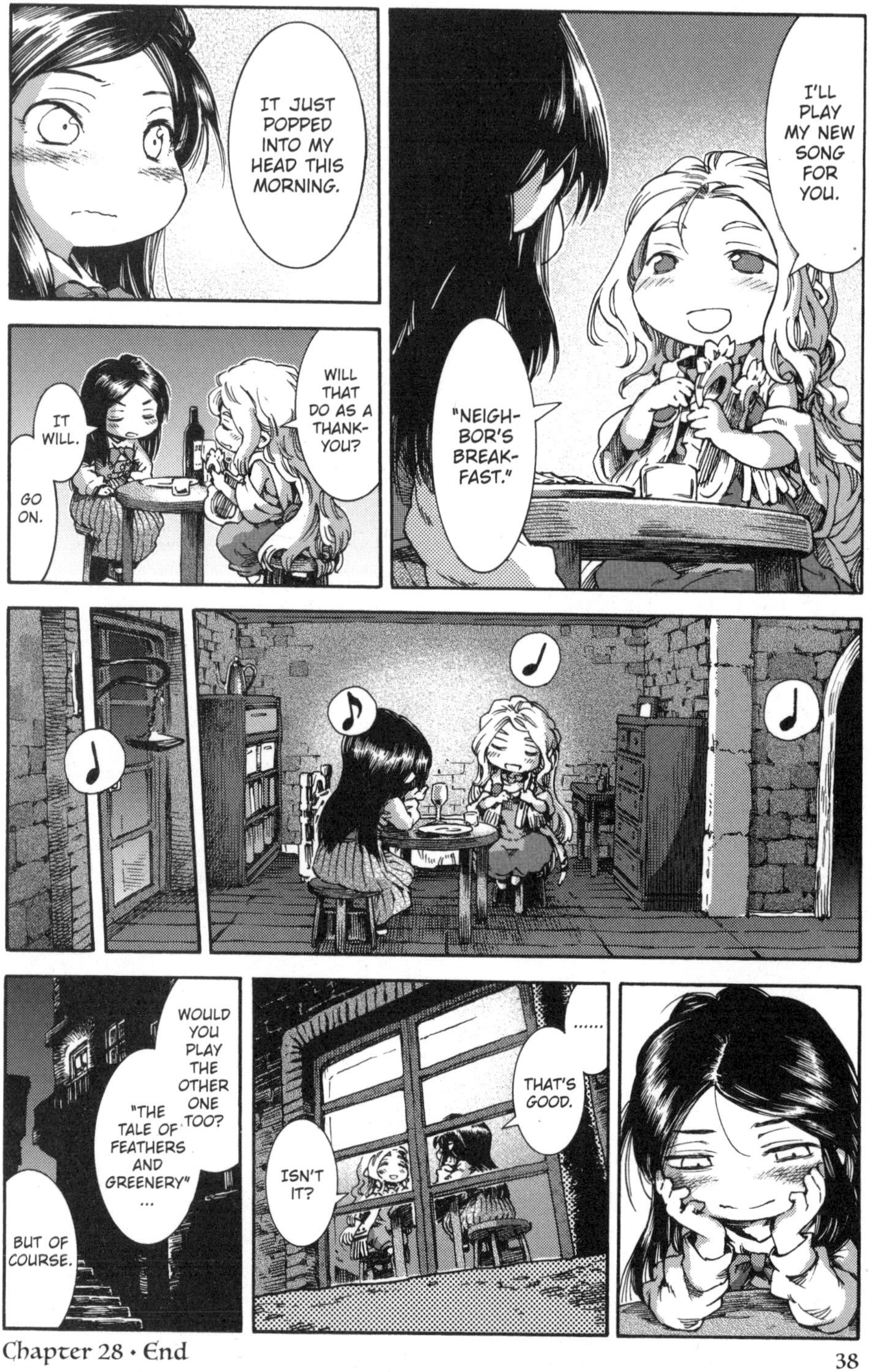
I'LL PLAY MY NEW SONG FOR YOU.
"NEIGHBOR'S BREAKFAST."
IT JUST POPPED INTO MY HEAD THIS MORNING.
WILL THAT DO AS A THANK-YOU?
IT WILL.
GO ON.
......
THAT'S GOOD.
ISN'T IT?
WOULD YOU PLAY THE OTHER ONE TOO?
"THE TALE OF FEATHERS AND GREENERY"...
BUT OF COURSE.

Chapter 28 • End

•*Column*• Underfoot Steps 28 / **Laika's Weekday**

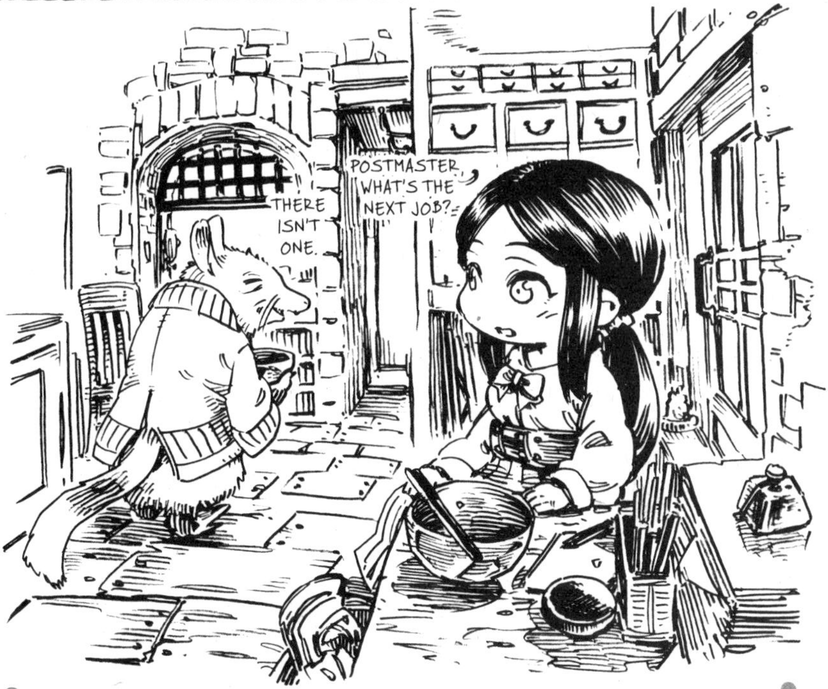
POSTMASTER, WHAT'S THE NEXT JOB?
THERE ISN'T ONE.

8:00 a.m. Breakfast
She usually makes do with pre-bought pastries.

9:00 a.m. Work
She works in the back at a small post office. There isn't much to do, and she has too much spare time.

12:30 p.m. Lunch
The new rice-bowl place next door is good, but she's concerned about her weight.

5:00 p.m. Home
On her way home, she buys groceries in town. Wine is cheaper at Honey Manor.

7:30 p.m. Dinner
She's been very into cooking with herbs lately. Her neighbor catches the scent.

11:00 p.m. Nightcap
Instead of going home, the neighbor keeps singing. (There have never been any complaints.)

1:00 a.m. Bed
When the neighbor doesn't stop singing, she's short on sleep the next day.

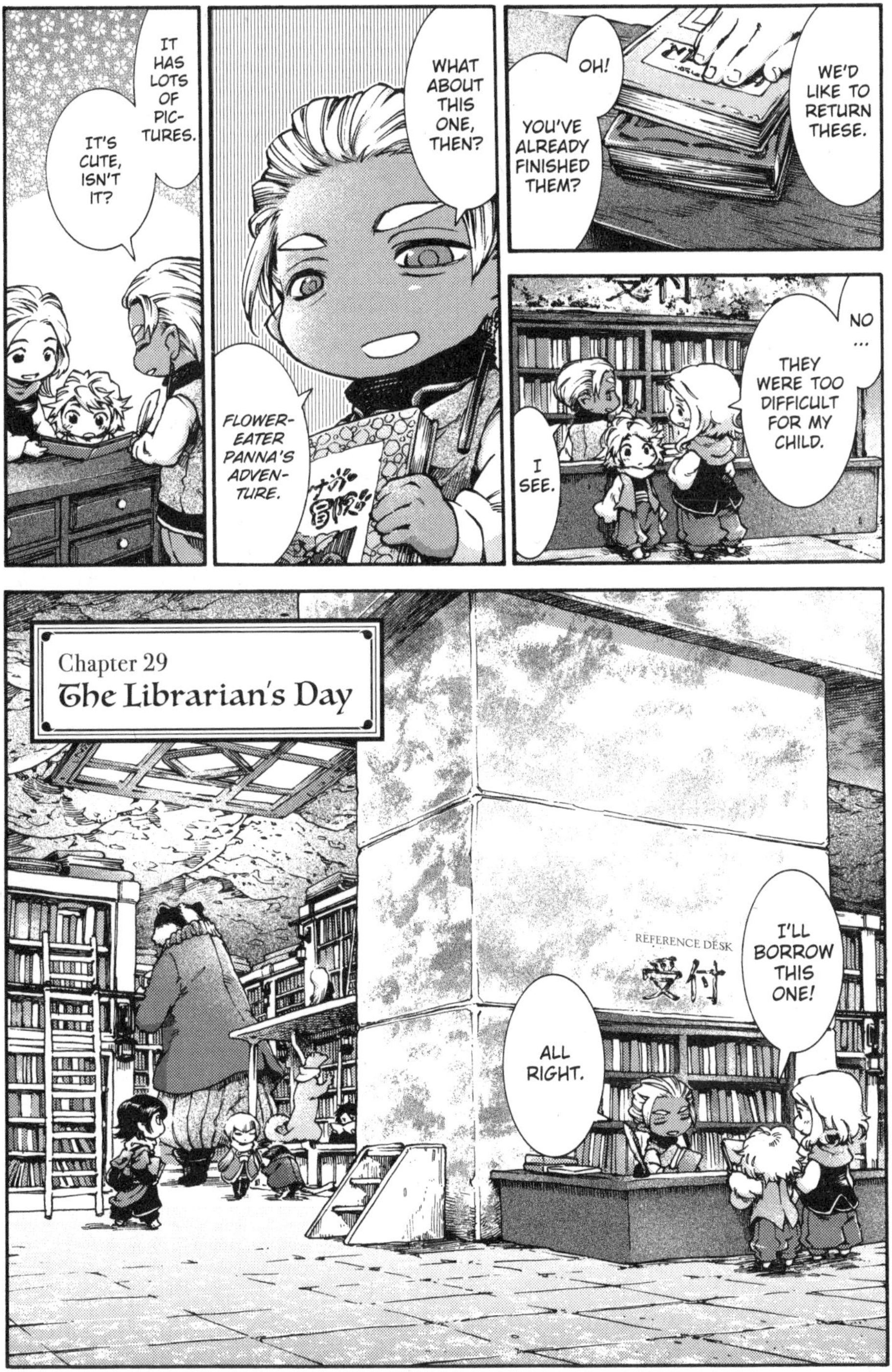
WE'D LIKE TO RETURN THESE.
OH!
YOU'VE ALREADY FINISHED THEM?
NO ... THEY WERE TOO DIFFICULT FOR MY CHILD.
I SEE.
WHAT ABOUT THIS ONE, THEN?
FLOWER-EATER PANNA'S ADVENTURE.
IT HAS LOTS OF PICTURES.
IT'S CUTE, ISN'T IT?
Chapter 29
The Librarian's Day
REFERENCE DESK
受付
I'LL BORROW THIS ONE!
ALL RIGHT.

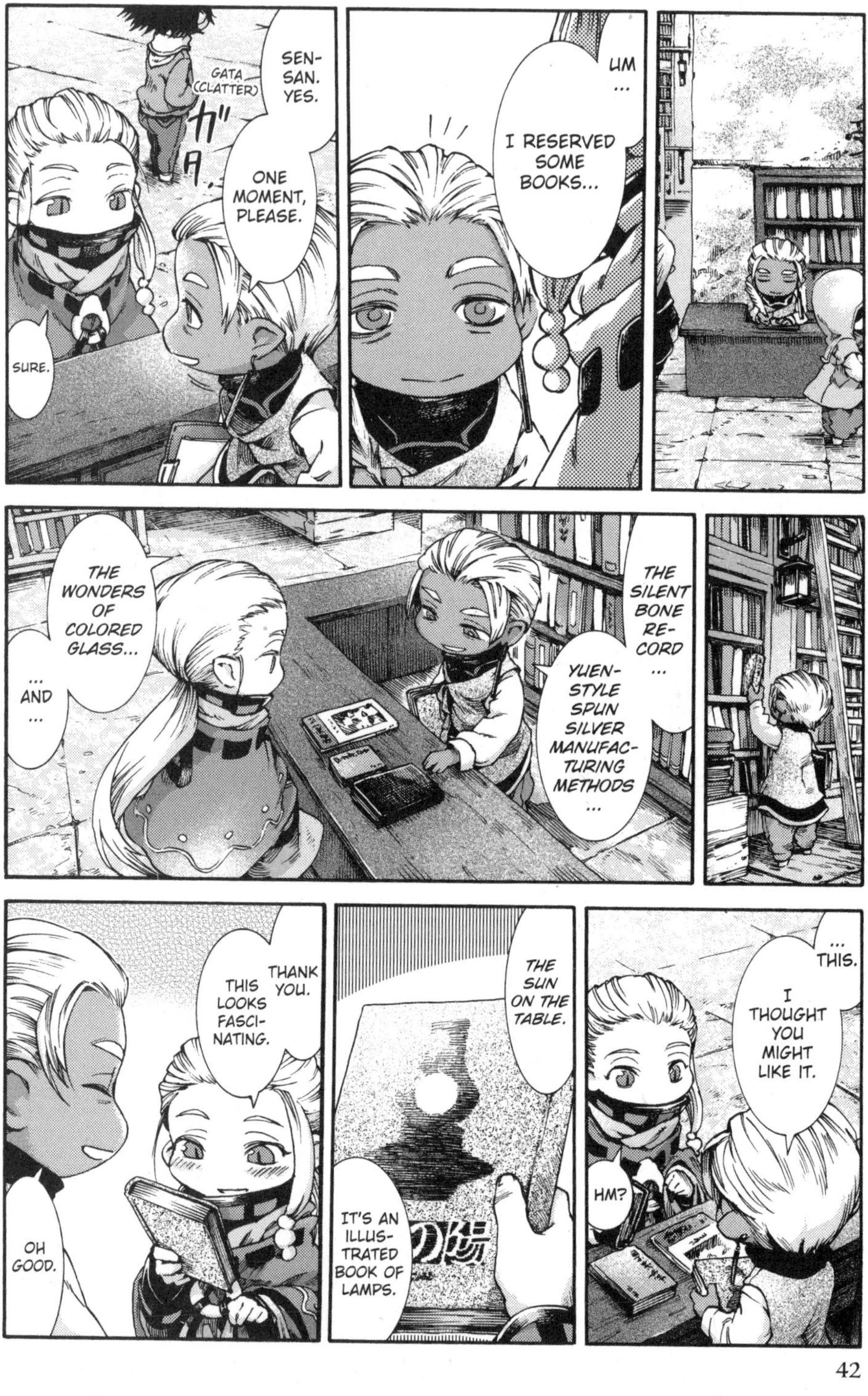
UM ... I RESERVED SOME BOOKS...
SEN-SAN. YES.
GATA (CLATTER)
ONE MOMENT, PLEASE.
SURE.
THE SILENT BONE RECORD ...
YUEN-STYLE SPUN SILVER MANUFACTURING METHODS ...
THE WONDERS OF COLORED GLASS...
... AND ...
... THIS.
I THOUGHT YOU MIGHT LIKE IT.
HM?
THE SUN ON THE TABLE.
IT'S AN ILLUSTRATED BOOK OF LAMPS.
THANK YOU.
THIS LOOKS FASCINATING.
OH GOOD.

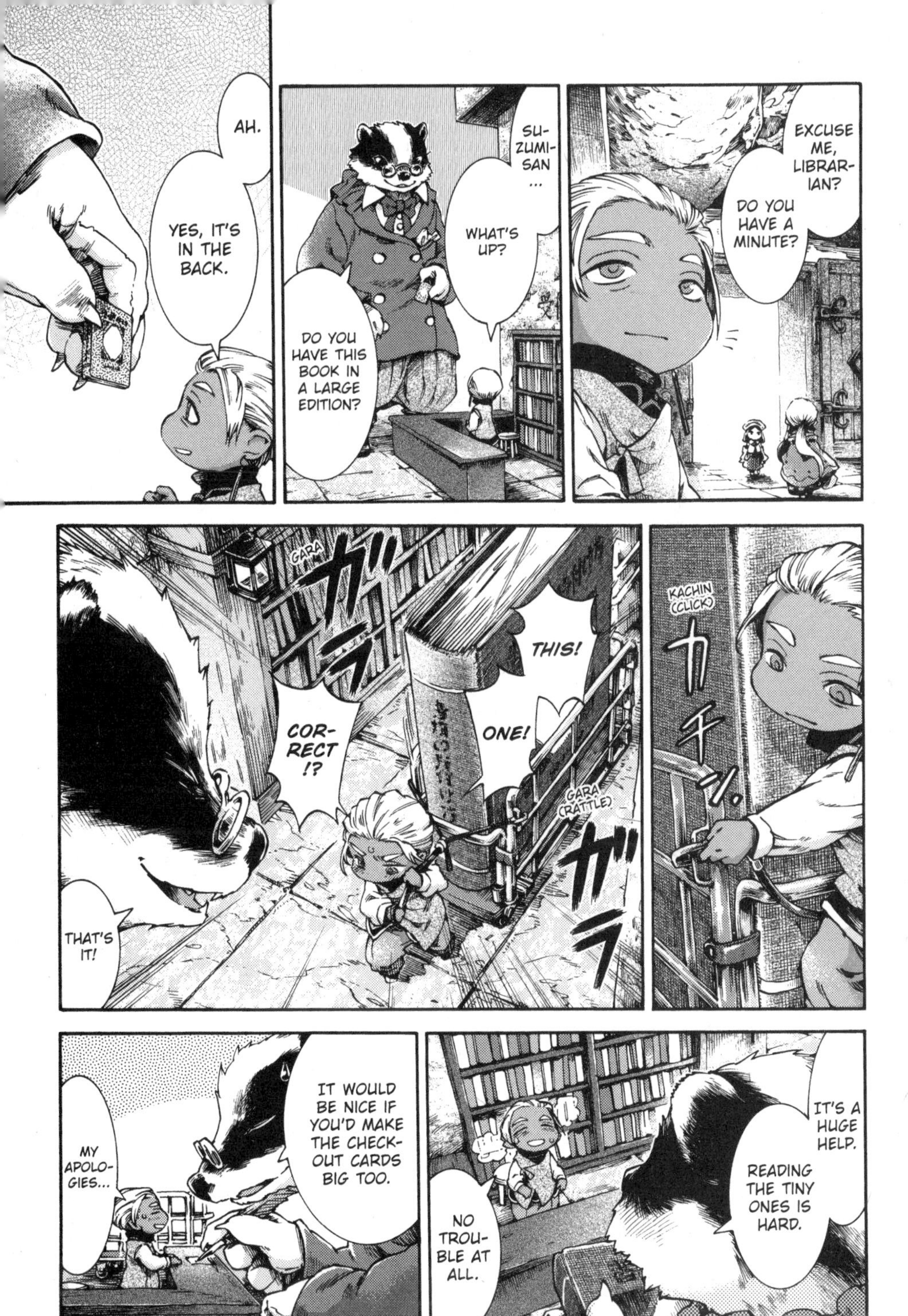
EXCUSE ME, LIBRARIAN?
DO YOU HAVE A MINUTE?
SU-ZUMI-SAN ...
WHAT'S UP?
DO YOU HAVE THIS BOOK IN A LARGE EDITION?
AH.
YES, IT'S IN THE BACK.
KACHIN (CLICK)
GARA
THIS! ONE!
CORRECT!?
GARA (RATTLE)
THAT'S IT!
IT'S A HUGE HELP.
READING THE TINY ONES IS HARD.
NO TROUBLE AT ALL.
IT WOULD BE NICE IF YOU'D MAKE THE CHECK-OUT CARDS BIG TOO.
MY APOLO-GIES...

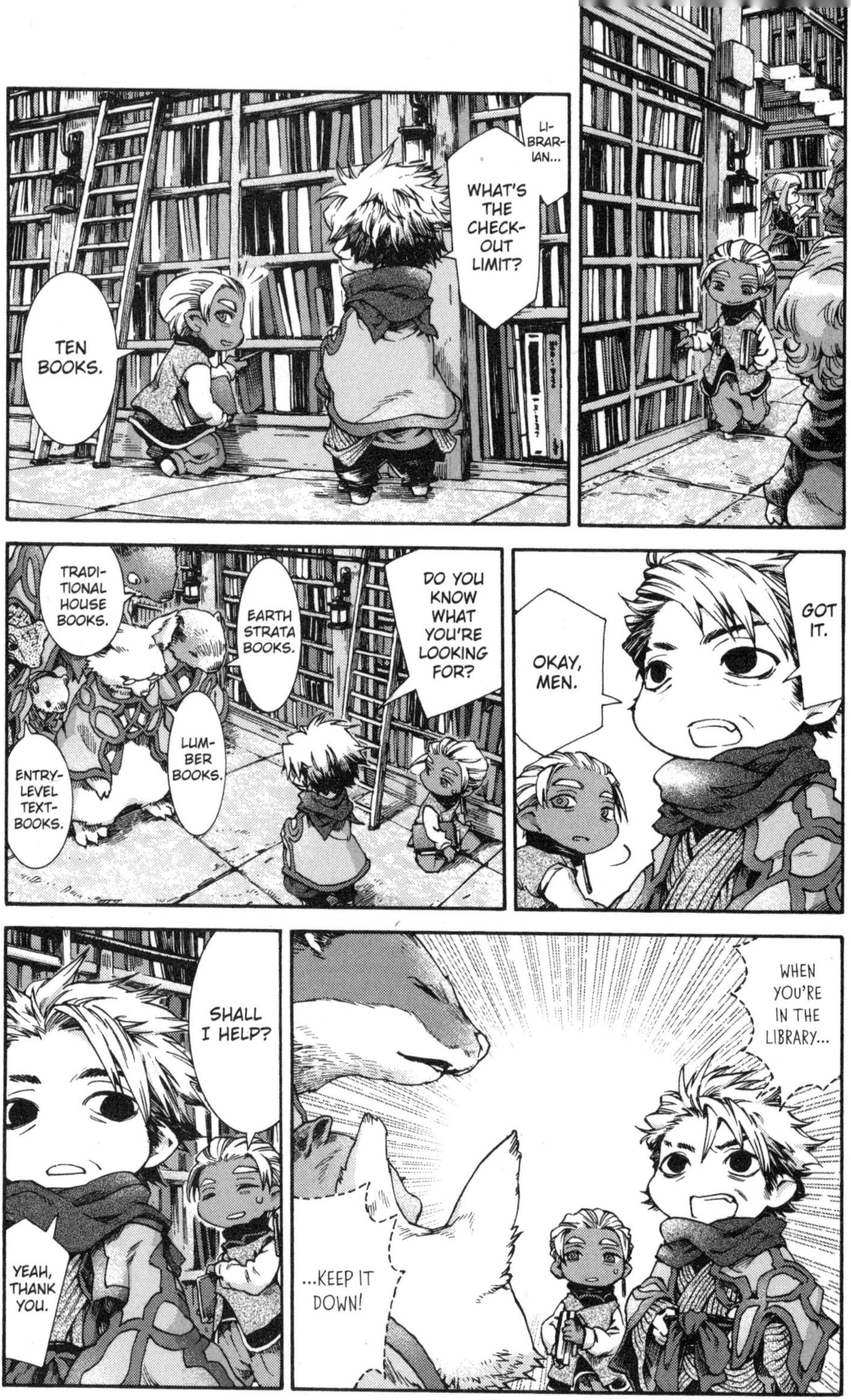
LI-BRAR-IAN...
WHAT'S THE CHECK-OUT LIMIT?
TEN BOOKS.
GOT IT.
OKAY, MEN.
DO YOU KNOW WHAT YOU'RE LOOKING FOR?
EARTH STRATA BOOKS.
TRADI-TIONAL HOUSE BOOKS.
LUM-BER BOOKS.
ENTRY-LEVEL TEXT-BOOKS.
WHEN YOU'RE IN THE LIBRARY...
...KEEP IT DOWN!
SHALL I HELP?
YEAH, THANK YOU.

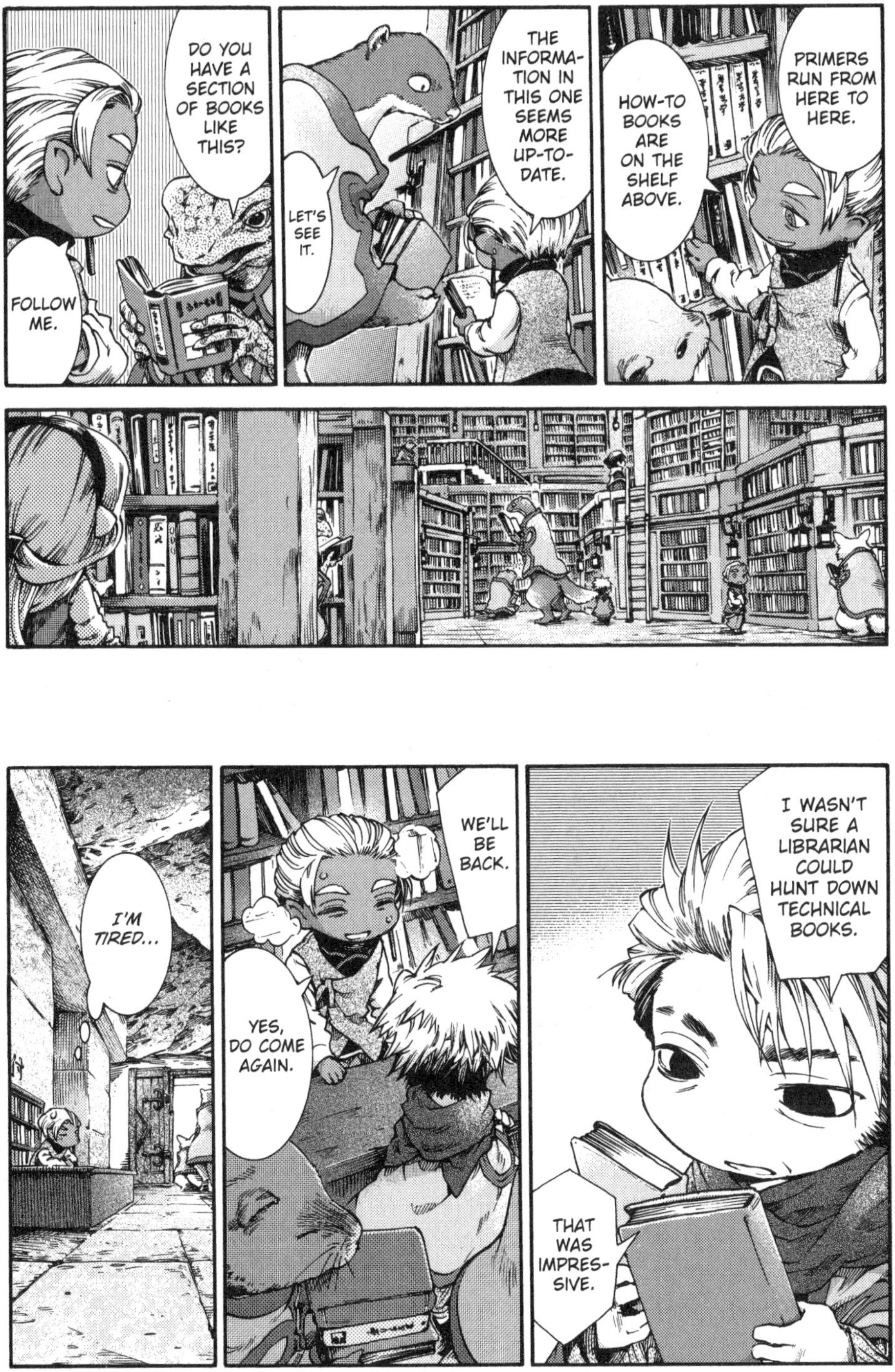
PRIMERS RUN FROM HERE TO HERE.
HOW-TO BOOKS ARE ON THE SHELF ABOVE.
THE INFORMATION IN THIS ONE SEEMS MORE UP-TO-DATE.
LET'S SEE IT.
DO YOU HAVE A SECTION OF BOOKS LIKE THIS?
FOLLOW ME.
I WASN'T SURE A LIBRARIAN COULD HUNT DOWN TECHNICAL BOOKS.
THAT WAS IMPRESSIVE.
WE'LL BE BACK.
YES, DO COME AGAIN.
I'M TIRED...

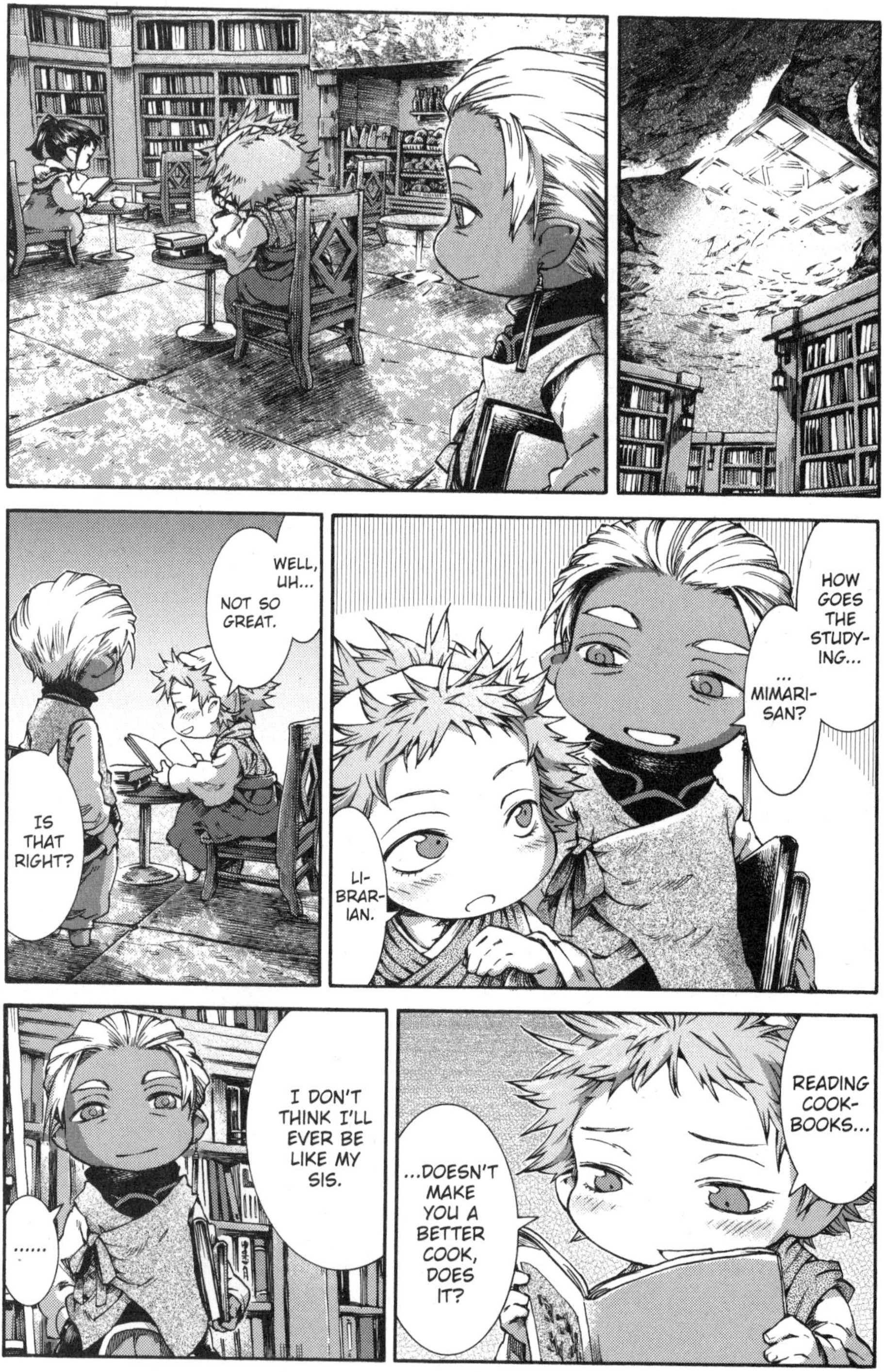
HOW GOES THE STUDYING... ...MIMARI-SAN?
LIBRARIAN.
WELL, UH... NOT SO GREAT.
IS THAT RIGHT?
READING COOKBOOKS...
...DOESN'T MAKE YOU A BETTER COOK, DOES IT?
I DON'T THINK I'LL EVER BE LIKE MY SIS.
......

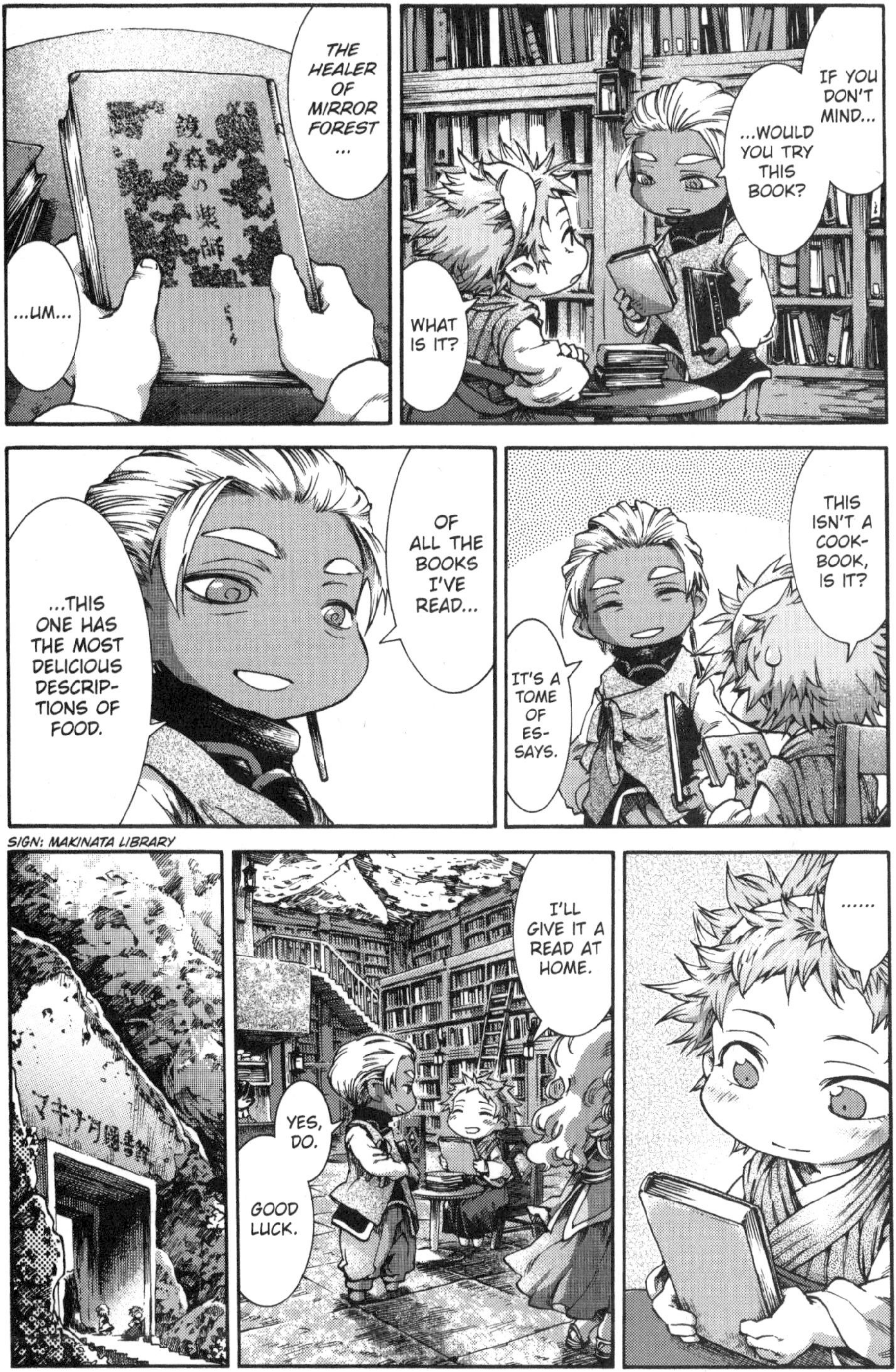
IF YOU DON'T MIND...
...WOULD YOU TRY THIS BOOK?
WHAT IS IT?
THE HEALER OF MIRROR FOREST...
...UM...
THIS ISN'T A COOKBOOK, IS IT?
IT'S A TOME OF ESSAYS.
OF ALL THE BOOKS I'VE READ...
...THIS ONE HAS THE MOST DELICIOUS DESCRIPTIONS OF FOOD.
......
I'LL GIVE IT A READ AT HOME.
YES, DO.
GOOD LUCK.
SIGN: MAKINATA LIBRARY

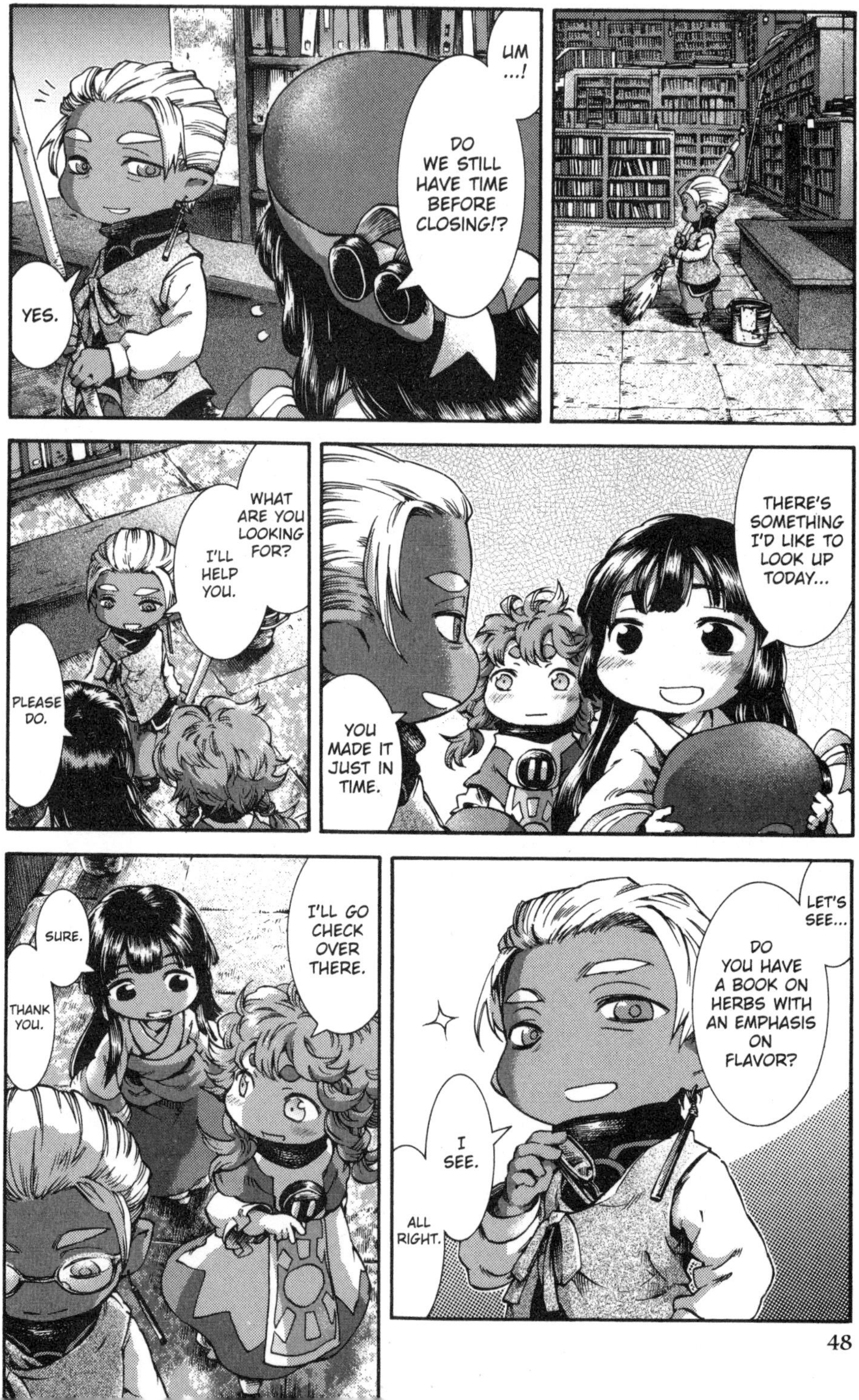
UM ...!
DO WE STILL HAVE TIME BEFORE CLOSING!?
YES.
THERE'S SOMETHING I'D LIKE TO LOOK UP TODAY...
YOU MADE IT JUST IN TIME.
WHAT ARE YOU LOOKING FOR?
I'LL HELP YOU.
PLEASE DO.
LET'S SEE...
DO YOU HAVE A BOOK ON HERBS WITH AN EMPHASIS ON FLAVOR?
I SEE.
ALL RIGHT.
I'LL GO CHECK OVER THERE.
SURE.
THANK YOU.

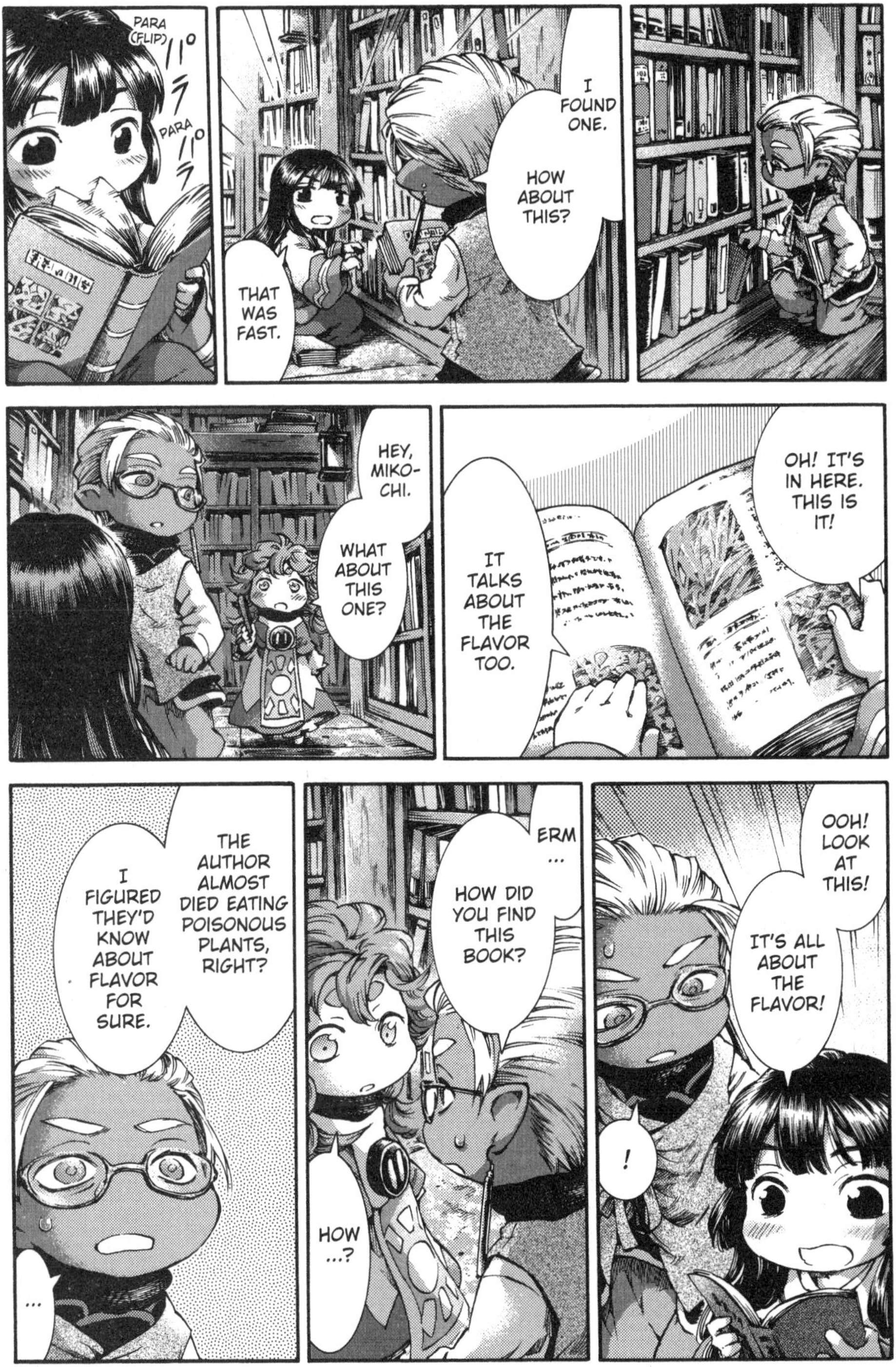
I FOUND ONE.
HOW ABOUT THIS?
THAT WAS FAST.
PARA (FLIP)
PARA
OH! IT'S IN HERE. THIS IS IT!
IT TALKS ABOUT THE FLAVOR TOO.
HEY, MIKO-CHI.
WHAT ABOUT THIS ONE?
OOH! LOOK AT THIS!
IT'S ALL ABOUT THE FLAVOR!
!
ERM...
HOW DID YOU FIND THIS BOOK?
HOW ...?
THE AUTHOR ALMOST DIED EATING POISONOUS PLANTS, RIGHT?
I FIGURED THEY'D KNOW ABOUT FLAVOR FOR SURE.
...

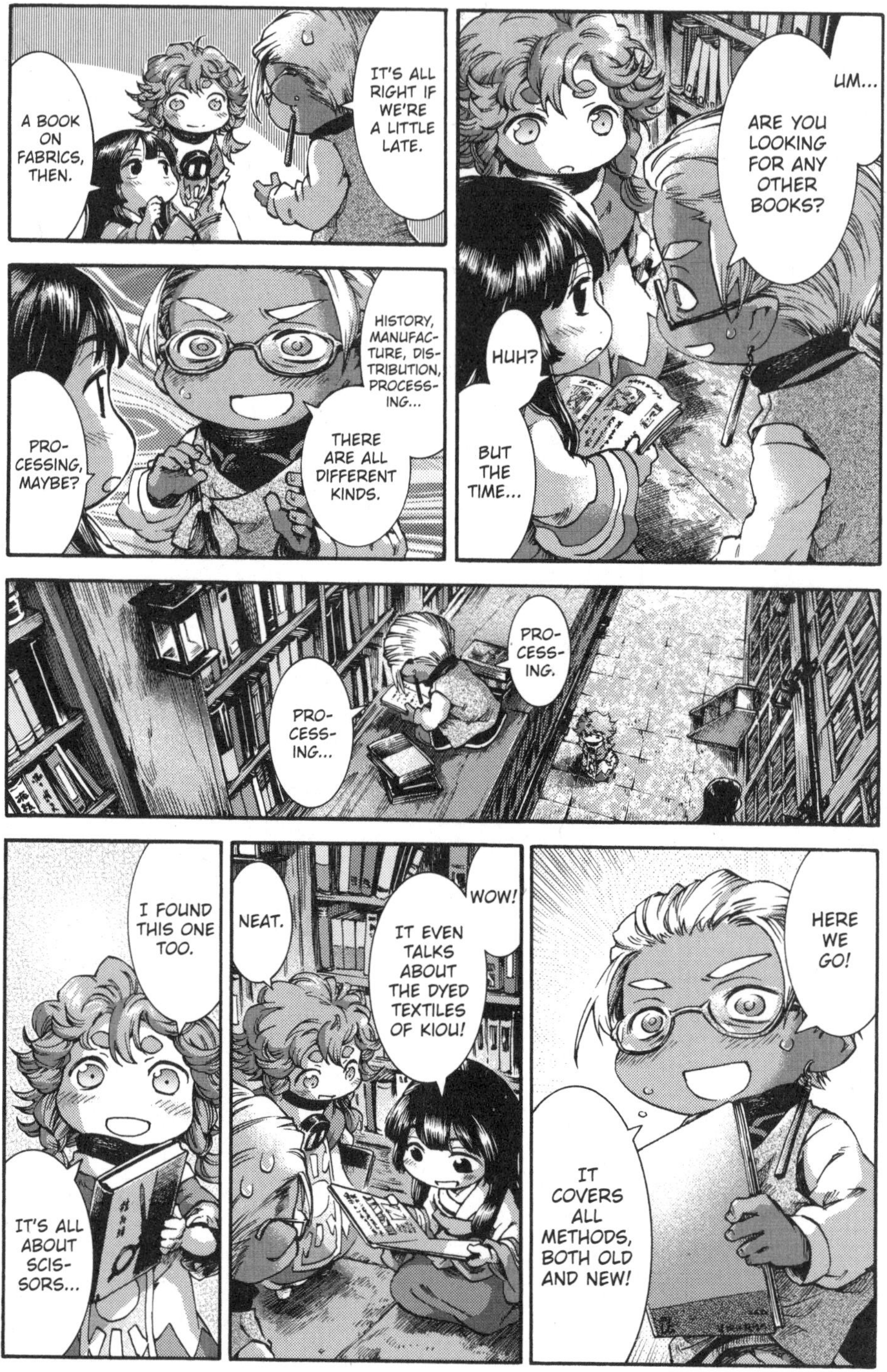
UM...
ARE YOU LOOKING FOR ANY OTHER BOOKS?
HUH?
BUT THE TIME...
IT'S ALL RIGHT IF WE'RE A LITTLE LATE.
A BOOK ON FABRICS, THEN.
HISTORY, MANUFAC-TURE, DIS-TRIBUTION, PROCESS-ING...
THERE ARE ALL DIFFERENT KINDS.
PRO-CESSING, MAYBE?
PRO-CESS-ING.
PRO-CESS-ING...
HERE WE GO!
IT COVERS ALL METHODS, BOTH OLD AND NEW!
WOW!
IT EVEN TALKS ABOUT THE DYED TEXTILES OF KIOU!
NEAT.
I FOUND THIS ONE TOO.
IT'S ALL ABOUT SCIS-SORS...

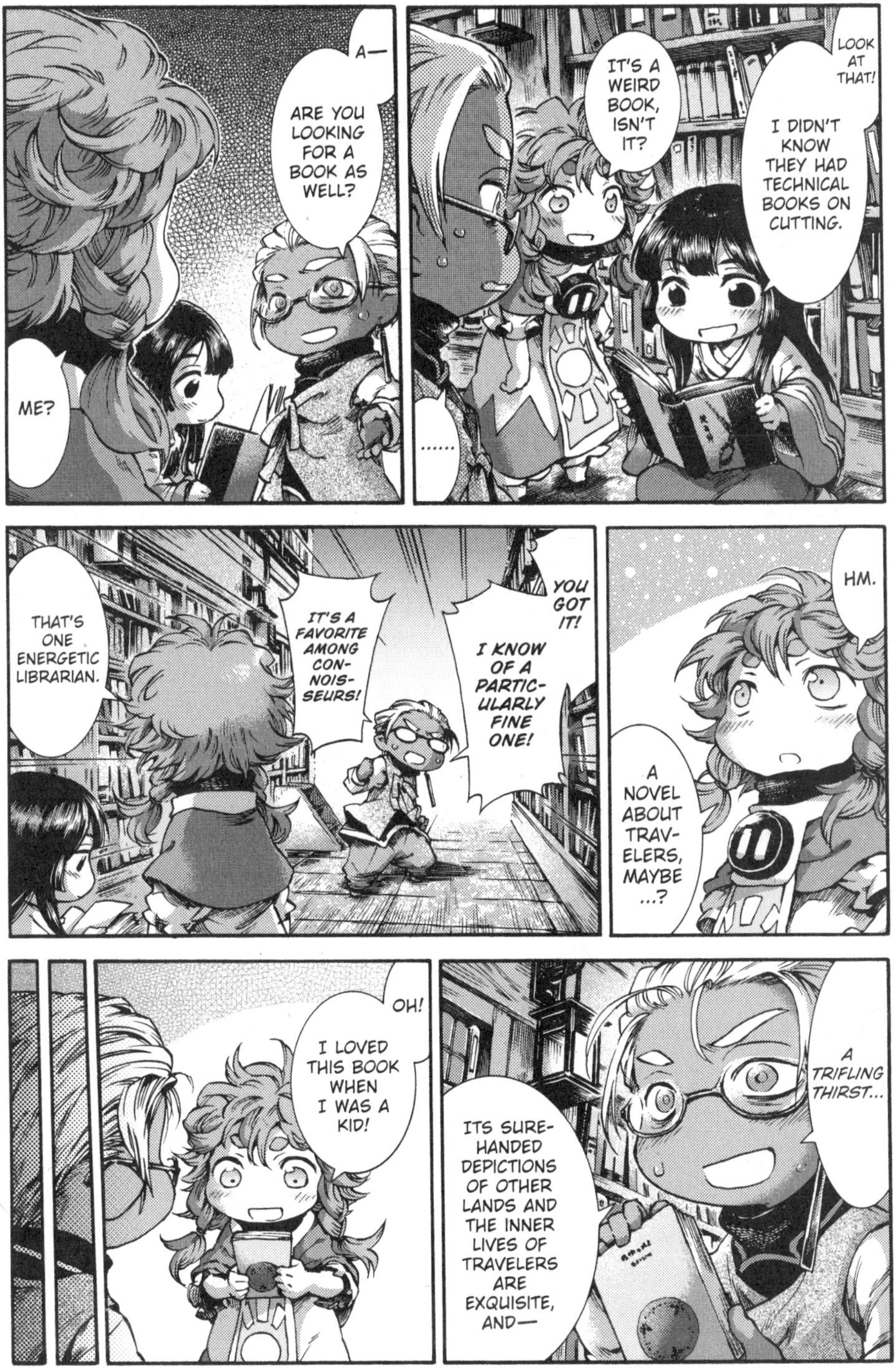
LOOK AT THAT!
I DIDN'T KNOW THEY HAD TECHNICAL BOOKS ON CUTTING.
IT'S A WEIRD BOOK, ISN'T IT?
......
A—
ARE YOU LOOKING FOR A BOOK AS WELL?
ME?
HM.
A NOVEL ABOUT TRAV-ELERS, MAYBE ...?
YOU GOT IT!
I KNOW OF A PARTIC-ULARLY FINE ONE!
IT'S A FAVORITE AMONG CON-NOIS-SEURS!
THAT'S ONE ENERGETIC LIBRARIAN.
A TRIFLING THIRST...
ITS SURE-HANDED DEPICTIONS OF OTHER LANDS AND THE INNER LIVES OF TRAVELERS ARE EXQUISITE, AND—
OH!
I LOVED THIS BOOK WHEN I WAS A KID!

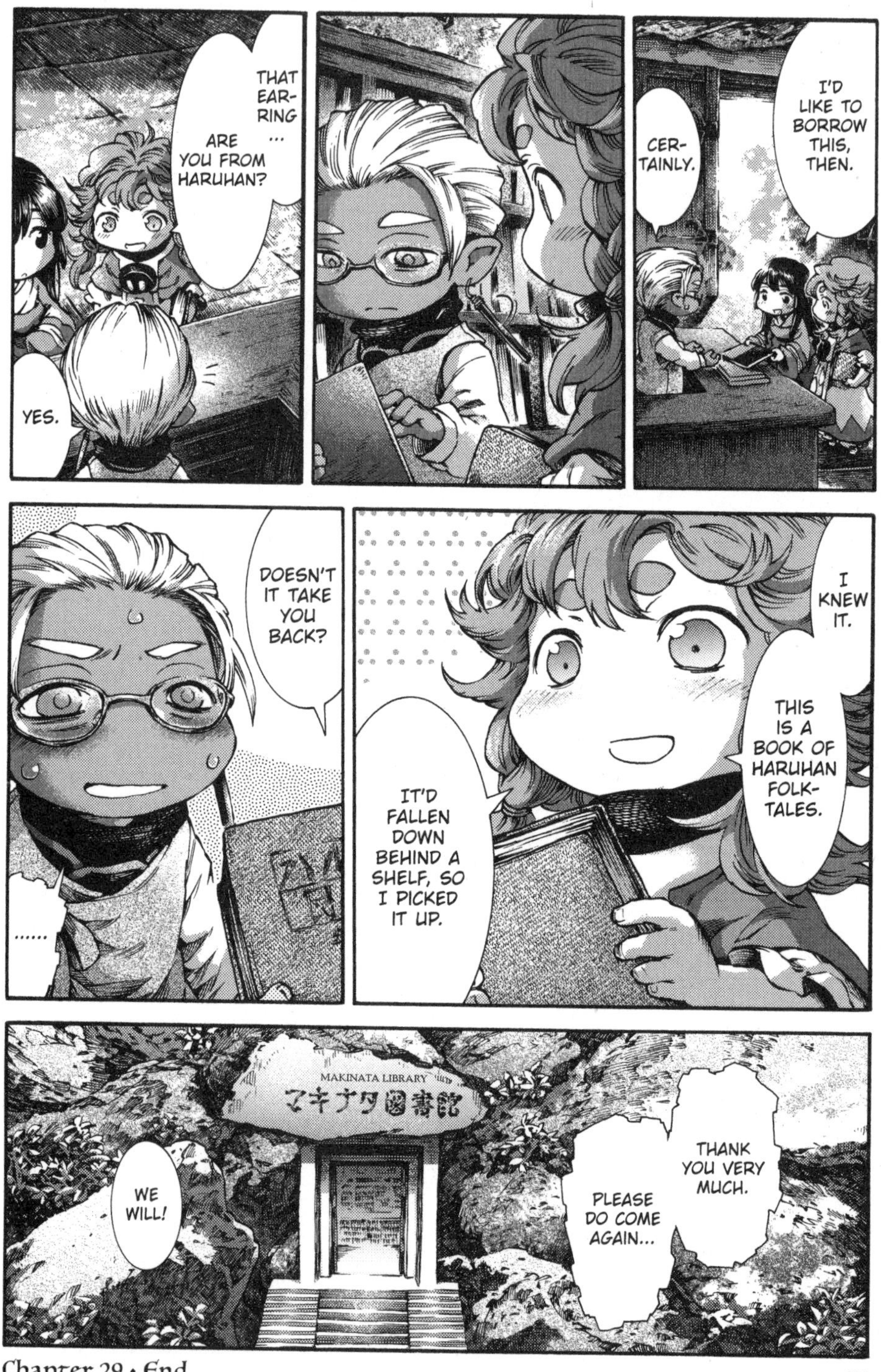
I'D LIKE TO BORROW THIS, THEN.
CER-TAINLY.
THAT EAR-RING ...
ARE YOU FROM HARUHAN?
YES.
I KNEW IT.
THIS IS A BOOK OF HARUHAN FOLK-TALES.
IT'D FALLEN DOWN BEHIND A SHELF, SO I PICKED IT UP.
DOESN'T IT TAKE YOU BACK?
......
MAKINATA LIBRARY
マキナタ図書館
THANK YOU VERY MUCH.
PLEASE DO COME AGAIN...
WE WILL!

Chapter 29 • End

Panna spoke, eyes filling with tears.

"I won't eat flowers anymore.
Otherwise, I'd lose my one and only friend."

The flower, now a mere stalk, looked at Panna and smiled.

"It's all right. You can eat me.
Take the seeds I gave you a minute ago and sow them here.
Next spring, come back, and bring your friends."

—An excerpt from *Flower-Eater Panna's Adventure*,
    from the Makinata library collection

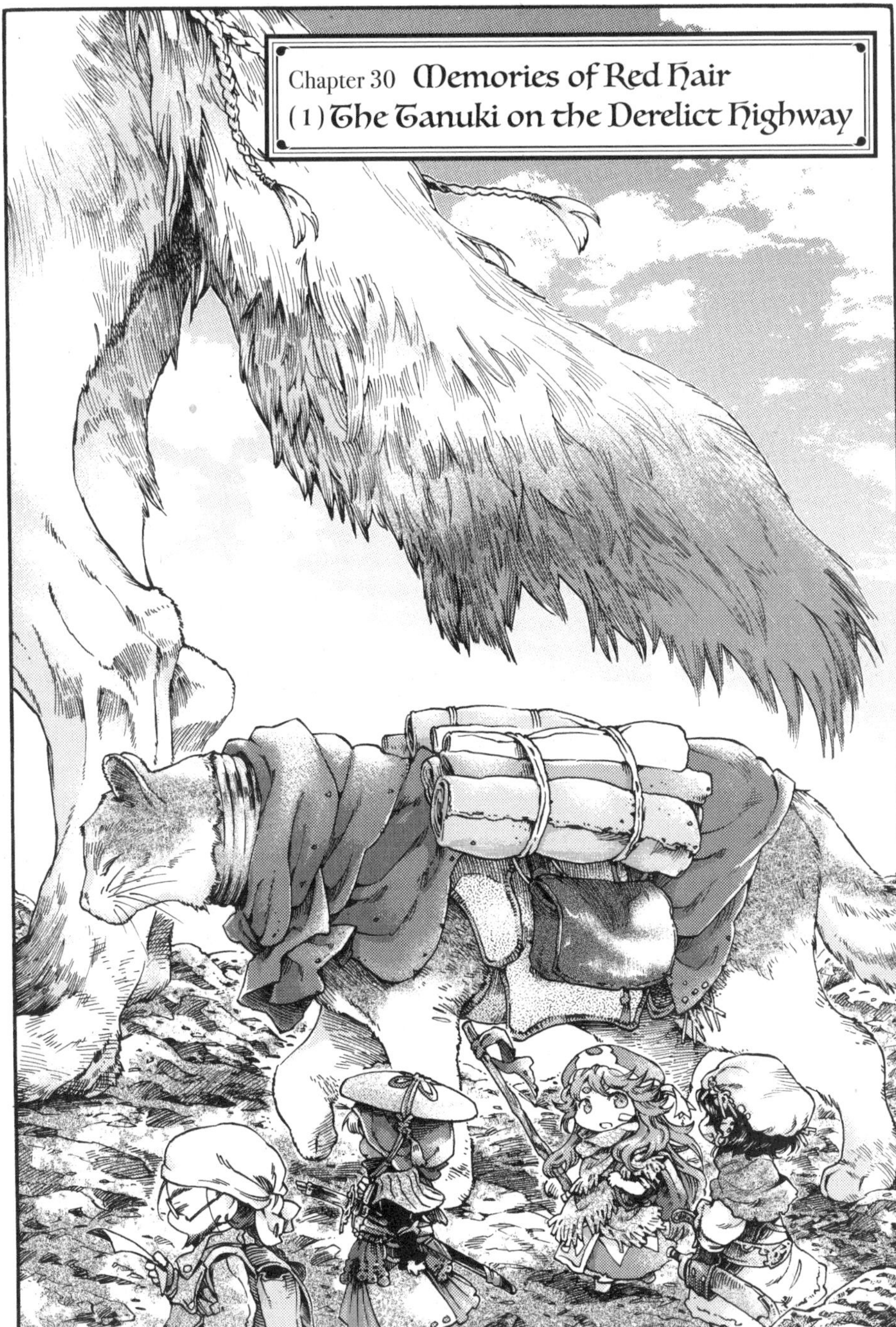
Chapter 30 Memories of Red Hair
(1) The Tanuki on the Derelict Highway

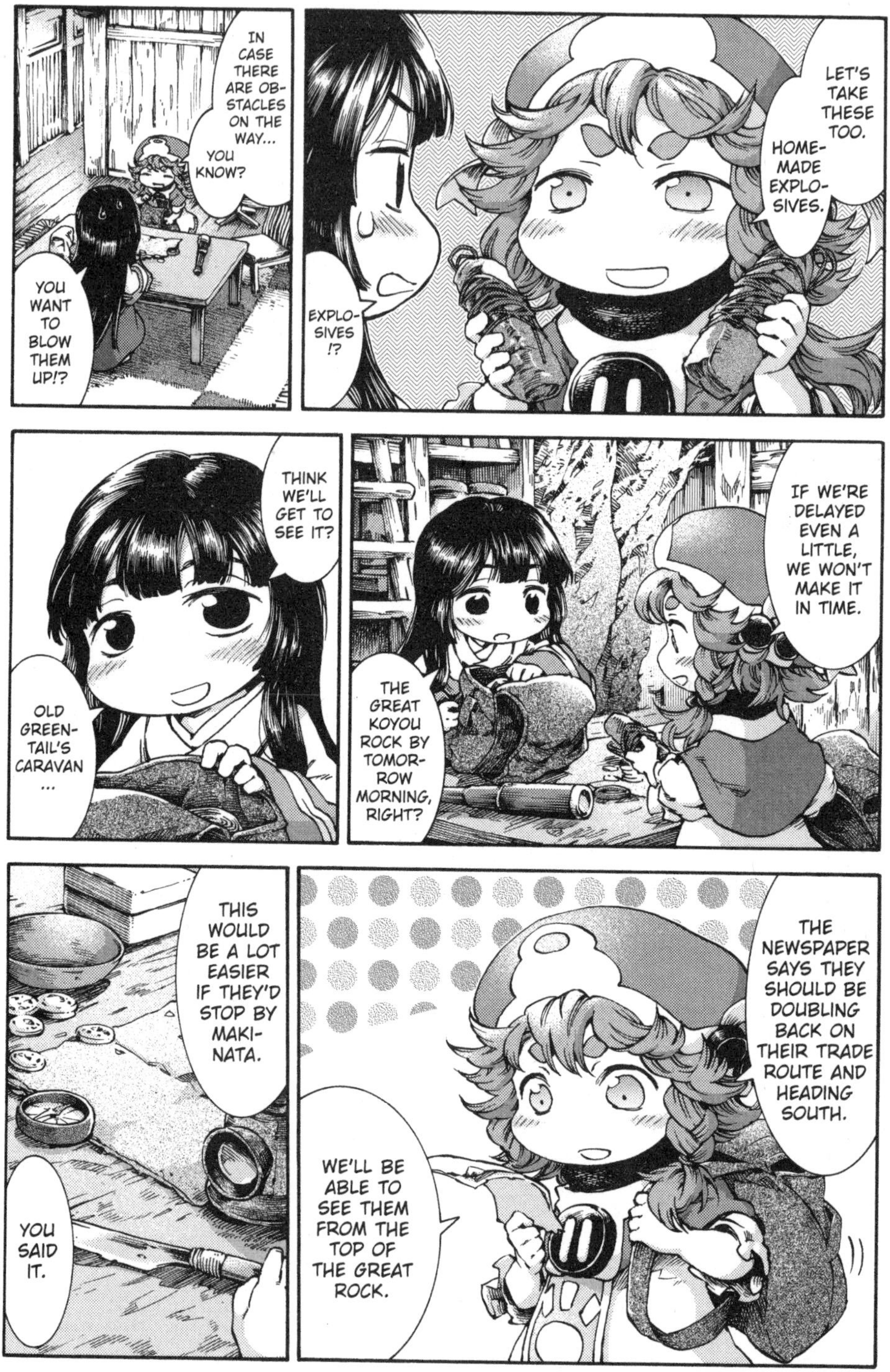
LET'S TAKE THESE TOO. HOMEMADE EXPLOSIVES.
EXPLOSIVES!?
IN CASE THERE ARE OBSTACLES ON THE WAY...
YOU KNOW?
YOU WANT TO BLOW THEM UP!?
IF WE'RE DELAYED EVEN A LITTLE, WE WON'T MAKE IT IN TIME.
THE GREAT KOYOU ROCK BY TOMORROW MORNING, RIGHT?
THINK WE'LL GET TO SEE IT?
OLD GREEN-TAIL'S CARAVAN...
THE NEWSPAPER SAYS THEY SHOULD BE DOUBLING BACK ON THEIR TRADE ROUTE AND HEADING SOUTH.
WE'LL BE ABLE TO SEE THEM FROM THE TOP OF THE GREAT ROCK.
THIS WOULD BE A LOT EASIER IF THEY'D STOP BY MAKINATA.
YOU SAID IT.

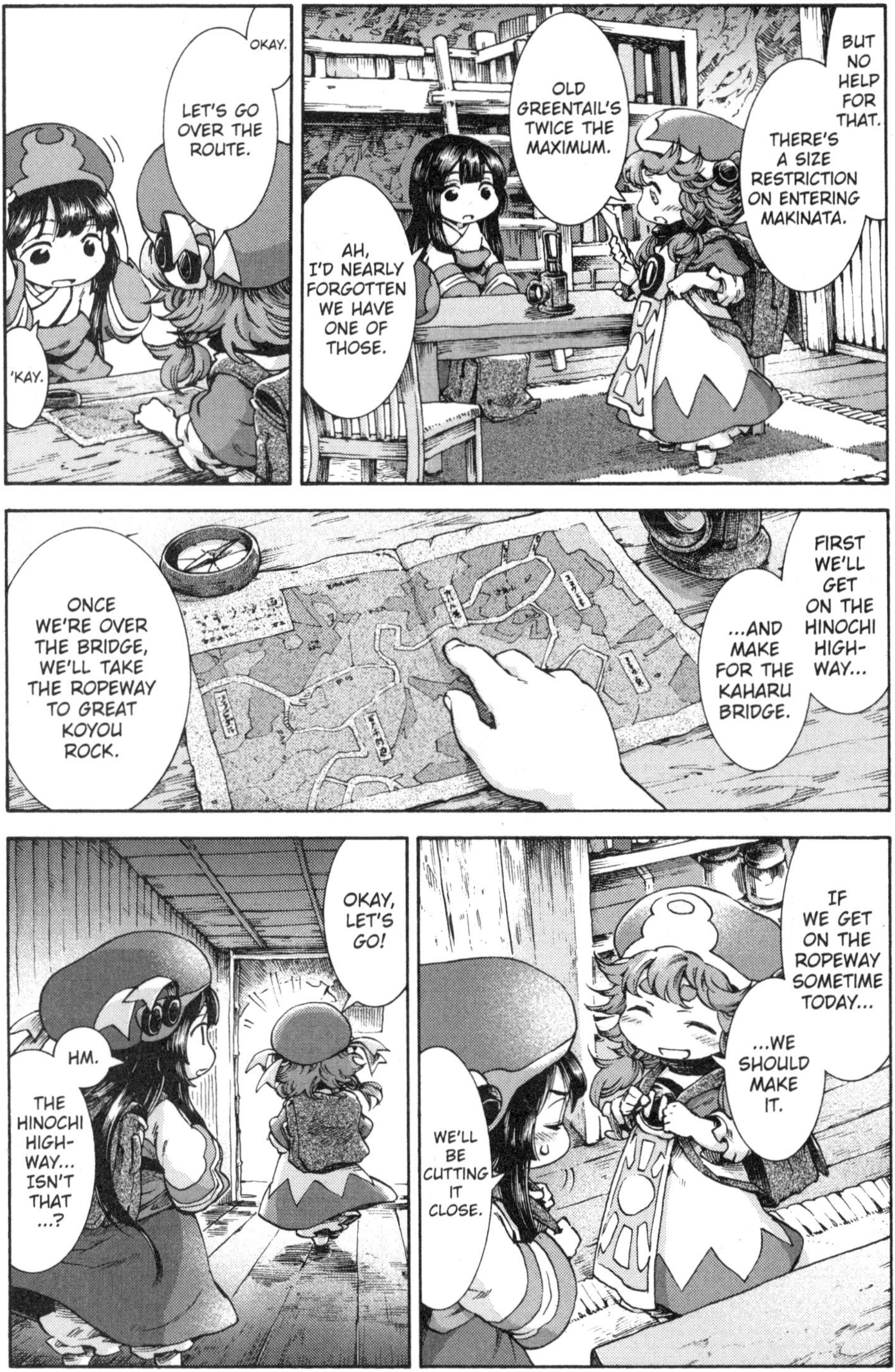
BUT NO HELP FOR THAT.
THERE'S A SIZE RESTRICTION ON ENTERING MAKINATA.
OLD GREENTAIL'S TWICE THE MAXIMUM.
AH, I'D NEARLY FORGOTTEN WE HAVE ONE OF THOSE.
OKAY.
LET'S GO OVER THE ROUTE.
'KAY.
FIRST WE'LL GET ON THE HINOCHI HIGHWAY...
...AND MAKE FOR THE KAHARU BRIDGE.
ONCE WE'RE OVER THE BRIDGE, WE'LL TAKE THE ROPEWAY TO GREAT KOYOU ROCK.
IF WE GET ON THE ROPEWAY SOMETIME TODAY...
...WE SHOULD MAKE IT.
WE'LL BE CUTTING IT CLOSE.
OKAY, LET'S GO!
HM.
THE HINOCHI HIGHWAY... ISN'T THAT ...?

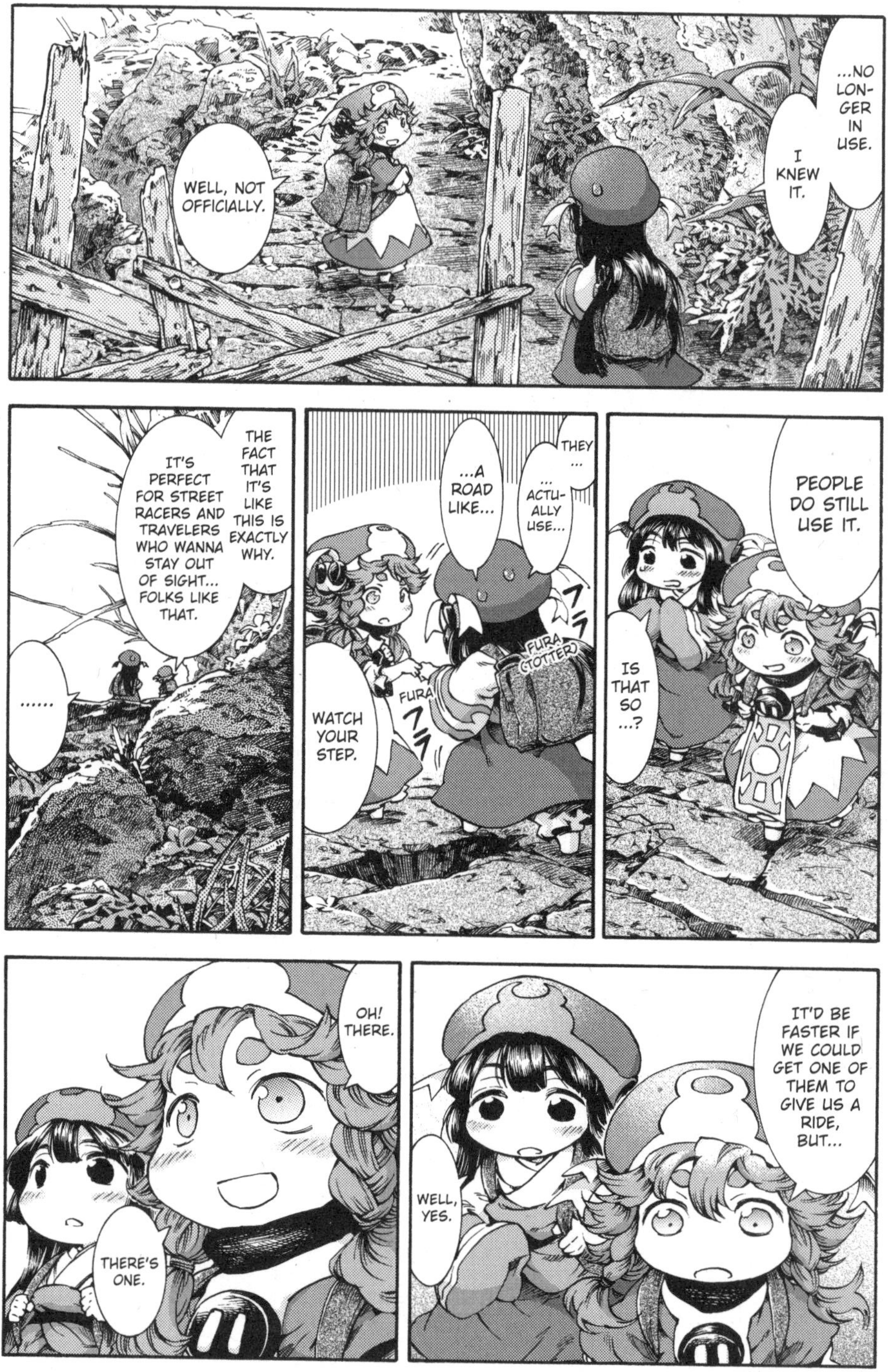
...NO LONGER IN USE.
I KNEW IT.
WELL, NOT OFFICIALLY.
PEOPLE DO STILL USE IT.
IS THAT SO ...?
THEY ...
... ACTUALLY USE...
...A ROAD LIKE...
FURA (TOTTER)
FURA
WATCH YOUR STEP.
THE FACT THAT IT'S LIKE THIS IS EXACTLY WHY.
IT'S PERFECT FOR STREET RACERS AND TRAVELERS WHO WANNA STAY OUT OF SIGHT... FOLKS LIKE THAT.
......
IT'D BE FASTER IF WE COULD GET ONE OF THEM TO GIVE US A RIDE, BUT...
WELL, YES.
OH! THERE.
THERE'S ONE.

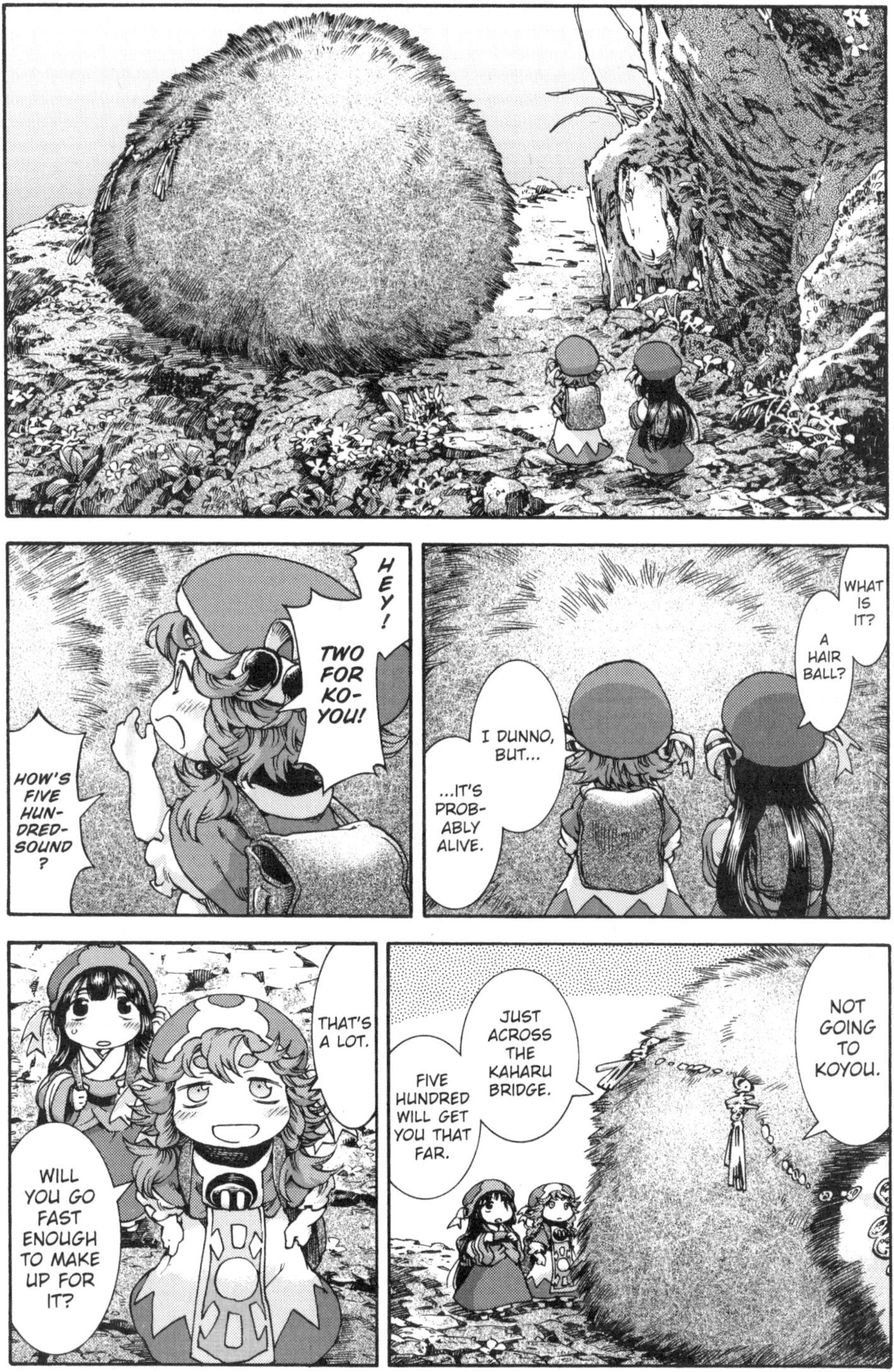
WHAT IS IT?
A HAIR BALL?
I DUNNO, BUT...
...IT'S PROBABLY ALIVE.
HEY!
TWO FOR KOYOU!
HOW'S FIVE HUNDRED SOUND?
NOT GOING TO KOYOU.
JUST ACROSS THE KAHARU BRIDGE.
FIVE HUNDRED WILL GET YOU THAT FAR.
THAT'S A LOT.
WILL YOU GO FAST ENOUGH TO MAKE UP FOR IT?

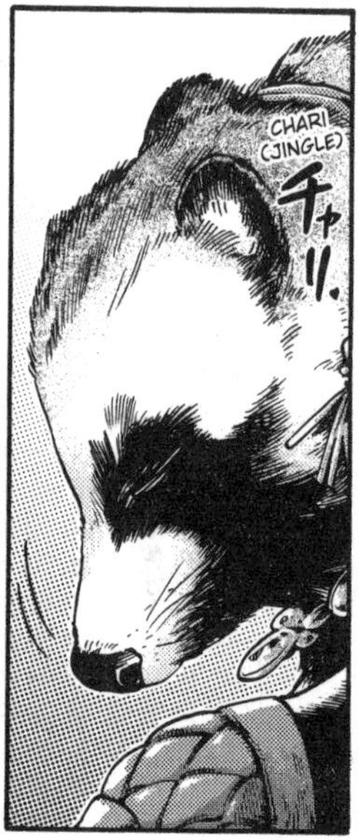
CHARI (JINGLE)
チャリ.
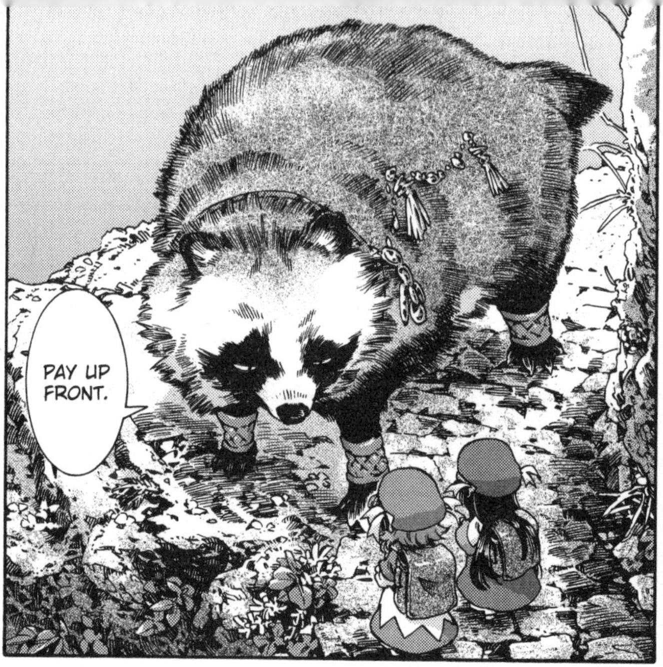
PAY UP FRONT.
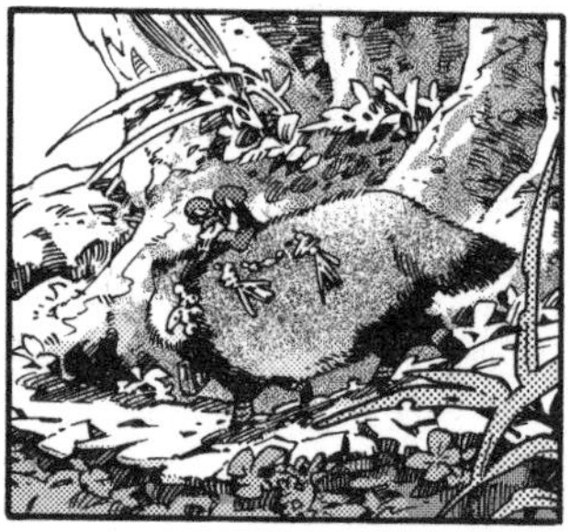
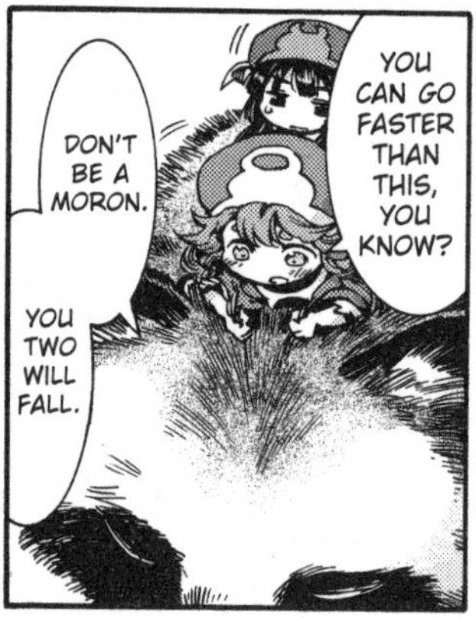
YOU CAN GO FASTER THAN THIS, YOU KNOW?
DON'T BE A MORON.
YOU TWO WILL FALL.
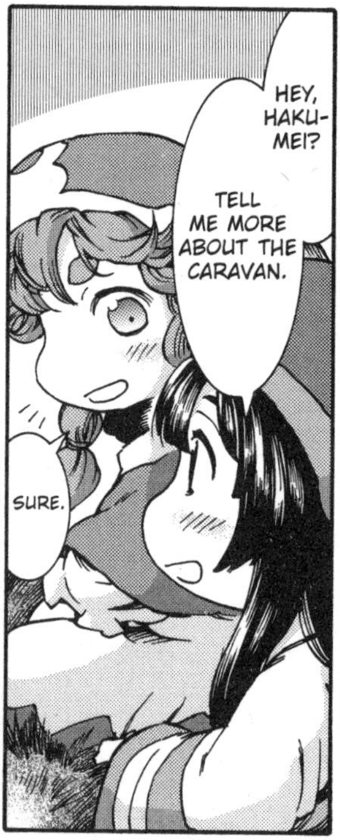
HEY, HAKU-MEI?
TELL ME MORE ABOUT THE CARAVAN.
SURE.
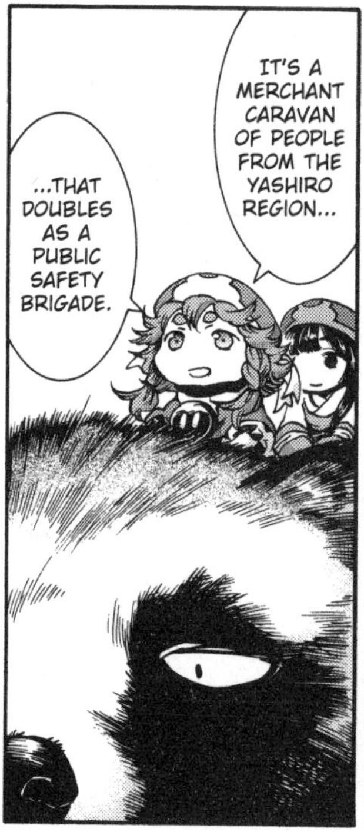
IT'S A MERCHANT CARAVAN OF PEOPLE FROM THE YASHIRO REGION...
...THAT DOUBLES AS A PUBLIC SAFETY BRIGADE.

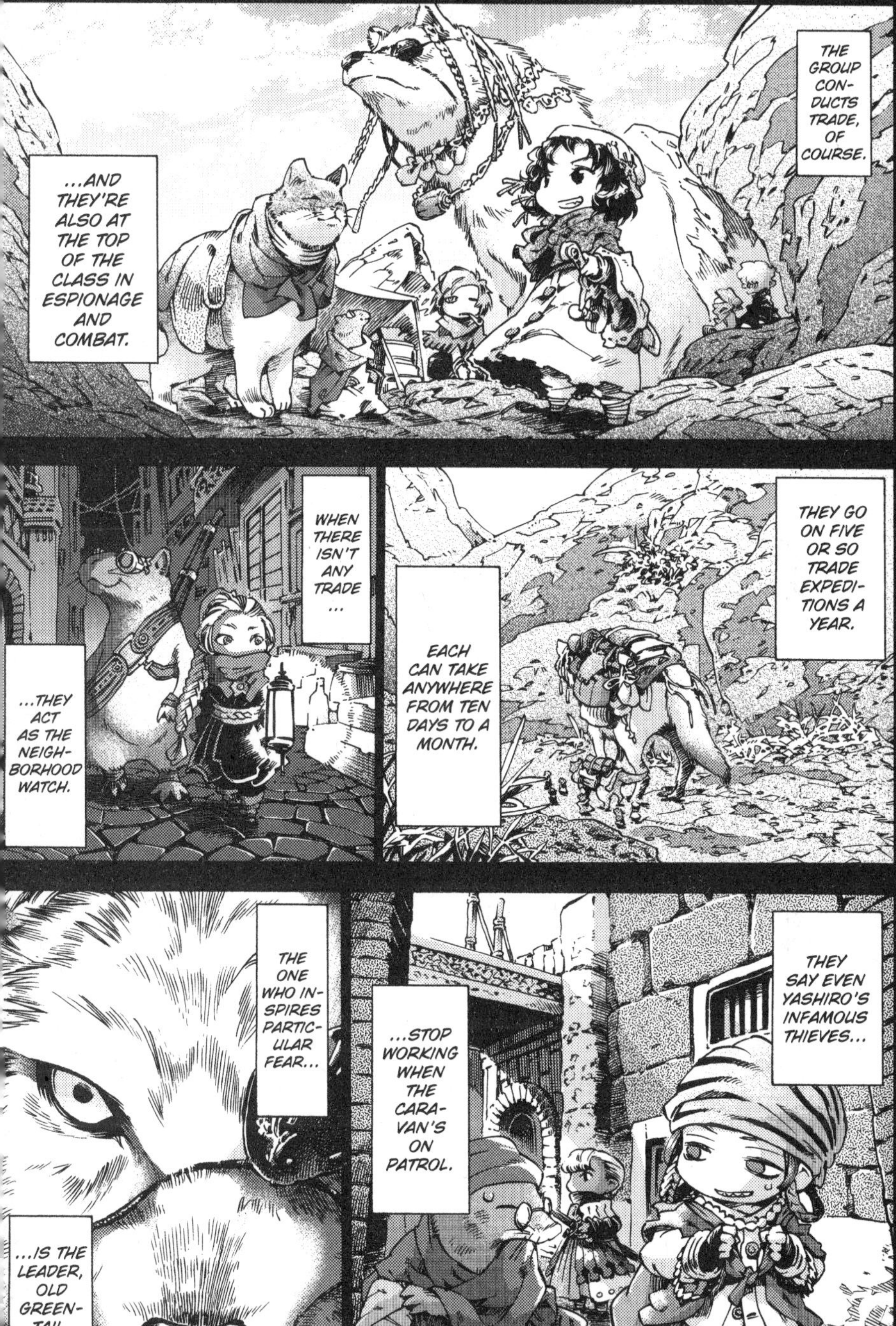
THE GROUP CONDUCTS TRADE, OF COURSE.
...AND THEY'RE ALSO AT THE TOP OF THE CLASS IN ESPIONAGE AND COMBAT.
THEY GO ON FIVE OR SO TRADE EXPEDITIONS A YEAR.
EACH CAN TAKE ANYWHERE FROM TEN DAYS TO A MONTH.
WHEN THERE ISN'T ANY TRADE...
...THEY ACT AS THE NEIGHBORHOOD WATCH.
THEY SAY EVEN YASHIRO'S INFAMOUS THIEVES...
...STOP WORKING WHEN THE CARAVAN'S ON PATROL.
THE ONE WHO INSPIRES PARTICULAR FEAR...
...IS THE LEADER, OLD GREENTAIL.

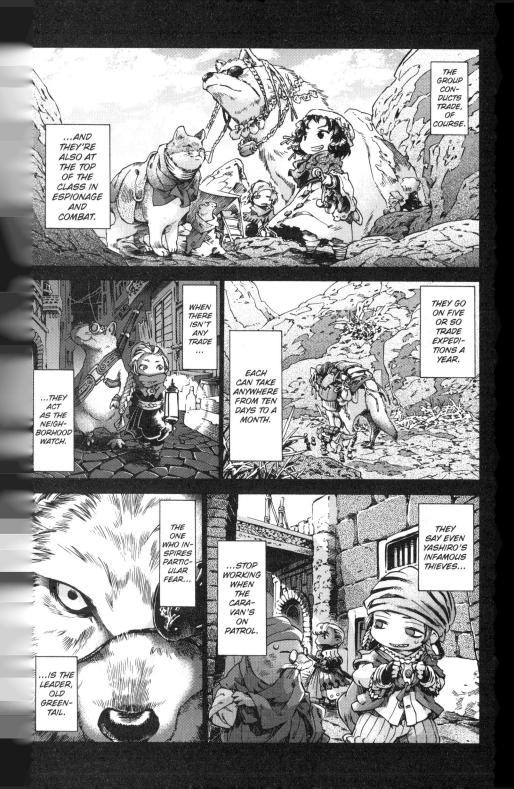

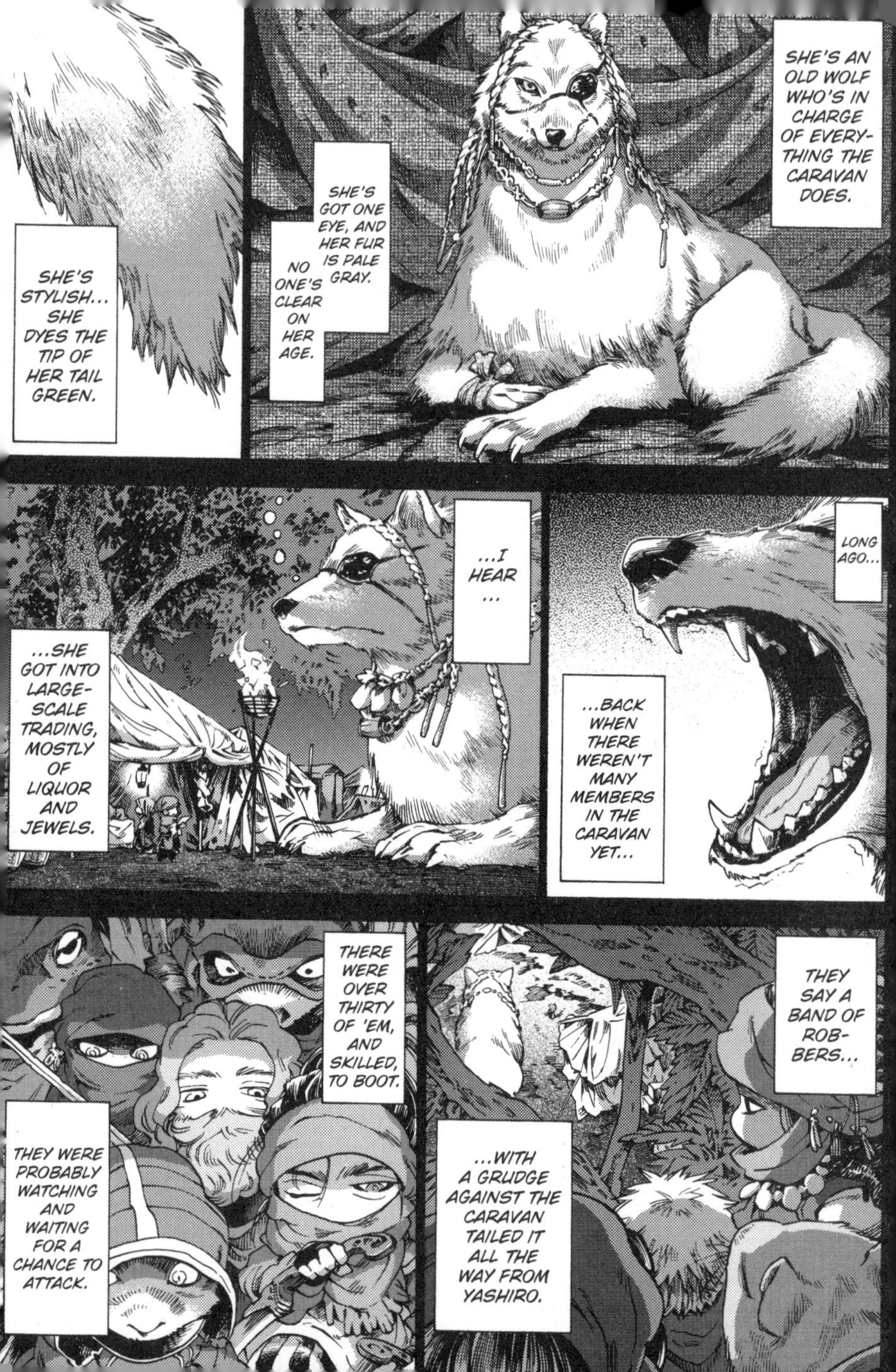
SHE'S AN OLD WOLF WHO'S IN CHARGE OF EVERYTHING THE CARAVAN DOES.
SHE'S GOT ONE EYE, AND HER FUR IS PALE GRAY.
NO ONE'S CLEAR ON HER AGE.
SHE'S STYLISH... SHE DYES THE TIP OF HER TAIL GREEN.
LONG AGO...
...BACK WHEN THERE WEREN'T MANY MEMBERS IN THE CARAVAN YET...
...I HEAR ...
...SHE GOT INTO LARGE-SCALE TRADING, MOSTLY OF LIQUOR AND JEWELS.
THEY SAY A BAND OF ROBBERS...
...WITH A GRUDGE AGAINST THE CARAVAN TAILED IT ALL THE WAY FROM YASHIRO.
THERE WERE OVER THIRTY OF 'EM, AND SKILLED, TO BOOT.
THEY WERE PROBABLY WATCHING AND WAITING FOR A CHANCE TO ATTACK.

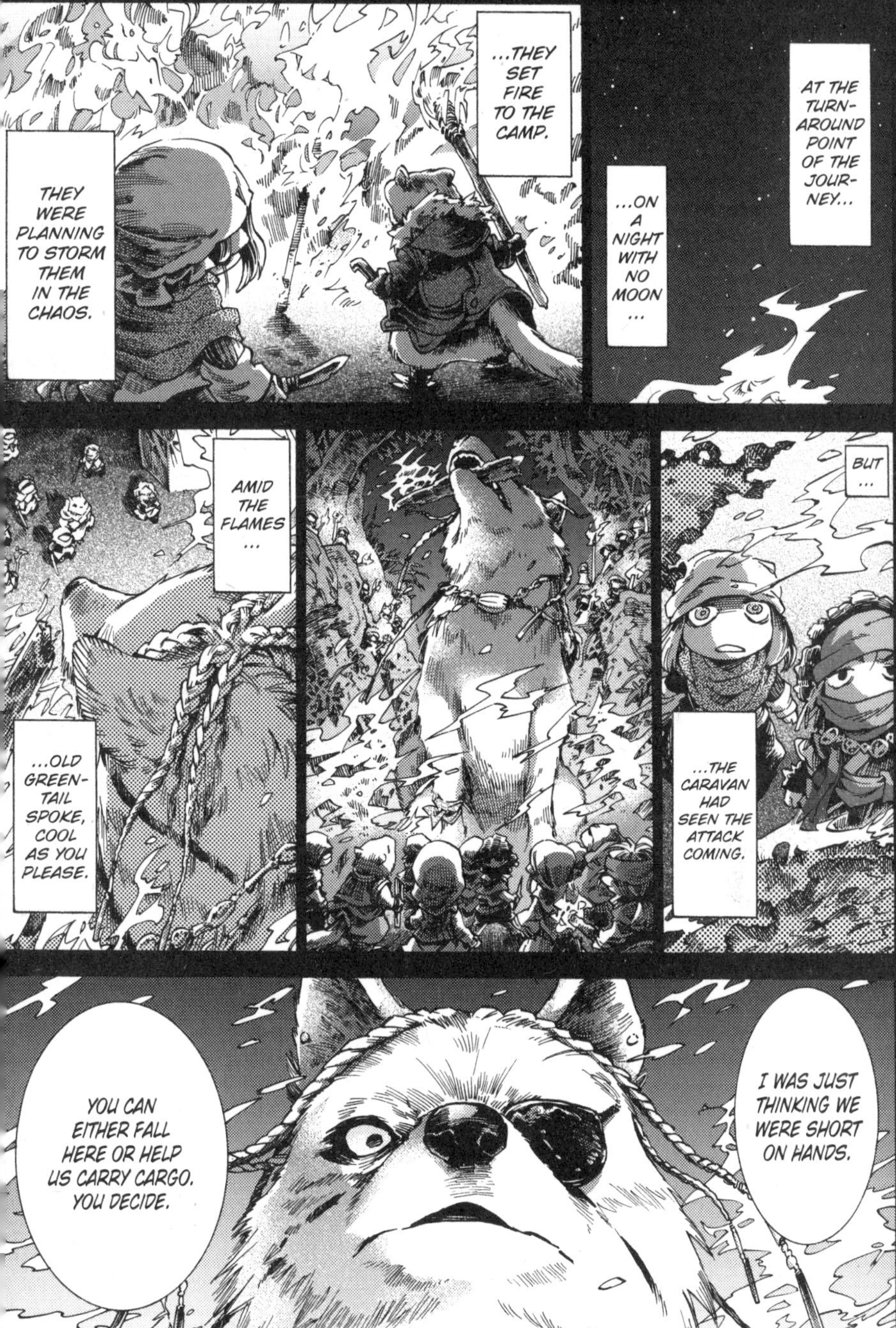
AT THE TURNAROUND POINT OF THE JOURNEY...
...ON A NIGHT WITH NO MOON...
...THEY SET FIRE TO THE CAMP.
THEY WERE PLANNING TO STORM THEM IN THE CHAOS.
BUT...
...THE CARAVAN HAD SEEN THE ATTACK COMING.
AMID THE FLAMES...
...OLD GREENTAIL SPOKE, COOL AS YOU PLEASE.
I WAS JUST THINKING WE WERE SHORT ON HANDS.
YOU CAN EITHER FALL HERE OR HELP US CARRY CARGO. YOU DECIDE.

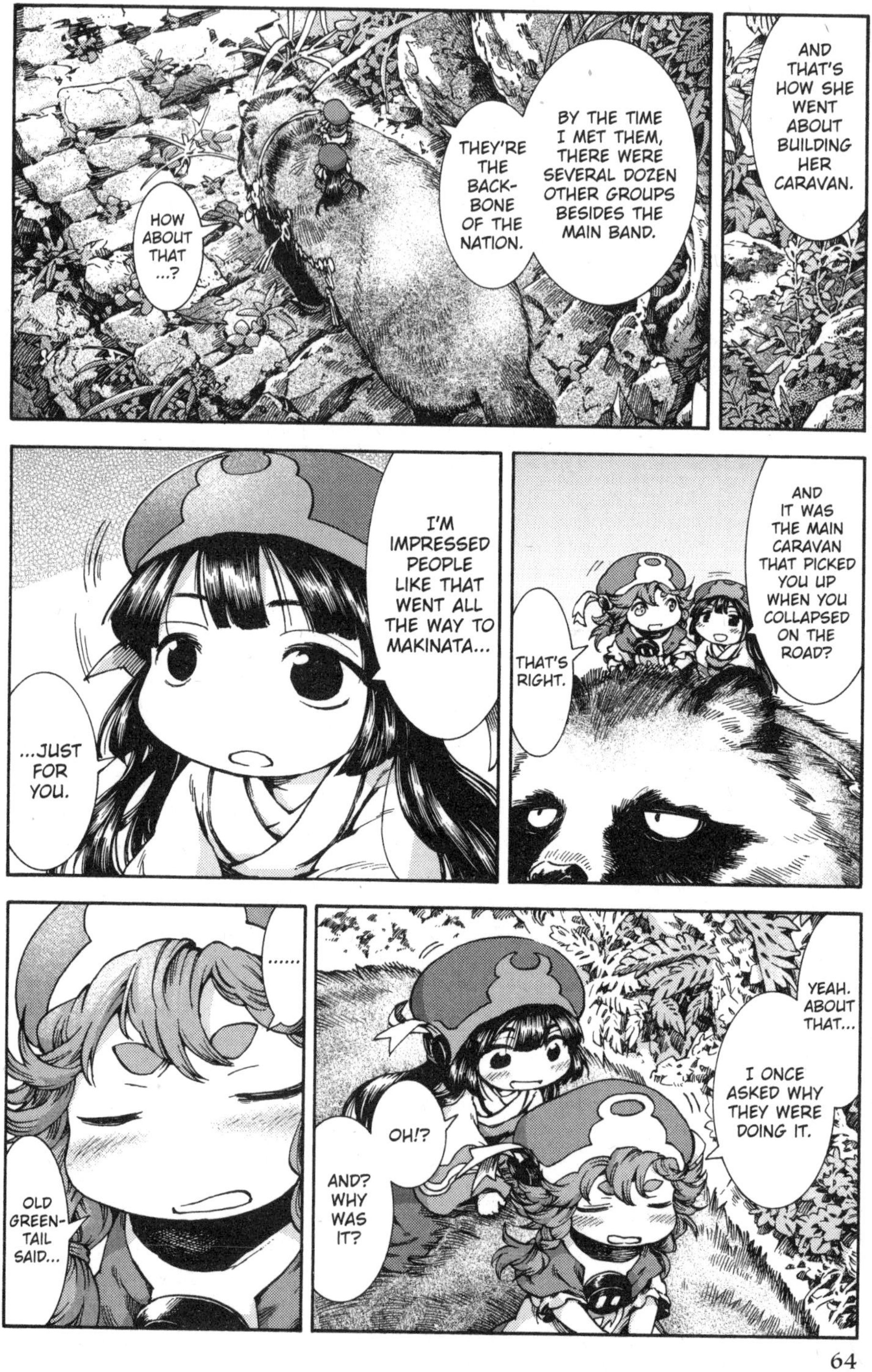
AND THAT'S HOW SHE WENT ABOUT BUILDING HER CARAVAN.
BY THE TIME I MET THEM, THERE WERE SEVERAL DOZEN OTHER GROUPS BESIDES THE MAIN BAND.
THEY'RE THE BACK-BONE OF THE NATION.
HOW ABOUT THAT ...?
AND IT WAS THE MAIN CARAVAN THAT PICKED YOU UP WHEN YOU COLLAPSED ON THE ROAD?
THAT'S RIGHT.
I'M IMPRESSED PEOPLE LIKE THAT WENT ALL THE WAY TO MAKINATA...
...JUST FOR YOU.
YEAH. ABOUT THAT...
I ONCE ASKED WHY THEY WERE DOING IT.
OH!?
AND? WHY WAS IT?
......
OLD GREEN-TAIL SAID...

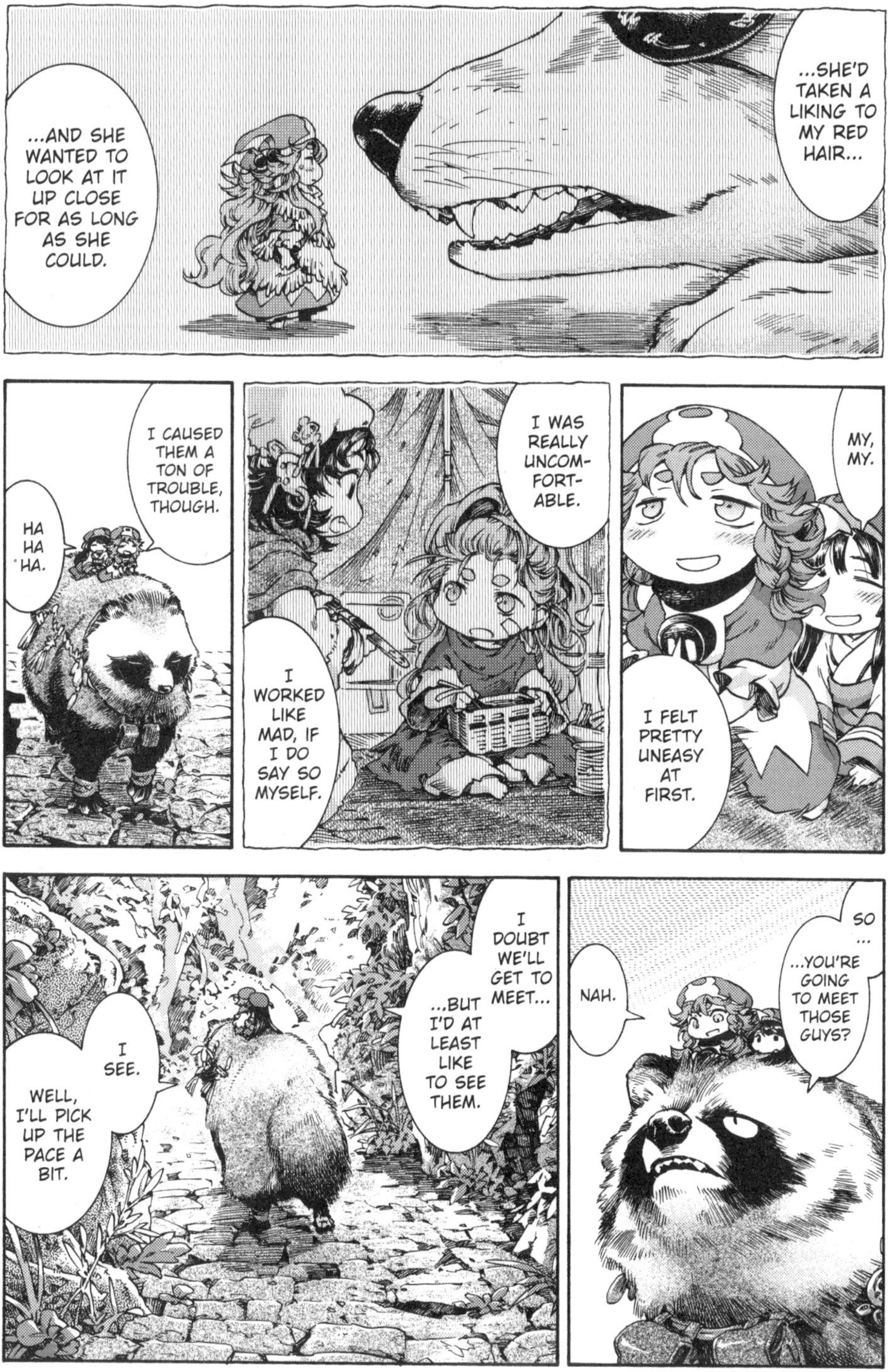
...SHE'D TAKEN A LIKING TO MY RED HAIR...
...AND SHE WANTED TO LOOK AT IT UP CLOSE FOR AS LONG AS SHE COULD.
MY, MY.
I FELT PRETTY UNEASY AT FIRST.
I WAS REALLY UNCOM-FORT-ABLE.
I WORKED LIKE MAD, IF I DO SAY SO MYSELF.
I CAUSED THEM A TON OF TROUBLE, THOUGH.
HA HA HA.
SO ...
...YOU'RE GOING TO MEET THOSE GUYS?
NAH.
I DOUBT WE'LL GET TO MEET...
...BUT I'D AT LEAST LIKE TO SEE THEM.
I SEE.
WELL, I'LL PICK UP THE PACE A BIT.

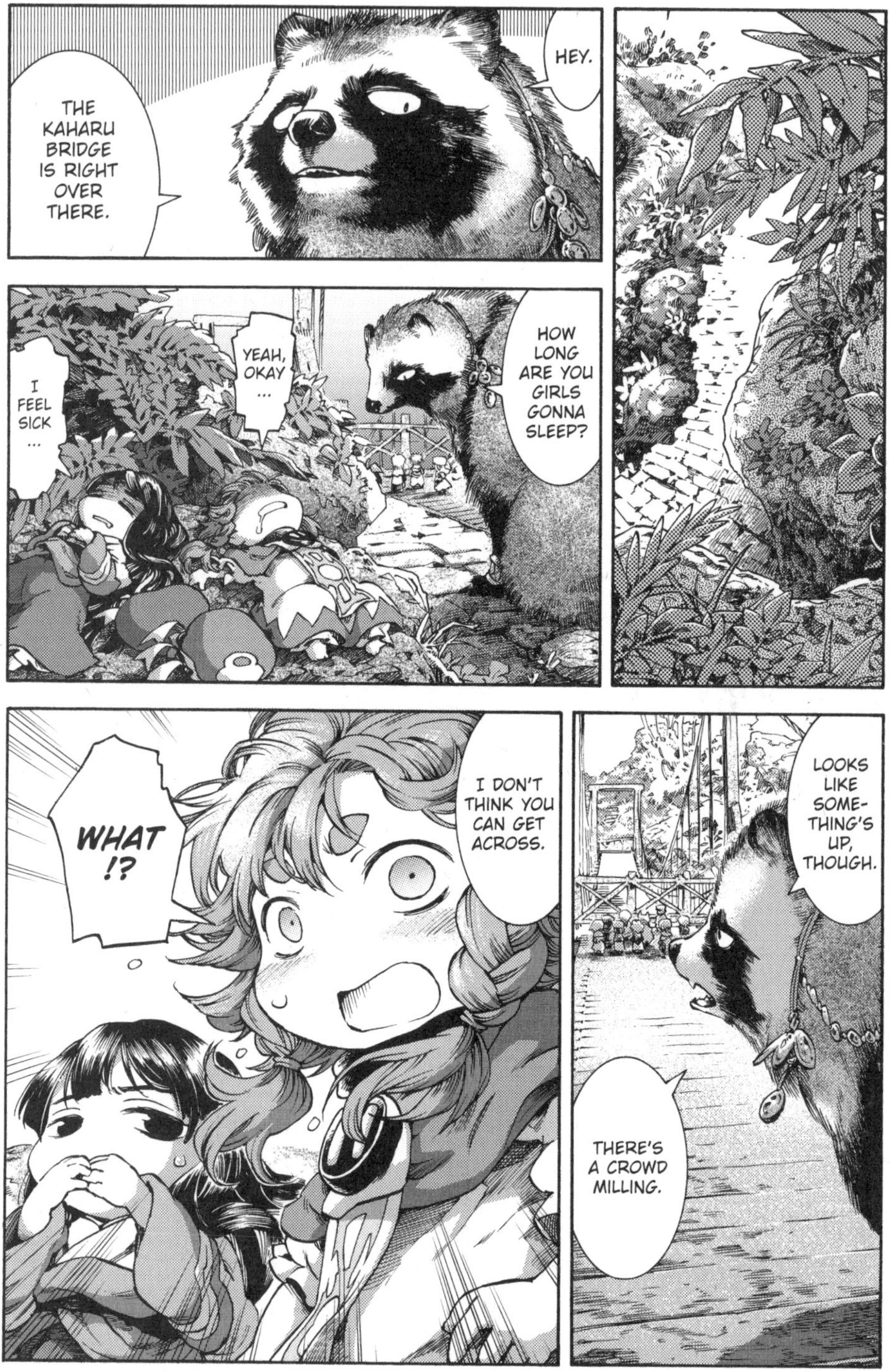
HEY.
THE KAHARU BRIDGE IS RIGHT OVER THERE.
HOW LONG ARE YOU GIRLS GONNA SLEEP?
YEAH, OKAY ...
I FEEL SICK ...
LOOKS LIKE SOME-THING'S UP, THOUGH.
THERE'S A CROWD MILLING.
I DON'T THINK YOU CAN GET ACROSS.
WHAT !?

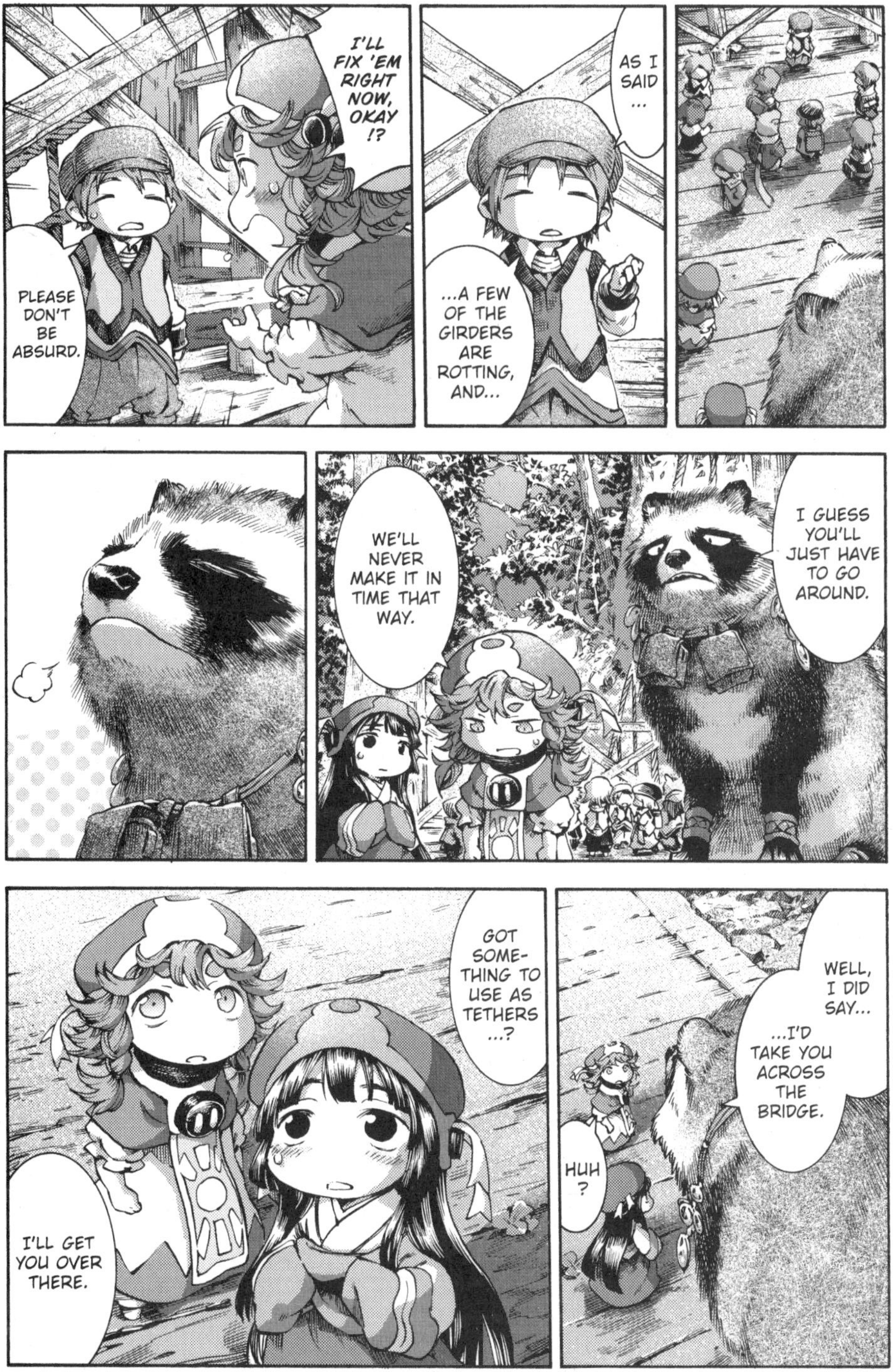
AS I SAID...
...A FEW OF THE GIRDERS ARE ROTTING, AND...
I'LL FIX 'EM RIGHT NOW, OKAY!?
PLEASE DON'T BE ABSURD.
I GUESS YOU'LL JUST HAVE TO GO AROUND.
WE'LL NEVER MAKE IT IN TIME THAT WAY.
WELL, I DID SAY...
...I'D TAKE YOU ACROSS THE BRIDGE.
HUH?
GOT SOMETHING TO USE AS TETHERS...?
I'LL GET YOU OVER THERE.

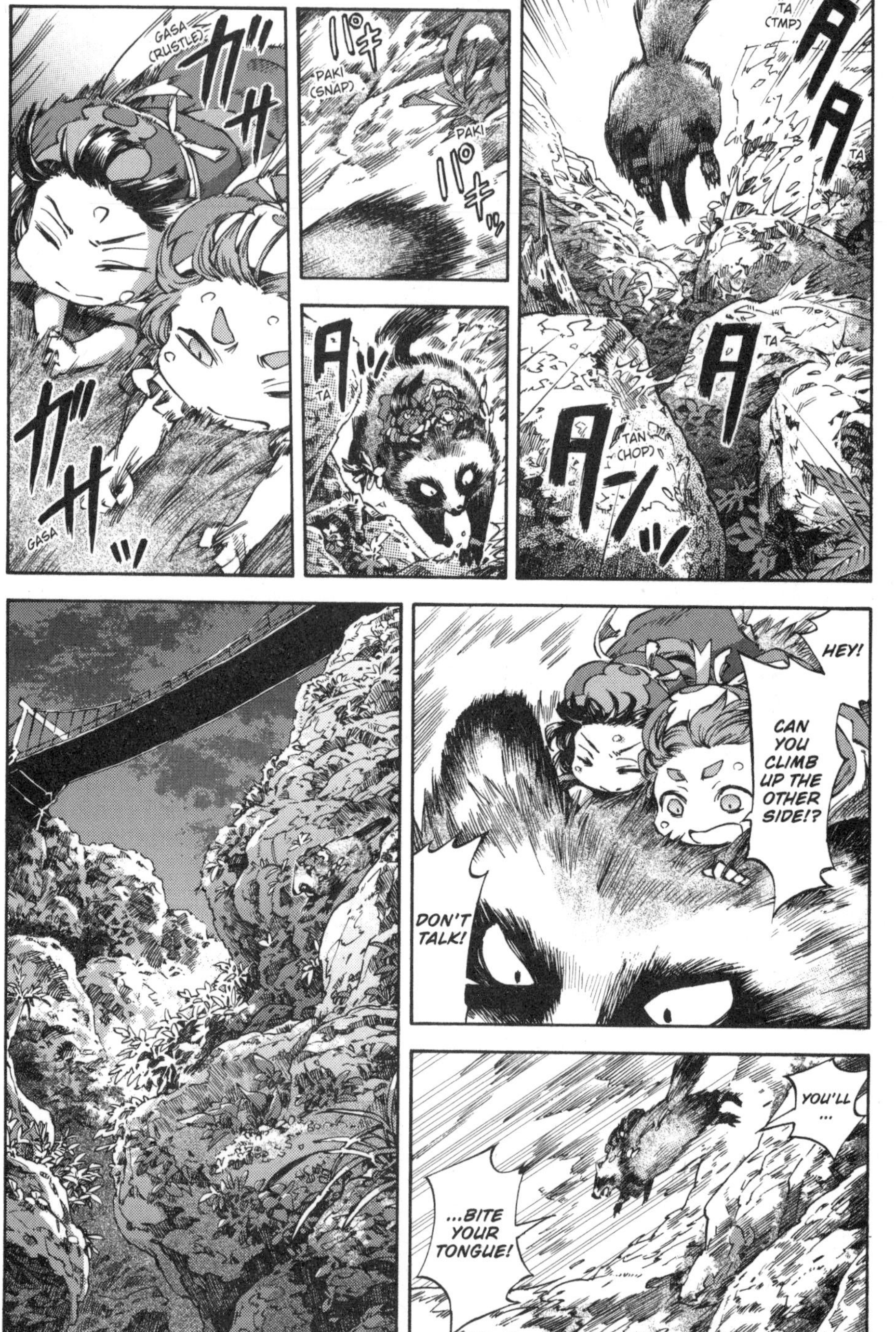
TA (TMP)
TA
TA
TAN (CHOP)
PAKI (SNAP)
PAKI
TA
GASA (RUSTLE)
GASA
HEY!
CAN YOU CLIMB UP THE OTHER SIDE!?
DON'T TALK!
YOU'LL ...
...BITE YOUR TONGUE!

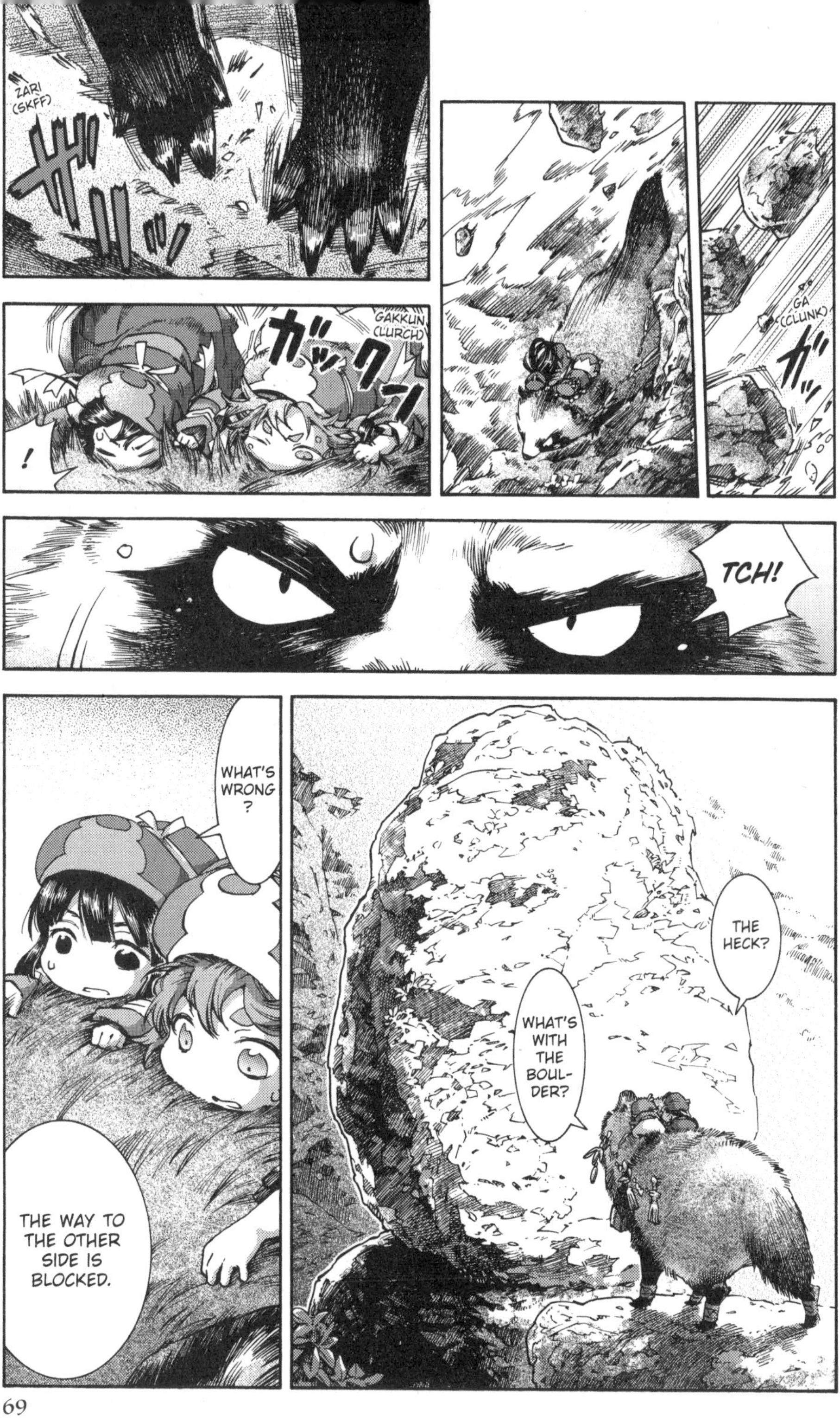
ZARI (SKFF)
GA (CLUNK)
GAKKUN (LURCH)
!
TCH!
THE HECK?
WHAT'S WITH THE BOULDER?
WHAT'S WRONG?
THE WAY TO THE OTHER SIDE IS BLOCKED.

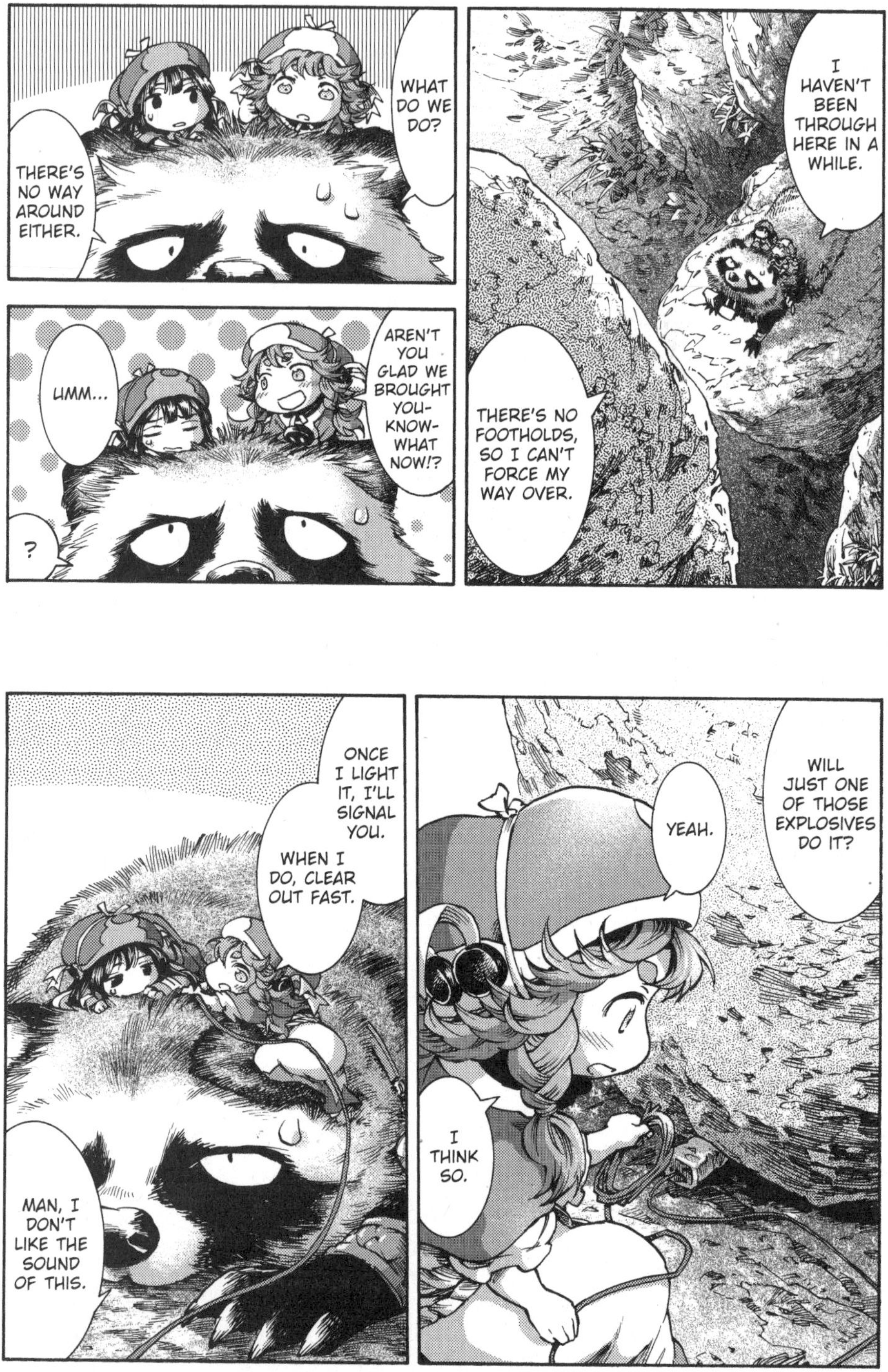
I HAVEN'T BEEN THROUGH HERE IN A WHILE.
THERE'S NO FOOTHOLDS, SO I CAN'T FORCE MY WAY OVER.
WHAT DO WE DO?
THERE'S NO WAY AROUND EITHER.
AREN'T YOU GLAD WE BROUGHT YOU-KNOW-WHAT NOW!?
UMM...
?
WILL JUST ONE OF THOSE EXPLOSIVES DO IT?
YEAH.
I THINK SO.
ONCE I LIGHT IT, I'LL SIGNAL YOU.
WHEN I DO, CLEAR OUT FAST.
MAN, I DON'T LIKE THE SOUND OF THIS.

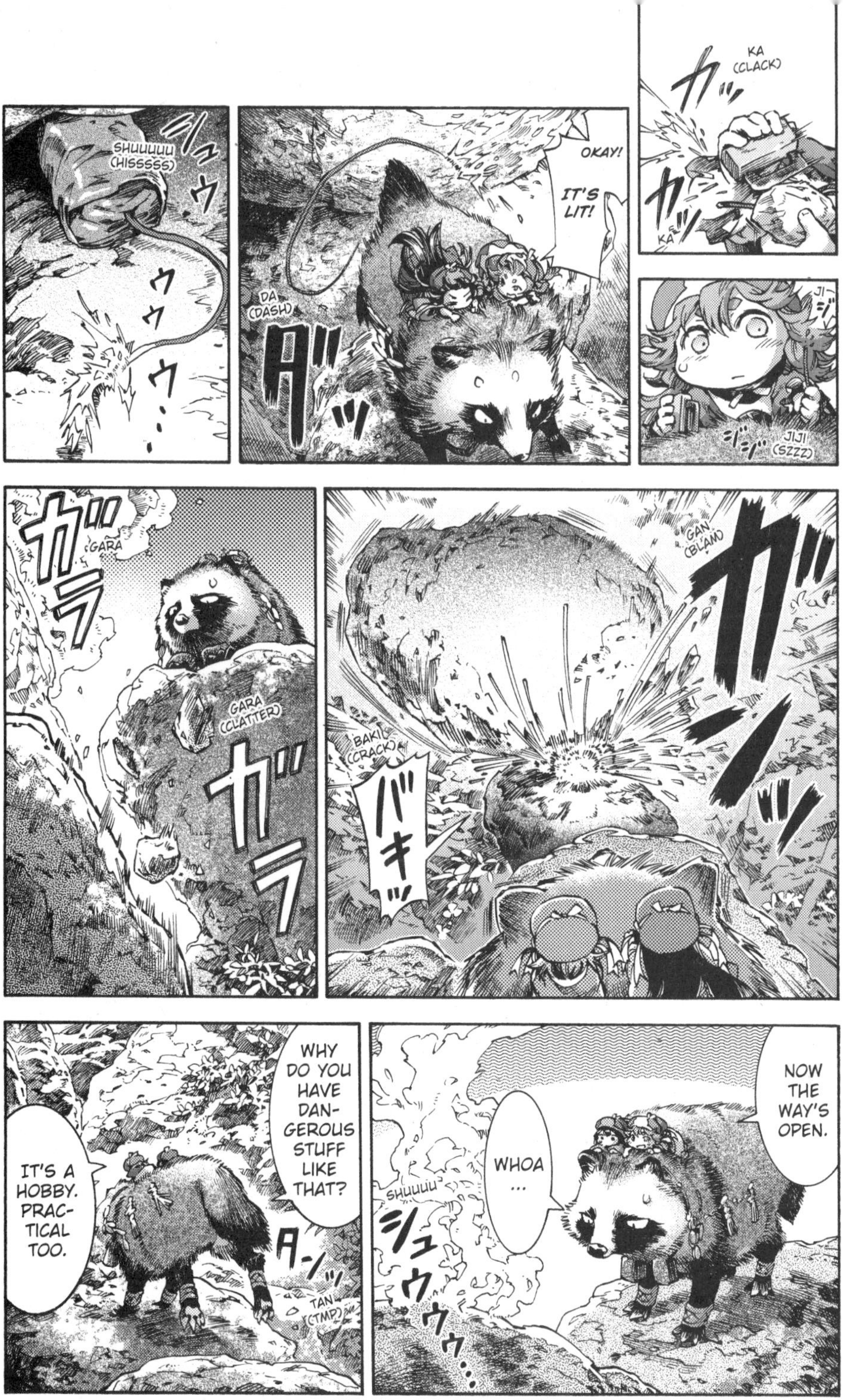
KA (CLACK)
KA
JI
JIJI (SZZZ)
OKAY!
IT'S LIT!
DA (DASH)
SHUUUUU (HISSSSS)
GAN (BLAM)
BAKI (CRACK)
GARA
GARA (CLATTER)
NOW THE WAY'S OPEN.
WHOA...
SHUUUU
WHY DO YOU HAVE DAN-GEROUS STUFF LIKE THAT?
IT'S A HOBBY. PRAC-TICAL TOO.
TAN (TMP)

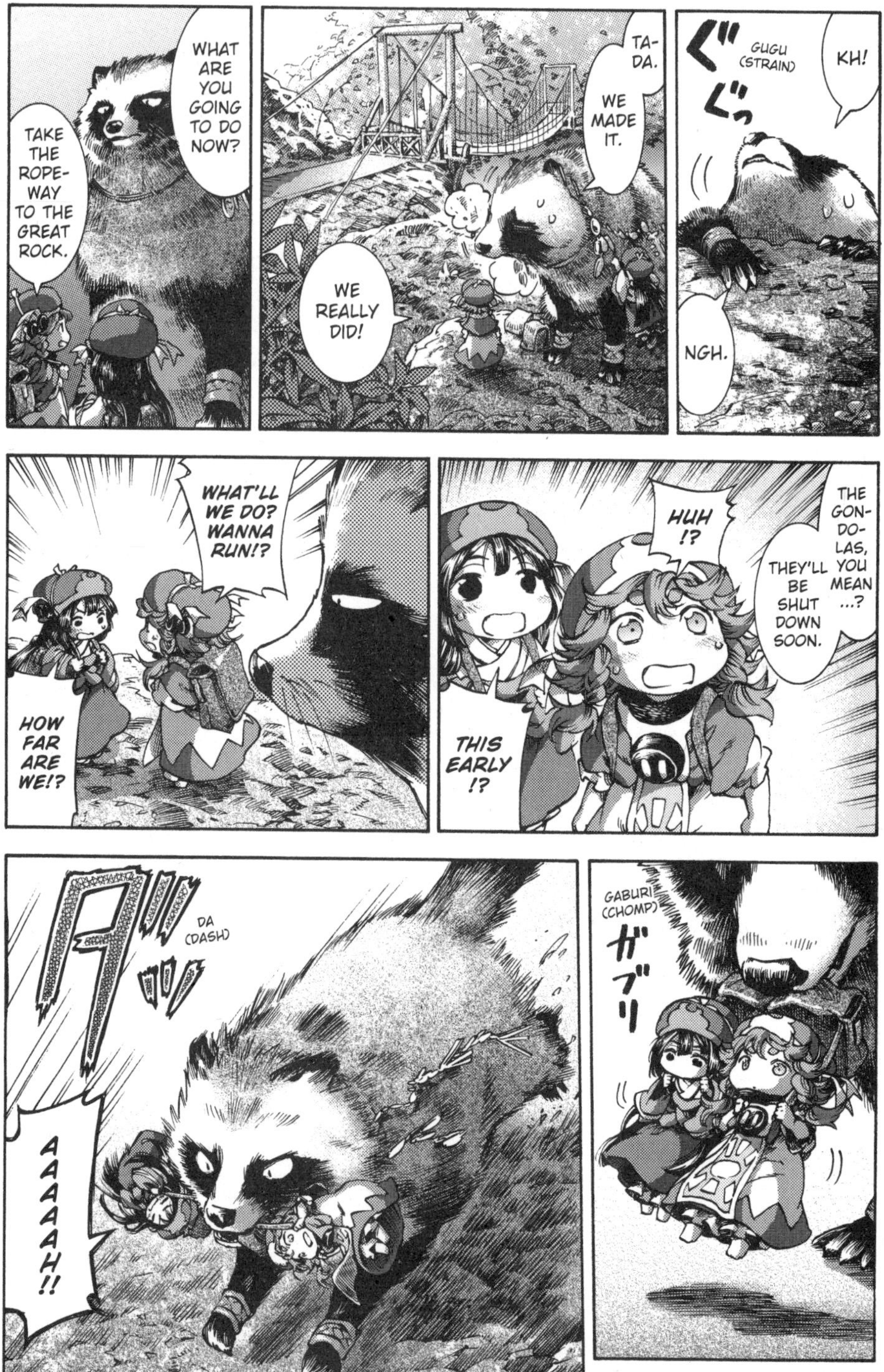
KH!
GUGU (STRAIN)
ぐぐっ
NGH.
TA-DA.
WE MADE IT.
WE REALLY DID!
WHAT ARE YOU GOING TO DO NOW?
TAKE THE ROPE-WAY TO THE GREAT ROCK.
THE GON-DO-LAS, YOU MEAN ...?
THEY'LL BE SHUT DOWN SOON.
HUH !?
THIS EARLY !?
WHAT'LL WE DO? WANNA RUN!?
HOW FAR ARE WE!?
GABURI (CHOMP)
ガブリ
DA (DASH)
AAAAAAH!!

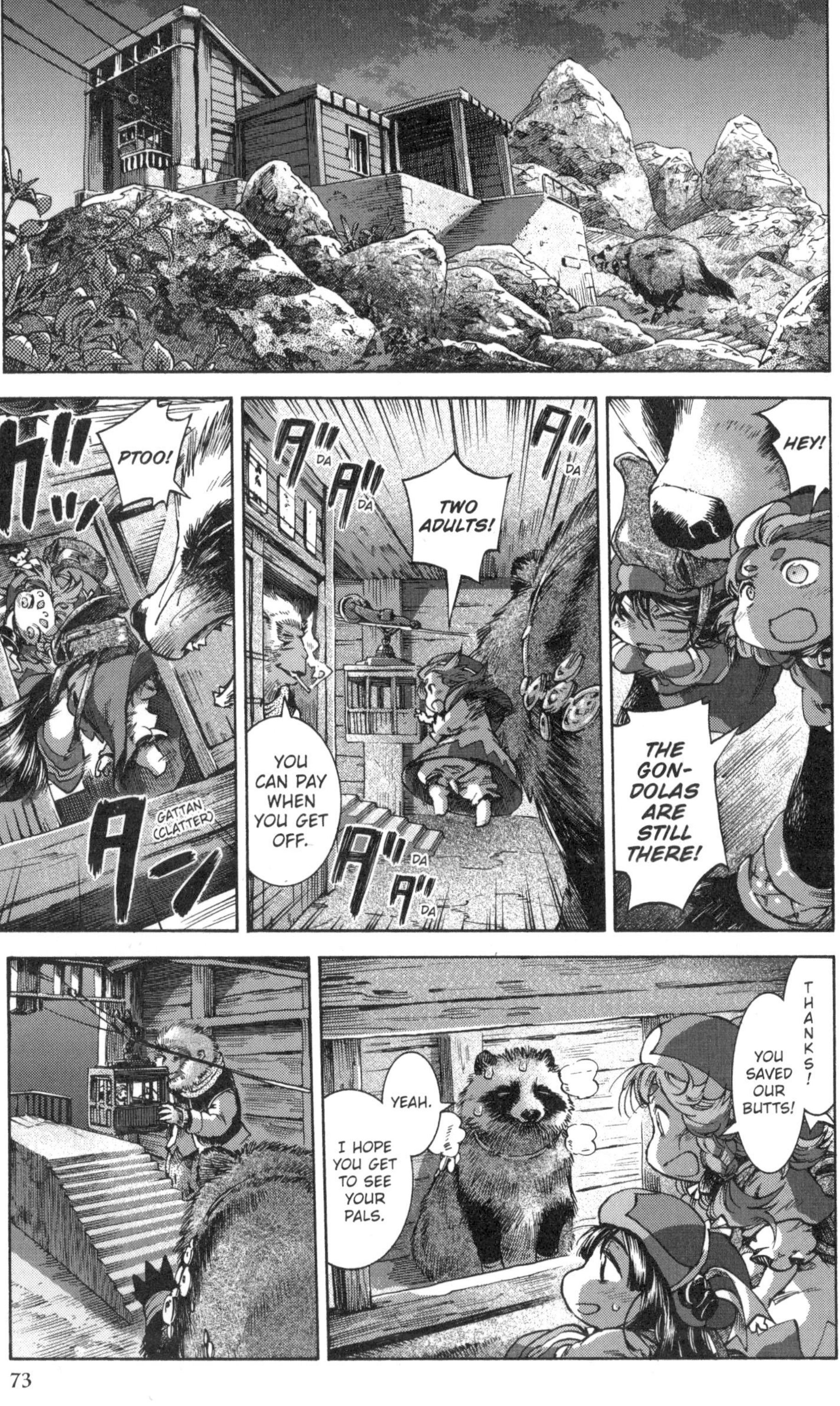
HEY!
THE GON-DOLAS ARE STILL THERE!
DA
DA
DA
TWO ADULTS!
YOU CAN PAY WHEN YOU GET OFF.
DA
DA
PTOO!
GATTAN (CLATTER)
THANKS!
YOU SAVED OUR BUTTS!
YEAH.
I HOPE YOU GET TO SEE YOUR PALS.

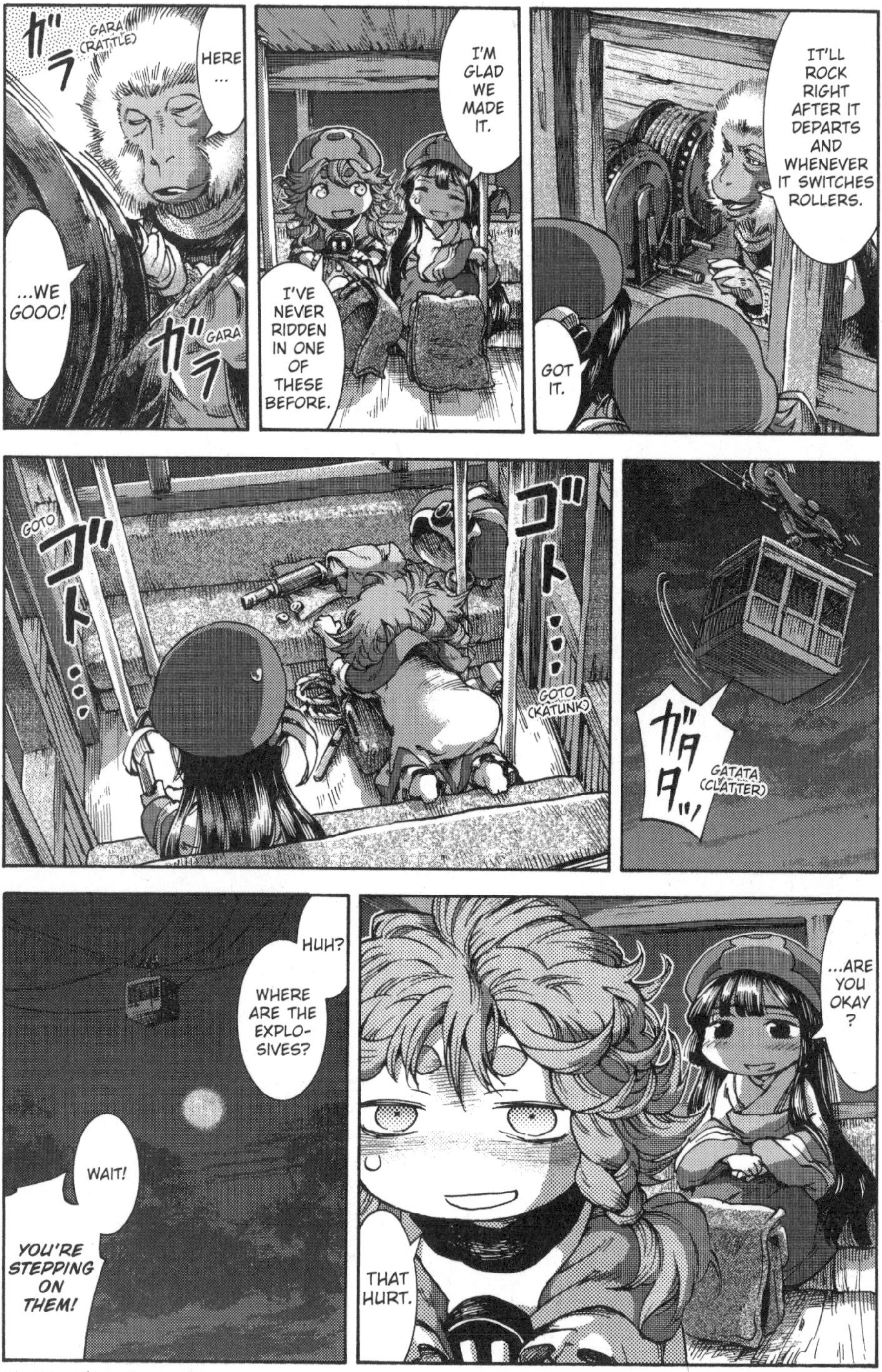
IT'LL ROCK RIGHT AFTER IT DEPARTS AND WHENEVER IT SWITCHES ROLLERS.
GOT IT.
I'M GLAD WE MADE IT.
I'VE NEVER RIDDEN IN ONE OF THESE BEFORE.
ガラ
GARA (RATTLE)
HERE...
...WE GOOO!
ガラ
GARA
ガタタッ
GATATA (CLATTER)
ゴト...
GOTO (KATUNK)
ゴト...
GOTO
...ARE YOU OKAY?
THAT HURT.
HUH?
WHERE ARE THE EXPLOSIVES?
WAIT!
YOU'RE STEPPING ON THEM!

To Be Continued...

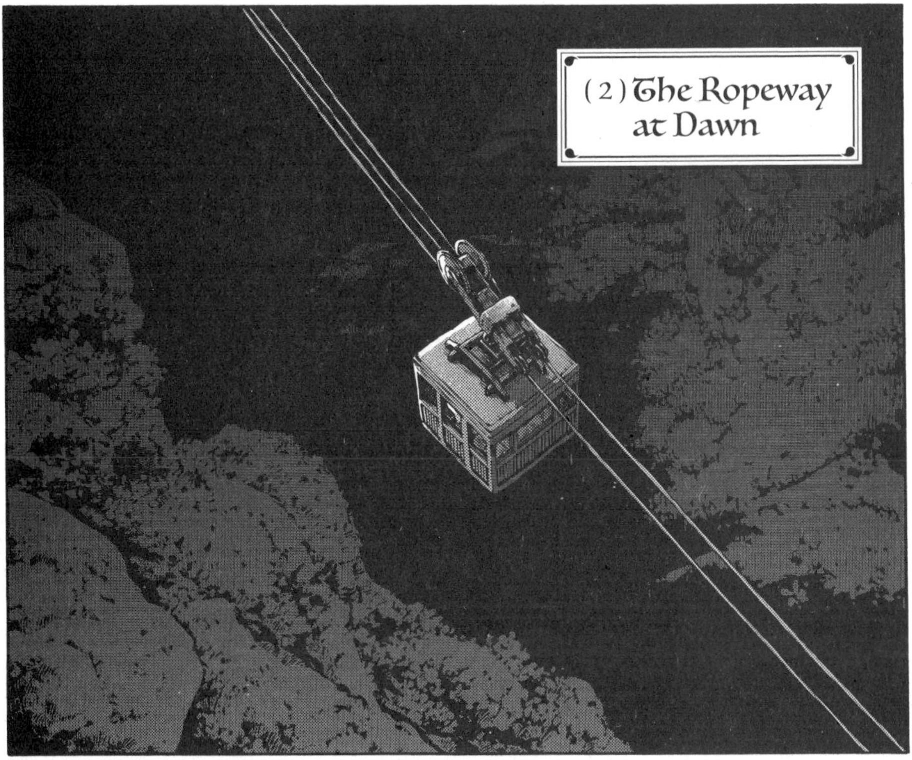
(2) The Ropeway at Dawn

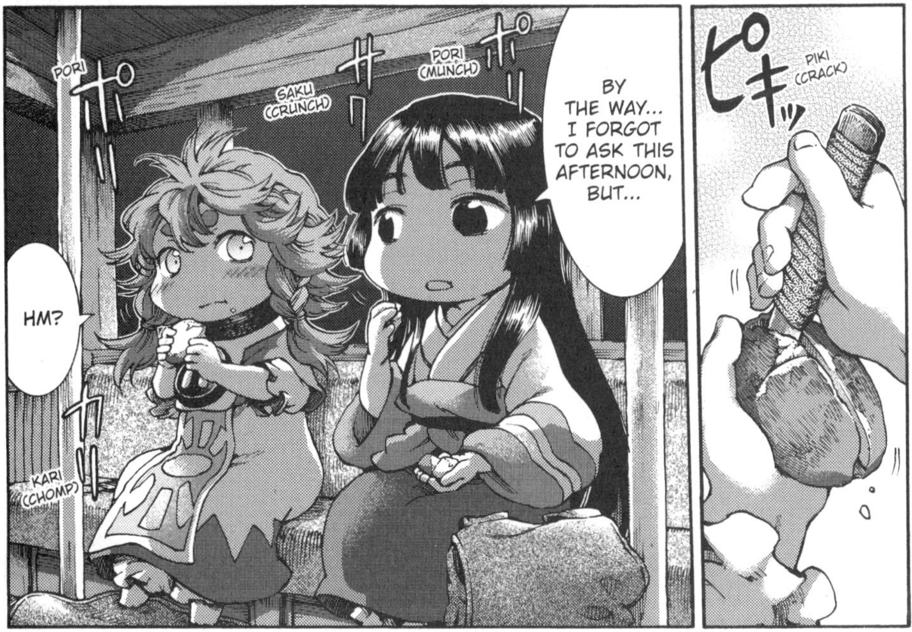
ピキッ
PIKI (CRACK)
BY THE WAY... I FORGOT TO ASK THIS AFTERNOON, BUT...
ポリ
PORI (MUNCH)
サク
SAKU (CRUNCH)
ポ
PORI
HM?
カリ
KARI (CHOMP)

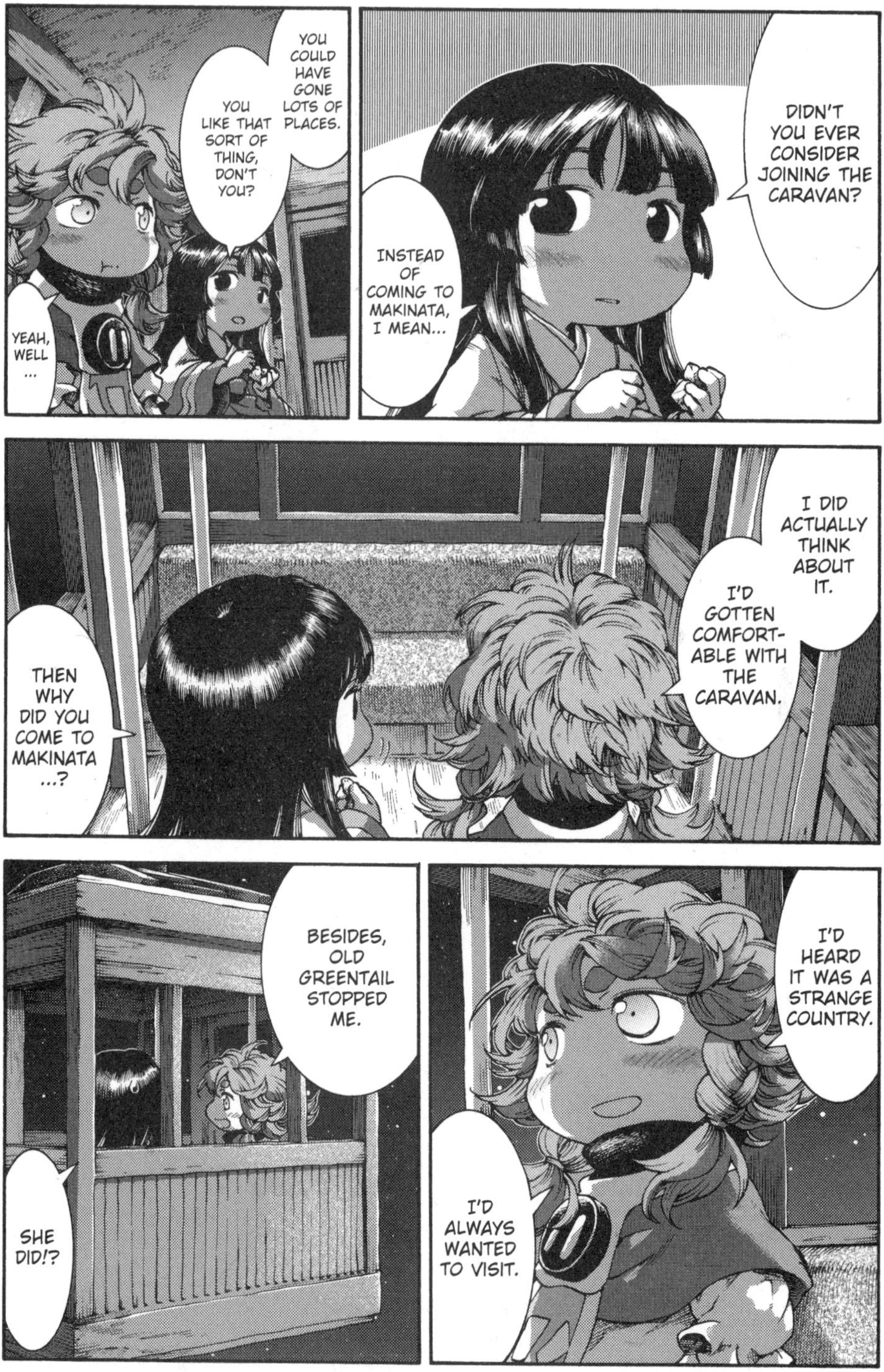
DIDN'T YOU EVER CONSIDER JOINING THE CARAVAN?
INSTEAD OF COMING TO MAKINATA, I MEAN...
YOU COULD HAVE GONE LOTS OF PLACES.
YOU LIKE THAT SORT OF THING, DON'T YOU?
YEAH, WELL ...
I DID ACTUALLY THINK ABOUT IT.
I'D GOTTEN COMFORT-ABLE WITH THE CARAVAN.
THEN WHY DID YOU COME TO MAKINATA ...?
I'D HEARD IT WAS A STRANGE COUNTRY.
I'D ALWAYS WANTED TO VISIT.
BESIDES, OLD GREENTAIL STOPPED ME.
SHE DID!?

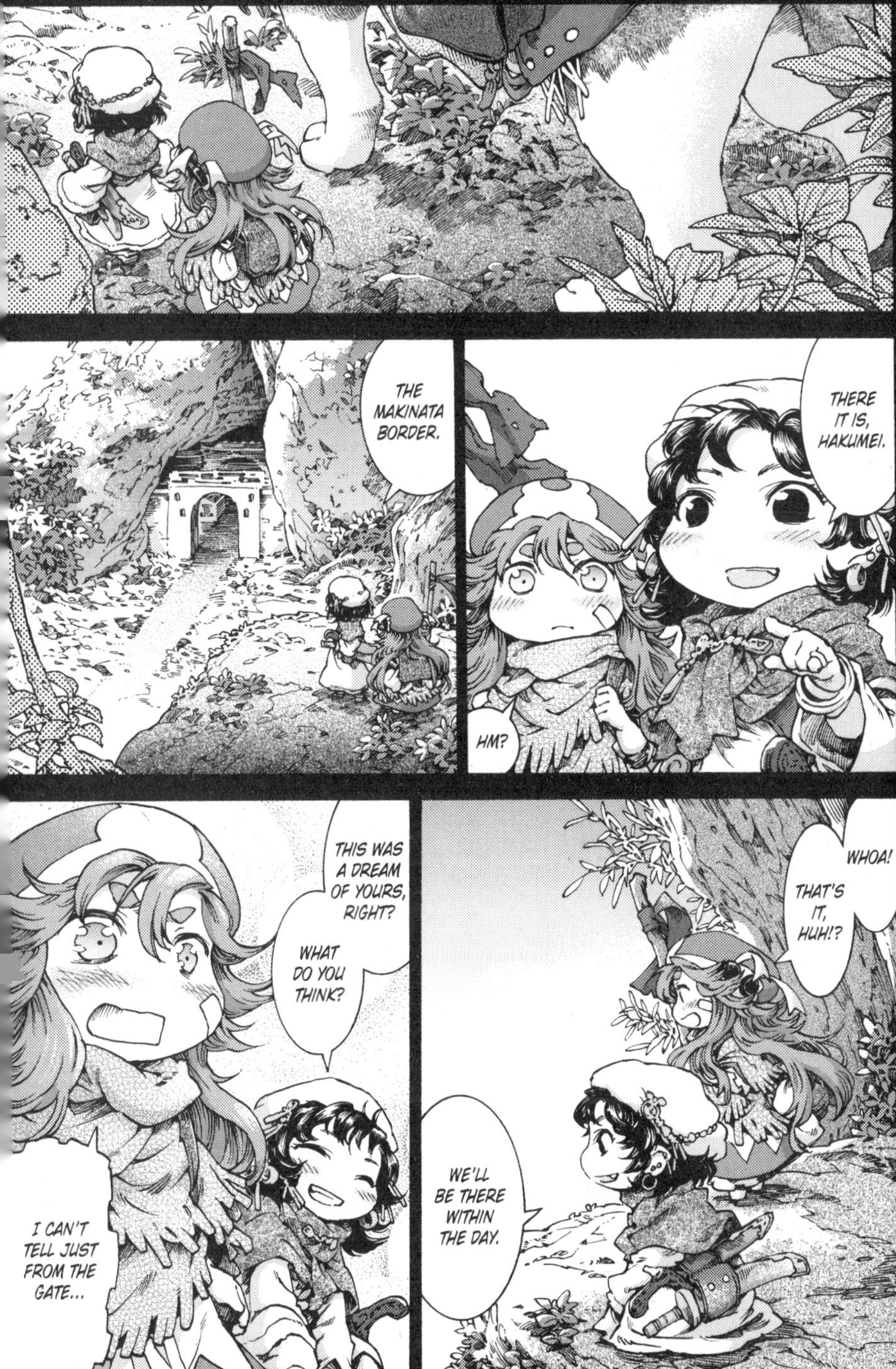
THERE IT IS, HAKUMEI.
HM?
THE MAKINATA BORDER.
WHOA!
THAT'S IT, HUH!?
WE'LL BE THERE WITHIN THE DAY.
THIS WAS A DREAM OF YOURS, RIGHT?
WHAT DO YOU THINK?
I CAN'T TELL JUST FROM THE GATE...

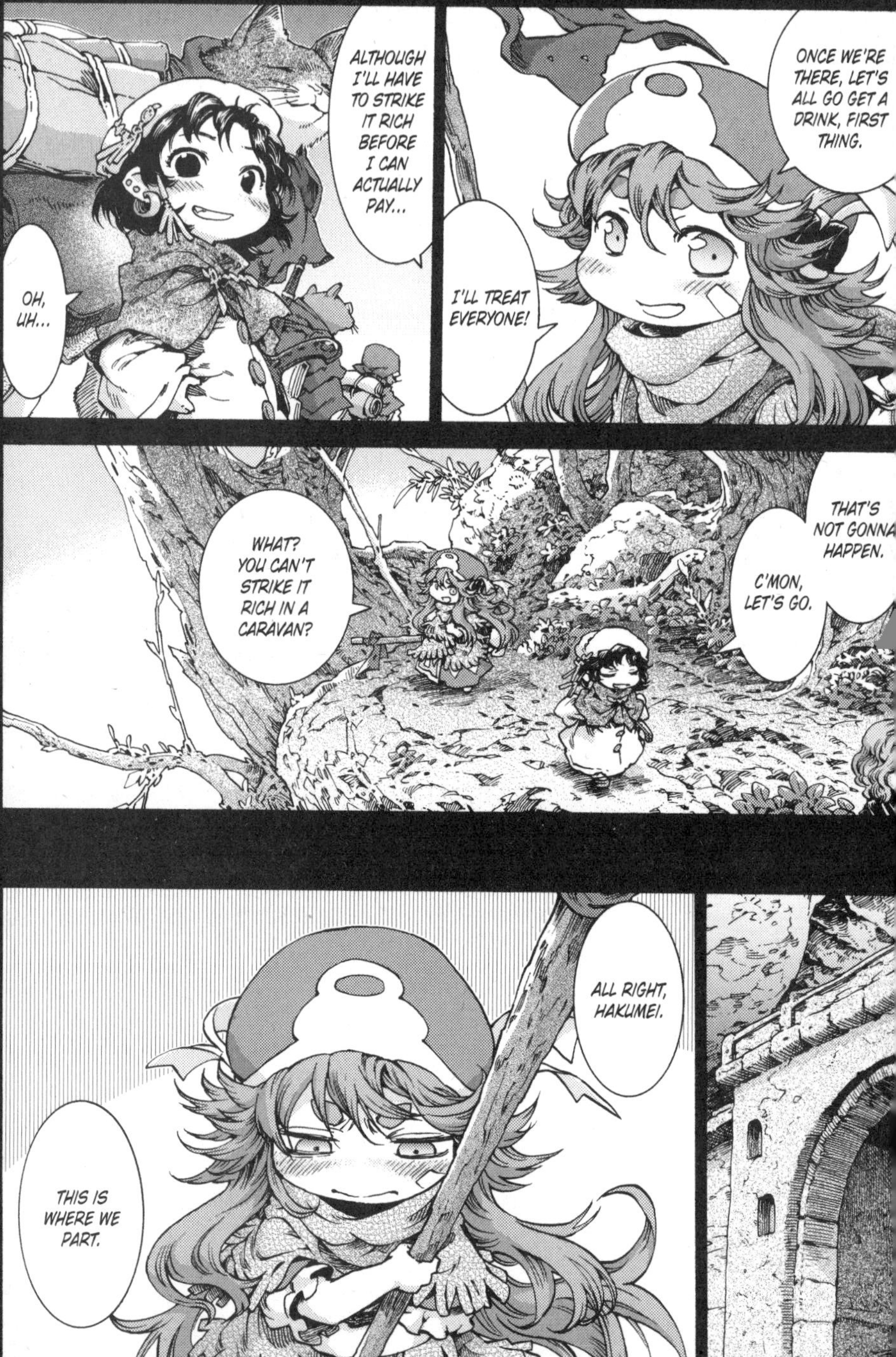
ONCE WE'RE THERE, LET'S ALL GO GET A DRINK, FIRST THING.
I'LL TREAT EVERYONE!
ALTHOUGH I'LL HAVE TO STRIKE IT RICH BEFORE I CAN ACTUALLY PAY...
OH, UH...
WHAT? YOU CAN'T STRIKE IT RICH IN A CARAVAN?
THAT'S NOT GONNA HAPPEN.
C'MON, LET'S GO.
ALL RIGHT, HAKUMEI.
THIS IS WHERE WE PART.

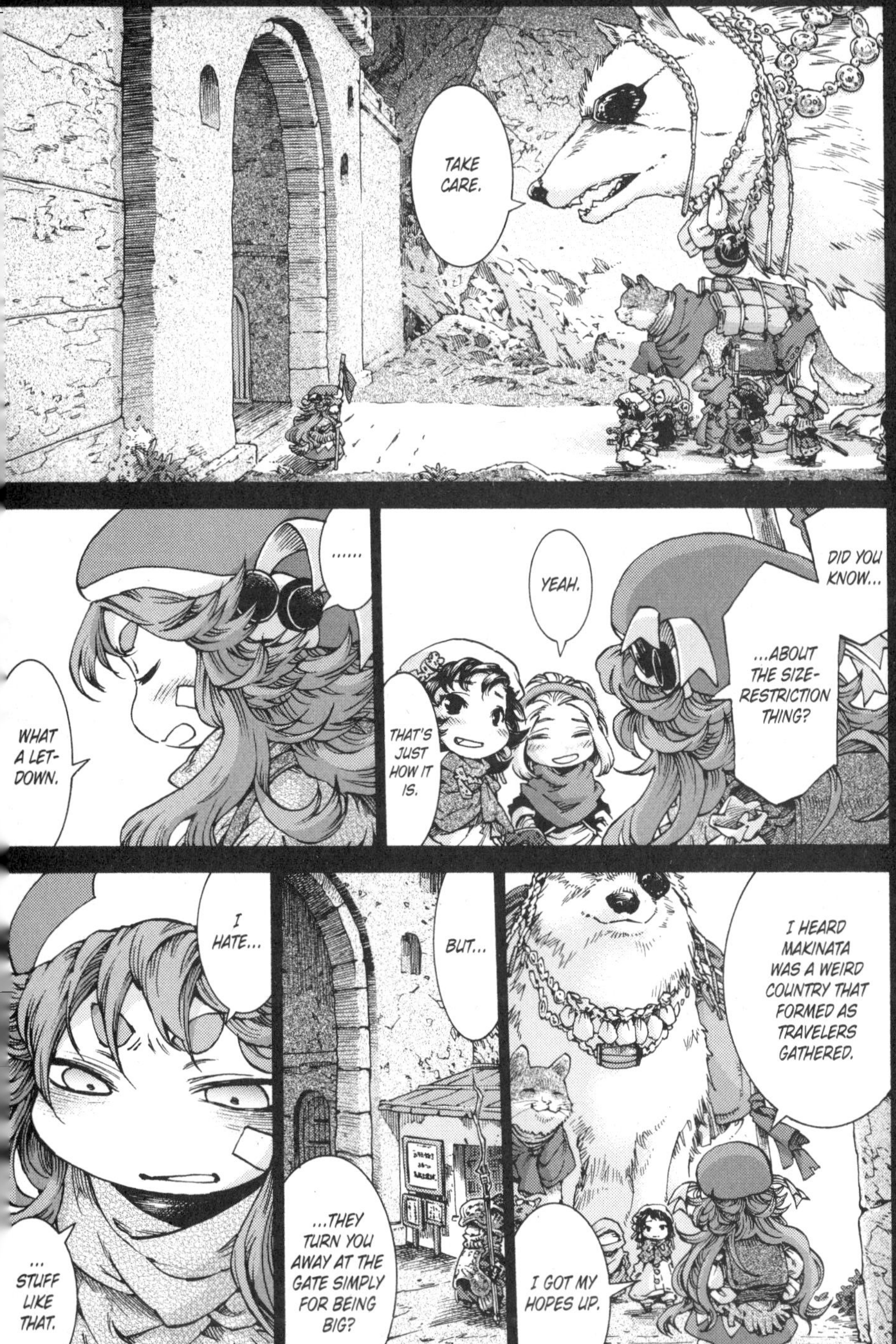
TAKE CARE.
DID YOU KNOW...
...ABOUT THE SIZE-RESTRICTION THING?
YEAH.
THAT'S JUST HOW IT IS.
......
WHAT A LET-DOWN.
I HEARD MAKINATA WAS A WEIRD COUNTRY THAT FORMED AS TRAVELERS GATHERED.
I GOT MY HOPES UP.
BUT...
...THEY TURN YOU AWAY AT THE GATE SIMPLY FOR BEING BIG?
I HATE...
...STUFF LIKE THAT.

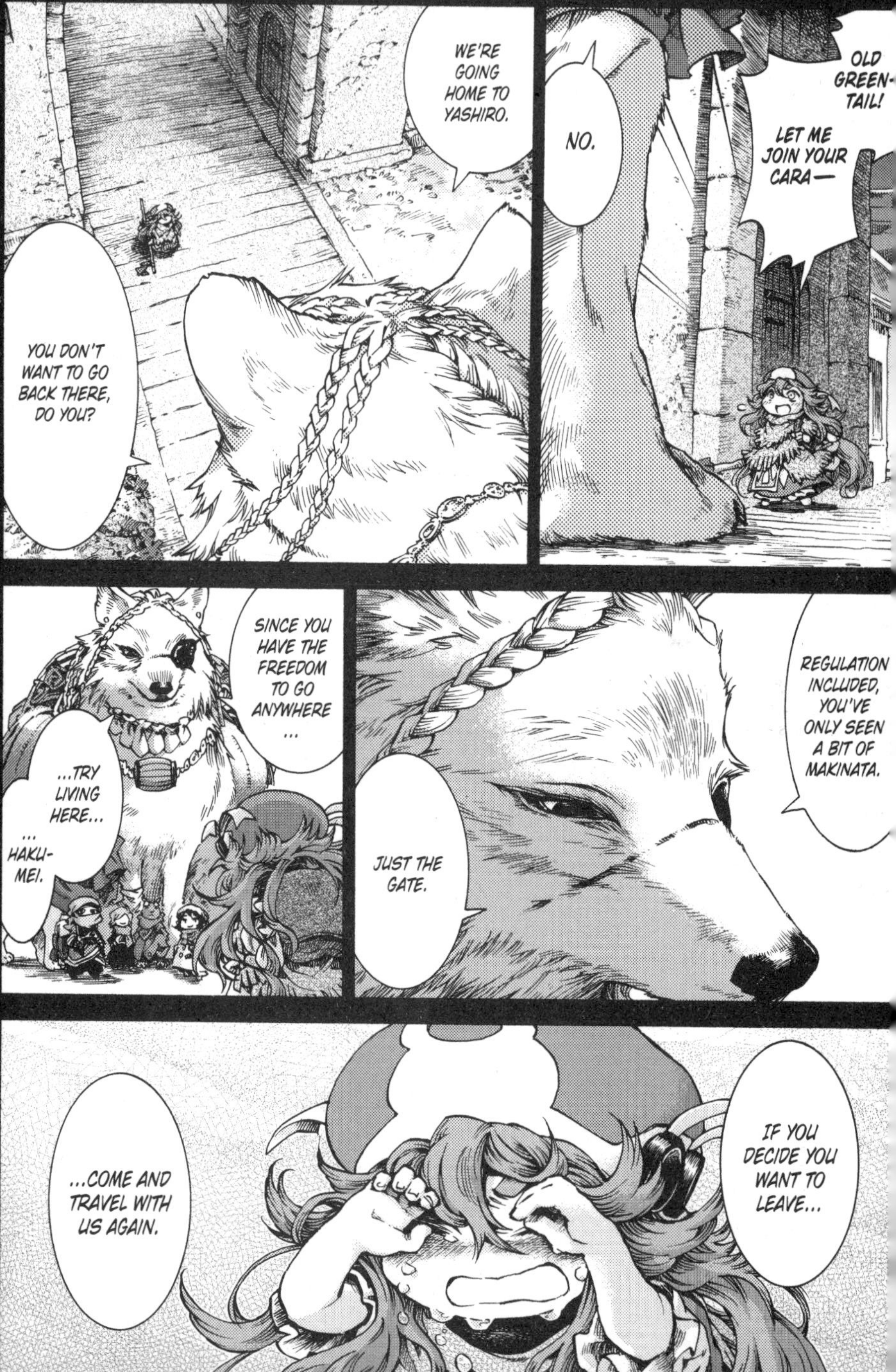
OLD GREEN-TAIL!
LET ME JOIN YOUR CARA—
NO.
WE'RE GOING HOME TO YASHIRO.
YOU DON'T WANT TO GO BACK THERE, DO YOU?
REGULATION INCLUDED, YOU'VE ONLY SEEN A BIT OF MAKINATA.
JUST THE GATE.
SINCE YOU HAVE THE FREEDOM TO GO ANYWHERE...
...TRY LIVING HERE...
...HAKUMEI.
IF YOU DECIDE YOU WANT TO LEAVE...
...COME AND TRAVEL WITH US AGAIN.

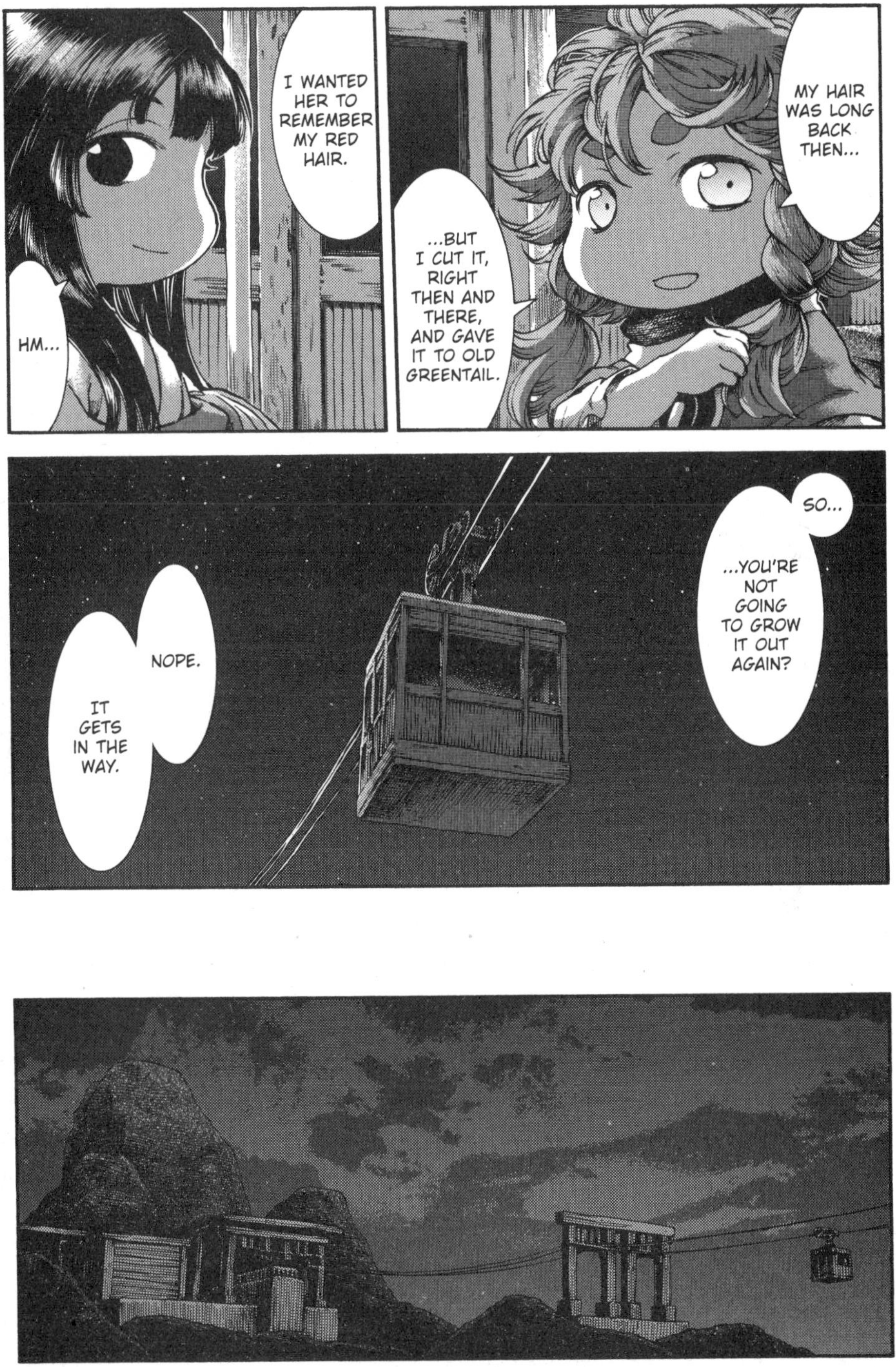
MY HAIR WAS LONG BACK THEN...
...BUT I CUT IT, RIGHT THEN AND THERE, AND GAVE IT TO OLD GREENTAIL.
I WANTED HER TO REMEMBER MY RED HAIR.
HM...
SO...
...YOU'RE NOT GOING TO GROW IT OUT AGAIN?
NOPE.
IT GETS IN THE WAY.

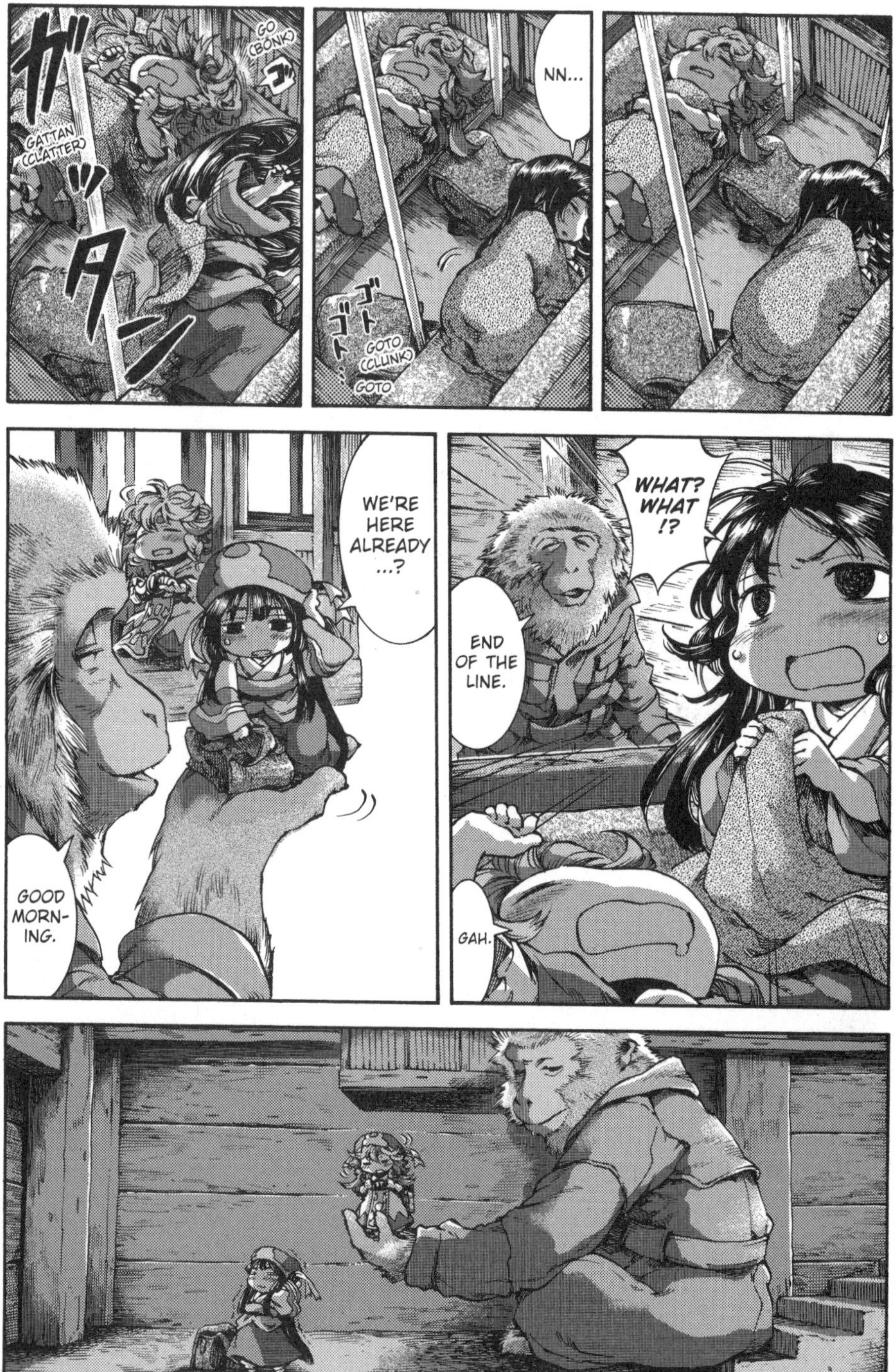
NN...
GOTO (CLUNK) GOTO
GO (BONK)
GATTAN (CLATTER)
WHAT? WHAT !?
END OF THE LINE.
GAH.
WE'RE HERE ALREADY ...?
GOOD MORNING.

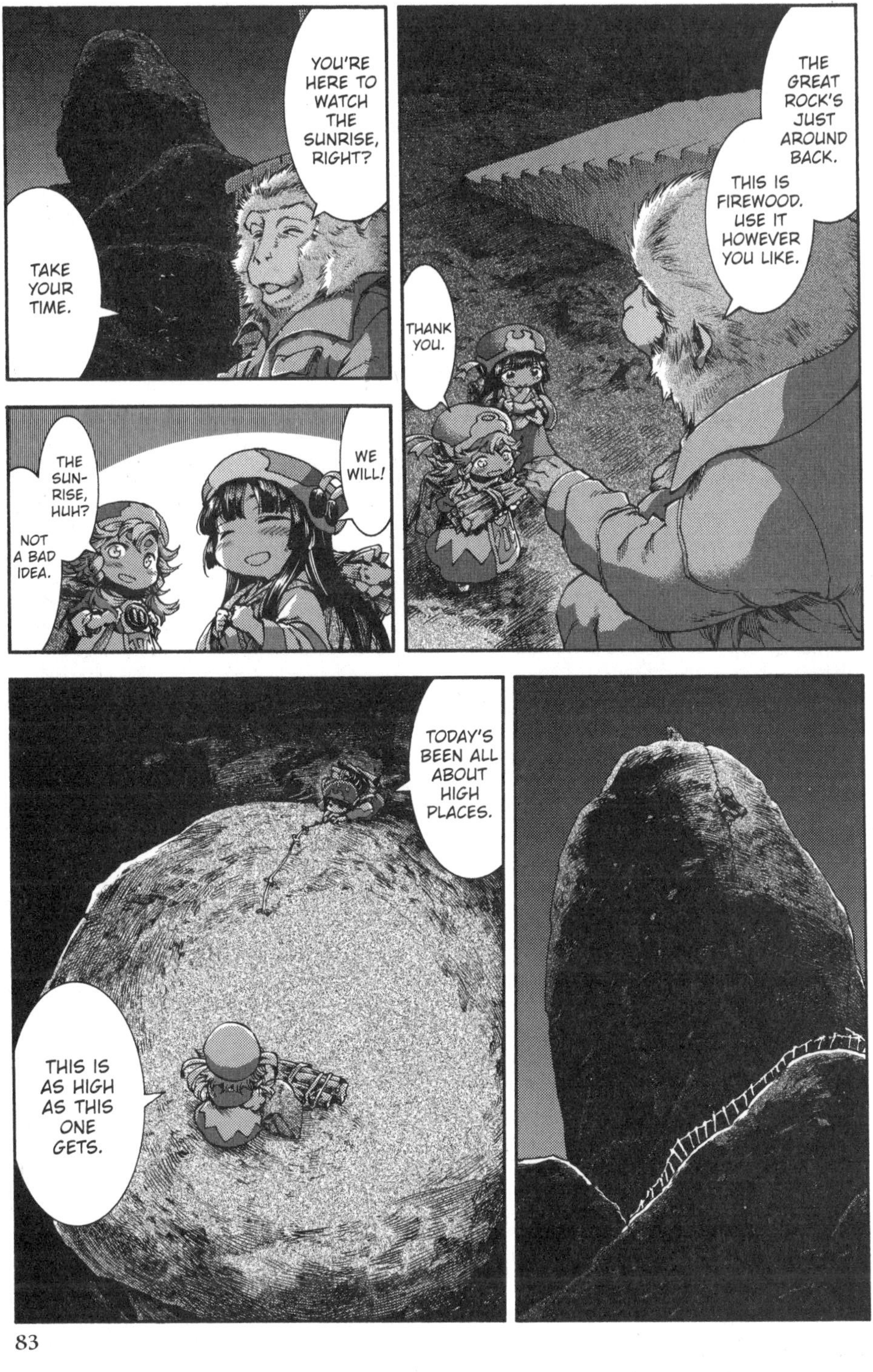
THE GREAT ROCK'S JUST AROUND BACK.
THIS IS FIREWOOD. USE IT HOWEVER YOU LIKE.
THANK YOU.
YOU'RE HERE TO WATCH THE SUNRISE, RIGHT?
TAKE YOUR TIME.
WE WILL!
THE SUN-RISE, HUH?
NOT A BAD IDEA.
TODAY'S BEEN ALL ABOUT HIGH PLACES.
THIS IS AS HIGH AS THIS ONE GETS.

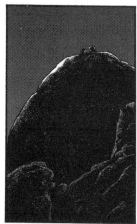

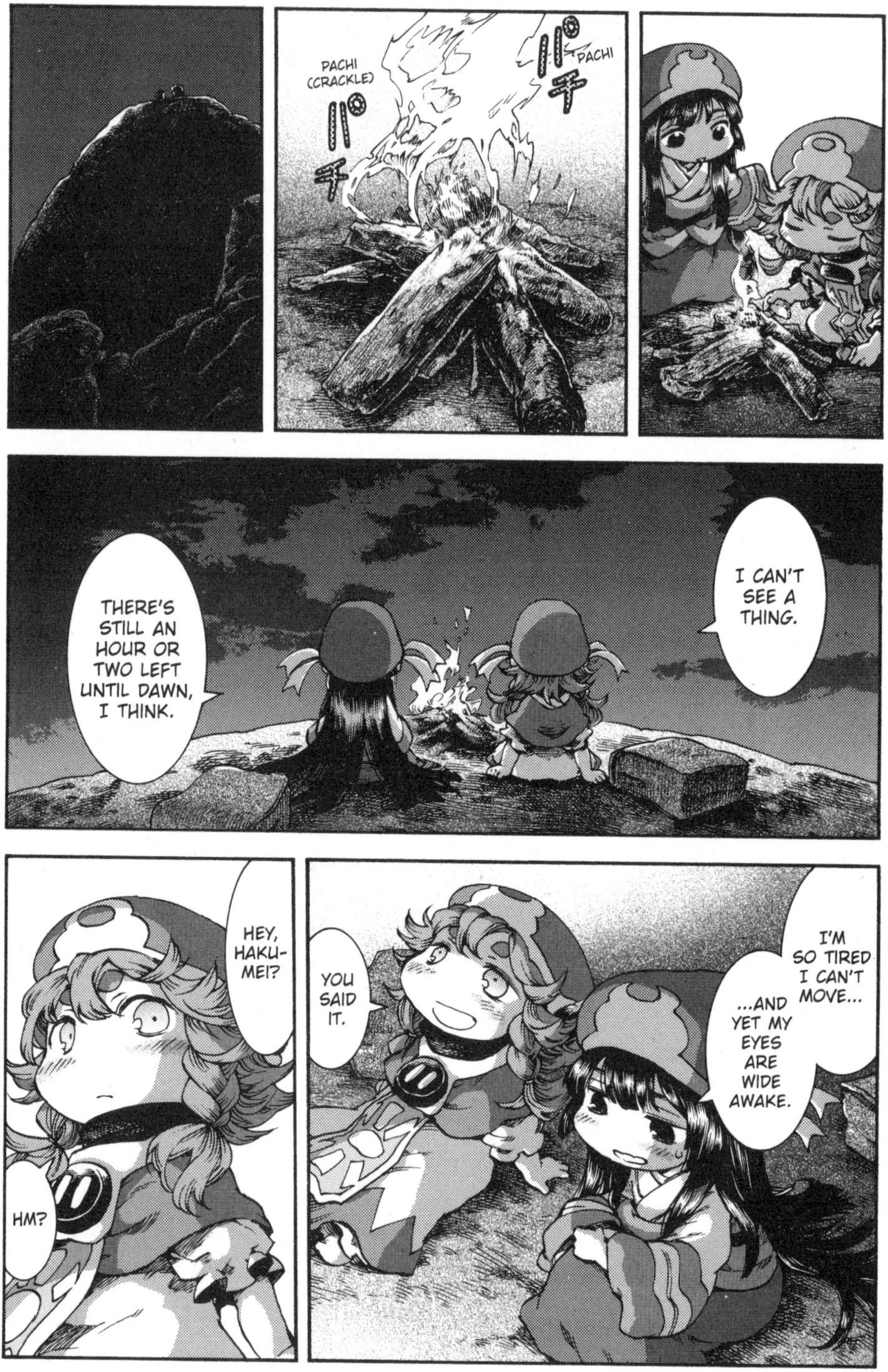
パチ
PACHI
PACHI (CRACKLE)
パチ
I CAN'T SEE A THING.
THERE'S STILL AN HOUR OR TWO LEFT UNTIL DAWN, I THINK.
I'M SO TIRED I CAN'T MOVE...
...AND YET MY EYES ARE WIDE AWAKE.
YOU SAID IT.
HEY, HAKU-MEI?
HM?

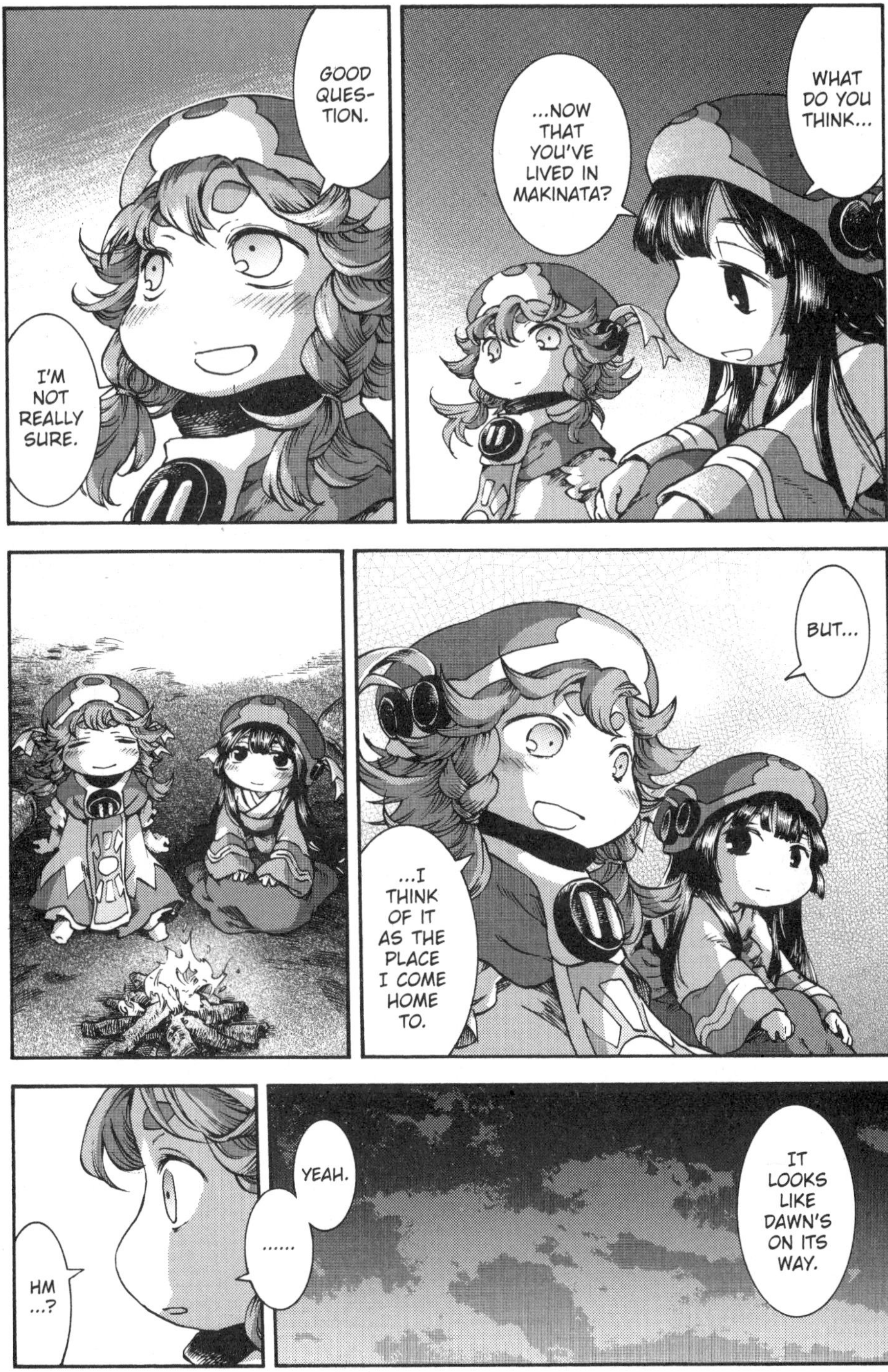
WHAT DO YOU THINK...
...NOW THAT YOU'VE LIVED IN MAKINATA?
GOOD QUES-TION.
I'M NOT REALLY SURE.
BUT...
...I THINK OF IT AS THE PLACE I COME HOME TO.
IT LOOKS LIKE DAWN'S ON ITS WAY.
YEAH.
......
HM ...?

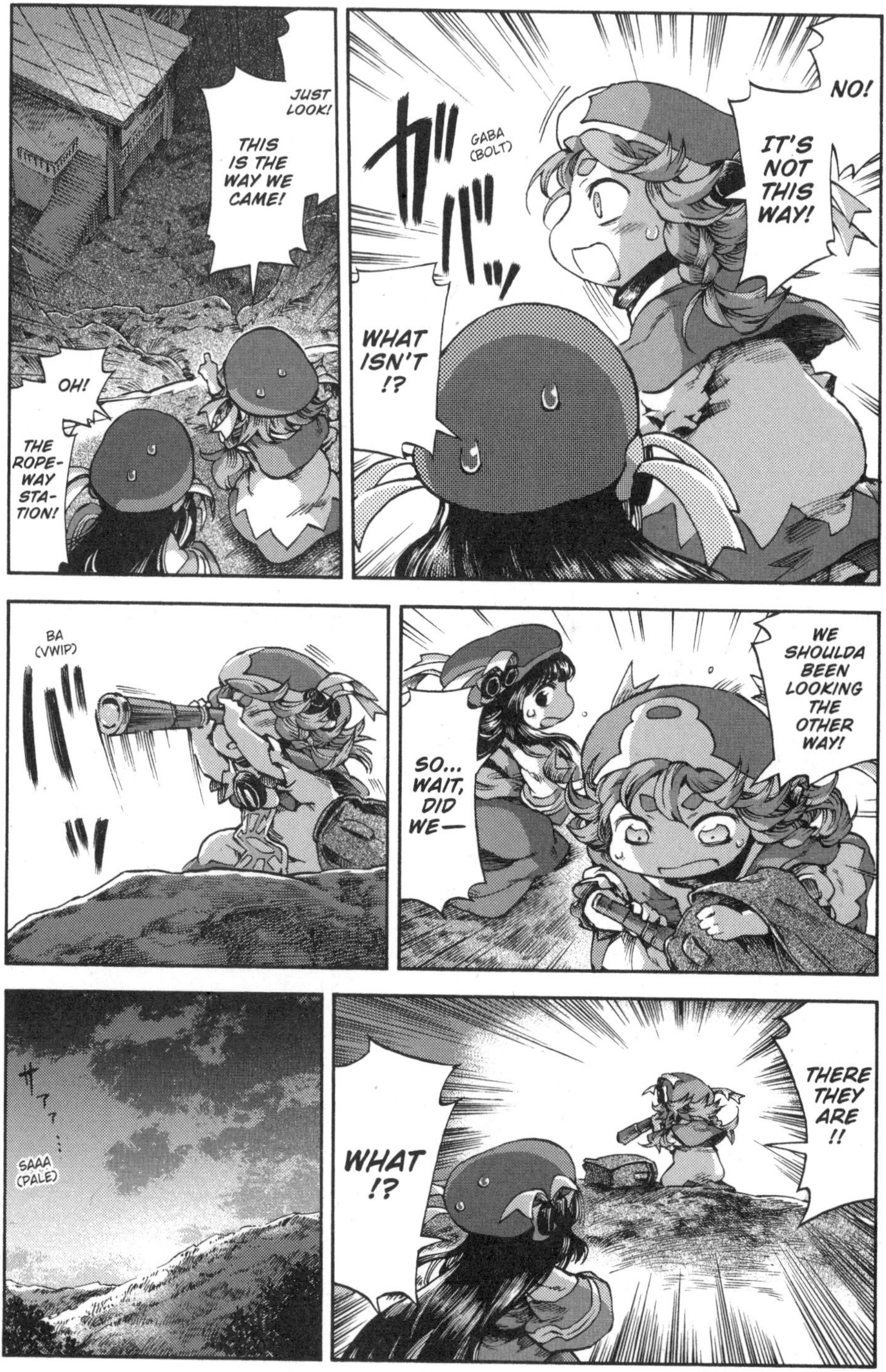
NO!
IT'S NOT THIS WAY!
GABA (BOLT)
WHAT ISN'T !?
JUST LOOK!
THIS IS THE WAY WE CAME!
OH!
THE ROPE-WAY STATION!
WE SHOULDA BEEN LOOKING THE OTHER WAY!
SO... WAIT, DID WE—
BA (VWIP)
THERE THEY ARE !!
WHAT !?
SAAA (PALE)

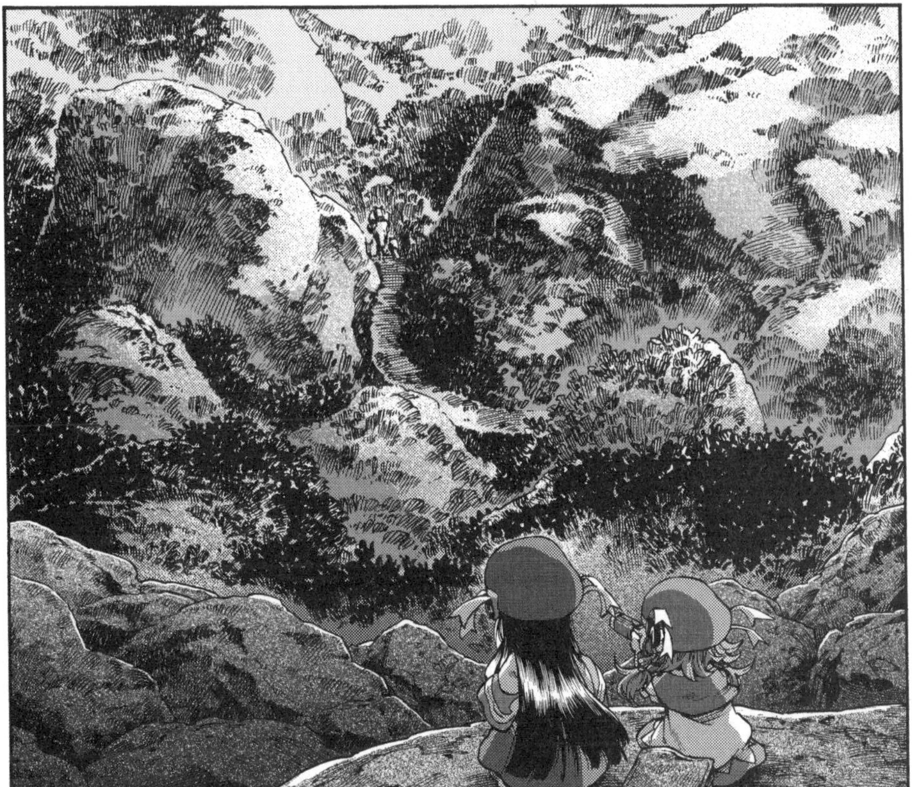

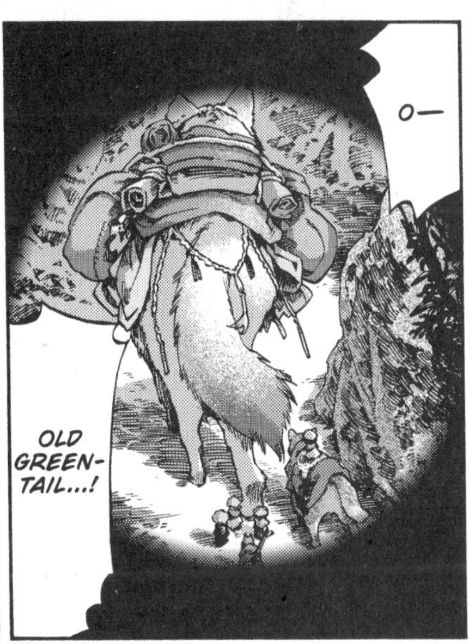
O—
OLD GREEN-TAIL...!

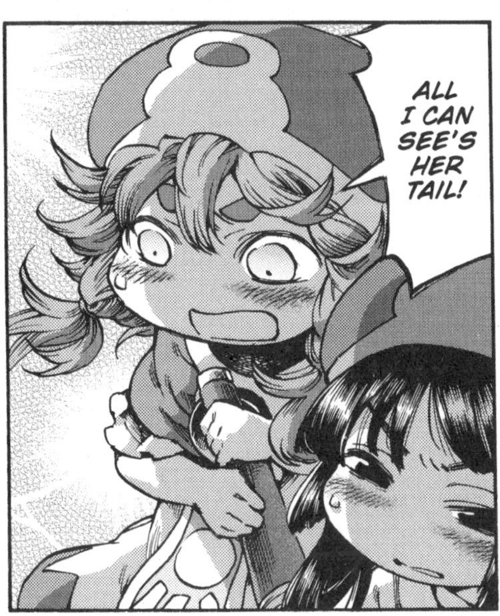
ALL I CAN SEE'S HER TAIL!

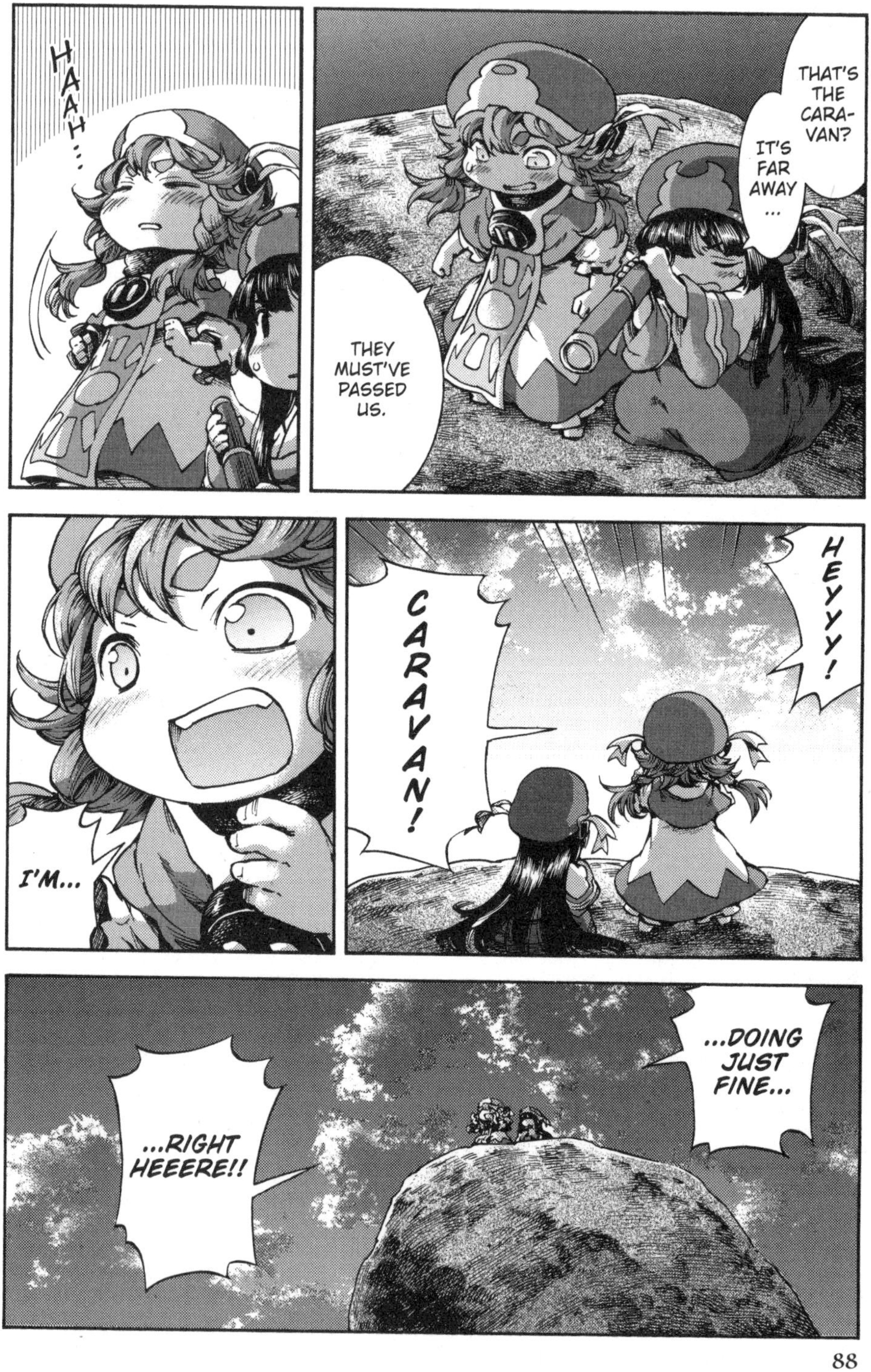

THAT'S THE CARAVAN?
IT'S FAR AWAY...
THEY MUST'VE PASSED US.
HAAH...
HEYYY!
CARAVAN!
I'M...
...DOING JUST FINE...
...RIGHT HEEERE!!

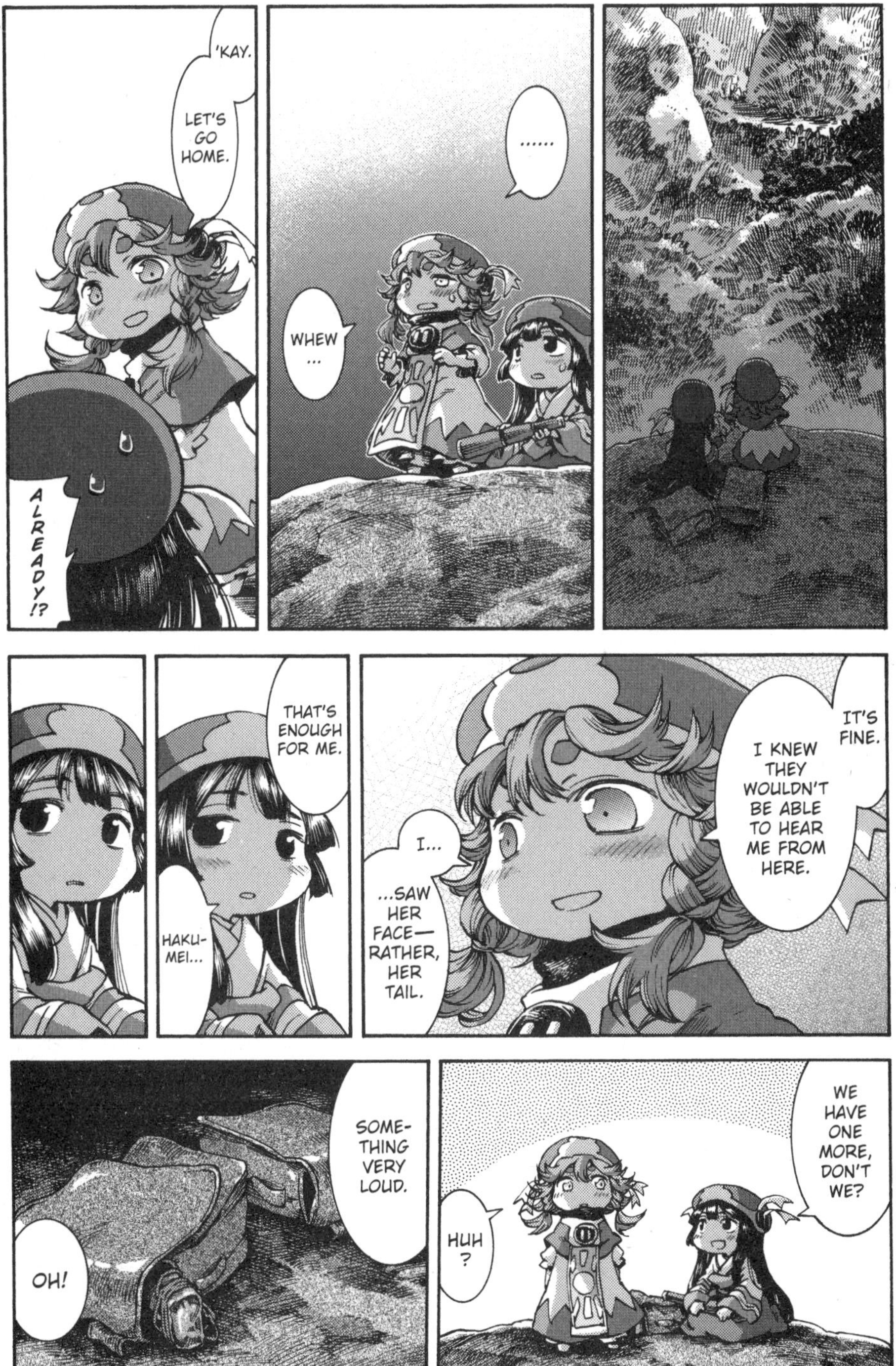
......
WHEW ...
'KAY.
LET'S GO HOME.
ALREADY!?
IT'S FINE.
I KNEW THEY WOULDN'T BE ABLE TO HEAR ME FROM HERE.
I...
...SAW HER FACE—RATHER, HER TAIL.
THAT'S ENOUGH FOR ME.
HAKU-MEI...
WE HAVE ONE MORE, DON'T WE?
HUH?
SOME-THING VERY LOUD.
OH!

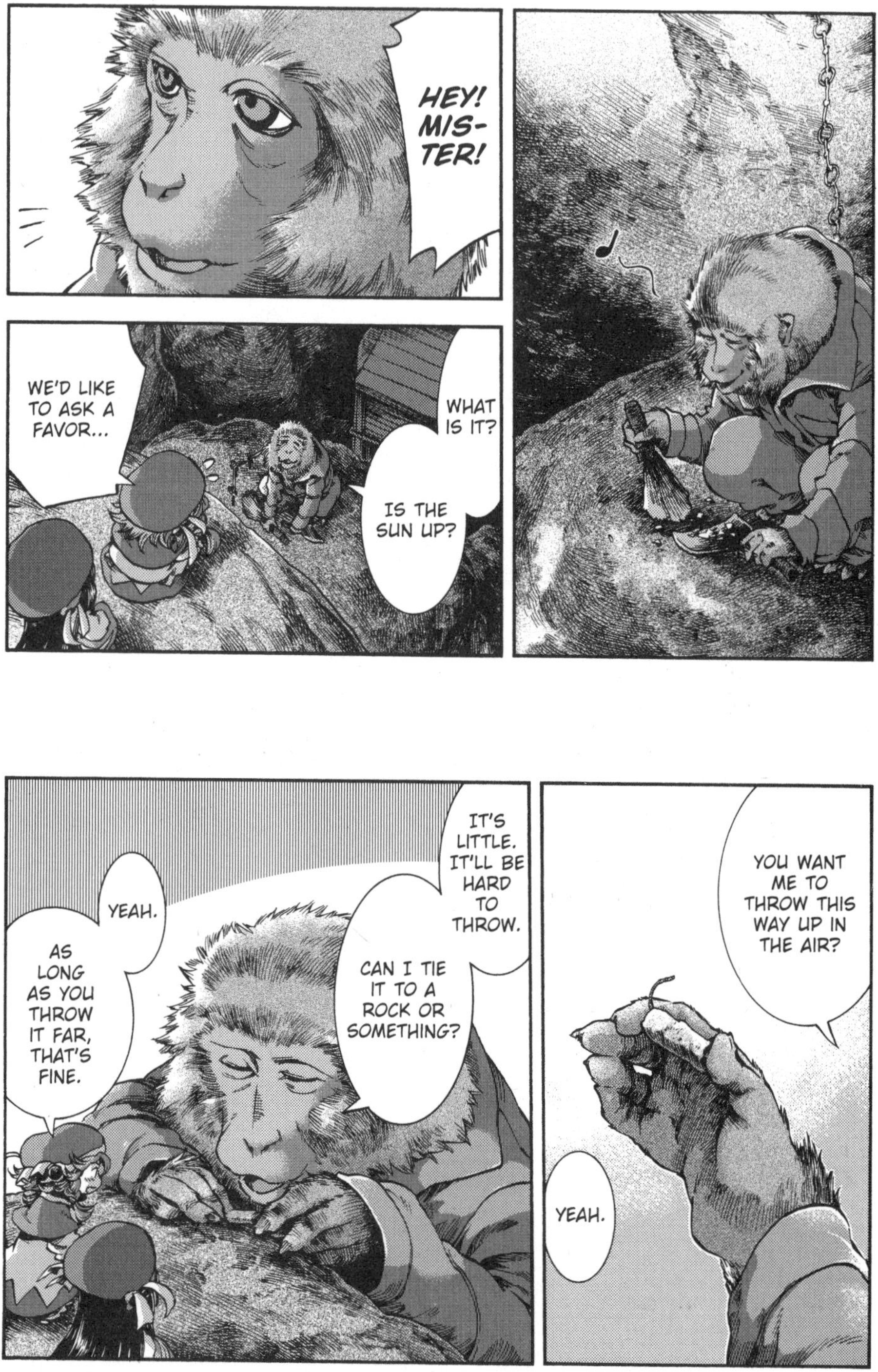
HEY! MIS-TER!
WHAT IS IT?
WE'D LIKE TO ASK A FAVOR...
IS THE SUN UP?
YOU WANT ME TO THROW THIS WAY UP IN THE AIR?
YEAH.
IT'S LITTLE. IT'LL BE HARD TO THROW.
CAN I TIE IT TO A ROCK OR SOMETHING?
YEAH.
AS LONG AS YOU THROW IT FAR, THAT'S FINE.

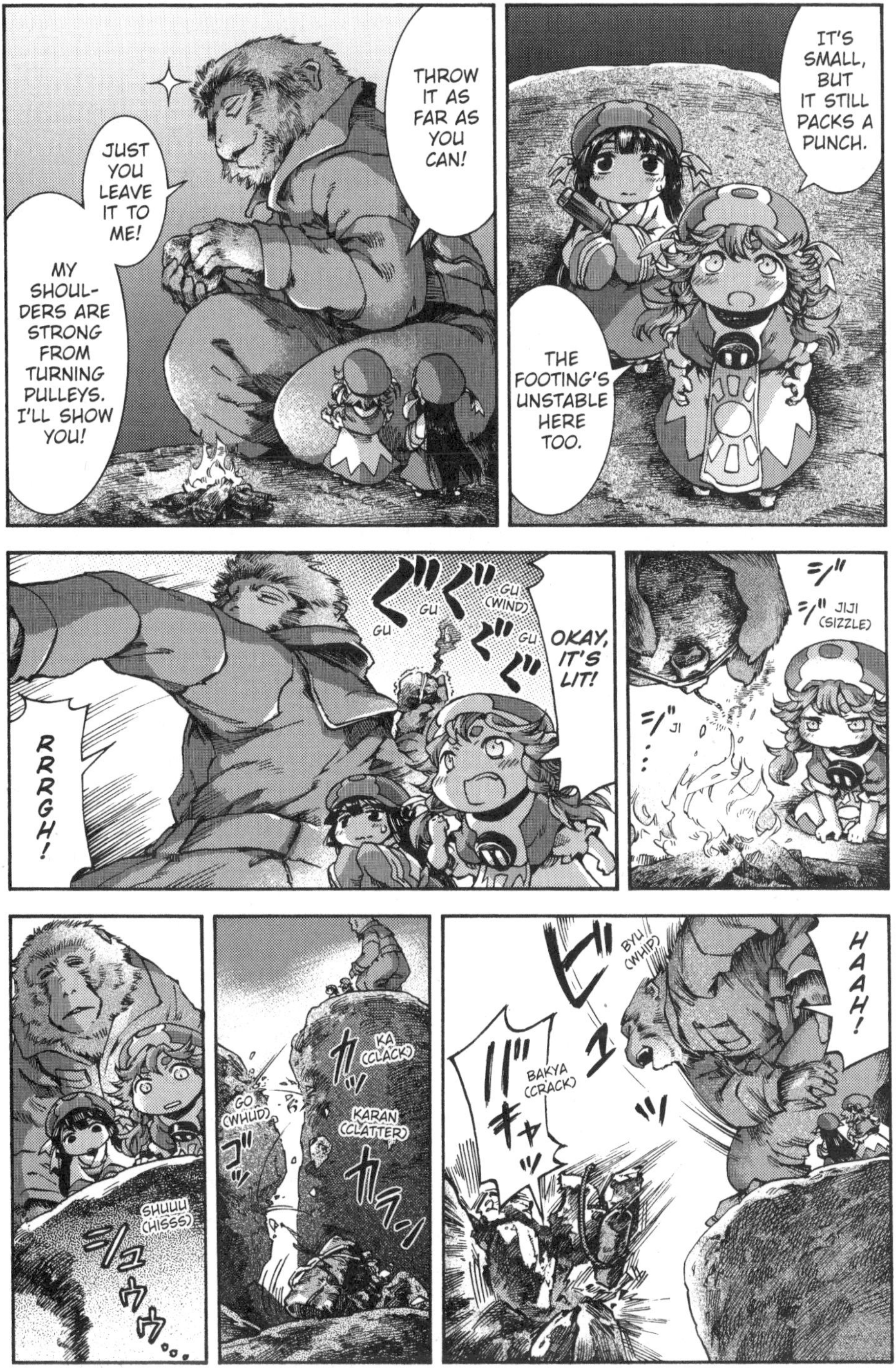
IT'S SMALL, BUT IT STILL PACKS A PUNCH.
THE FOOTING'S UNSTABLE HERE TOO.
THROW IT AS FAR AS YOU CAN!
JUST YOU LEAVE IT TO ME!
MY SHOUL-DERS ARE STRONG FROM TURNING PULLEYS. I'LL SHOW YOU!
JIJI (SIZZLE)
JI
OKAY, IT'S LIT!
GU GU GU GU (WIND)
RRRGH!
HAAAH!
BYU (WHIP)
BAKYA (CRACK)
KA (CLACK)
GO (WHUD)
KARAN (CLATTER)
SHUUU (HISSS)

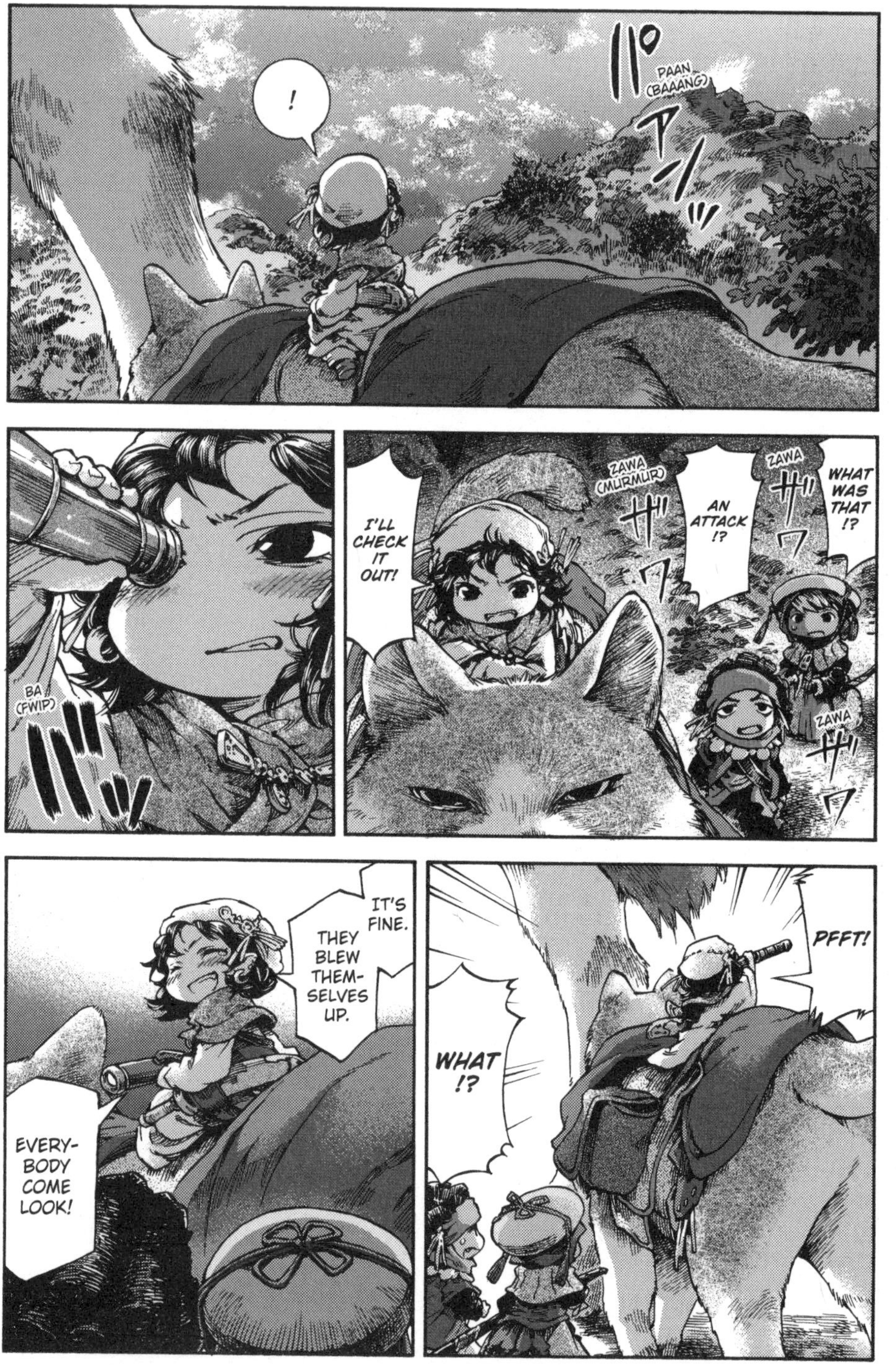
!
PAAN (BAAANG)
WHAT WAS THAT!?
ZAWA
AN ATTACK!?
ZAWA (MURMUR)
I'LL CHECK IT OUT!
ZAWA
BA (FWIP)
PFFT!
WHAT!?
IT'S FINE.
THEY BLEW THEMSELVES UP.
EVERYBODY COME LOOK!

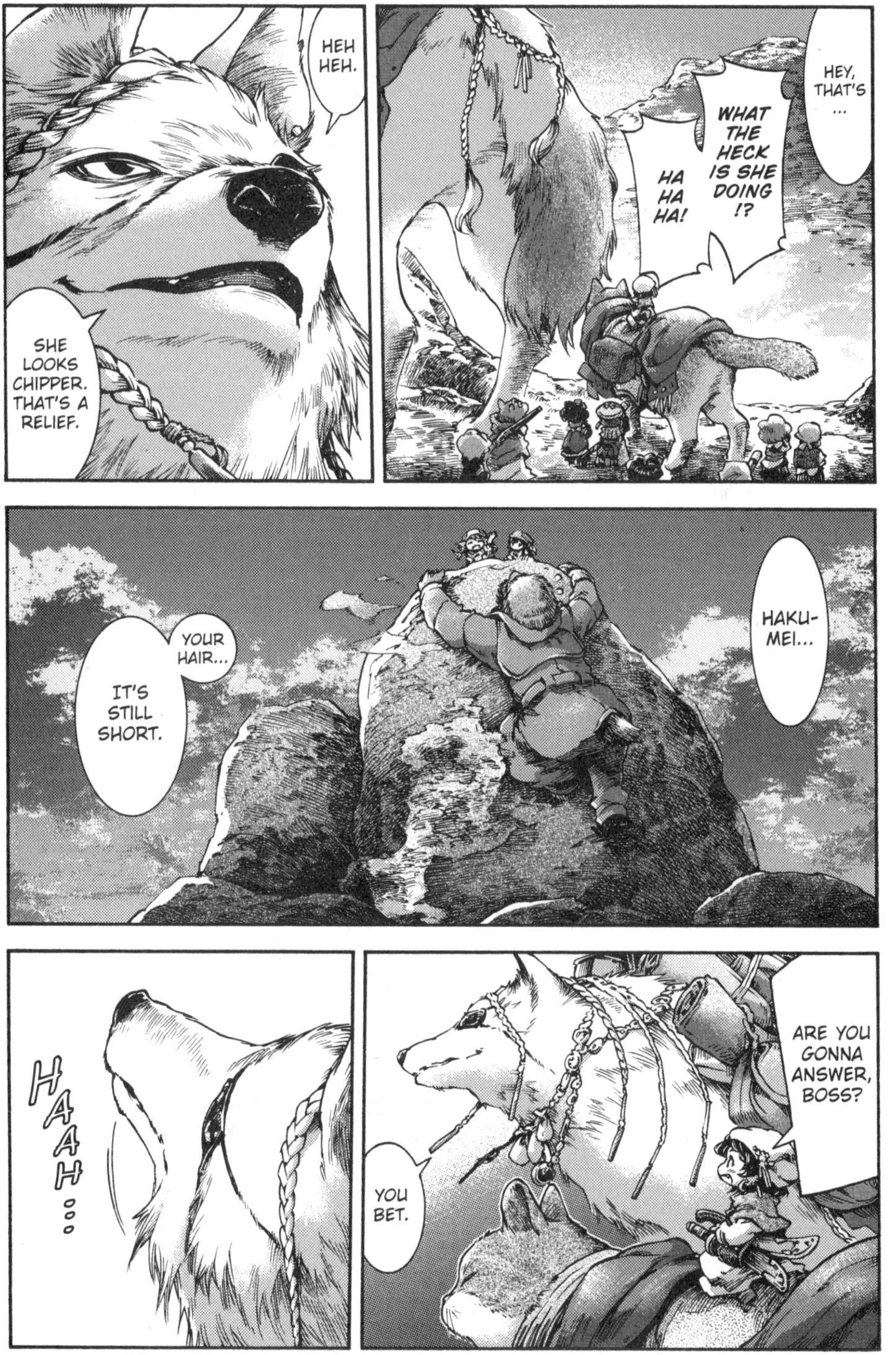
HEY, THAT'S ...
WHAT THE HECK IS SHE DOING !?
HA HA HA!
HEH HEH.
SHE LOOKS CHIPPER. THAT'S A RELIEF.
HAKU-MEI...
YOUR HAIR...
IT'S STILL SHORT.
ARE YOU GONNA ANSWER, BOSS?
YOU BET.
HAAH...

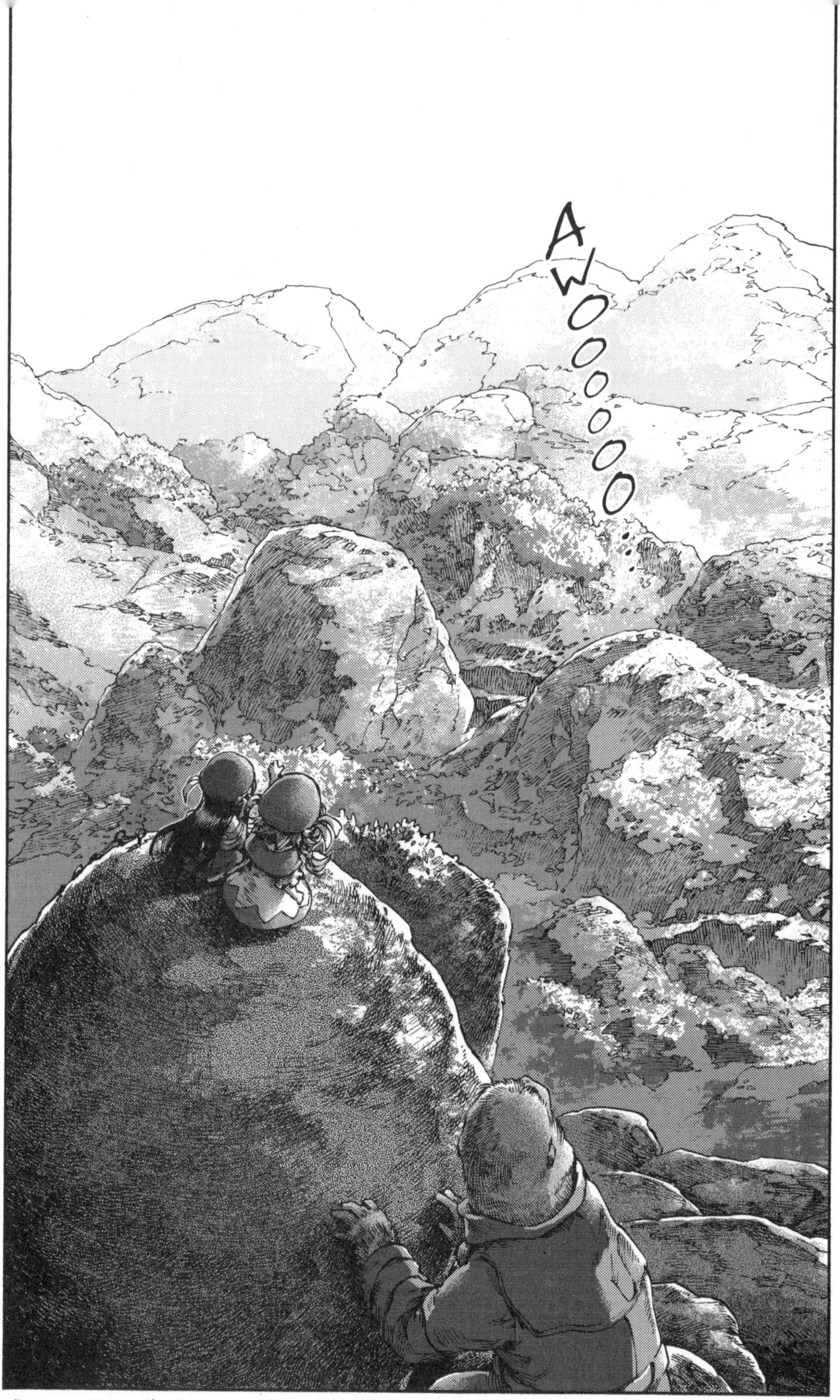
AWOOOOOO...

Chapter 30 • End

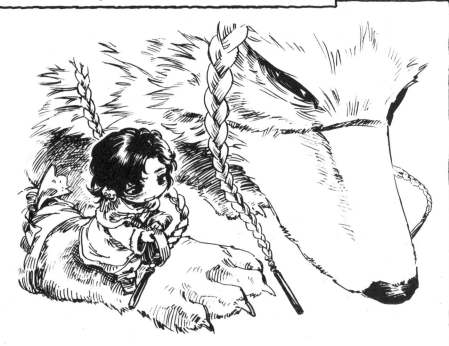

"Boss, is about here good?"

"Put it a little lower, please."

"It keeps coming apart. Want me to braid it?"

"That's up to you."

"When the sun hits it, it really does shine bright red, doesn't it?"

"Is it too showy, do you think?"

"You're already plenty showy, boss. Hey, don't move."

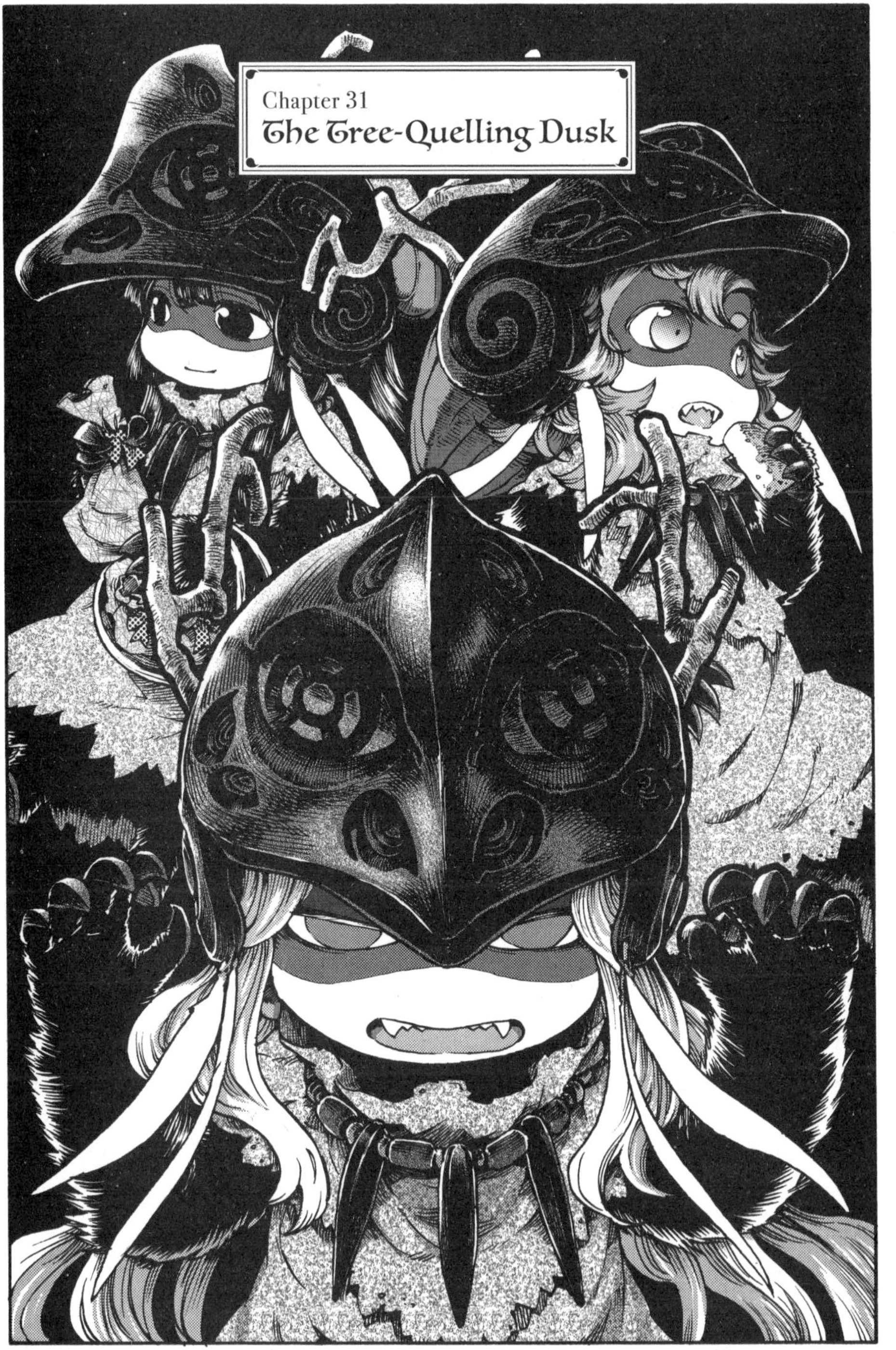
Chapter 31
The Tree-Quelling Dusk

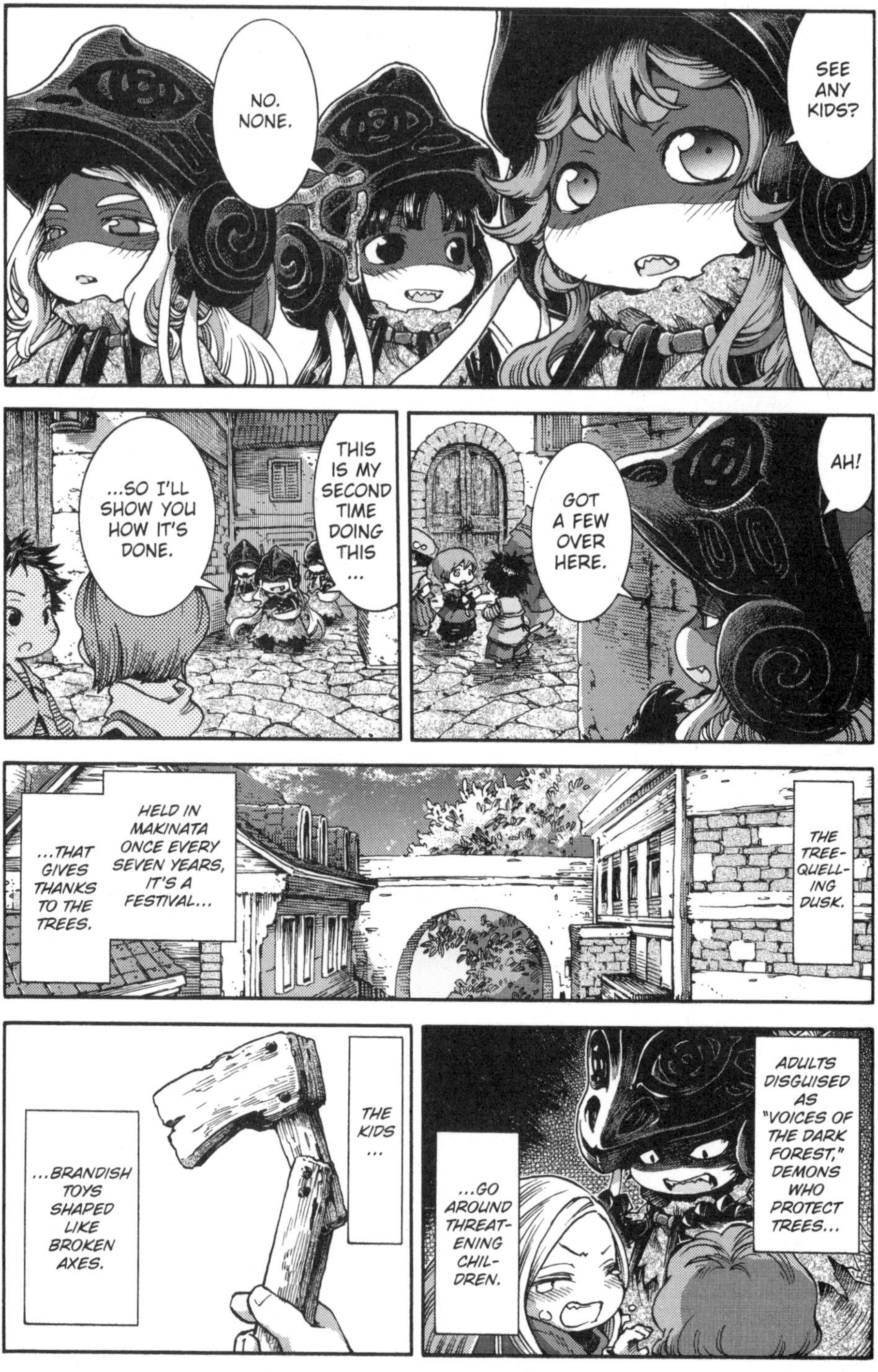
SEE ANY KIDS?
NO. NONE.
AH!
GOT A FEW OVER HERE.
THIS IS MY SECOND TIME DOING THIS...
...SO I'LL SHOW YOU HOW IT'S DONE.
THE TREE-QUELLING DUSK.
HELD IN MAKINATA ONCE EVERY SEVEN YEARS, IT'S A FESTIVAL...
...THAT GIVES THANKS TO THE TREES.
ADULTS DISGUISED AS "VOICES OF THE DARK FOREST," DEMONS WHO PROTECT TREES...
...GO AROUND THREAT-ENING CHIL-DREN.
THE KIDS...
...BRANDISH TOYS SHAPED LIKE BROKEN AXES.

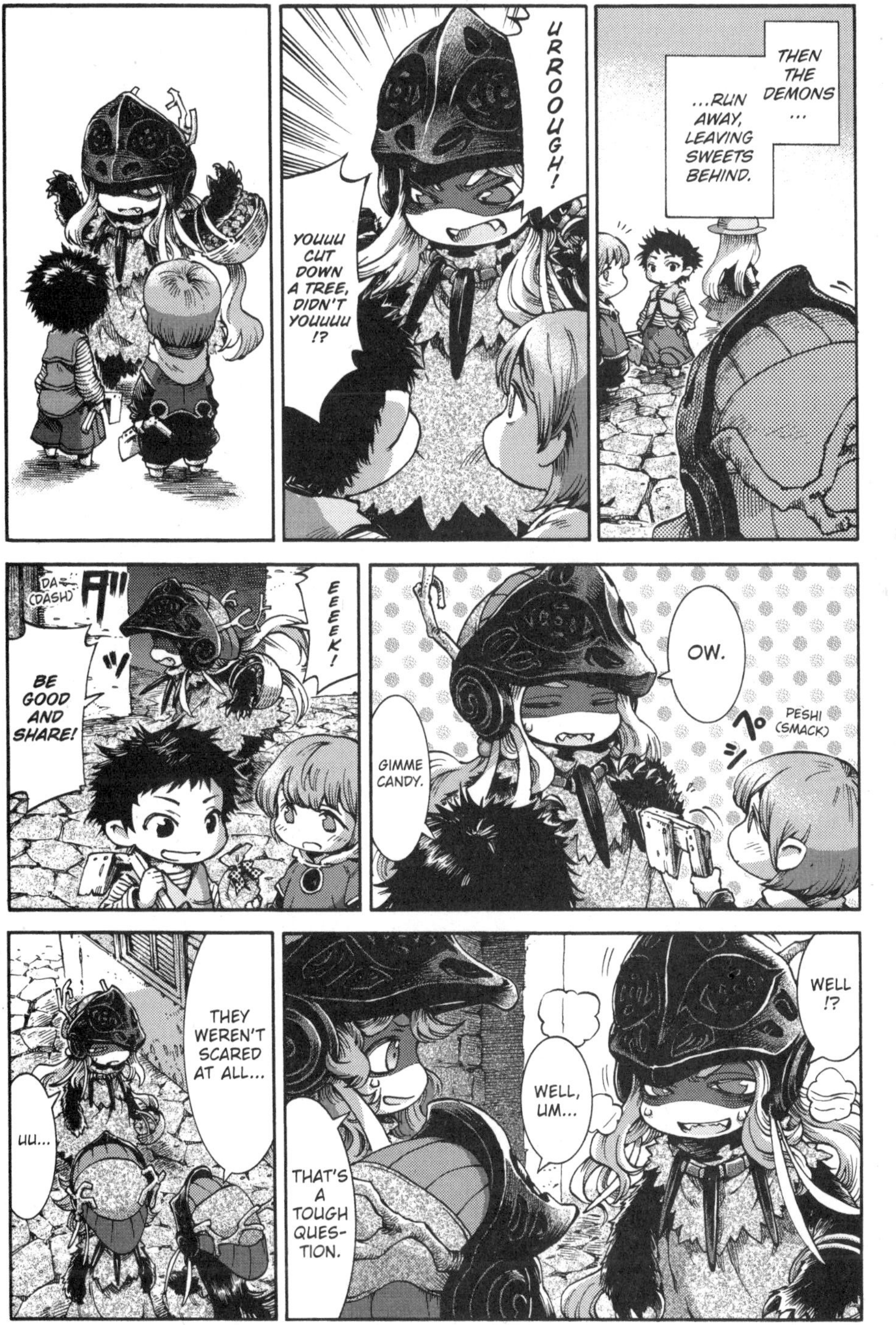
THEN THE DEMONS...
...RUN AWAY, LEAVING SWEETS BEHIND.
URROOUGH!
YOUUU CUT DOWN A TREE, DIDN'T YOUUUU!?
OW.
PESHI (SMACK)
GIMME CANDY.
EEEEK!
DA (DASH)
BE GOOD AND SHARE!
WELL!?
WELL, UM...
THAT'S A TOUGH QUESTION.
THEY WEREN'T SCARED AT ALL...
UU...

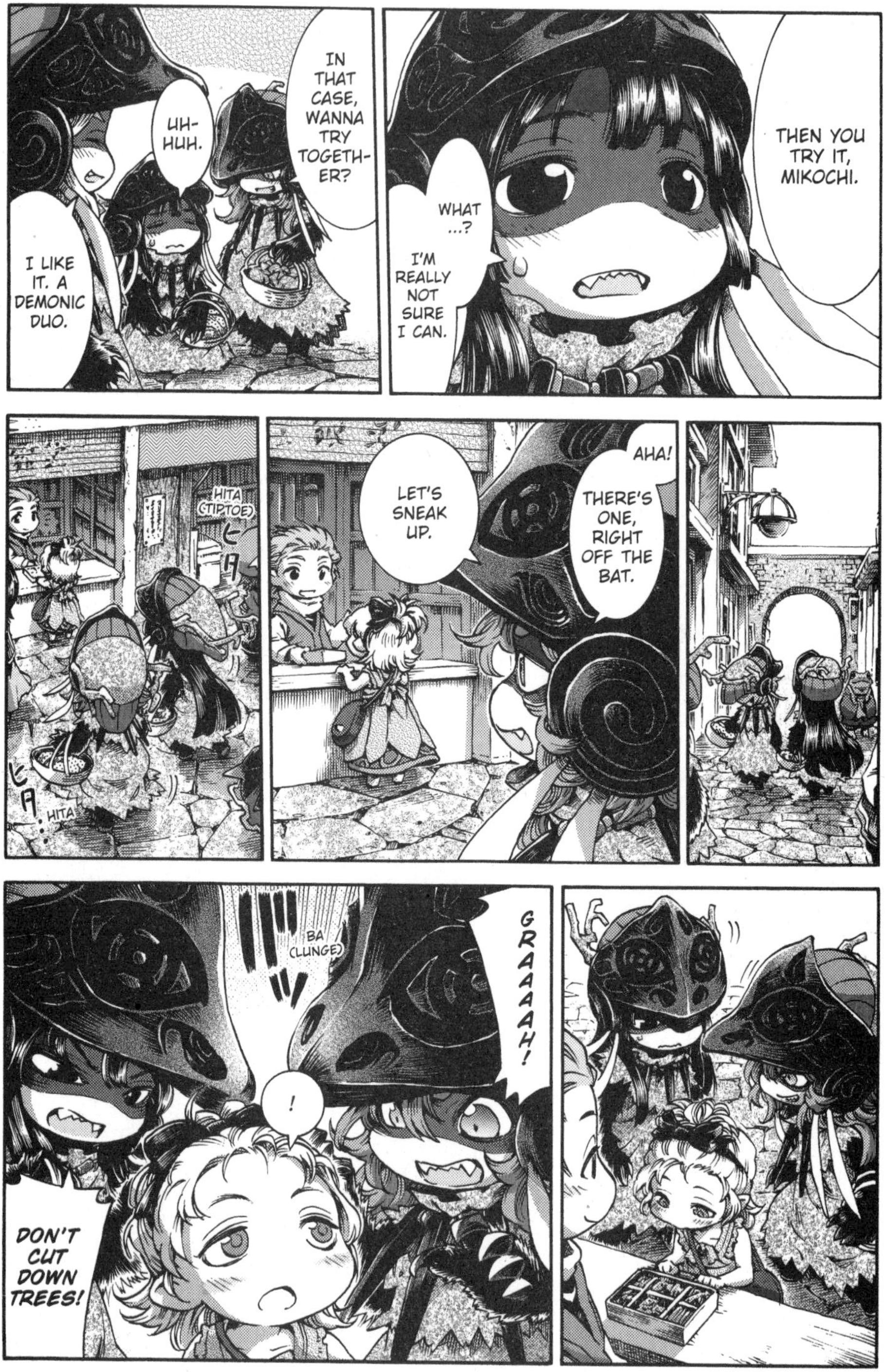
THEN YOU TRY IT, MIKOCHI.
WHAT ...?
I'M REALLY NOT SURE I CAN.
IN THAT CASE, WANNA TRY TOGETHER?
UH-HUH.
I LIKE IT. A DEMONIC DUO.
AHA!
THERE'S ONE, RIGHT OFF THE BAT.
LET'S SNEAK UP.
HITA (TIPTOE)
ヒタ
ヒタ...
HITA
GRAAAAH!
BA (LUNGE)
!
DON'T CUT DOWN TREES!

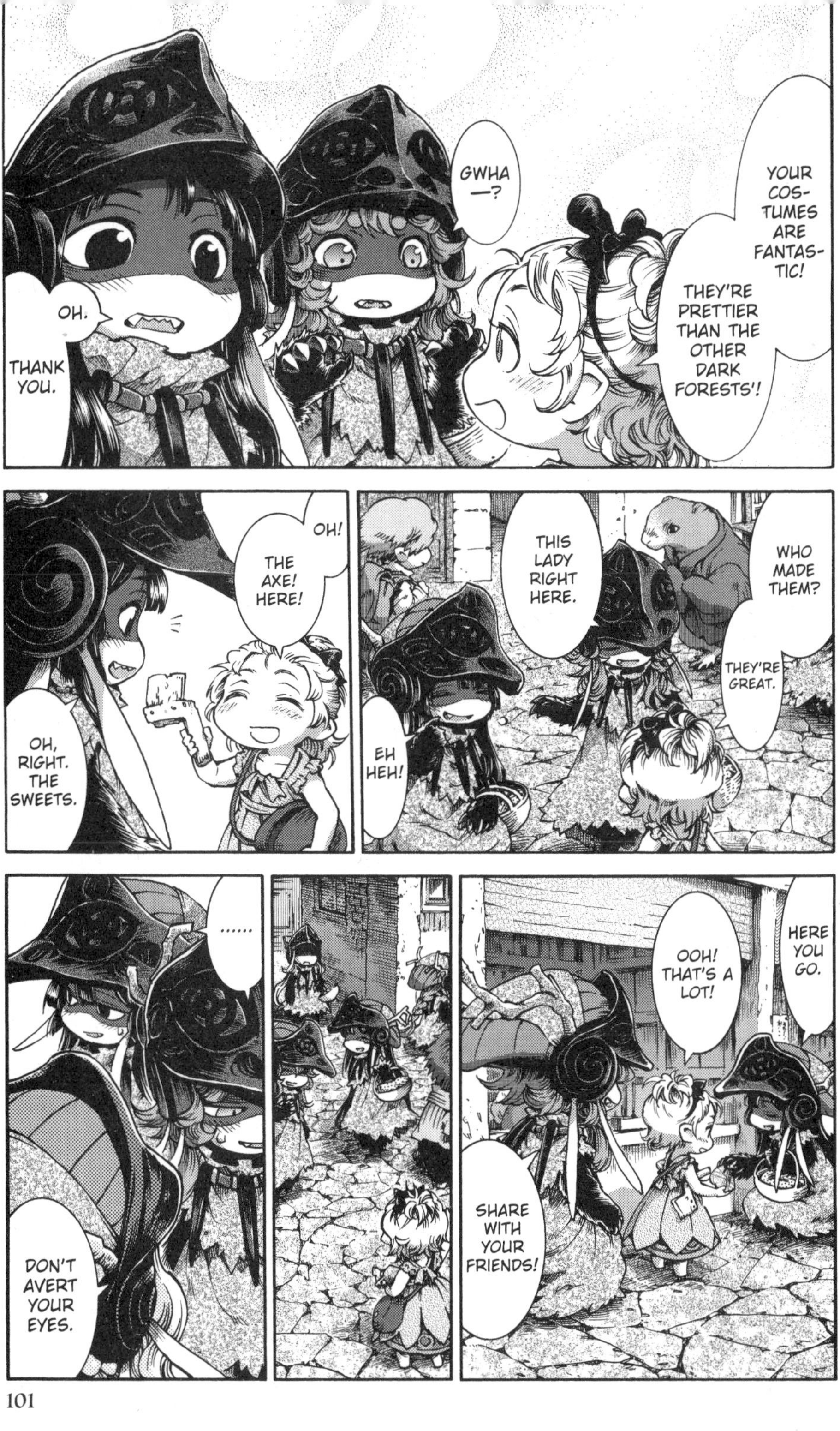
YOUR COS-TUMES ARE FANTAS-TIC!
THEY'RE PRETTIER THAN THE OTHER DARK FORESTS'!
GWHA—?
OH.
THANK YOU.
WHO MADE THEM?
THEY'RE GREAT.
THIS LADY RIGHT HERE.
EH HEH!
OH!
THE AXE! HERE!
OH, RIGHT. THE SWEETS.
HERE YOU GO.
OOH! THAT'S A LOT!
SHARE WITH YOUR FRIENDS!
......
DON'T AVERT YOUR EYES.

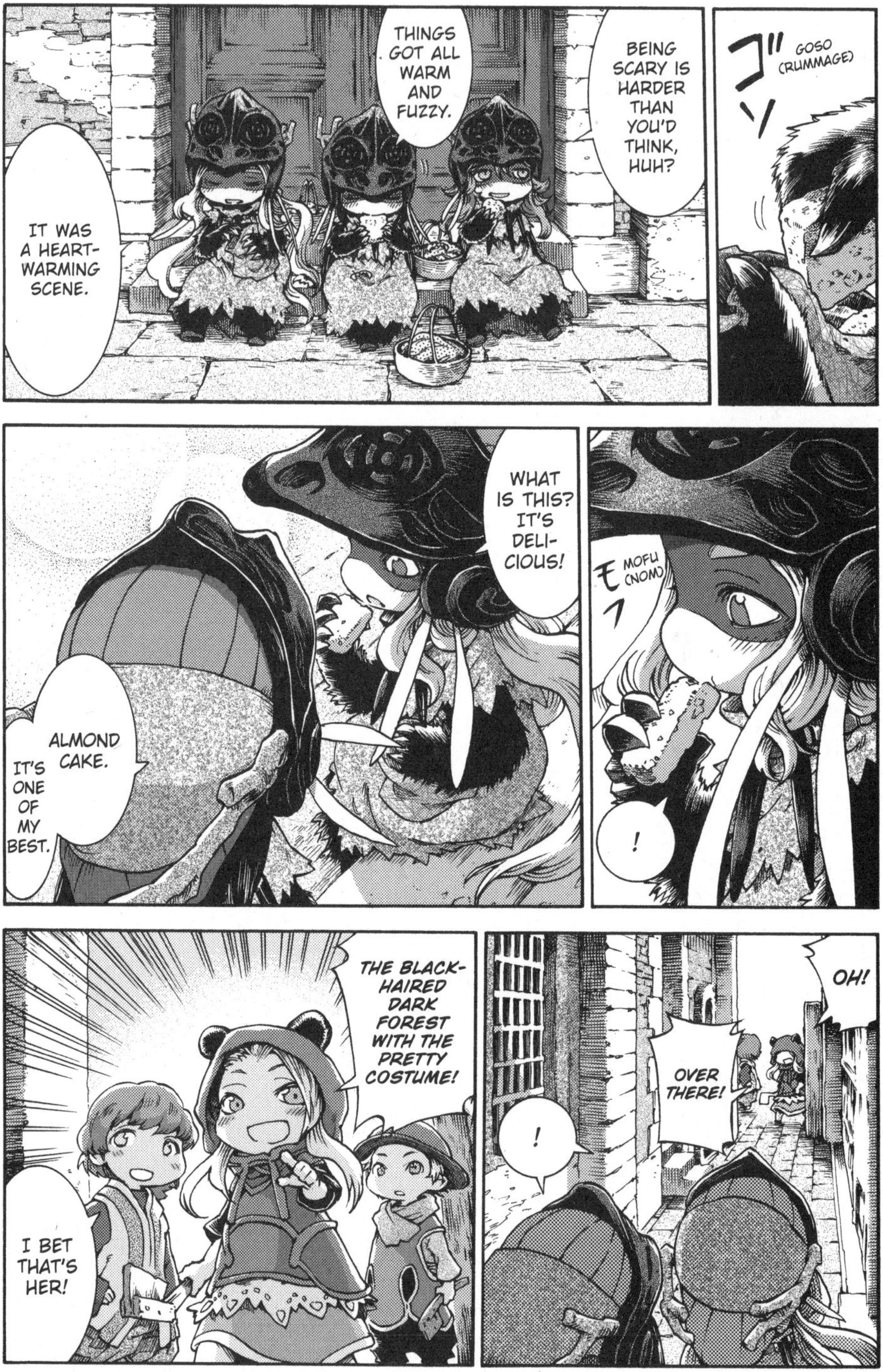
ゴソ
GOSO (RUMMAGE)
BEING SCARY IS HARDER THAN YOU'D THINK, HUH?
THINGS GOT ALL WARM AND FUZZY.
IT WAS A HEART-WARMING SCENE.
モフ
MOFU (NOM)
!
WHAT IS THIS? IT'S DELI-CIOUS!
ALMOND CAKE.
IT'S ONE OF MY BEST.
OH!
OVER THERE!
!
THE BLACK-HAIRED DARK FOREST WITH THE PRETTY COSTUME!
I BET THAT'S HER!

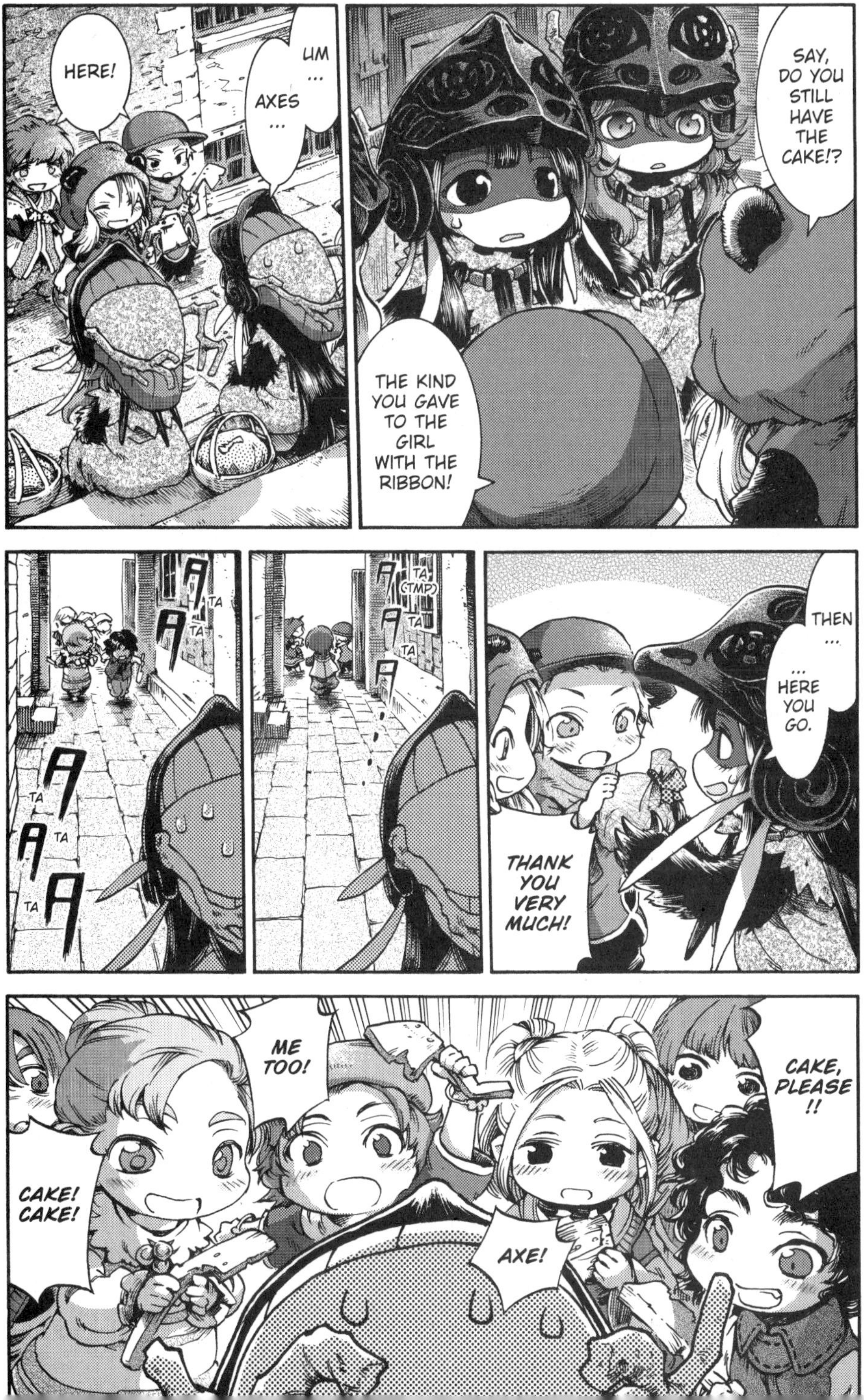
SAY, DO YOU STILL HAVE THE CAKE!?
THE KIND YOU GAVE TO THE GIRL WITH THE RIBBON!
UM ... AXES ...
HERE!
THEN ...
... HERE YOU GO.
THANK YOU VERY MUCH!
TA (TMP)
TA
TA
TA
TA
TA
TA
TA
CAKE, PLEASE !!
ME TOO!
AXE!
CAKE! CAKE!

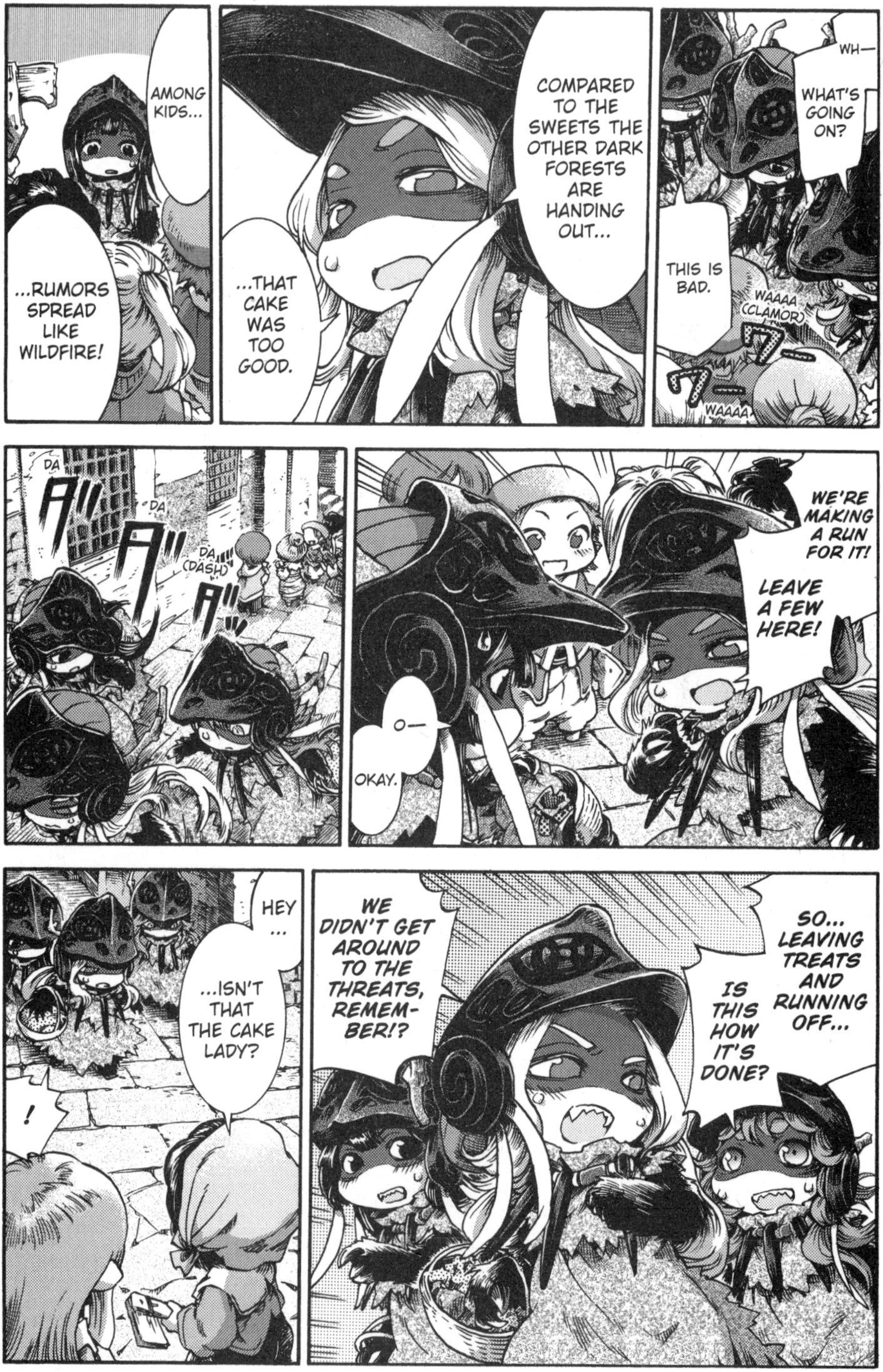
WH—
WHAT'S GOING ON?
THIS IS BAD.
WAAAA (CLAMOR)
WAAAA
COMPARED TO THE SWEETS THE OTHER DARK FORESTS ARE HANDING OUT...
...THAT CAKE WAS TOO GOOD.
AMONG KIDS...
...RUMORS SPREAD LIKE WILDFIRE!
WE'RE MAKING A RUN FOR IT!
LEAVE A FEW HERE!
O—
OKAY.
DA
DA
DA (DASH)
SO... LEAVING TREATS AND RUNNING OFF...
IS THIS HOW IT'S DONE?
WE DIDN'T GET AROUND TO THE THREATS, REMEMBER!?
HEY ...
...ISN'T THAT THE CAKE LADY?
!

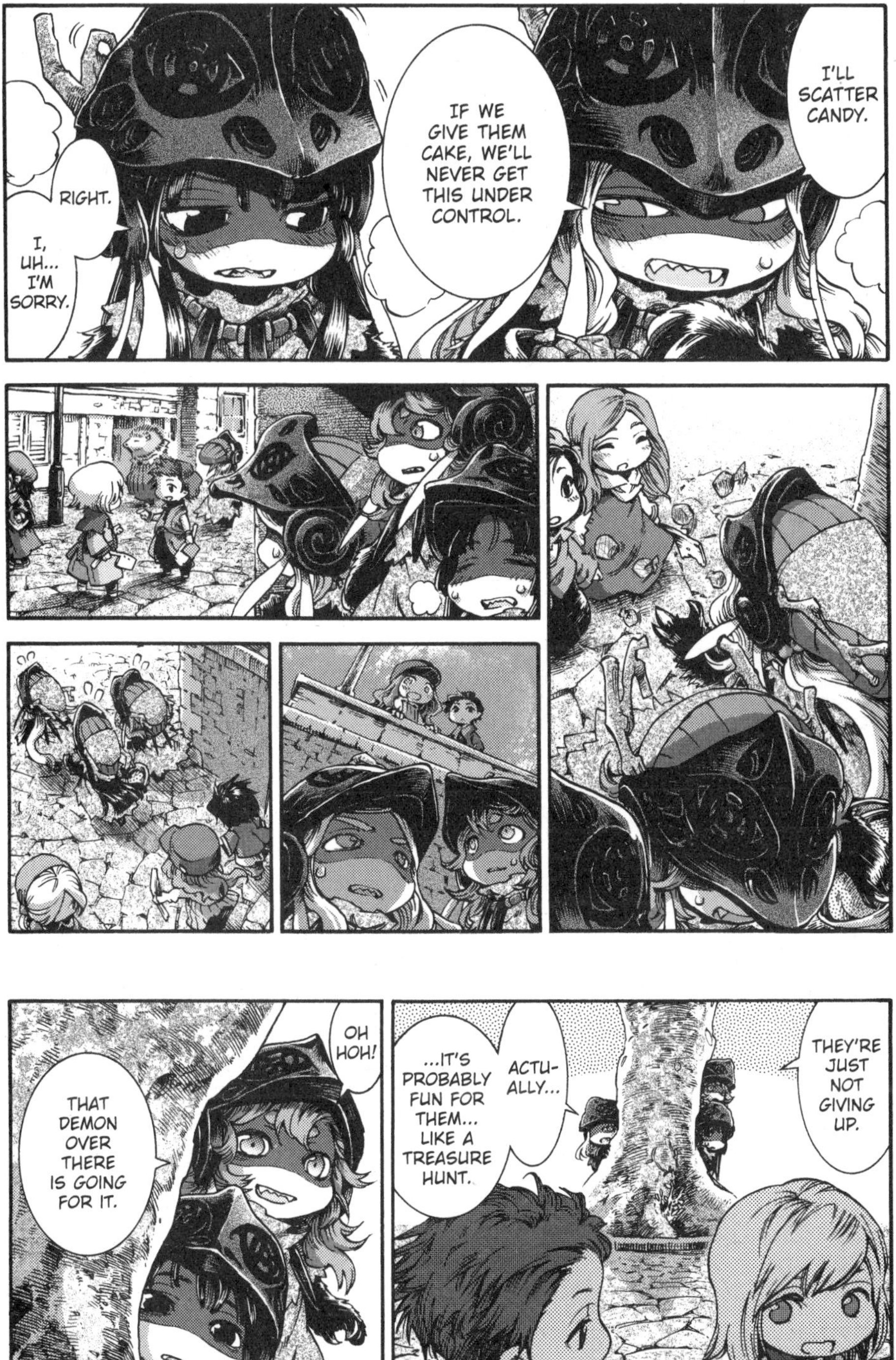
I'LL SCATTER CANDY.
IF WE GIVE THEM CAKE, WE'LL NEVER GET THIS UNDER CONTROL.
RIGHT.
I, UH... I'M SORRY.
THEY'RE JUST NOT GIVING UP.
ACTU-ALLY...
...IT'S PROBABLY FUN FOR THEM... LIKE A TREASURE HUNT.
OH HOH!
THAT DEMON OVER THERE IS GOING FOR IT.

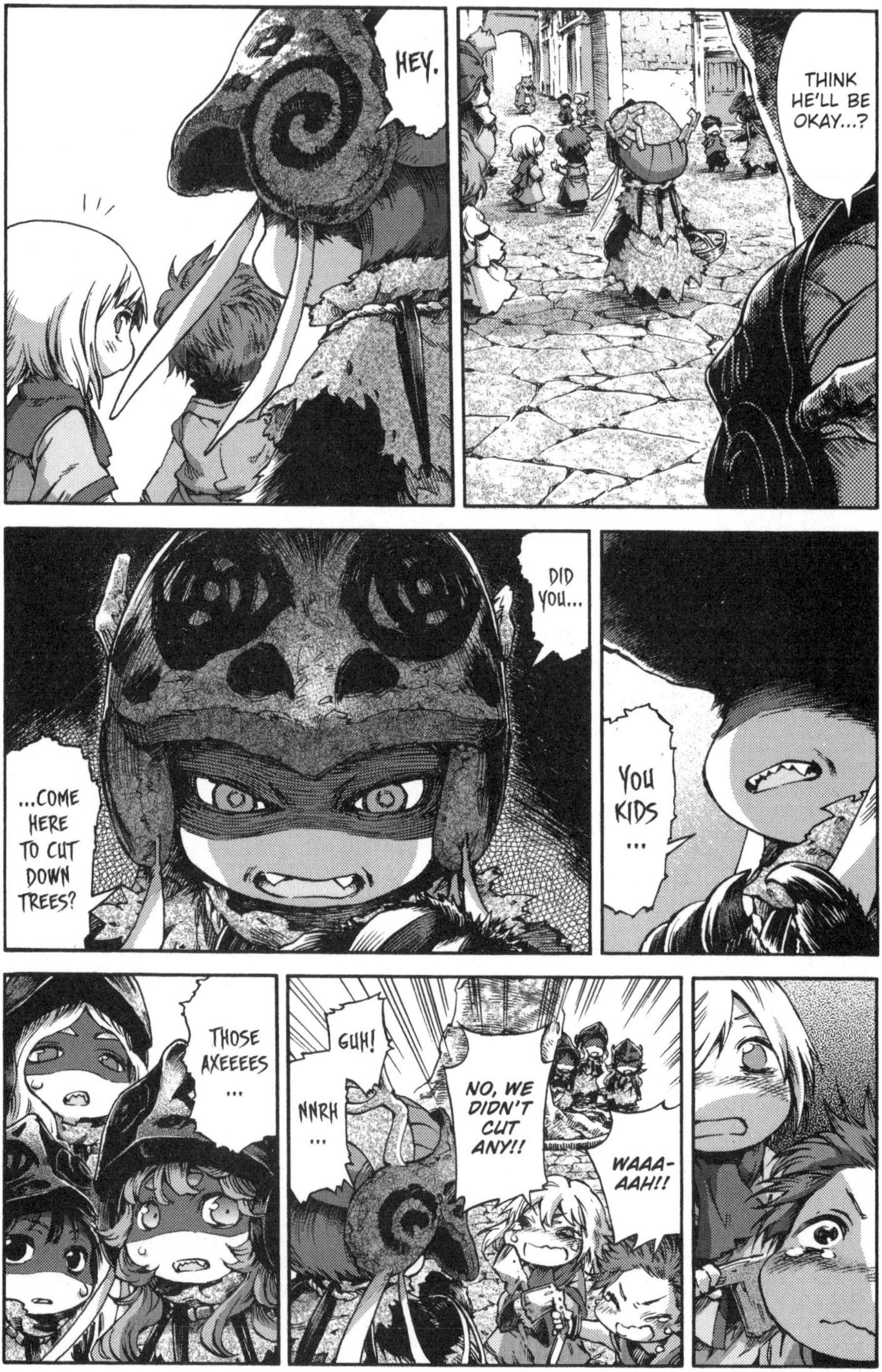
THINK HE'LL BE OKAY...?
HEY.
YOU KIDS ...
DID YOU...
...COME HERE TO CUT DOWN TREES?
WAAA-AAH!!
NO, WE DIDN'T CUT ANY!!
GUH!
NNRH ...
THOSE AXEEEES ...

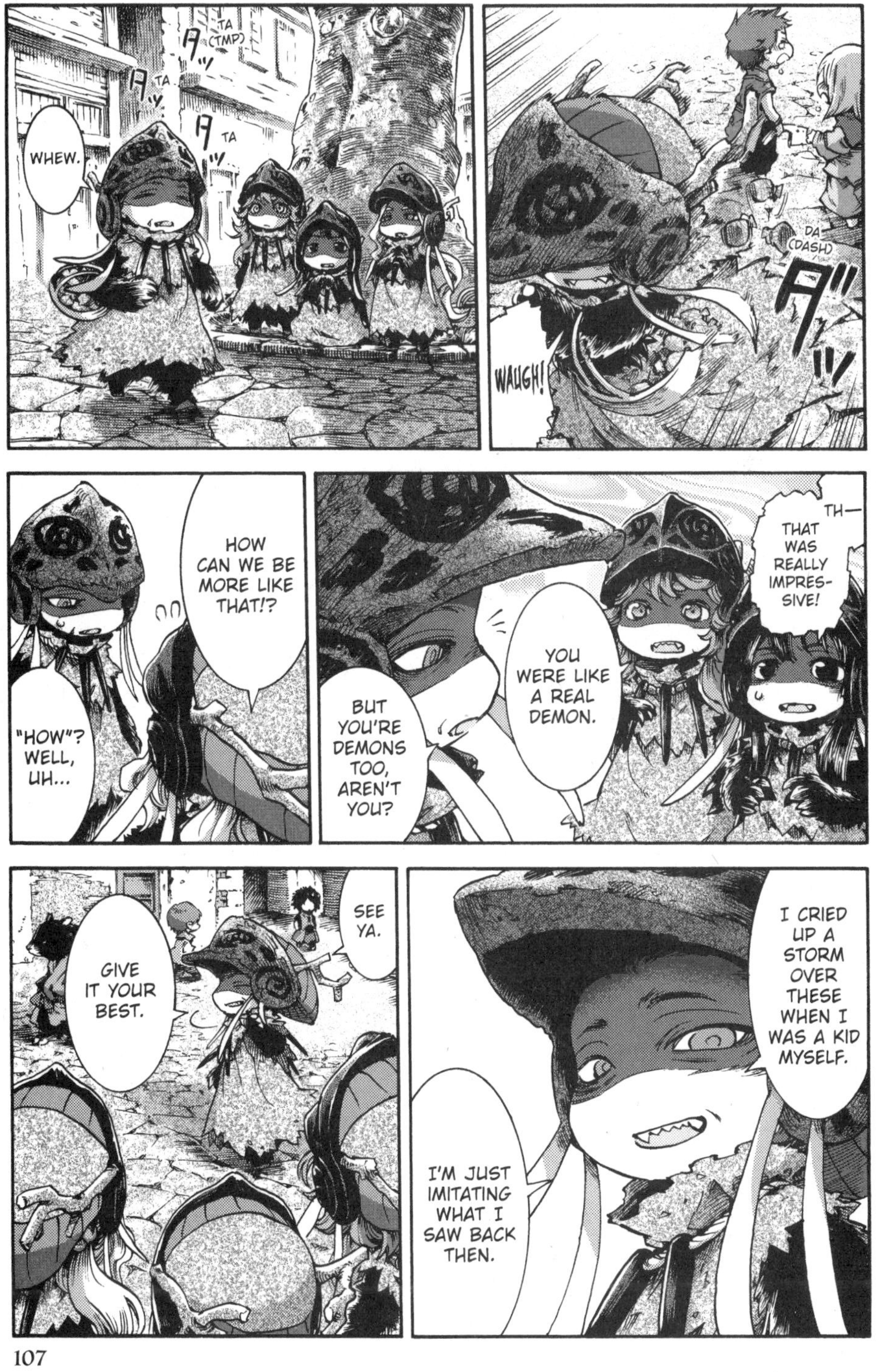
DA (DASH)
WAUGH!
TA (TMP)
TA
TA
WHEW.
TH— THAT WAS REALLY IMPRESSIVE!
YOU WERE LIKE A REAL DEMON.
BUT YOU'RE DEMONS TOO, AREN'T YOU?
HOW CAN WE BE MORE LIKE THAT!?
"HOW"? WELL, UH...
I CRIED UP A STORM OVER THESE WHEN I WAS A KID MYSELF.
I'M JUST IMITATING WHAT I SAW BACK THEN.
SEE YA.
GIVE IT YOUR BEST.

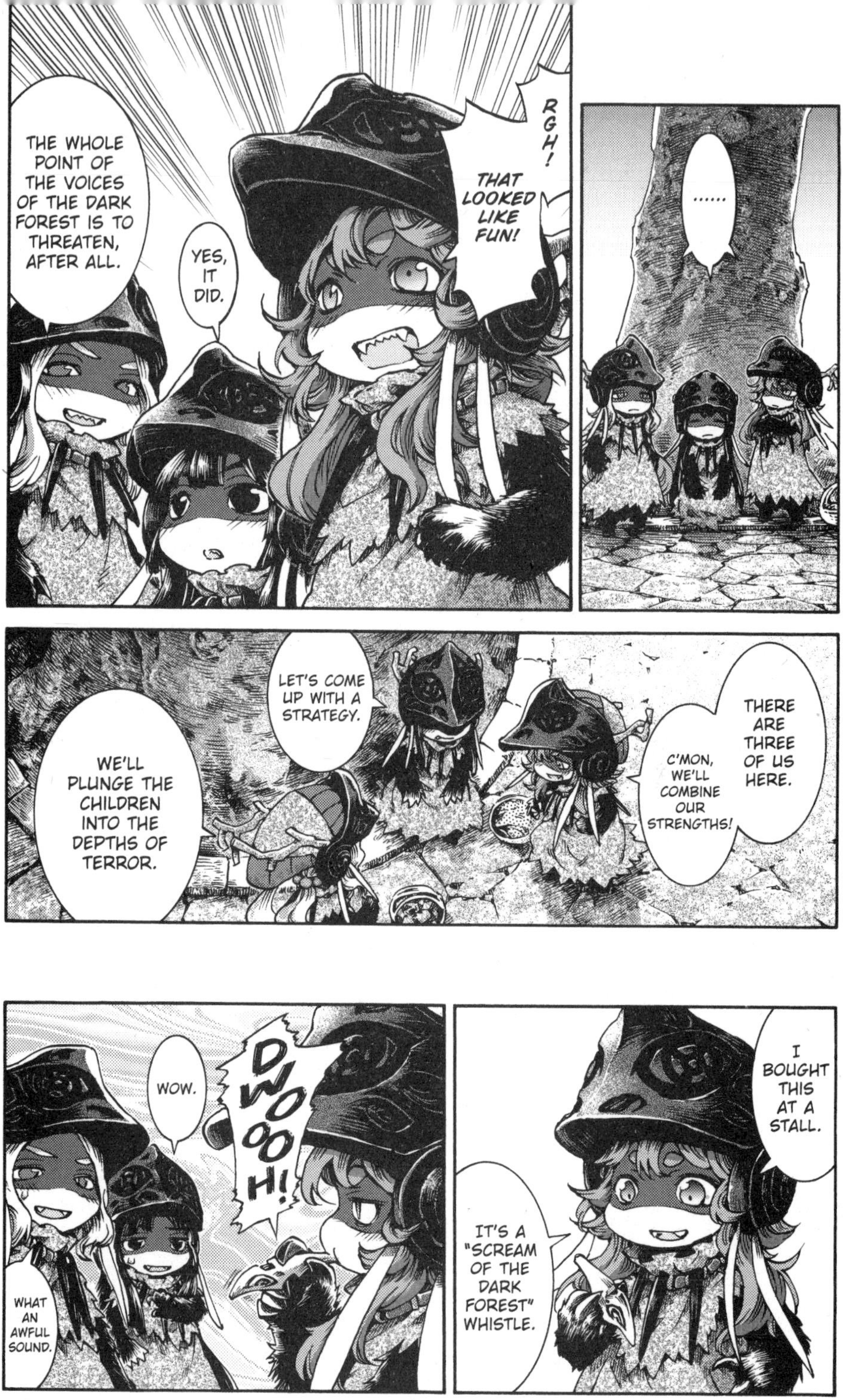
......
RGH!
THAT LOOKED LIKE FUN!
YES, IT DID.
THE WHOLE POINT OF THE VOICES OF THE DARK FOREST IS TO THREATEN, AFTER ALL.
THERE ARE THREE OF US HERE.
C'MON, WE'LL COMBINE OUR STRENGTHS!
LET'S COME UP WITH A STRATEGY.
WE'LL PLUNGE THE CHILDREN INTO THE DEPTHS OF TERROR.
I BOUGHT THIS AT A STALL.
IT'S A "SCREAM OF THE DARK FOREST" WHISTLE.
DWOOOH!
WOW.
WHAT AN AWFUL SOUND.

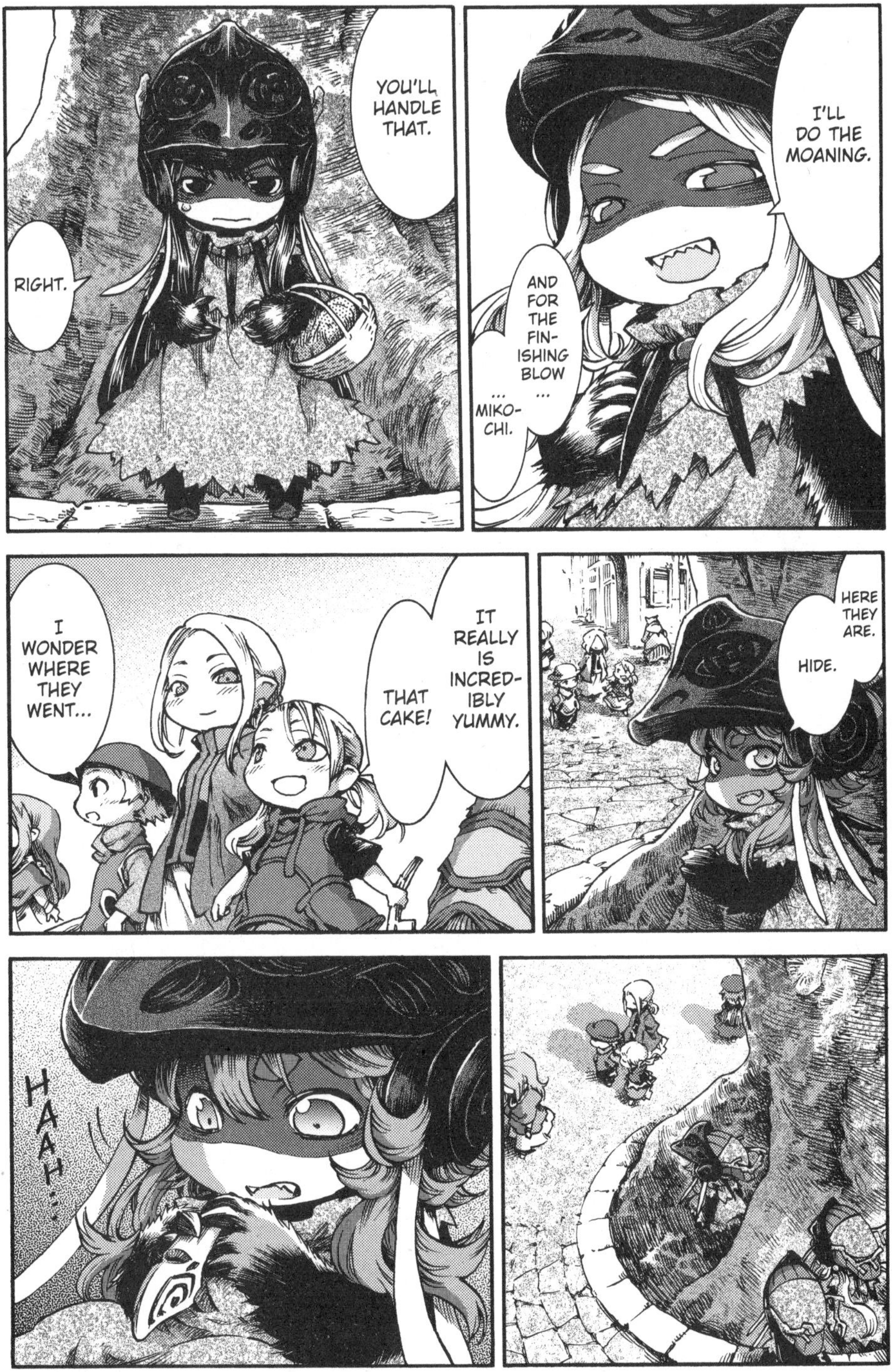
I'LL DO THE MOANING.
AND FOR THE FIN-ISHING BLOW ... ... MIKO-CHI.
YOU'LL HANDLE THAT.
RIGHT.
HERE THEY ARE.
HIDE.
IT REALLY IS INCRED-IBLY YUMMY.
THAT CAKE!
I WONDER WHERE THEY WENT...
HAAH...

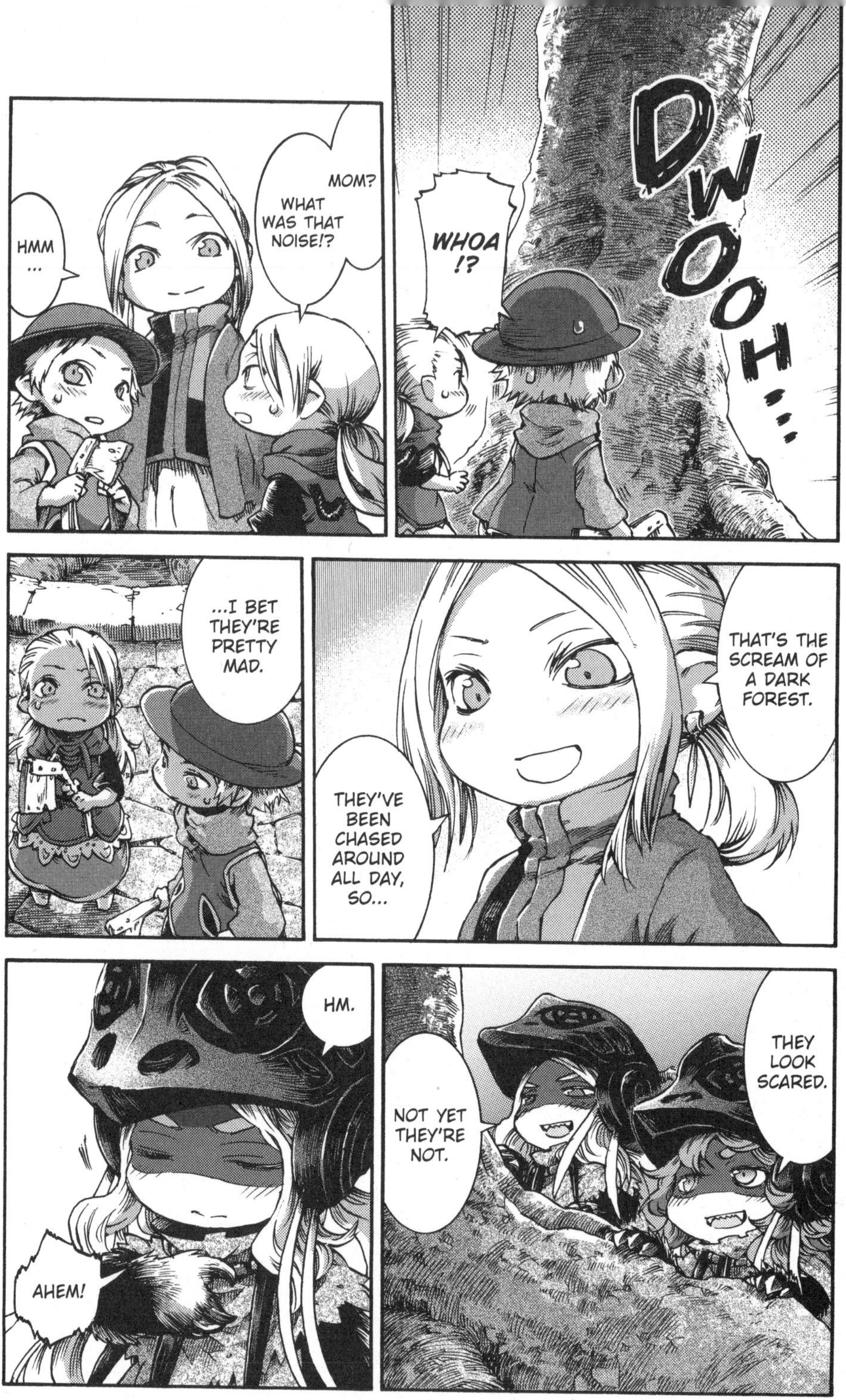
DWOOOH...
WHOA!?
MOM? WHAT WAS THAT NOISE!?
HMM...
THAT'S THE SCREAM OF A DARK FOREST.
THEY'VE BEEN CHASED AROUND ALL DAY, SO...
...I BET THEY'RE PRETTY MAD.
THEY LOOK SCARED.
NOT YET THEY'RE NOT.
HM.
AHEM!

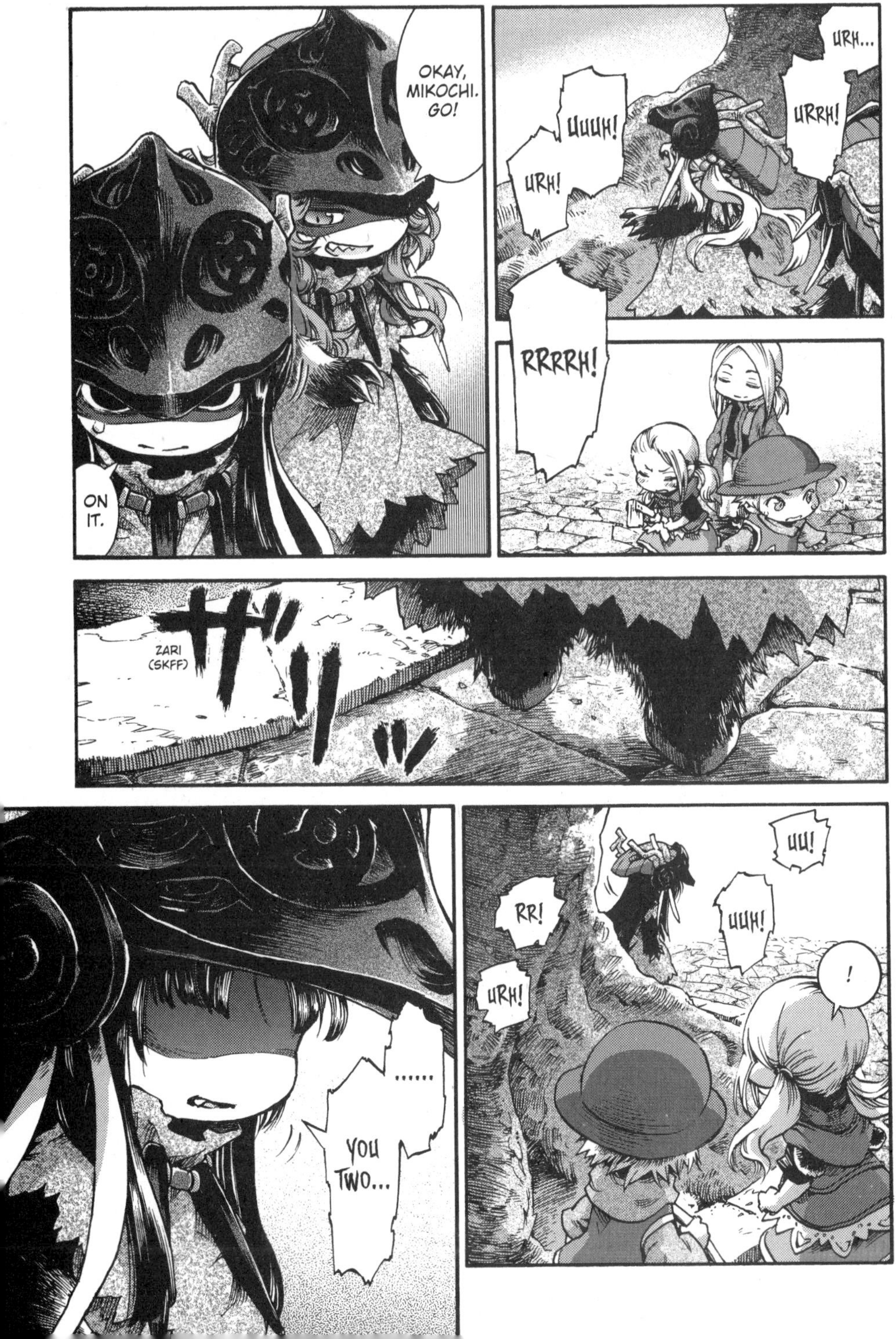
URH...
URRH!
UUUH!
URH!
RRRRH!
OKAY, MIKOCHI. GO!
ON IT.
ZARI (SKFF)
UU!
UUH!
RR!
URH!
!
......
YOU TWO...

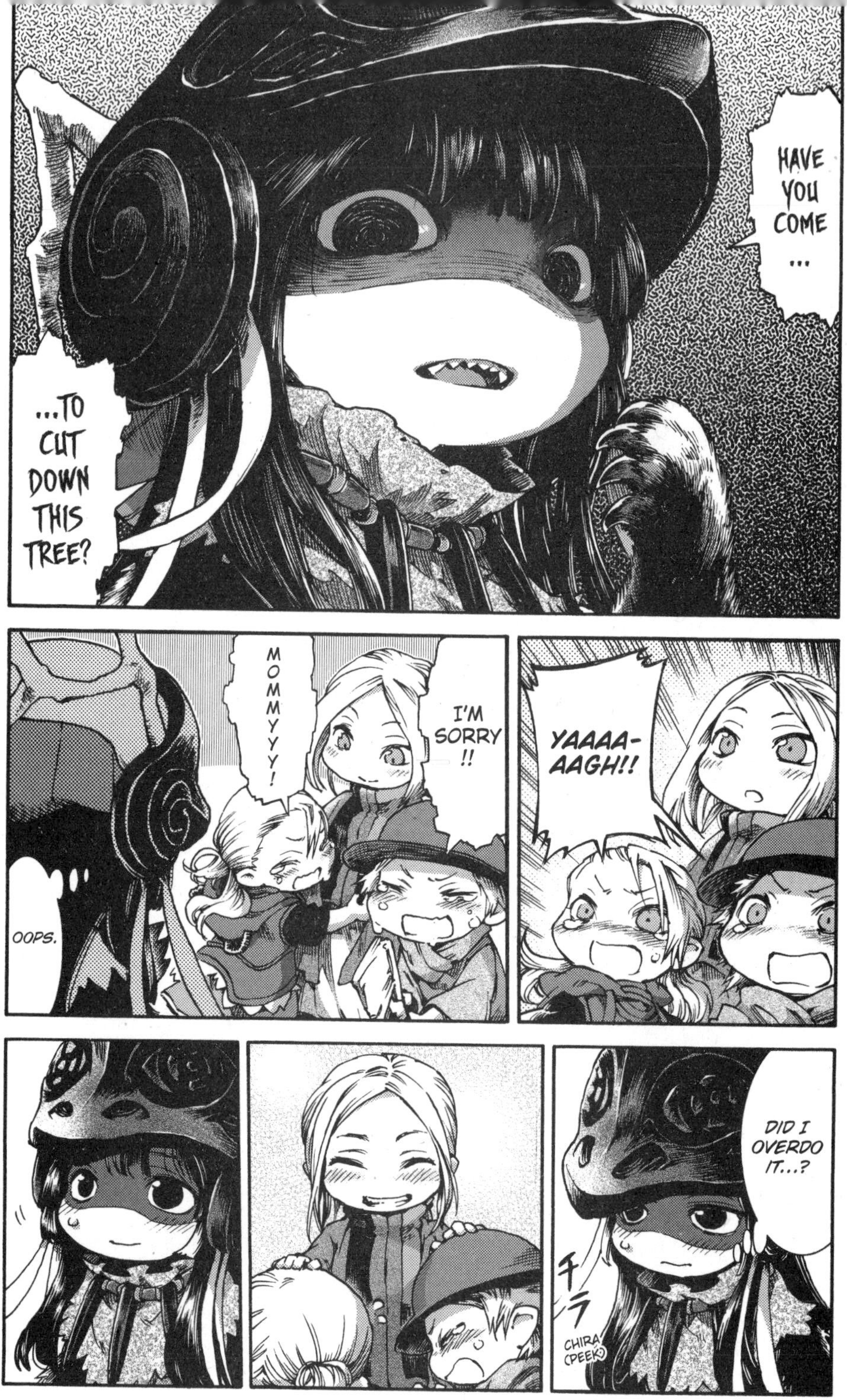
HAVE YOU COME...
...TO CUT DOWN THIS TREE?
YAAAA-AAGH!!
I'M SORRY!!
MOMMYYY!
OOPS.
DID I OVERDO IT...?
チラ
CHIRA (PEEK)

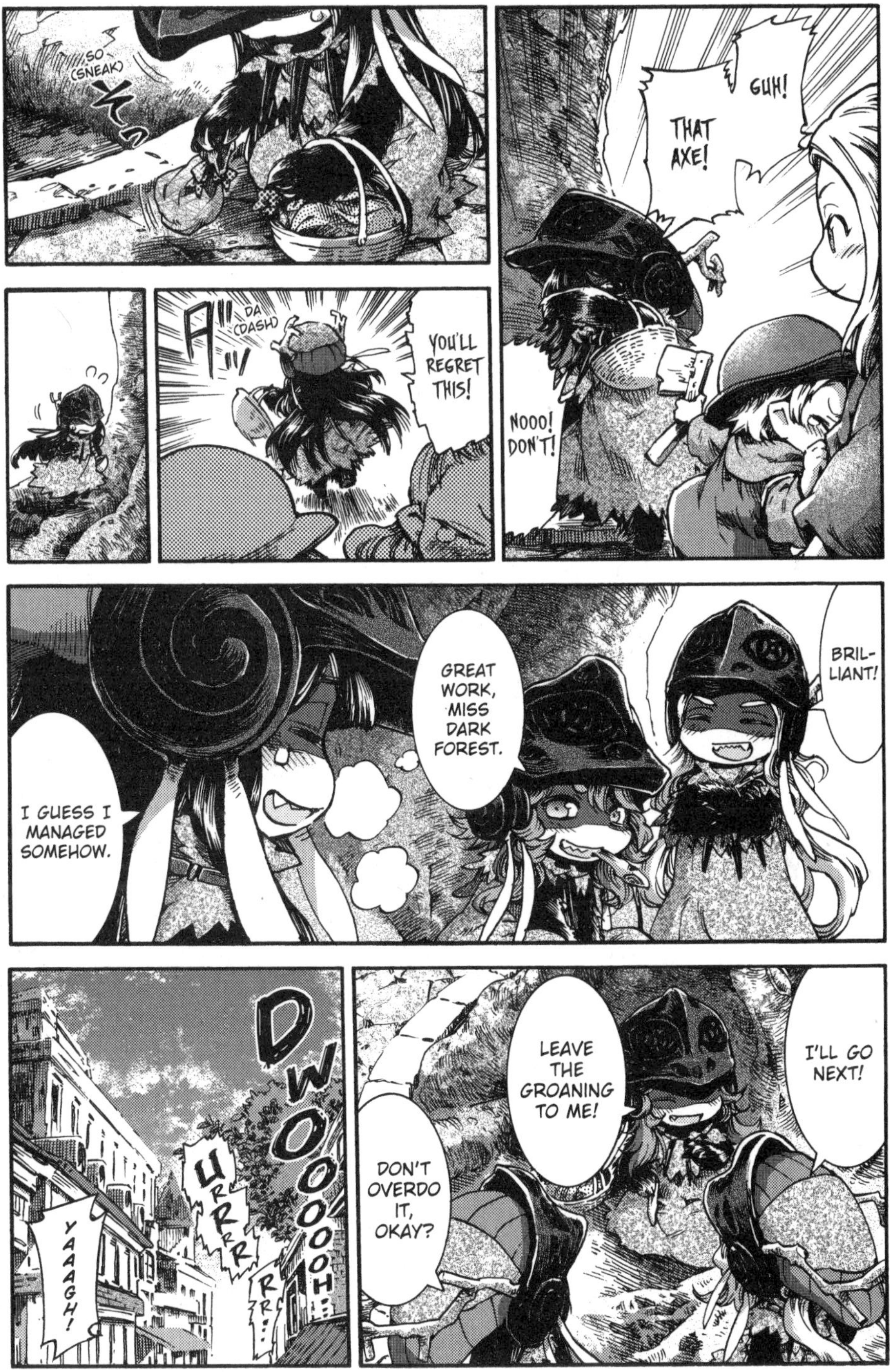
GUH!
THAT AXE!
NOOO! DON'T!
SO (SNEAK) そっ
DA (DASH)
YOU'LL REGRET THIS!
BRIL-LIANT!
GREAT WORK, MISS DARK FOREST.
I GUESS I MANAGED SOMEHOW.
I'LL GO NEXT!
LEAVE THE GROANING TO ME!
DON'T OVERDO IT, OKAY?
DWOOOOOOH...
URRRR RR...
YAAAGH!

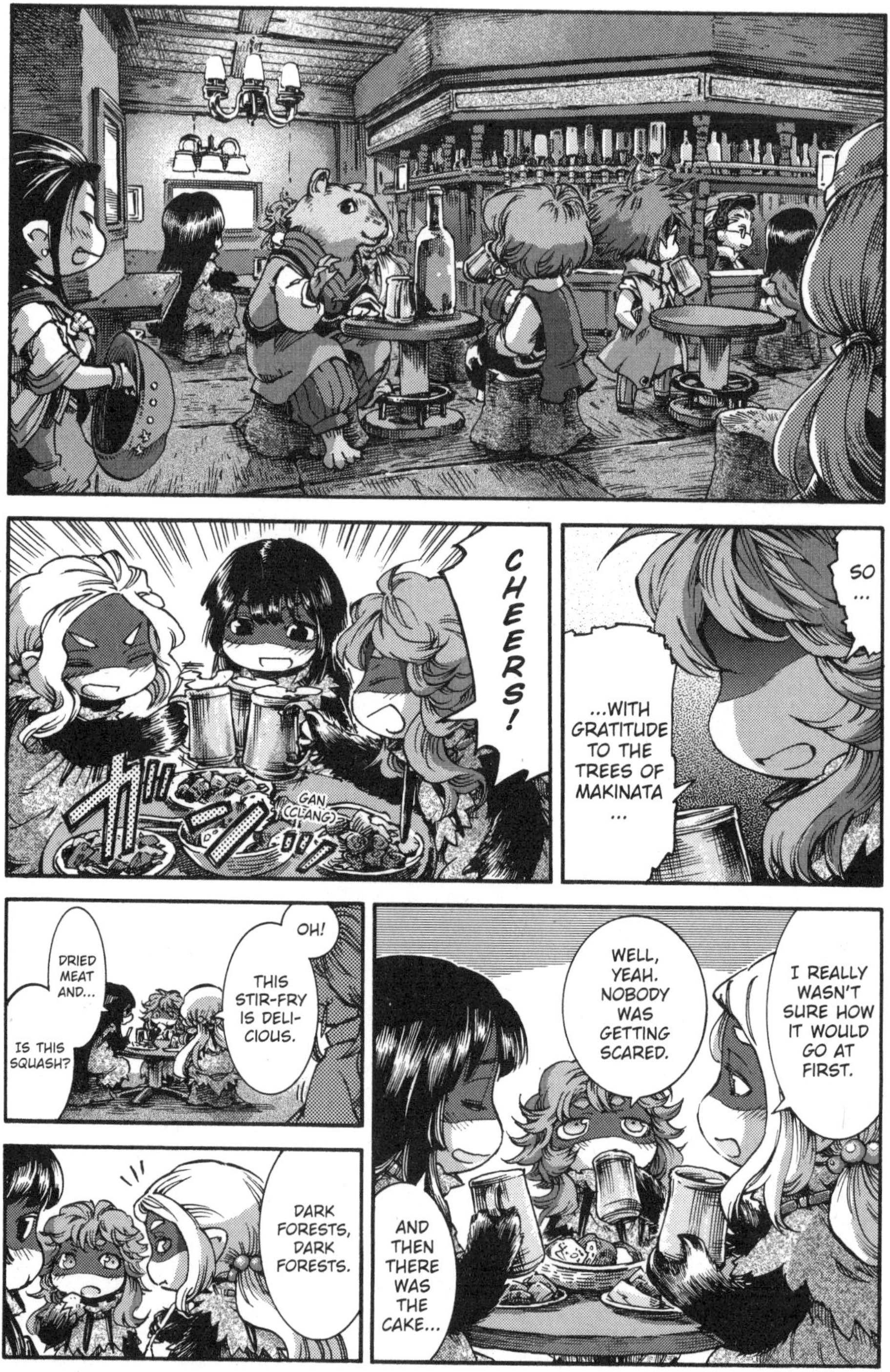
SO ...
...WITH GRATITUDE TO THE TREES OF MAKINATA ...
CHEERS!
GAN (CLANG)
I REALLY WASN'T SURE HOW IT WOULD GO AT FIRST.
WELL, YEAH. NOBODY WAS GETTING SCARED.
AND THEN THERE WAS THE CAKE...
OH!
THIS STIR-FRY IS DELI-CIOUS.
DRIED MEAT AND...
IS THIS SQUASH?
DARK FORESTS, DARK FORESTS.

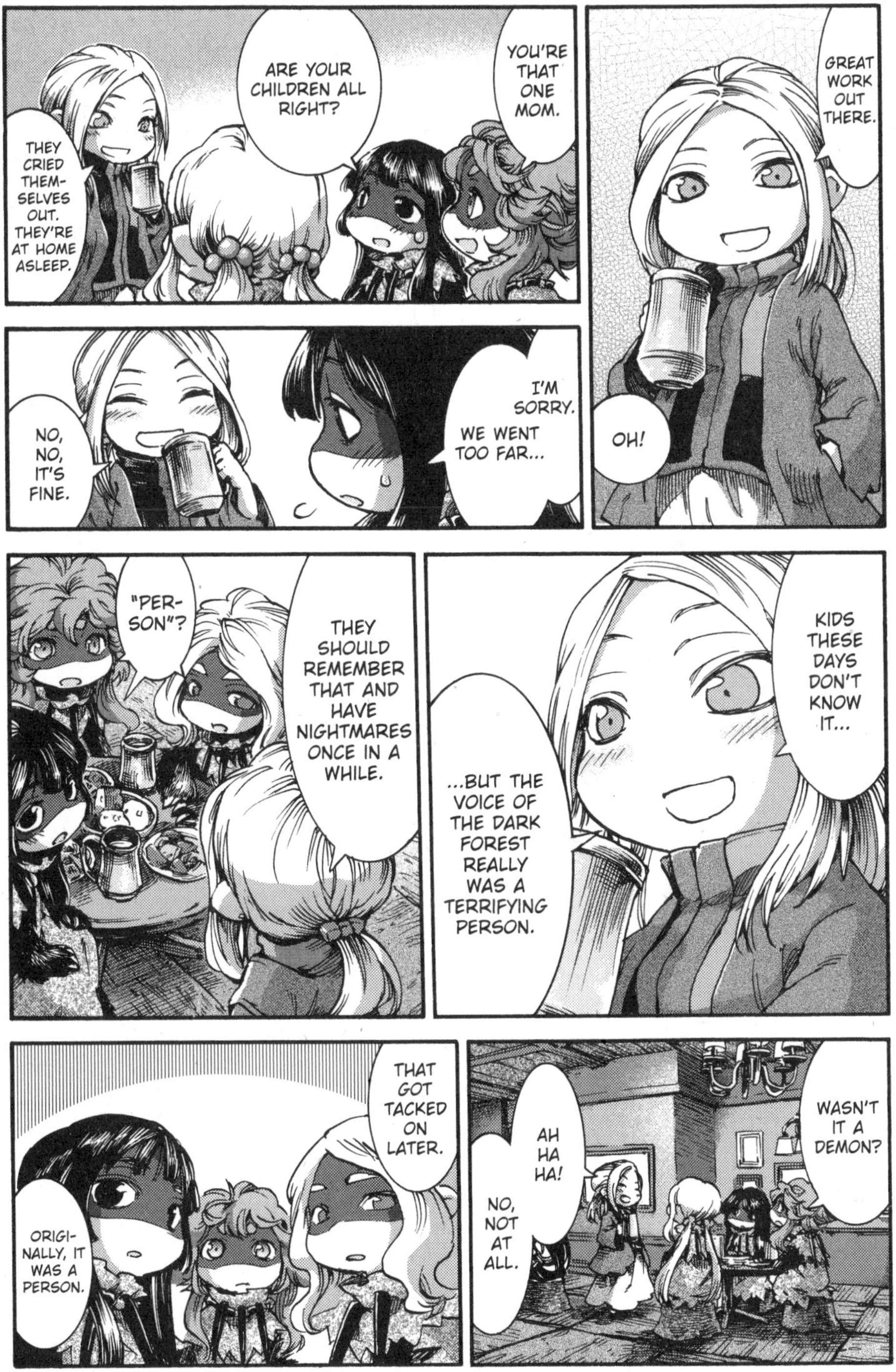
GREAT WORK OUT THERE.
OH!
YOU'RE THAT ONE MOM.
ARE YOUR CHILDREN ALL RIGHT?
THEY CRIED THEM-SELVES OUT. THEY'RE AT HOME ASLEEP.
I'M SORRY. WE WENT TOO FAR...
NO, NO, IT'S FINE.
KIDS THESE DAYS DON'T KNOW IT...
...BUT THE VOICE OF THE DARK FOREST REALLY WAS A TERRIFYING PERSON.
THEY SHOULD REMEMBER THAT AND HAVE NIGHTMARES ONCE IN A WHILE.
"PER-SON"?
WASN'T IT A DEMON?
AH HA HA!
NO, NOT AT ALL.
THAT GOT TACKED ON LATER.
ORIGI-NALLY, IT WAS A PERSON.

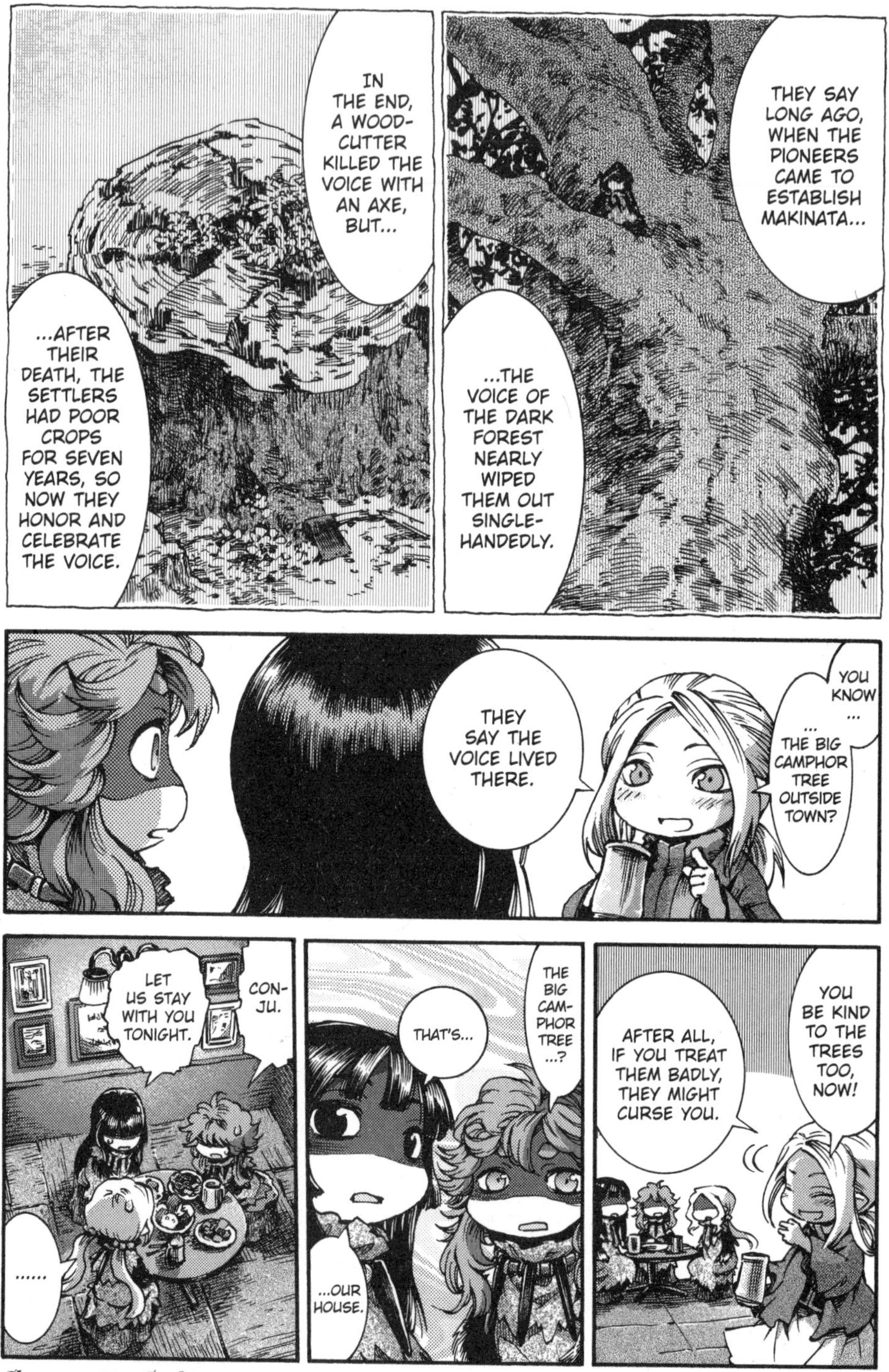
THEY SAY LONG AGO, WHEN THE PIONEERS CAME TO ESTABLISH MAKINATA...
...THE VOICE OF THE DARK FOREST NEARLY WIPED THEM OUT SINGLE-HANDEDLY.
IN THE END, A WOOD-CUTTER KILLED THE VOICE WITH AN AXE, BUT...
...AFTER THEIR DEATH, THE SETTLERS HAD POOR CROPS FOR SEVEN YEARS, SO NOW THEY HONOR AND CELEBRATE THE VOICE.
YOU KNOW... ...THE BIG CAMPHOR TREE OUTSIDE TOWN?
THEY SAY THE VOICE LIVED THERE.
YOU BE KIND TO THE TREES TOO, NOW!
AFTER ALL, IF YOU TREAT THEM BADLY, THEY MIGHT CURSE YOU.
THE BIG CAMPHOR TREE...?
THAT'S...
...OUR HOUSE.
CON-JU.
LET US STAY WITH YOU TONIGHT.
......

Chapter 31 • End

Material referencing the Voice of the Dark Forest is extremely limited. The woodcutter who killed them left no testimony, and the others had their hands full trying to rebuild the pioneer group and deal with the aftermath of the affair.

Of the handful of notes left by witnesses, all of them mention:

- A head with a beak-like shape
- Coarse body hair
- A terrifying voice

The festival is conducted in costumes that were designed based on these notes.

Chapter 32

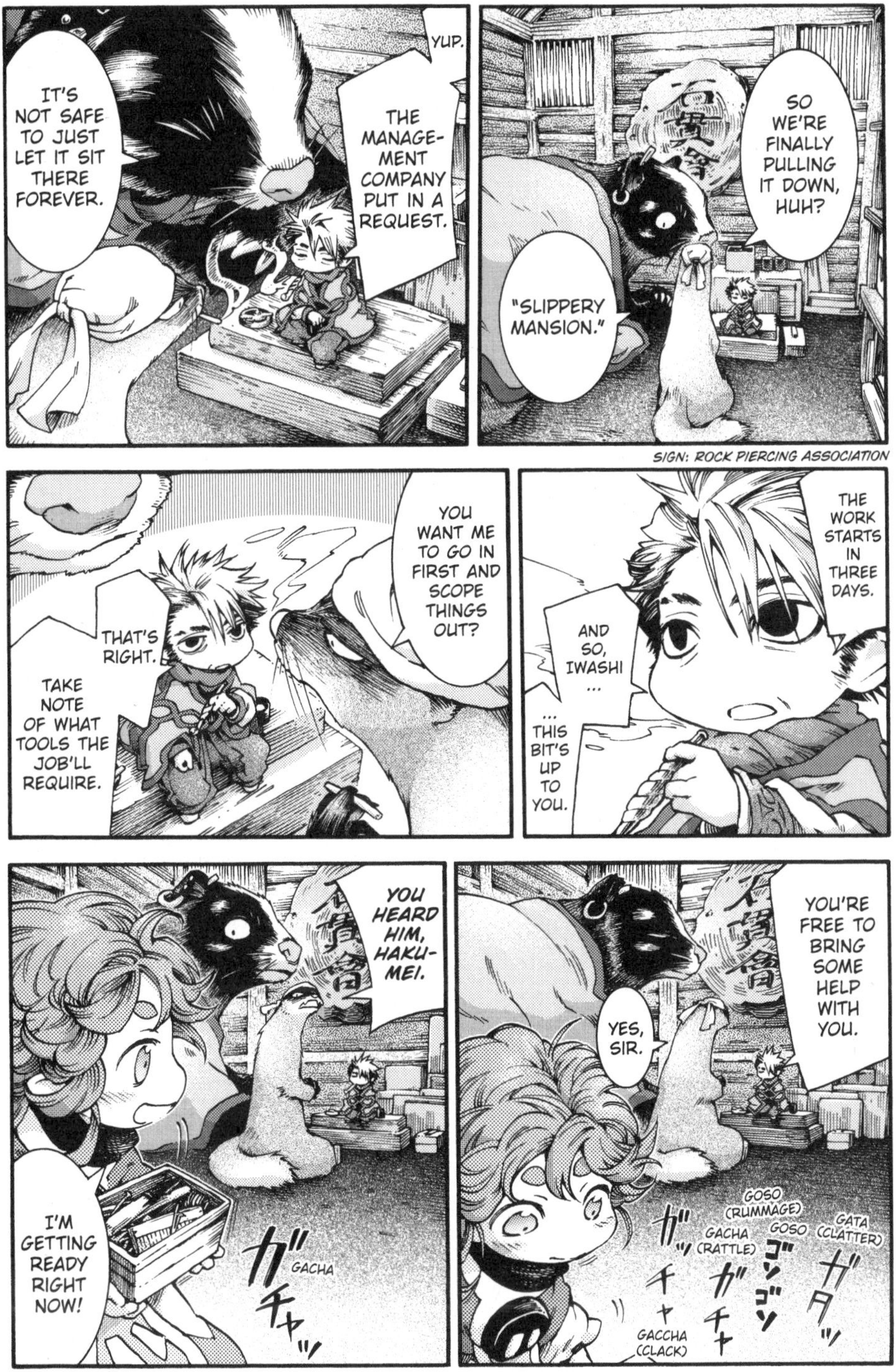
SO WE'RE FINALLY PULLING IT DOWN, HUH?
"SLIPPERY MANSION."
YUP.
THE MANAGEMENT COMPANY PUT IN A REQUEST.
IT'S NOT SAFE TO JUST LET IT SIT THERE FOREVER.
SIGN: ROCK PIERCING ASSOCIATION
THE WORK STARTS IN THREE DAYS.
AND SO, IWASHI...
...THIS BIT'S UP TO YOU.
YOU WANT ME TO GO IN FIRST AND SCOPE THINGS OUT?
THAT'S RIGHT.
TAKE NOTE OF WHAT TOOLS THE JOB'LL REQUIRE.
YOU'RE FREE TO BRING SOME HELP WITH YOU.
YES, SIR.
GOSO (RUMMAGE) GOSO
GATA (CLATTER)
GACHA (RATTLE)
GACCHA (CLACK)
YOU HEARD HIM, HAKUMEI.
I'M GETTING READY RIGHT NOW!
GACHA

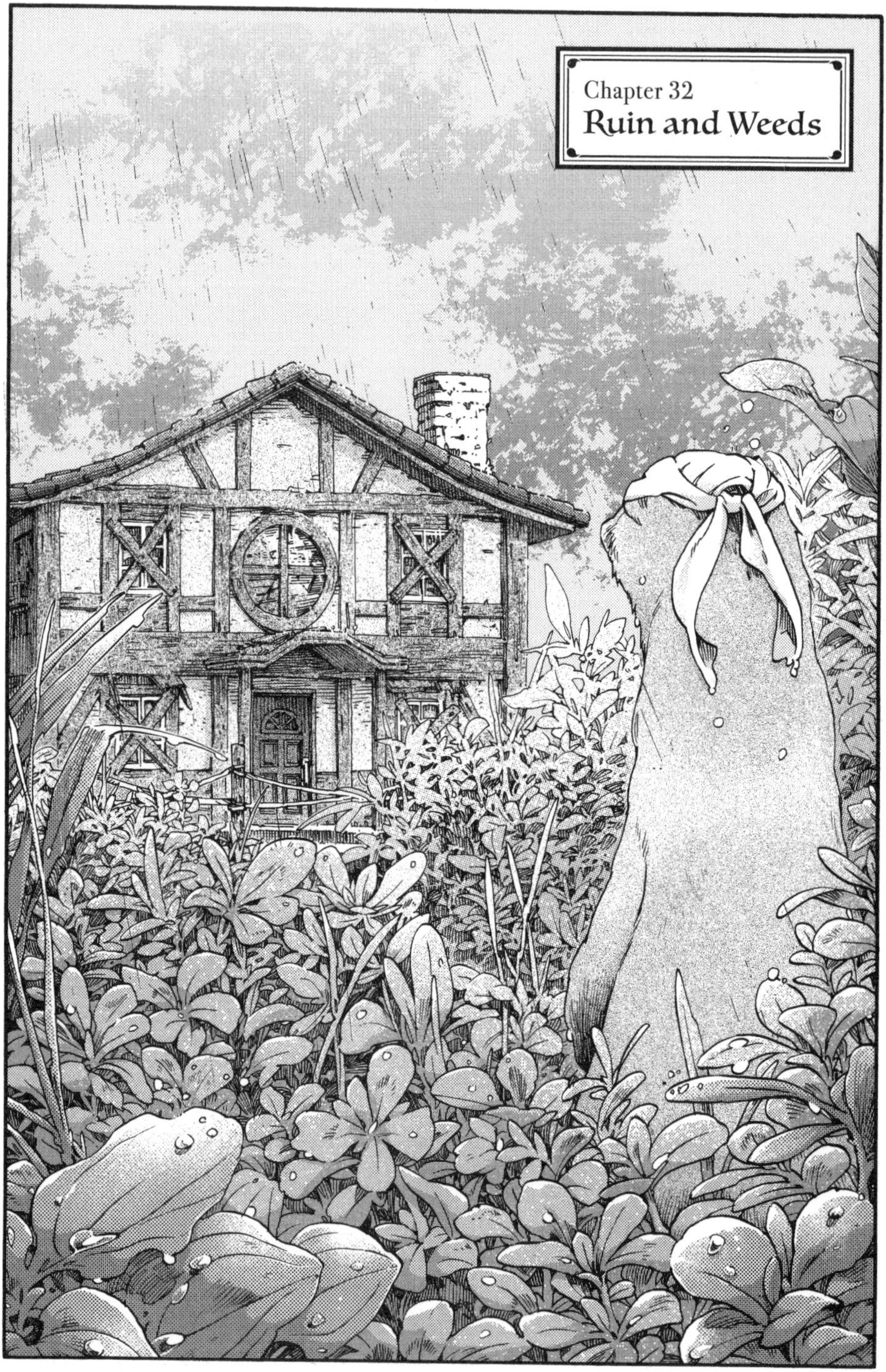
Chapter 32
Ruin and Weeds

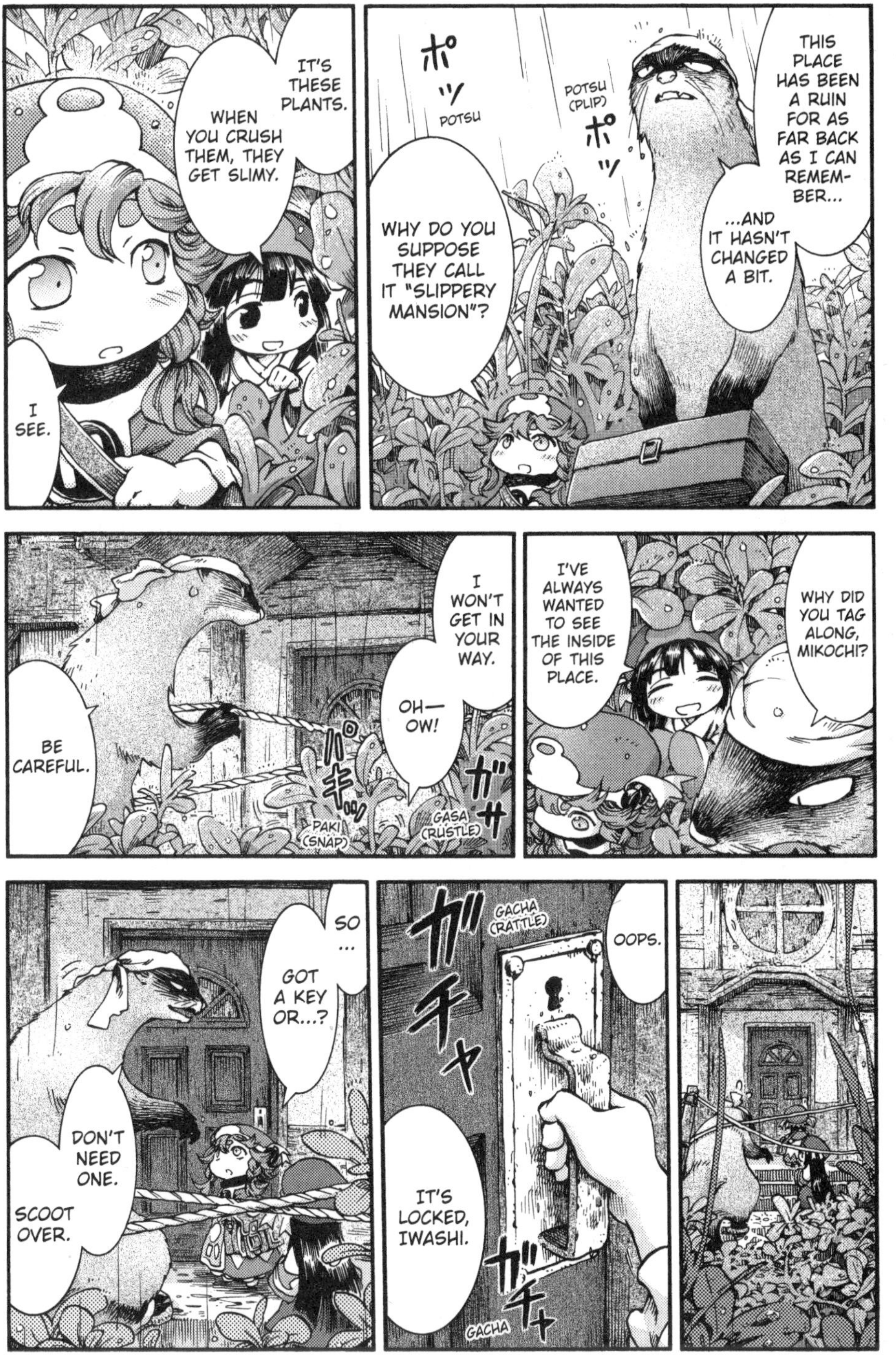
THIS PLACE HAS BEEN A RUIN FOR AS FAR BACK AS I CAN REMEMBER...
...AND IT HASN'T CHANGED A BIT.
ポツ
POTSU (PLIP)
WHY DO YOU SUPPOSE THEY CALL IT "SLIPPERY MANSION"?
ポツ
POTSU
IT'S THESE PLANTS.
WHEN YOU CRUSH THEM, THEY GET SLIMY.
I SEE.
WHY DID YOU TAG ALONG, MIKOCHI?
I'VE ALWAYS WANTED TO SEE THE INSIDE OF THIS PLACE.
I WON'T GET IN YOUR WAY.
OH—OW!
ガサ
GASA (RUSTLE)
パキッ
PAKI (SNAP)
BE CAREFUL.
OOPS.
ガチャ
GACHA (RATTLE)
IT'S LOCKED, IWASHI.
ガチャ
GACHA
SO ...
GOT A KEY OR...?
DON'T NEED ONE.
SCOOT OVER.

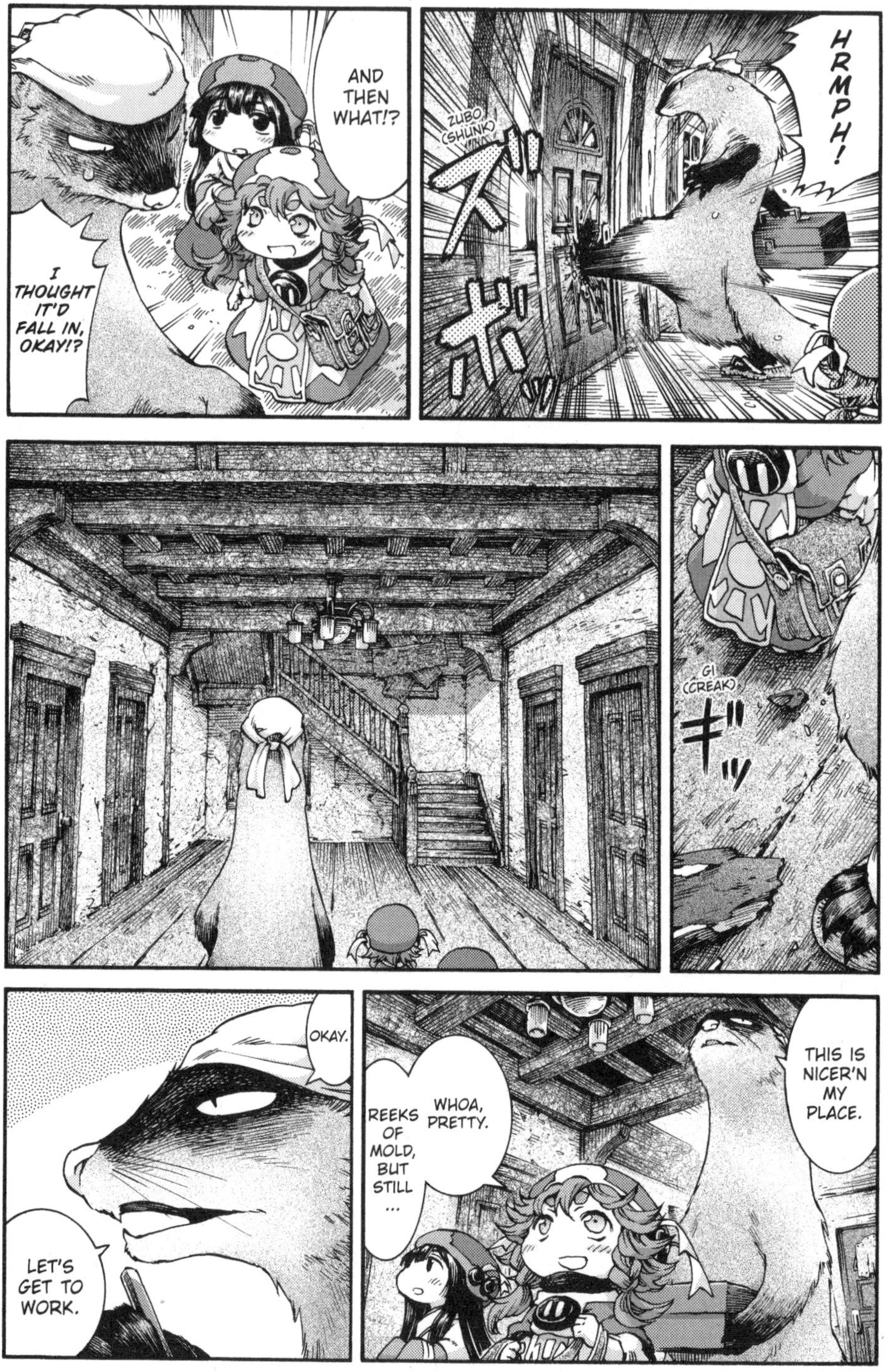
HRMPH!
ZUBO (SHUNK)
AND THEN WHAT!?
I THOUGHT IT'D FALL IN, OKAY!?
GI (CREAK)
THIS IS NICER'N MY PLACE.
WHOA, PRETTY.
REEKS OF MOLD, BUT STILL ...
OKAY.
LET'S GET TO WORK.

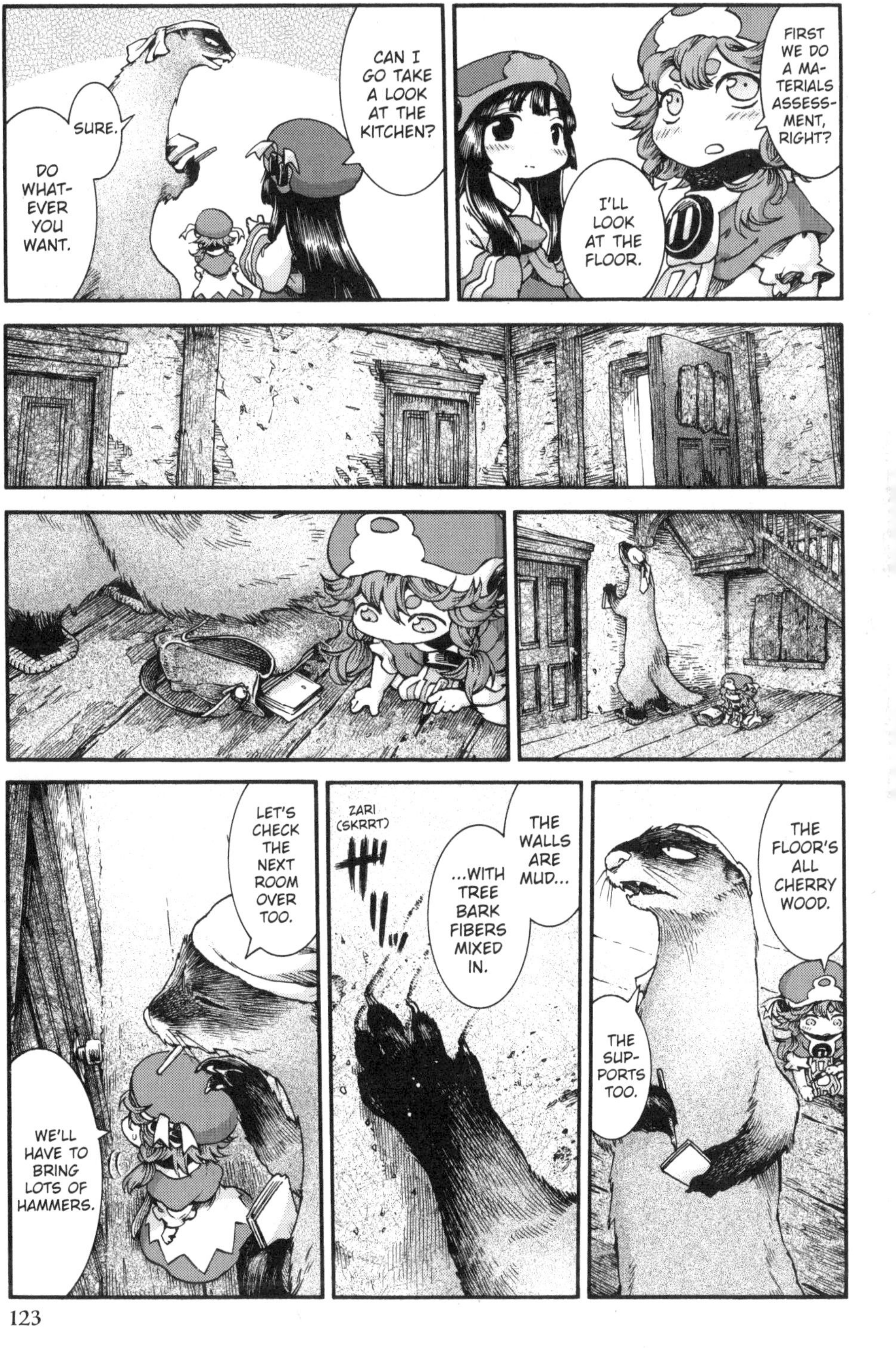
FIRST WE DO A MATERIALS ASSESSMENT, RIGHT?
I'LL LOOK AT THE FLOOR.
CAN I GO TAKE A LOOK AT THE KITCHEN?
SURE.
DO WHATEVER YOU WANT.
THE FLOOR'S ALL CHERRY WOOD.
THE SUPPORTS TOO.
THE WALLS ARE MUD...
...WITH TREE BARK FIBERS MIXED IN.
ZARI (SKRRT)
LET'S CHECK THE NEXT ROOM OVER TOO.
WE'LL HAVE TO BRING LOTS OF HAMMERS.

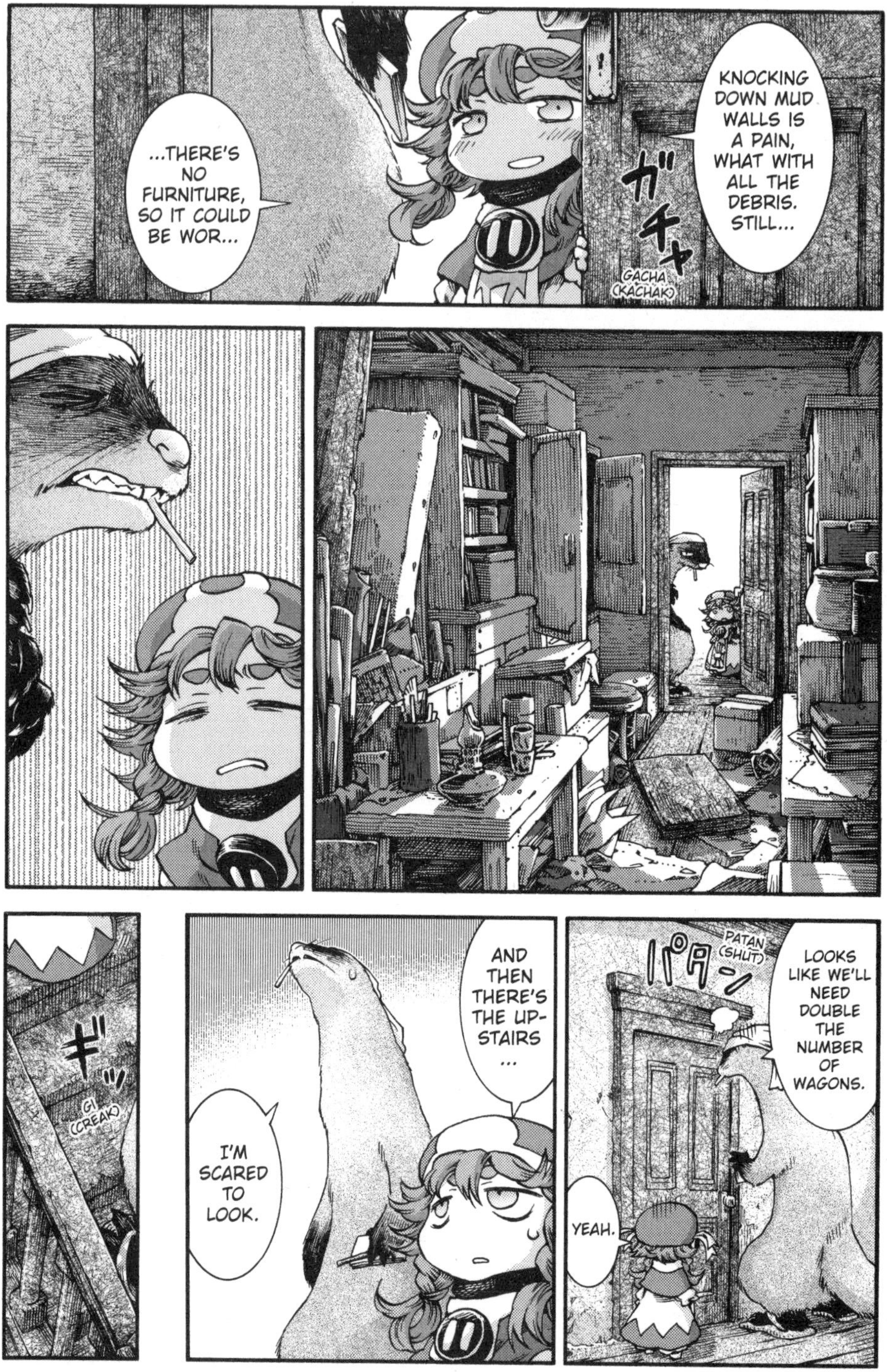
KNOCKING DOWN MUD WALLS IS A PAIN, WHAT WITH ALL THE DEBRIS. STILL...
ガチャ
GACHA (KACHAK)
...THERE'S NO FURNITURE, SO IT COULD BE WOR...
パターン
PATAN (SHUT)
LOOKS LIKE WE'LL NEED DOUBLE THE NUMBER OF WAGONS.
YEAH.
AND THEN THERE'S THE UP-STAIRS ...
I'M SCARED TO LOOK.
ギッ
GI (CREAK)

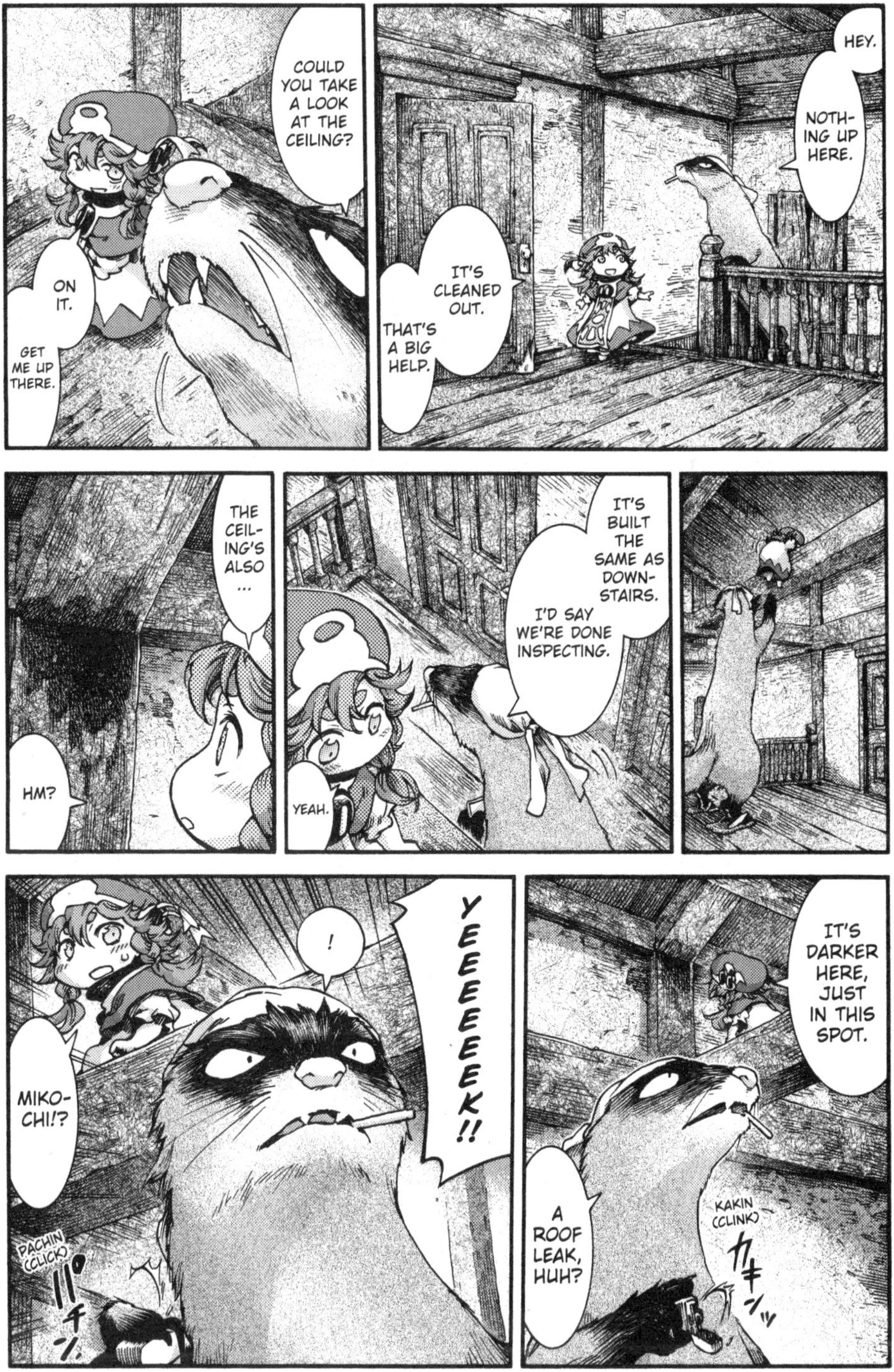
HEY.
NOTHING UP HERE.
IT'S CLEANED OUT.
THAT'S A BIG HELP.
COULD YOU TAKE A LOOK AT THE CEILING?
ON IT.
GET ME UP THERE.
IT'S BUILT THE SAME AS DOWNSTAIRS.
I'D SAY WE'RE DONE INSPECTING.
YEAH.
THE CEILING'S ALSO ...
HM?
IT'S DARKER HERE, JUST IN THIS SPOT.
A ROOF LEAK, HUH?
KAKIN (CLINK)
カキンッ
YEEEEEEEK!!
!
MIKOCHI!?
PACHIN (CLICK)
パチン

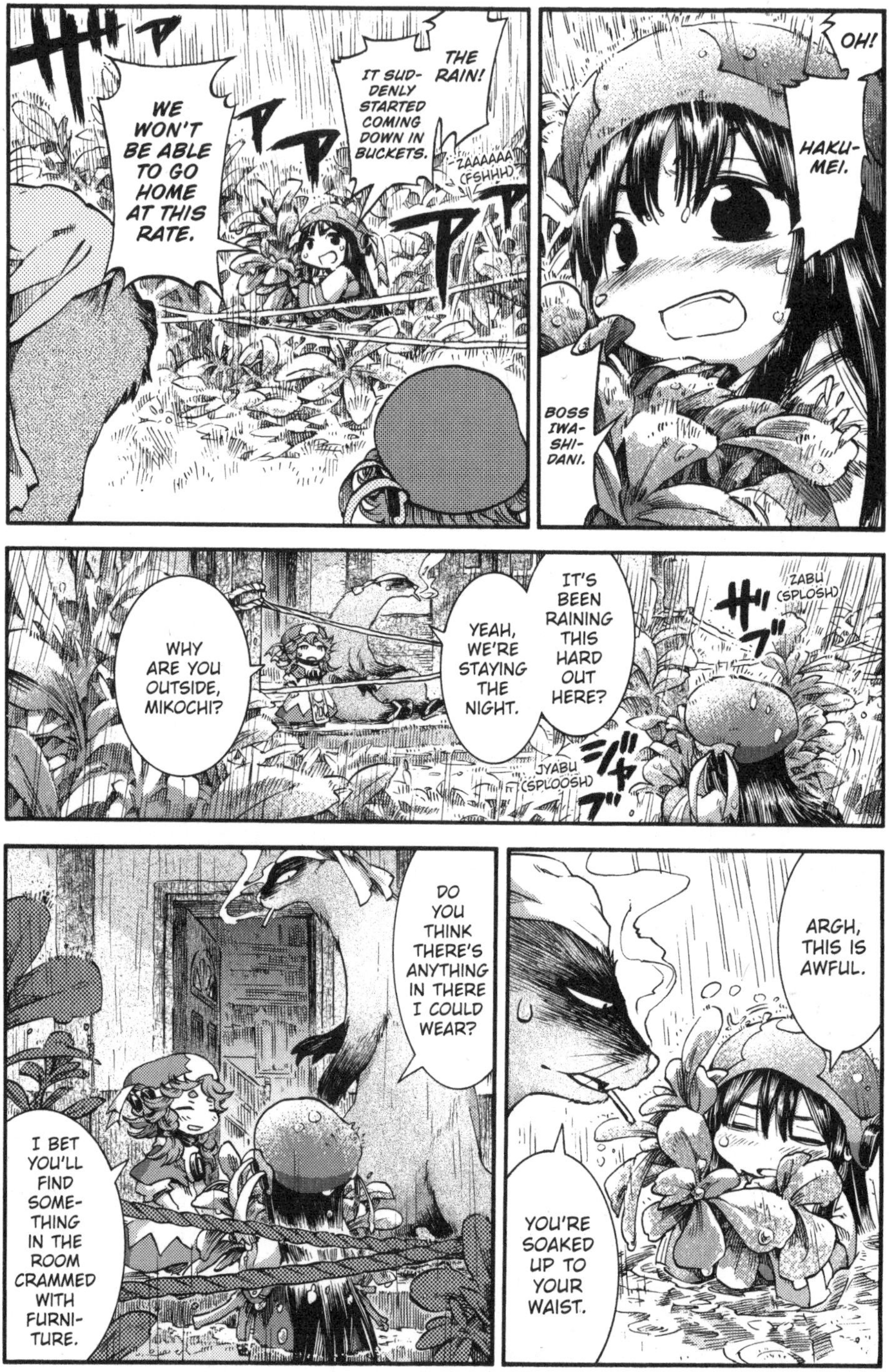
OH!
HAKUMEI.
BOSS IWASHIDANI.
THE RAIN!
IT SUDDENLY STARTED COMING DOWN IN BUCKETS.
ZAAAAAA (FSHHH)
WE WON'T BE ABLE TO GO HOME AT THIS RATE.
ZABU (SPLOSH)
IT'S BEEN RAINING THIS HARD OUT HERE?
YEAH, WE'RE STAYING THE NIGHT.
WHY ARE YOU OUTSIDE, MIKOCHI?
JYABU (SPLOOSH)
ARGH, THIS IS AWFUL.
YOU'RE SOAKED UP TO YOUR WAIST.
DO YOU THINK THERE'S ANYTHING IN THERE I COULD WEAR?
I BET YOU'LL FIND SOMETHING IN THE ROOM CRAMMED WITH FURNITURE.

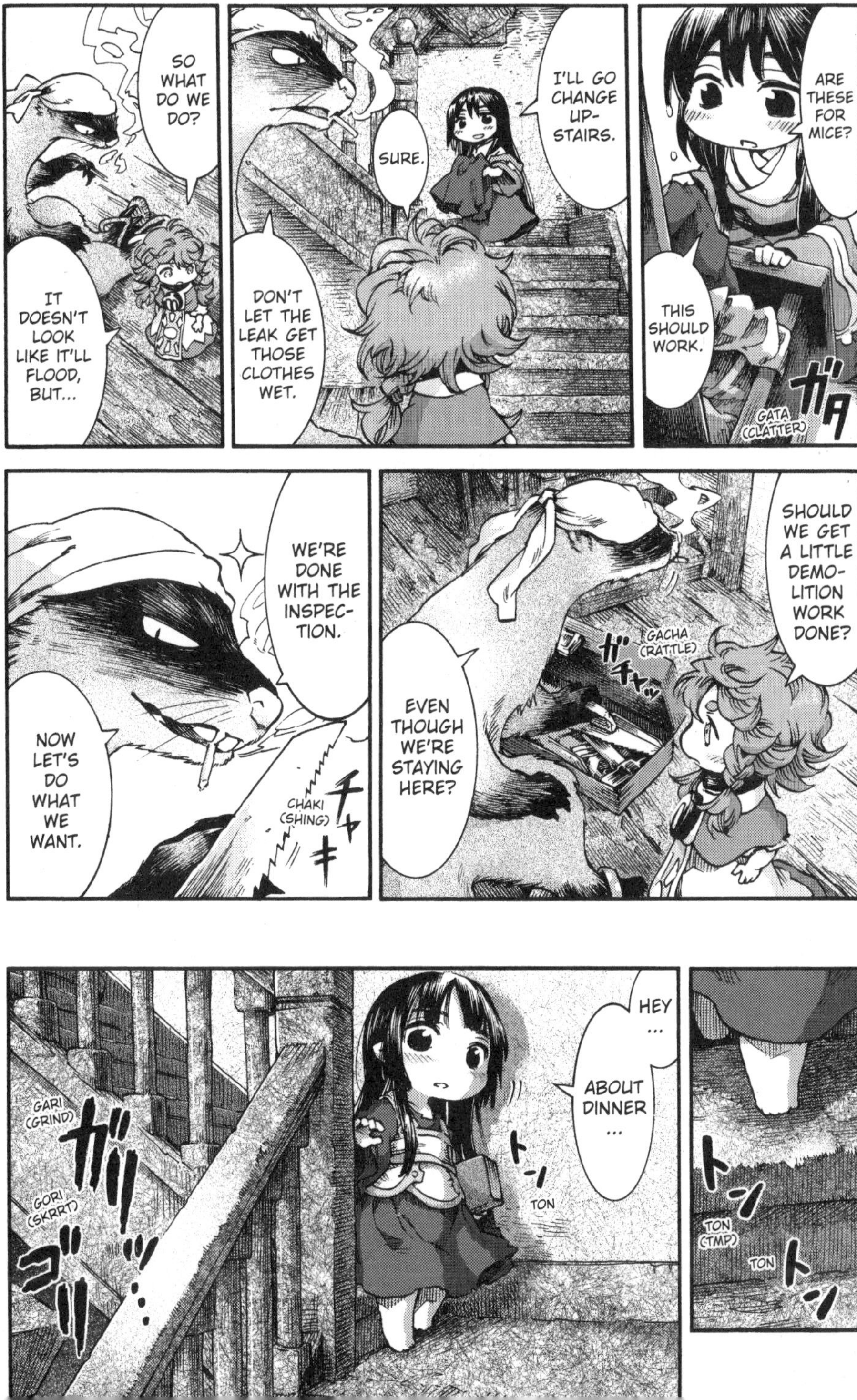
ARE THESE FOR MICE?
THIS SHOULD WORK.
GATA (CLATTER)
I'LL GO CHANGE UP-STAIRS.
SURE.
DON'T LET THE LEAK GET THOSE CLOTHES WET.
SO WHAT DO WE DO?
IT DOESN'T LOOK LIKE IT'LL FLOOD, BUT...
SHOULD WE GET A LITTLE DEMO-LITION WORK DONE?
GACHA (RATTLE)
EVEN THOUGH WE'RE STAYING HERE?
WE'RE DONE WITH THE INSPEC-TION.
NOW LET'S DO WHAT WE WANT.
CHAKI (SHING)
TON (TMP)
TON
HEY...
ABOUT DINNER...
TON
GARI (GRIND)
GORI (SKRRT)

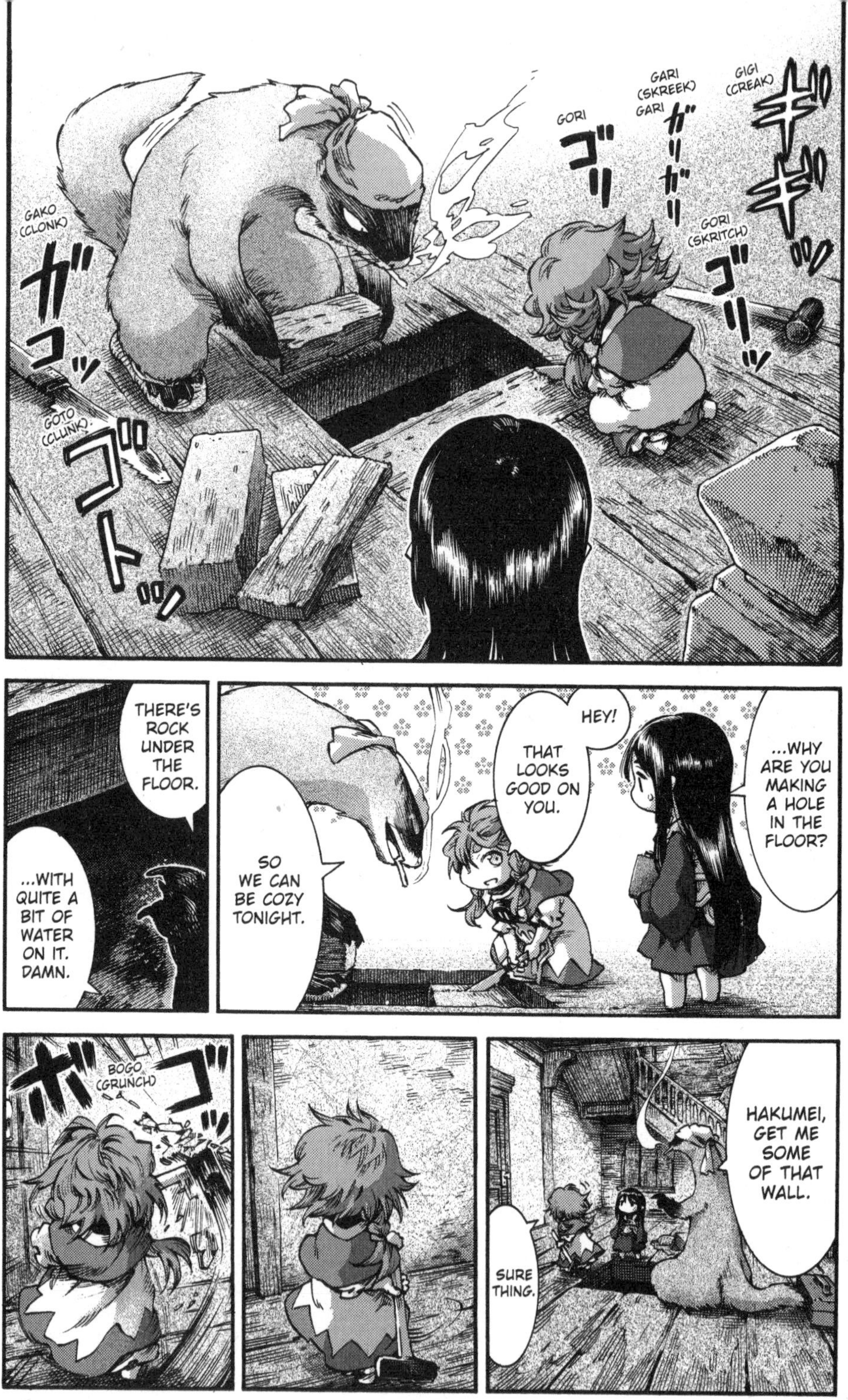
GIGI (CREAK)
GARI (SKREEK) GARI
GORI
GORI (SKRITCH)
GAKO (CLONK)
GOTO (CLUNK)
...WHY ARE YOU MAKING A HOLE IN THE FLOOR?
HEY!
THAT LOOKS GOOD ON YOU.
SO WE CAN BE COZY TONIGHT.
THERE'S ROCK UNDER THE FLOOR.
...WITH QUITE A BIT OF WATER ON IT. DAMN.
HAKUMEI, GET ME SOME OF THAT WALL.
SURE THING.
BOGO (GRUNCH)

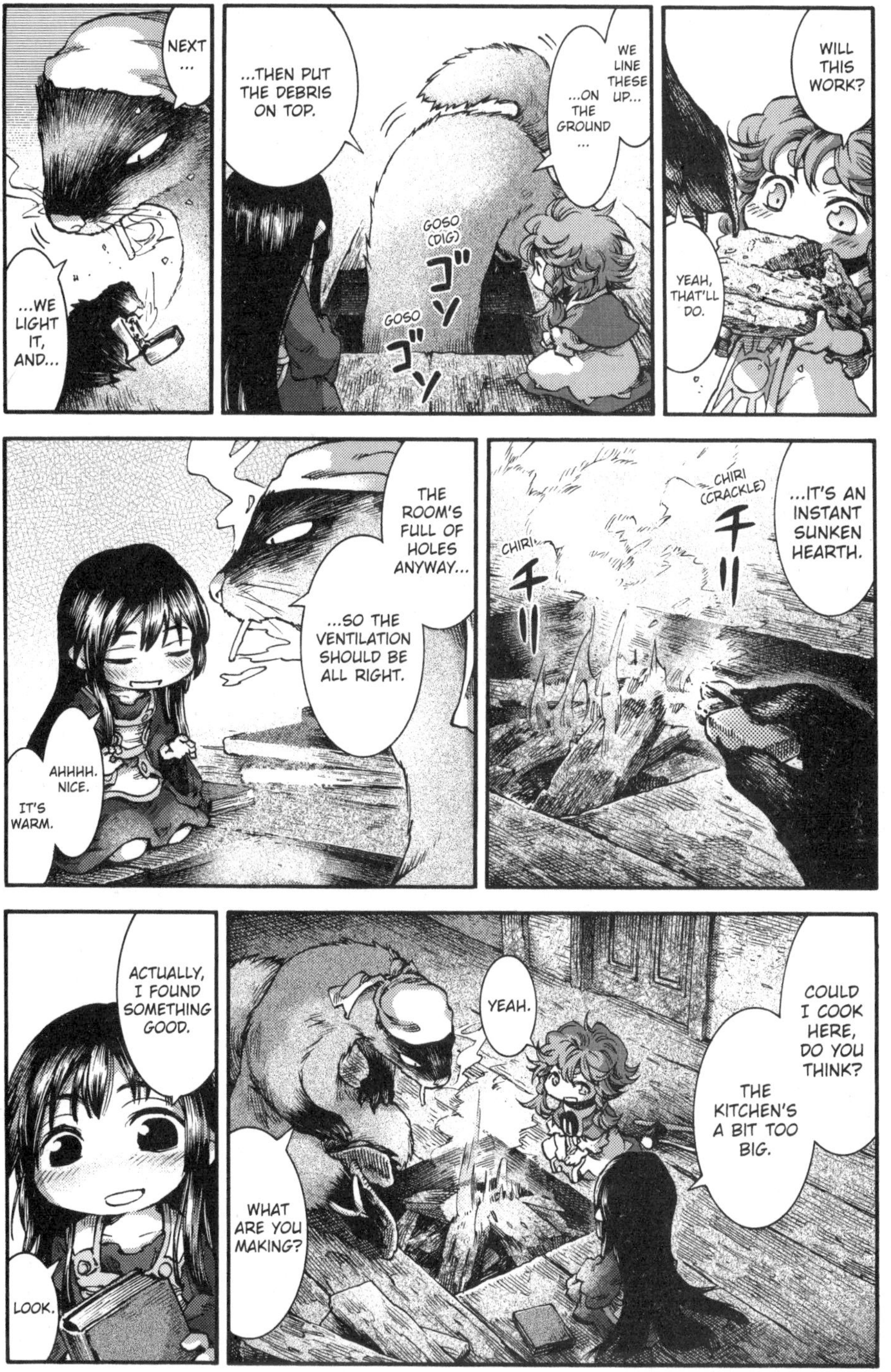
WILL THIS WORK?
YEAH, THAT'LL DO.
WE LINE THESE UP...
...ON THE GROUND...
GOSO (DIG)
ゴソ
GOSO
ゴソ
...THEN PUT THE DEBRIS ON TOP.
NEXT...
...WE LIGHT IT, AND...
...IT'S AN INSTANT SUNKEN HEARTH.
CHIRI (CRACKLE)
チリ
CHIRI
チリ
THE ROOM'S FULL OF HOLES ANYWAY...
...SO THE VENTILATION SHOULD BE ALL RIGHT.
AHHHH. NICE.
IT'S WARM.
COULD I COOK HERE, DO YOU THINK?
THE KITCHEN'S A BIT TOO BIG.
YEAH.
WHAT ARE YOU MAKING?
ACTUALLY, I FOUND SOMETHING GOOD.
LOOK.

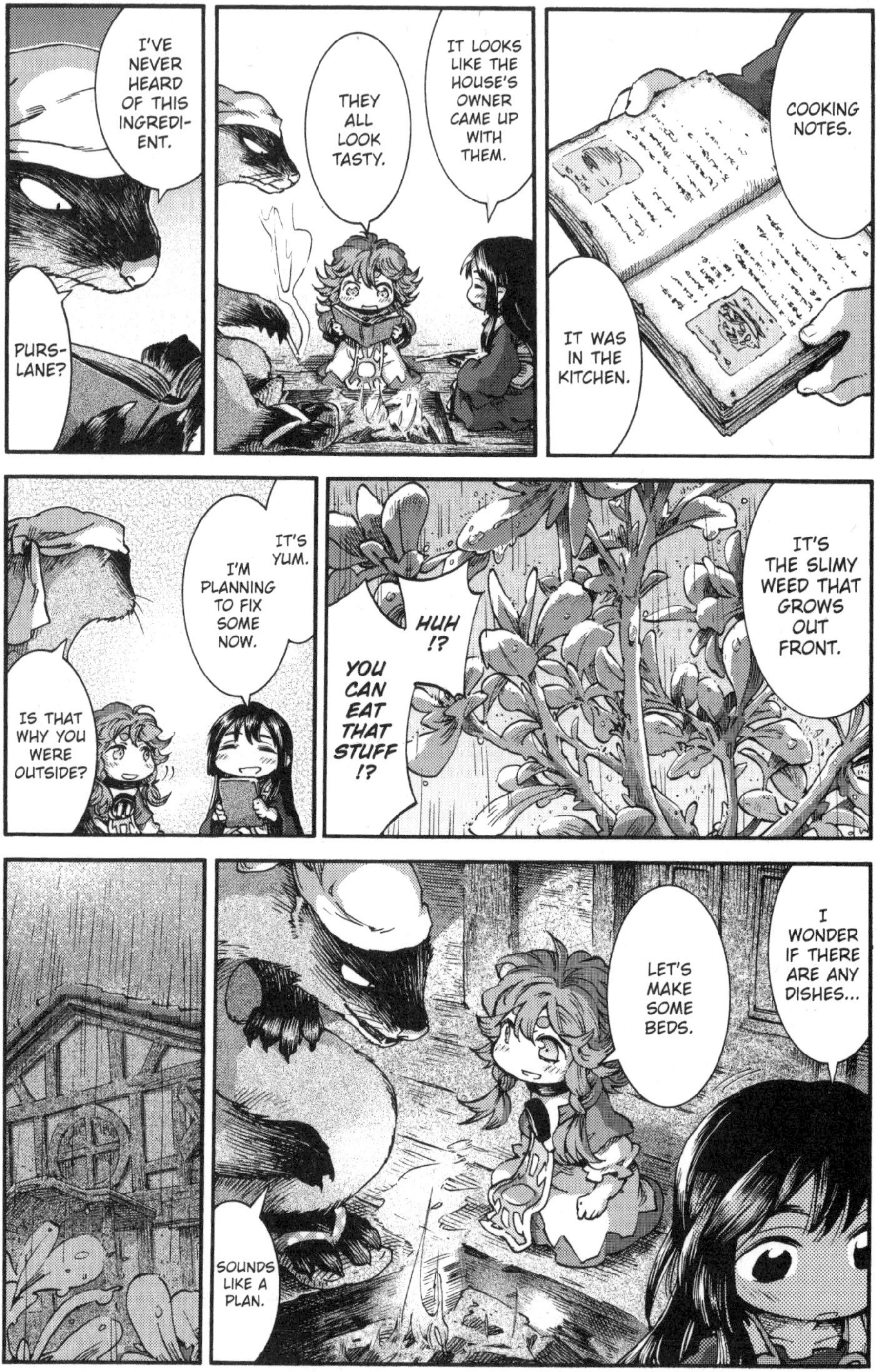
COOKING NOTES.
IT WAS IN THE KITCHEN.
IT LOOKS LIKE THE HOUSE'S OWNER CAME UP WITH THEM.
THEY ALL LOOK TASTY.
I'VE NEVER HEARD OF THIS INGREDI-ENT.
PURS-LANE?
IT'S THE SLIMY WEED THAT GROWS OUT FRONT.
HUH!?
YOU CAN EAT THAT STUFF!?
IT'S YUM.
I'M PLANNING TO FIX SOME NOW.
IS THAT WHY YOU WERE OUTSIDE?
I WONDER IF THERE ARE ANY DISHES...
LET'S MAKE SOME BEDS.
SOUNDS LIKE A PLAN.

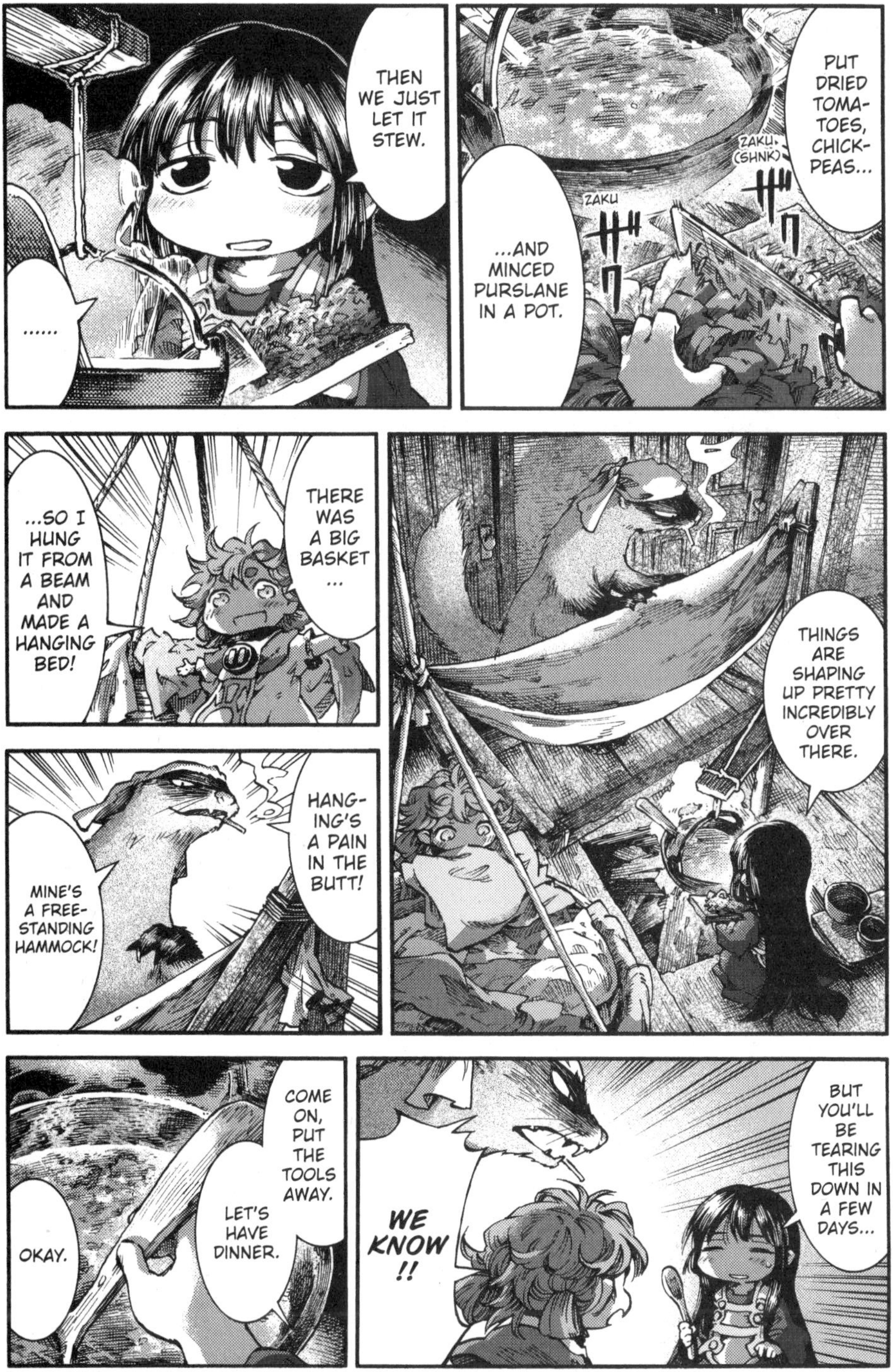
PUT DRIED TOMATOES, CHICKPEAS...
ZAKU (SHNK)
ZAKU
...AND MINCED PURSLANE IN A POT.
THEN WE JUST LET IT STEW.
......
THINGS ARE SHAPING UP PRETTY INCREDIBLY OVER THERE.
THERE WAS A BIG BASKET...
...SO I HUNG IT FROM A BEAM AND MADE A HANGING BED!
HANGING'S A PAIN IN THE BUTT!
MINE'S A FREE-STANDING HAMMOCK!
BUT YOU'LL BE TEARING THIS DOWN IN A FEW DAYS...
WE KNOW!!
COME ON, PUT THE TOOLS AWAY.
LET'S HAVE DINNER.
OKAY.

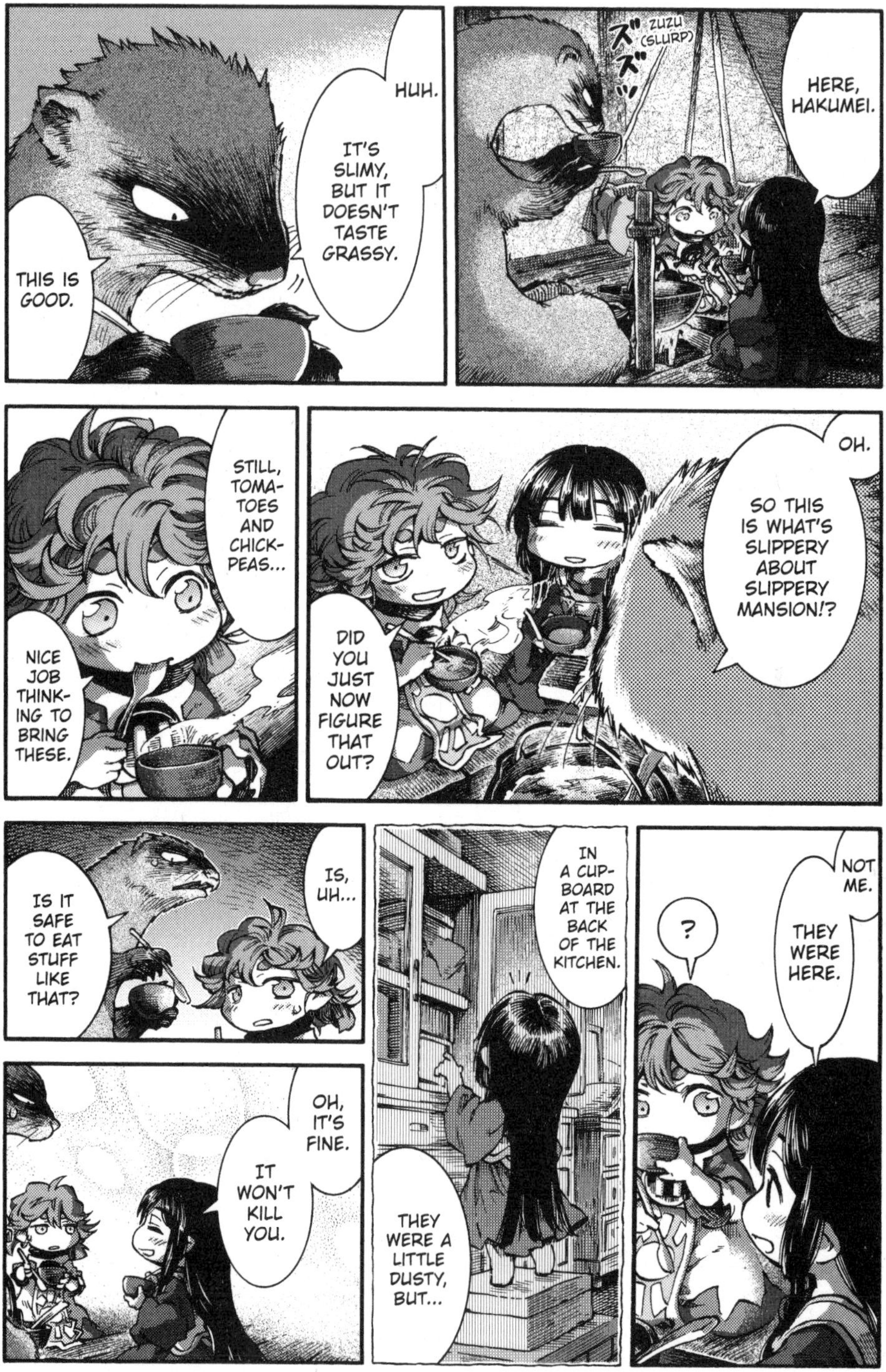
HERE, HAKUMEI.
ズズッ
ZUZU (SLURP)
HUH.
IT'S SLIMY, BUT IT DOESN'T TASTE GRASSY.
THIS IS GOOD.
OH.
SO THIS IS WHAT'S SLIPPERY ABOUT SLIPPERY MANSION!?
DID YOU JUST NOW FIGURE THAT OUT?
STILL, TOMA-TOES AND CHICK-PEAS...
NICE JOB THINK-ING TO BRING THESE.
NOT ME.
THEY WERE HERE.
?
IN A CUP-BOARD AT THE BACK OF THE KITCHEN.
THEY WERE A LITTLE DUSTY, BUT...
IS, UH...
IS IT SAFE TO EAT STUFF LIKE THAT?
OH, IT'S FINE.
IT WON'T KILL YOU.

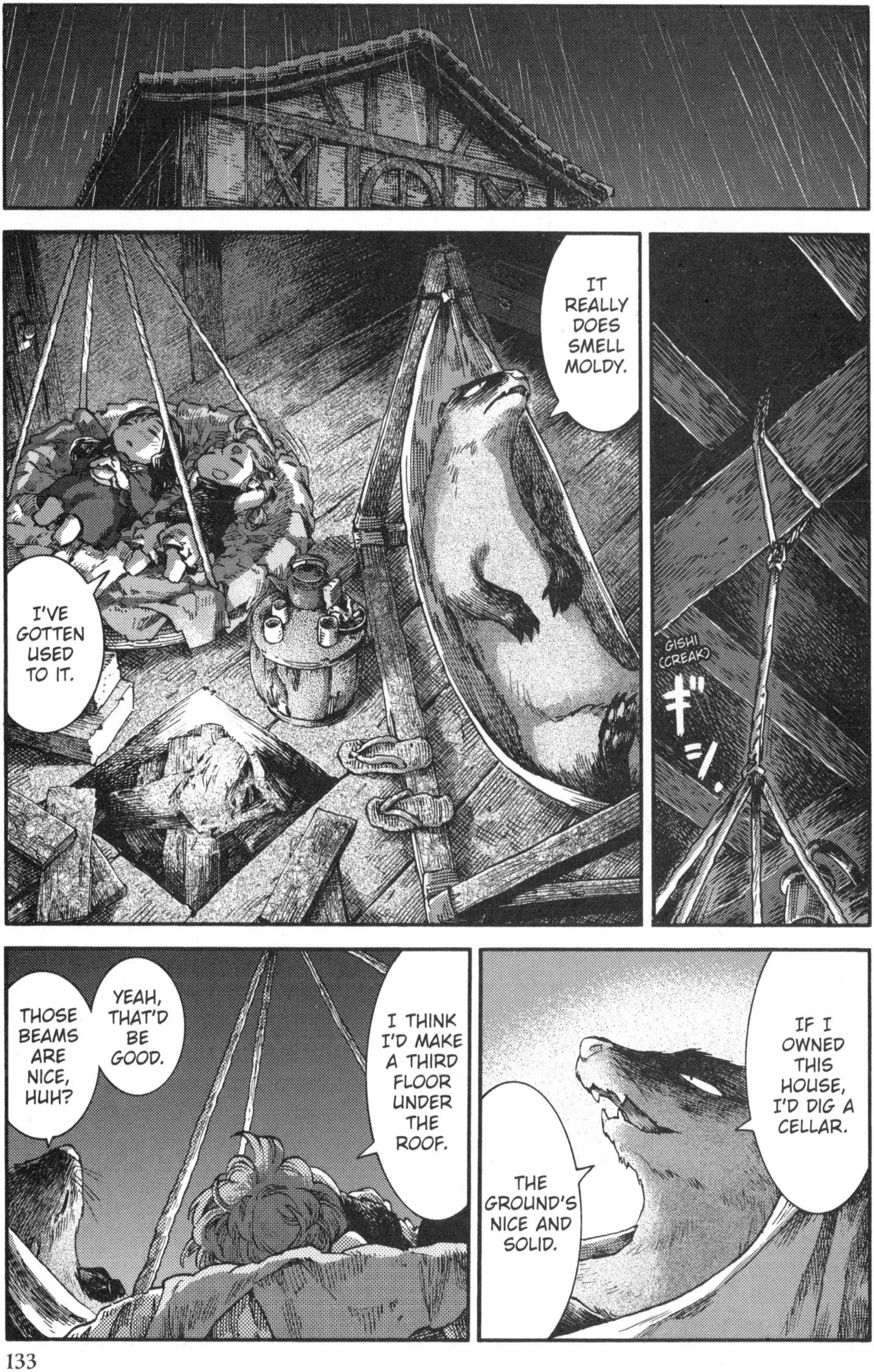
GISHI (CREAK)
ギシッ
IT REALLY DOES SMELL MOLDY.
I'VE GOTTEN USED TO IT.
IF I OWNED THIS HOUSE, I'D DIG A CELLAR.
THE GROUND'S NICE AND SOLID.
I THINK I'D MAKE A THIRD FLOOR UNDER THE ROOF.
YEAH, THAT'D BE GOOD.
THOSE BEAMS ARE NICE, HUH?

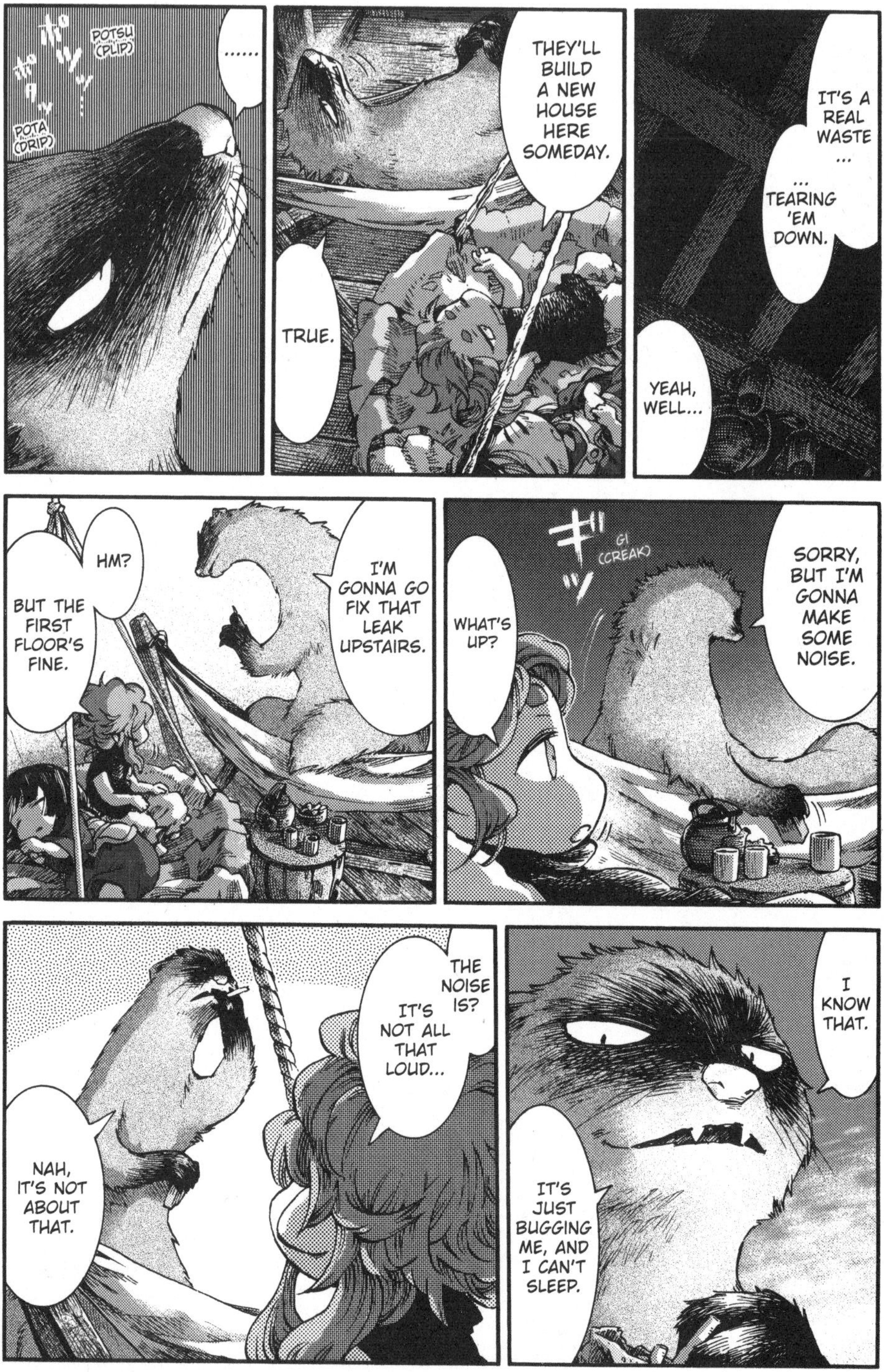
POTSU (PLIP)
POTA (DRIP)
......
THEY'LL BUILD A NEW HOUSE HERE SOMEDAY.
TRUE.
IT'S A REAL WASTE ...
... TEARING 'EM DOWN.
YEAH, WELL...
I'M GONNA GO FIX THAT LEAK UPSTAIRS.
HM?
BUT THE FIRST FLOOR'S FINE.
SORRY, BUT I'M GONNA MAKE SOME NOISE.
GI (CREAK)
WHAT'S UP?
THE NOISE IS?
IT'S NOT ALL THAT LOUD...
NAH, IT'S NOT ABOUT THAT.
I KNOW THAT.
IT'S JUST BUGGING ME, AND I CAN'T SLEEP.

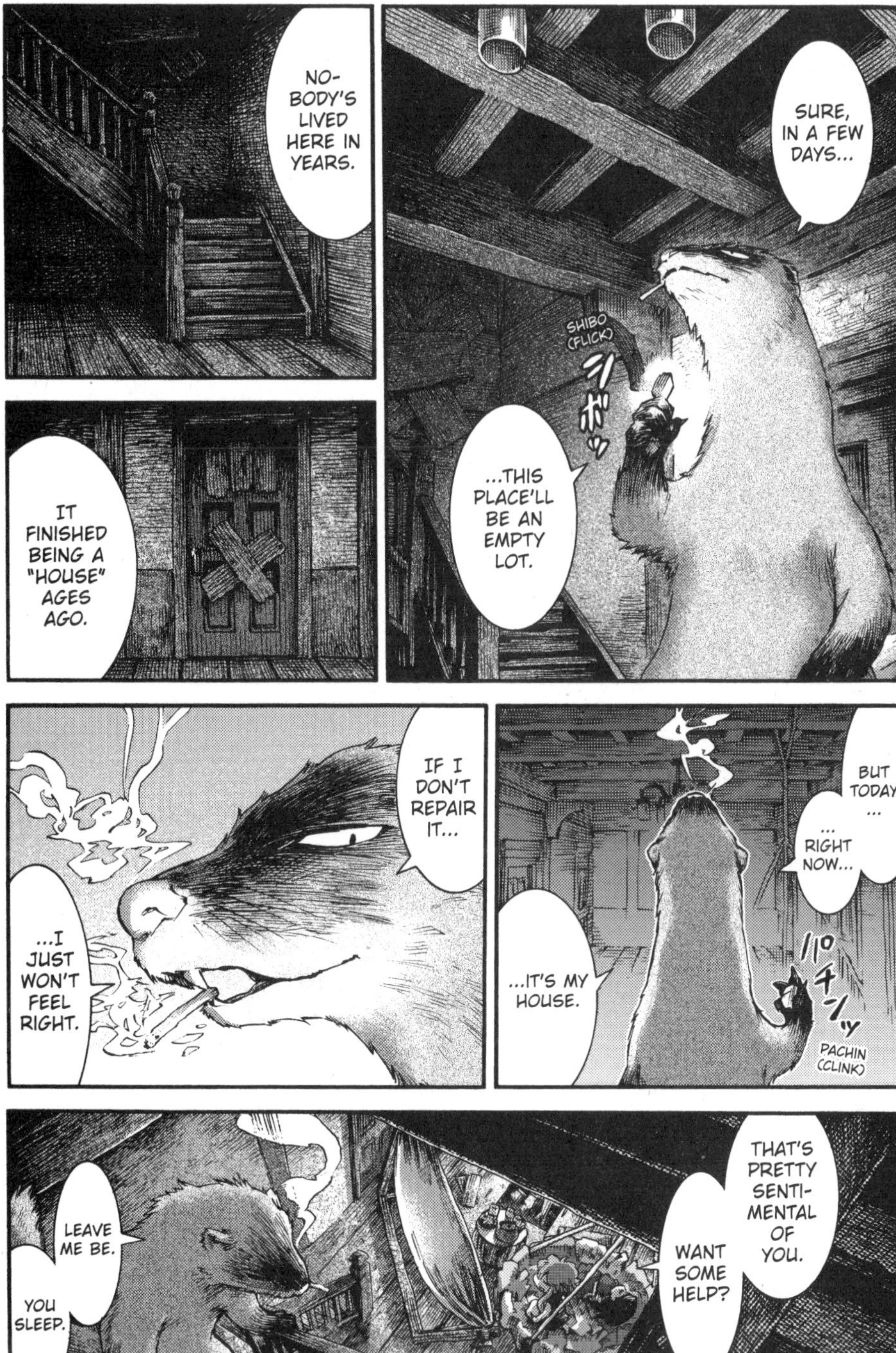
NO-BODY'S LIVED HERE IN YEARS.
IT FINISHED BEING A "HOUSE" AGES AGO.
SURE, IN A FEW DAYS...
SHIBO (FLICK)
...THIS PLACE'LL BE AN EMPTY LOT.
BUT TODAY...
...RIGHT NOW...
PACHIN (CLINK)
...IT'S MY HOUSE.
IF I DON'T REPAIR IT...
...I JUST WON'T FEEL RIGHT.
THAT'S PRETTY SENTI-MENTAL OF YOU.
WANT SOME HELP?
LEAVE ME BE.
YOU SLEEP.

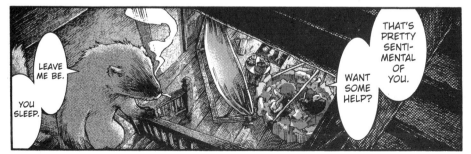

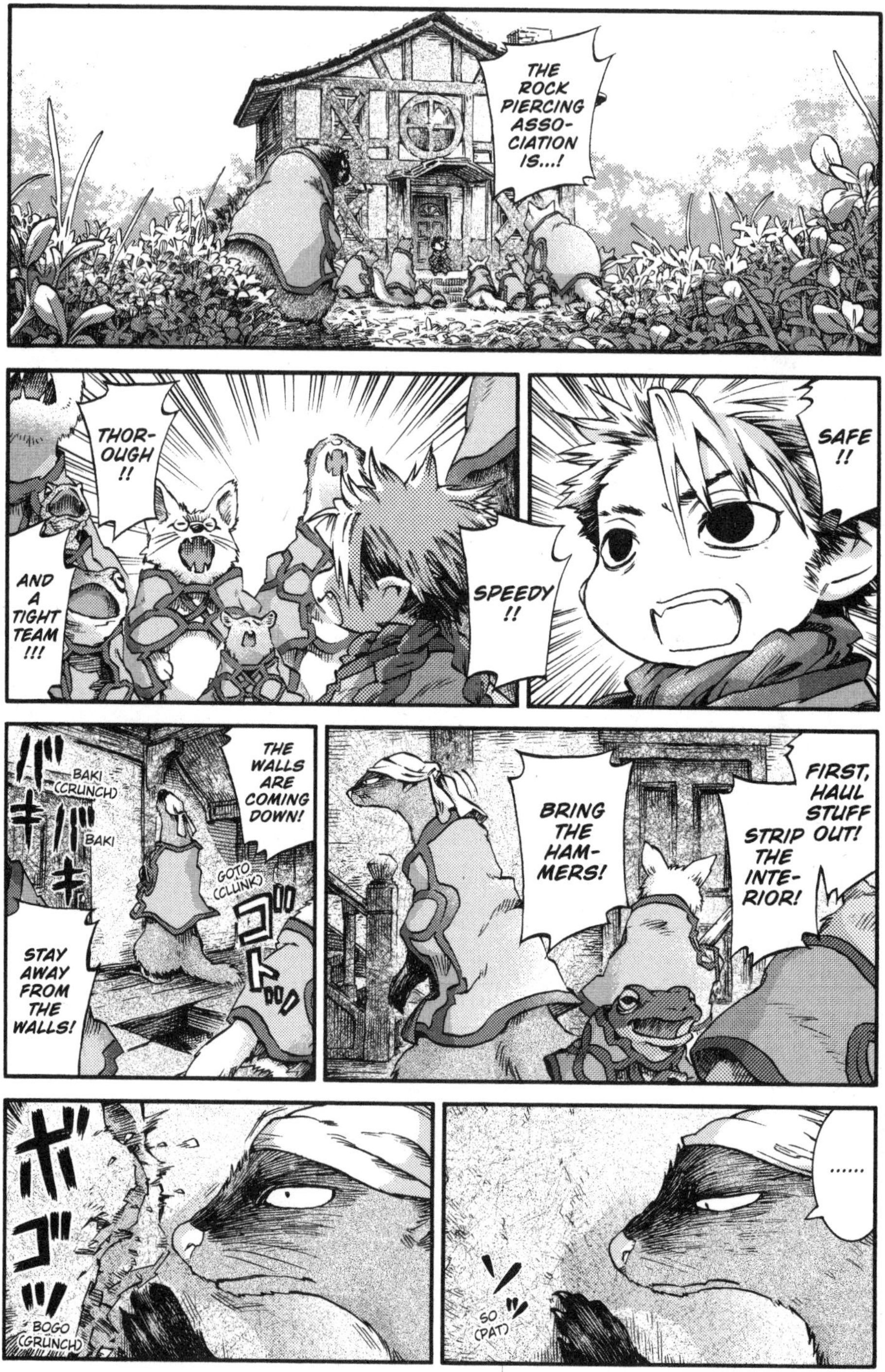
THE ROCK PIERCING ASSO-CIATION IS...!
SAFE!!
SPEEDY!!
THOR-OUGH!!
AND A TIGHT TEAM!!!
FIRST, HAUL STUFF OUT!
STRIP THE INTE-RIOR!
BRING THE HAM-MERS!
THE WALLS ARE COMING DOWN!
バキ
BAKI (CRUNCH)
バキ
BAKI
ゴトッ
GOTO (CLUNK)
STAY AWAY FROM THE WALLS!
......
ソッ
SO (PAT)
ボゴッ
BOGO (GRÜNCH)

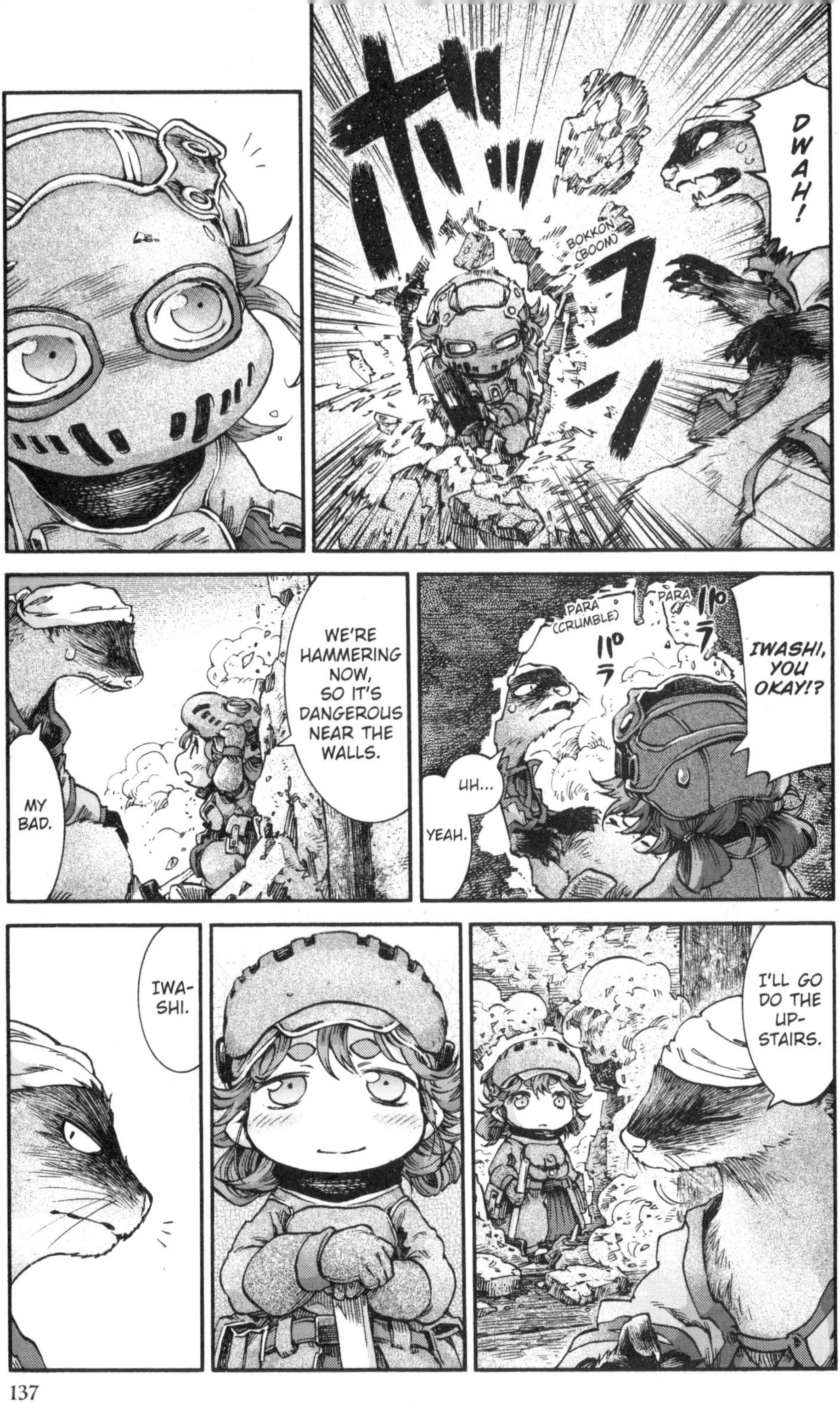
DWAH!
BOKKON (BOOM)
PARA (CRUMBLE)
PARA
IWASHI, YOU OKAY!?
UH...
YEAH.
WE'RE HAMMERING NOW, SO IT'S DANGEROUS NEAR THE WALLS.
MY BAD.
I'LL GO DO THE UP-STAIRS.
IWA-SHI.

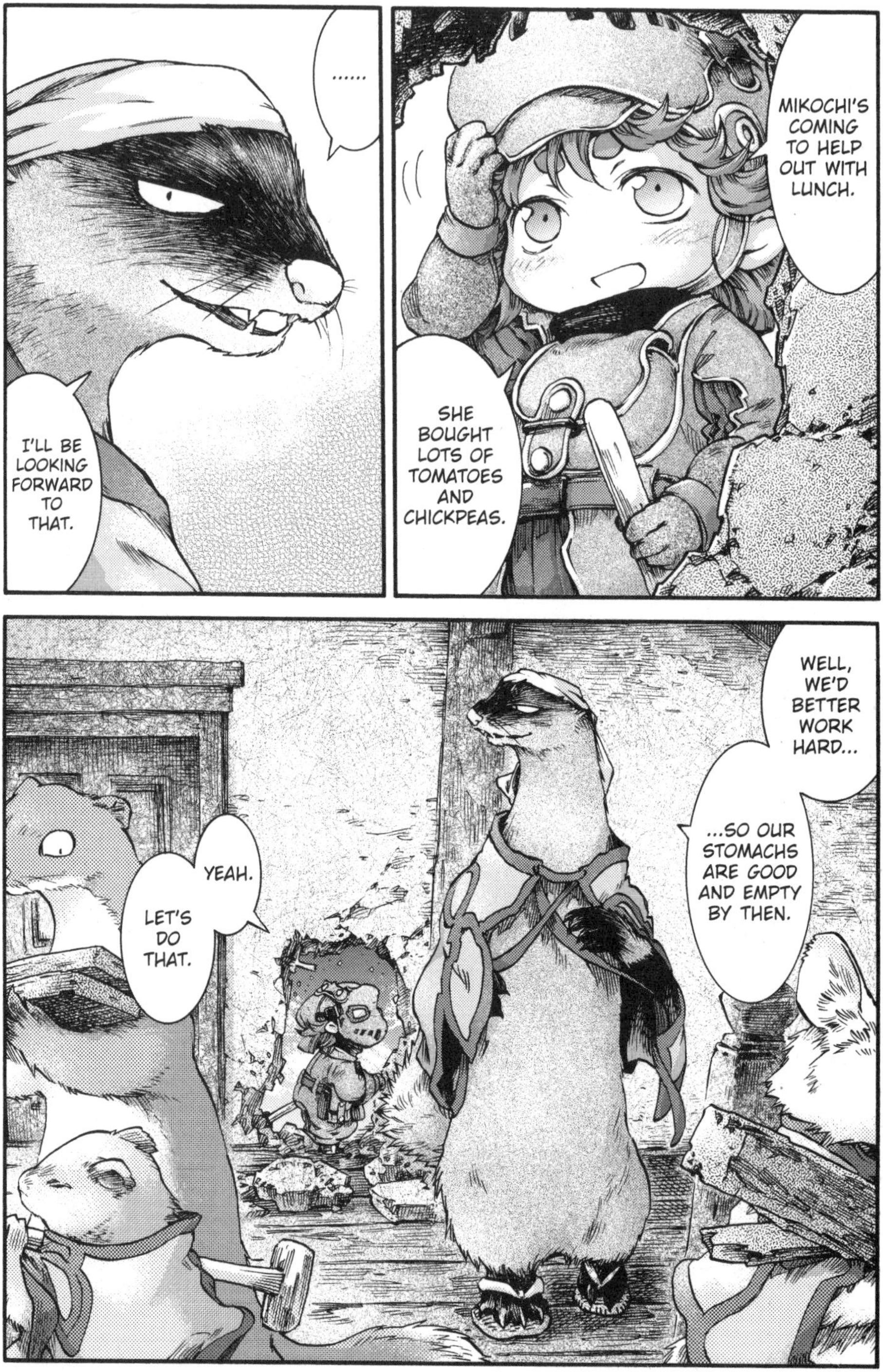
MIKOCHI'S COMING TO HELP OUT WITH LUNCH.
SHE BOUGHT LOTS OF TOMATOES AND CHICKPEAS.
......
I'LL BE LOOKING FORWARD TO THAT.
WELL, WE'D BETTER WORK HARD...
...SO OUR STOMACHS ARE GOOD AND EMPTY BY THEN.
YEAH.
LET'S DO THAT.

Chapter 32 • End

"This stuff's better than it was last time. Is that 'cos the ingredients are fresh?"

"I'd say it's because you've been doing physical labor, wouldn't you?"

"Oh hey, Iwashi, did you hear? They say they've got a buyer for this property."

"Yeah, I heard the neighbors are going to put up an assembly hall. Think we'll get that job soon?"

"I'd like to make a third floor in the attic and dig a cellar under it...and I want a canopy on the hammock."

"They're not building the place the way you want it, you know."

Chapter 33
A Metropolitan Life

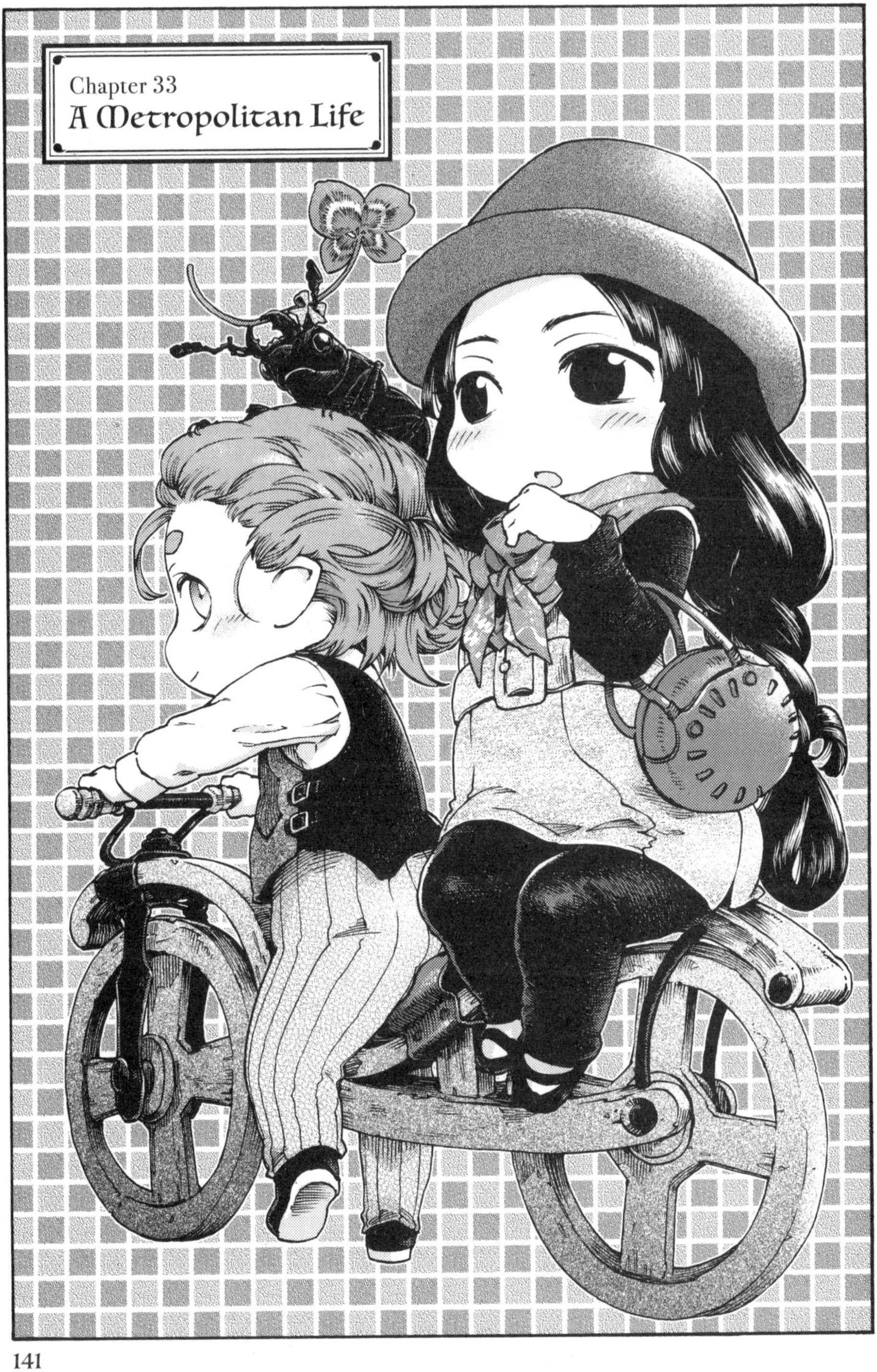

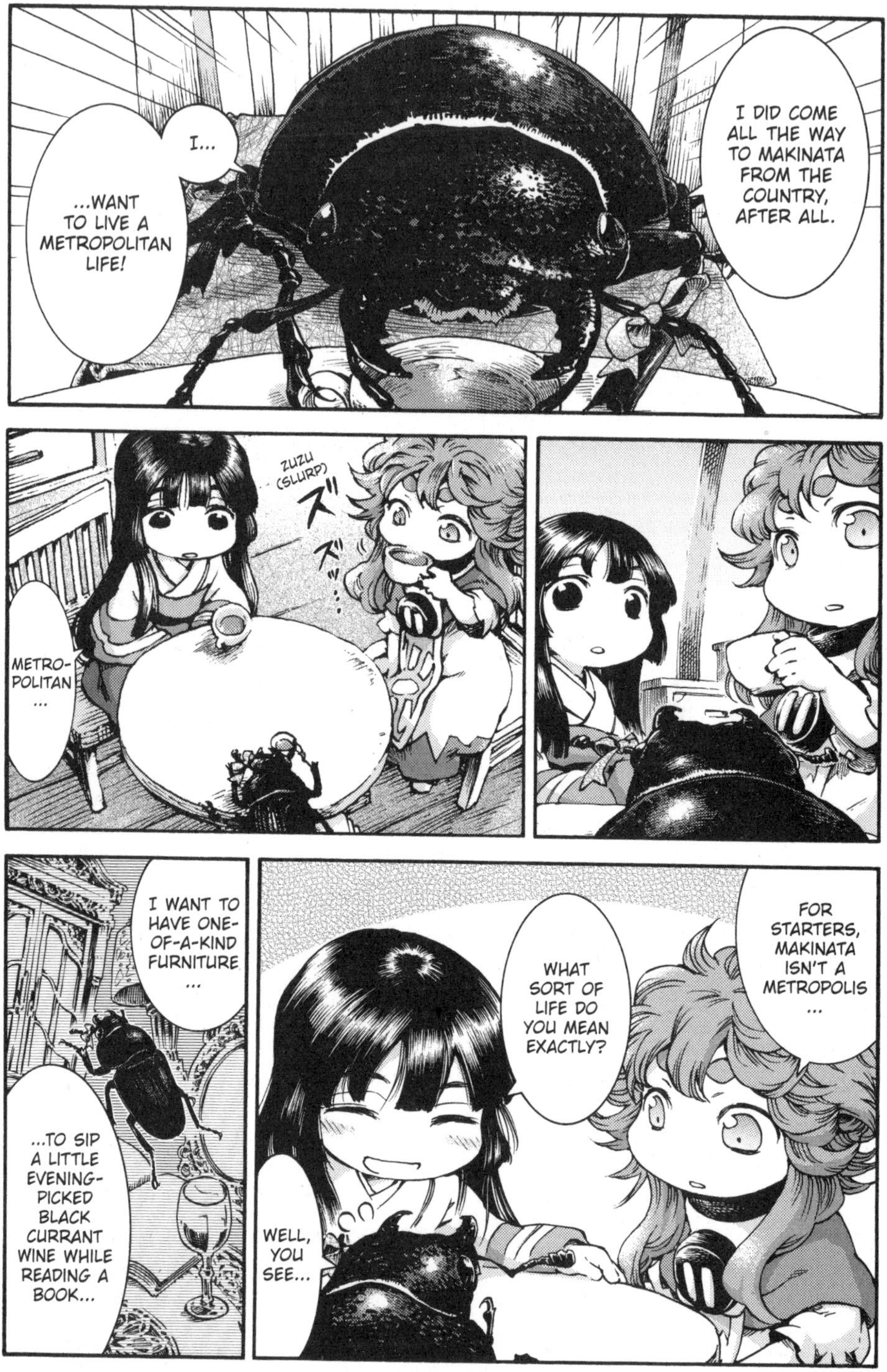
I DID COME ALL THE WAY TO MAKINATA FROM THE COUNTRY, AFTER ALL.
I...
...WANT TO LIVE A METROPOLITAN LIFE!
ZUZU (SLURP)
METRO-POLITAN...
FOR STARTERS, MAKINATA ISN'T A METROPOLIS...
WHAT SORT OF LIFE DO YOU MEAN EXACTLY?
WELL, YOU SEE...
I WANT TO HAVE ONE-OF-A-KIND FURNITURE...
...TO SIP A LITTLE EVENING-PICKED BLACK CURRANT WINE WHILE READING A BOOK...

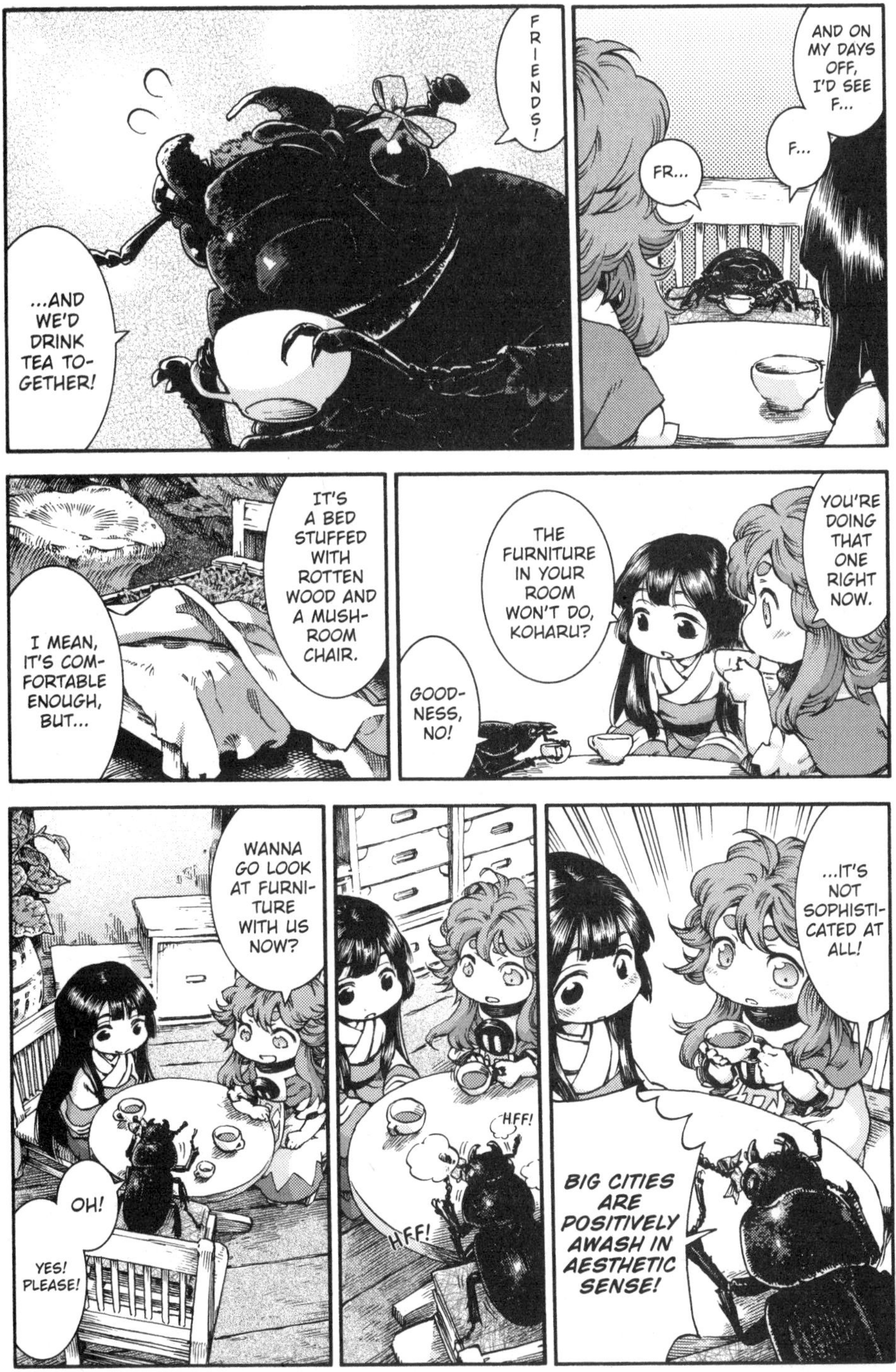
AND ON MY DAYS OFF, I'D SEE F...
F...
FR...
FRIENDS!
...AND WE'D DRINK TEA TOGETHER!
YOU'RE DOING THAT ONE RIGHT NOW.
THE FURNITURE IN YOUR ROOM WON'T DO, KOHARU?
GOODNESS, NO!
IT'S A BED STUFFED WITH ROTTEN WOOD AND A MUSHROOM CHAIR.
I MEAN, IT'S COMFORTABLE ENOUGH, BUT...
...IT'S NOT SOPHISTICATED AT ALL!
BIG CITIES ARE POSITIVELY AWASH IN AESTHETIC SENSE!
HFF!
HFF!
WANNA GO LOOK AT FURNITURE WITH US NOW?
OH!
YES! PLEASE!

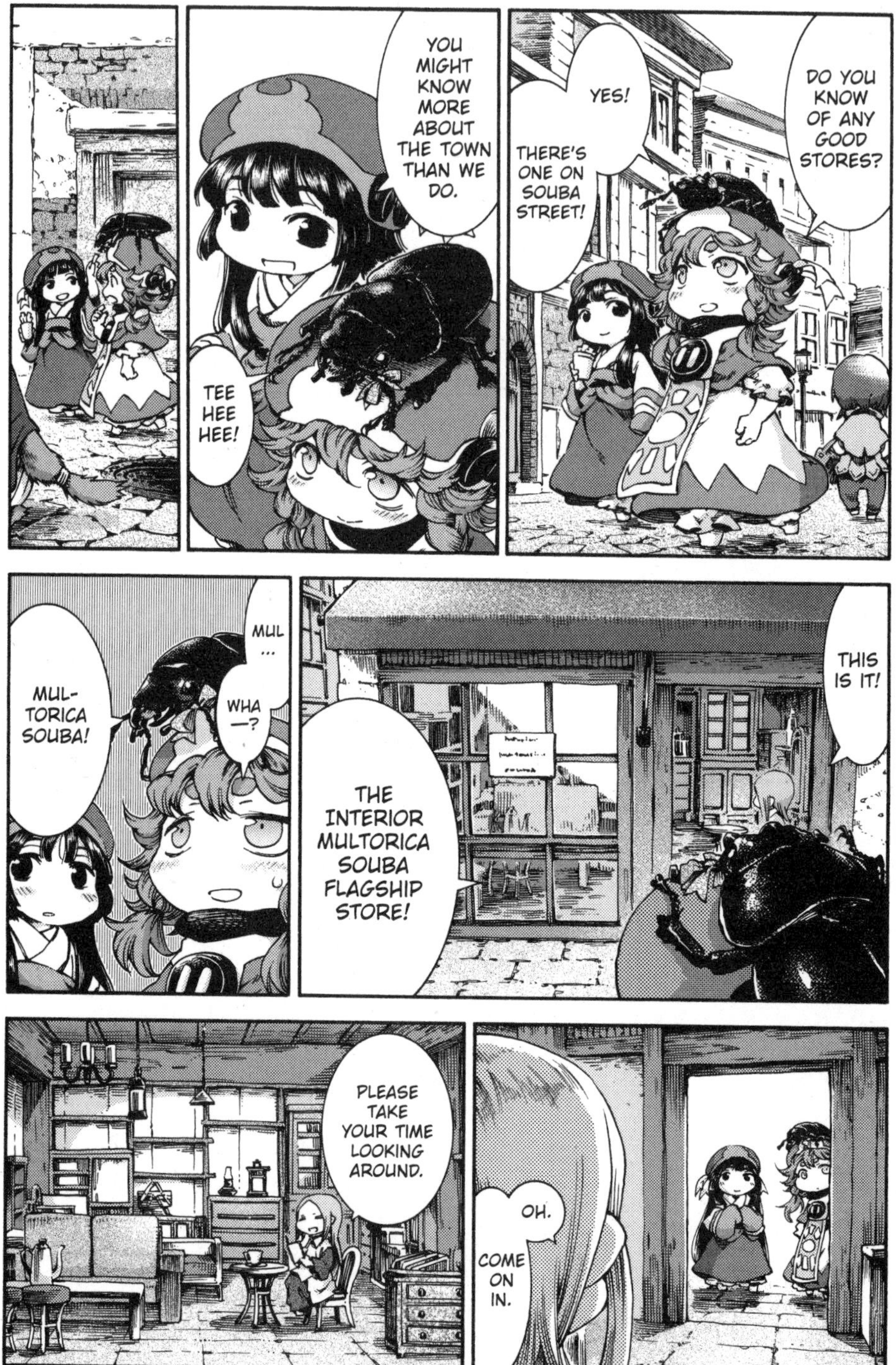
DO YOU KNOW OF ANY GOOD STORES?
YES!
THERE'S ONE ON SOUBA STREET!
YOU MIGHT KNOW MORE ABOUT THE TOWN THAN WE DO.
TEE HEE HEE!
THIS IS IT!
THE INTERIOR MULTORICA SOUBA FLAGSHIP STORE!
MUL...
WHA—?
MUL-TORICA SOUBA!
OH.
COME ON IN.
PLEASE TAKE YOUR TIME LOOKING AROUND.

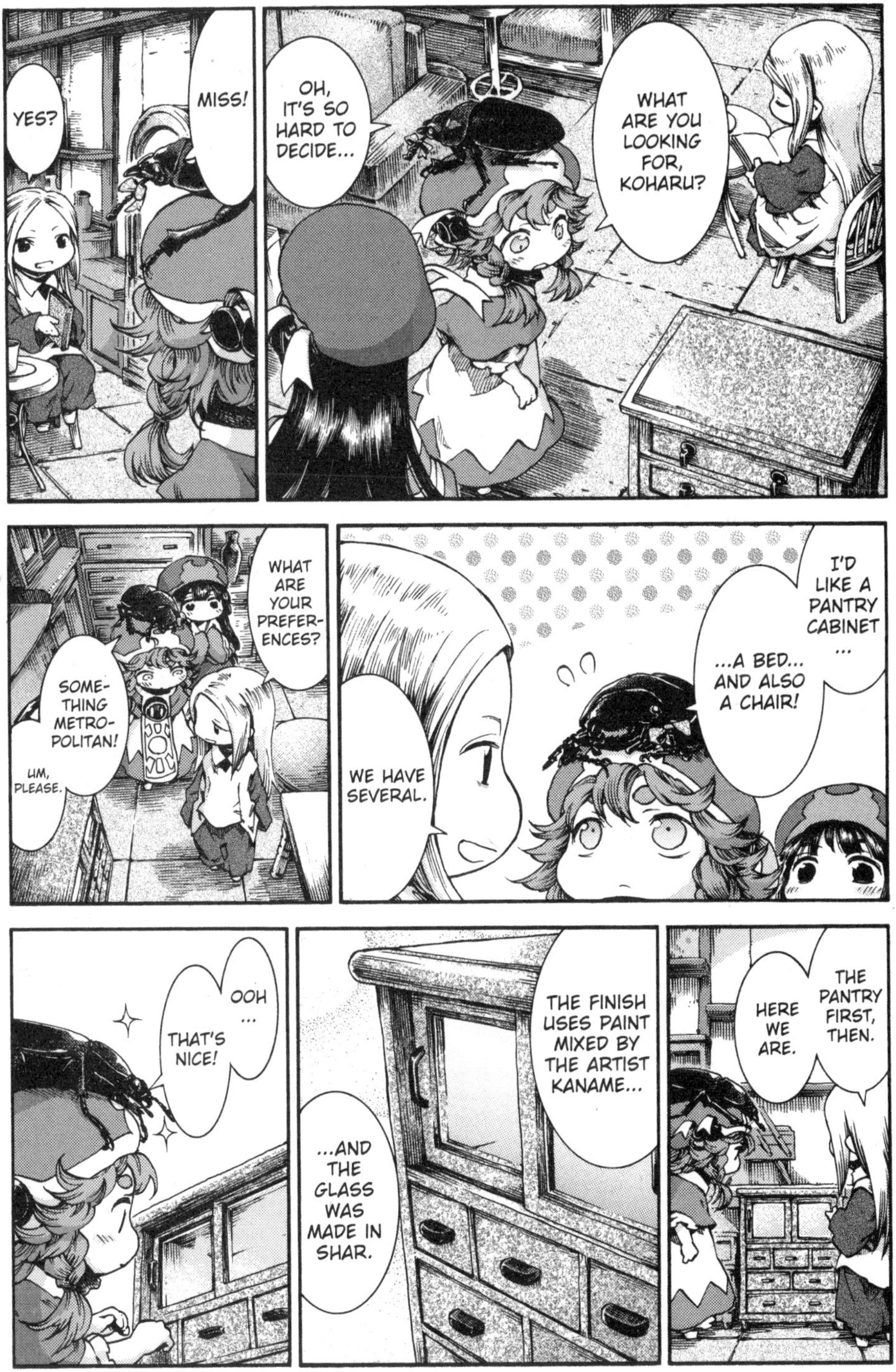
WHAT ARE YOU LOOKING FOR, KOHARU?
OH, IT'S SO HARD TO DECIDE...
MISS!
YES?
I'D LIKE A PANTRY CABINET...
...A BED... AND ALSO A CHAIR!
WE HAVE SEVERAL.
WHAT ARE YOUR PREFERENCES?
SOMETHING METROPOLITAN!
UM, PLEASE.
THE PANTRY FIRST, THEN.
HERE WE ARE.
THE FINISH USES PAINT MIXED BY THE ARTIST KANAME...
...AND THE GLASS WAS MADE IN SHAR.
OOH...
THAT'S NICE!

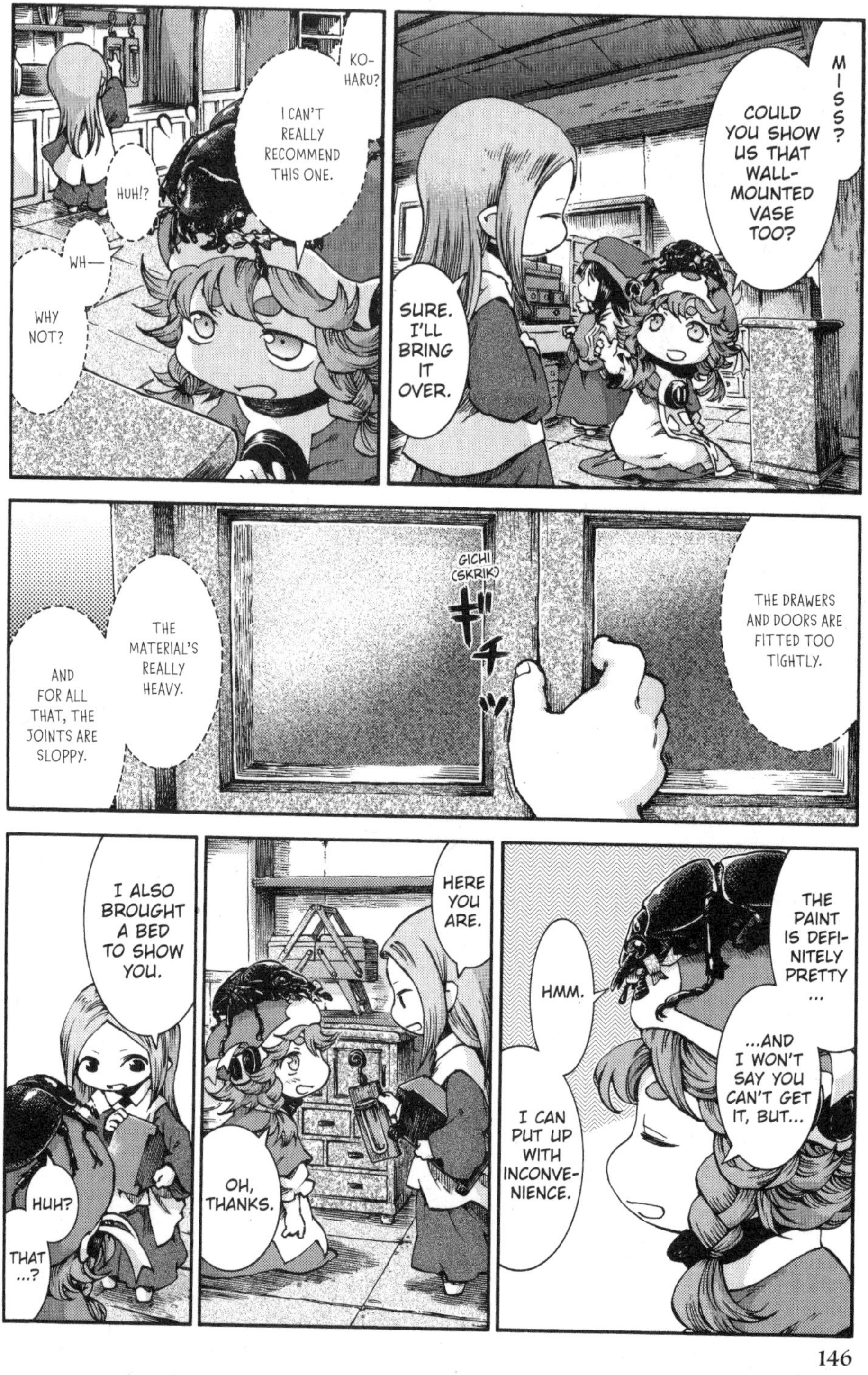
MISS?
COULD YOU SHOW US THAT WALL-MOUNTED VASE TOO?
SURE. I'LL BRING IT OVER.
KO-HARU?
I CAN'T REALLY RECOMMEND THIS ONE.
HUH!?
WH—
WHY NOT?
THE DRAWERS AND DOORS ARE FITTED TOO TIGHTLY.
GICHI (SKRIK)
THE MATERIAL'S REALLY HEAVY.
AND FOR ALL THAT, THE JOINTS ARE SLOPPY.
THE PAINT IS DEFINITELY PRETTY...
...AND I WON'T SAY YOU CAN'T GET IT, BUT...
HMM.
I CAN PUT UP WITH INCONVENIENCE.
HERE YOU ARE.
OH, THANKS.
I ALSO BROUGHT A BED TO SHOW YOU.
HUH?
THAT ...?

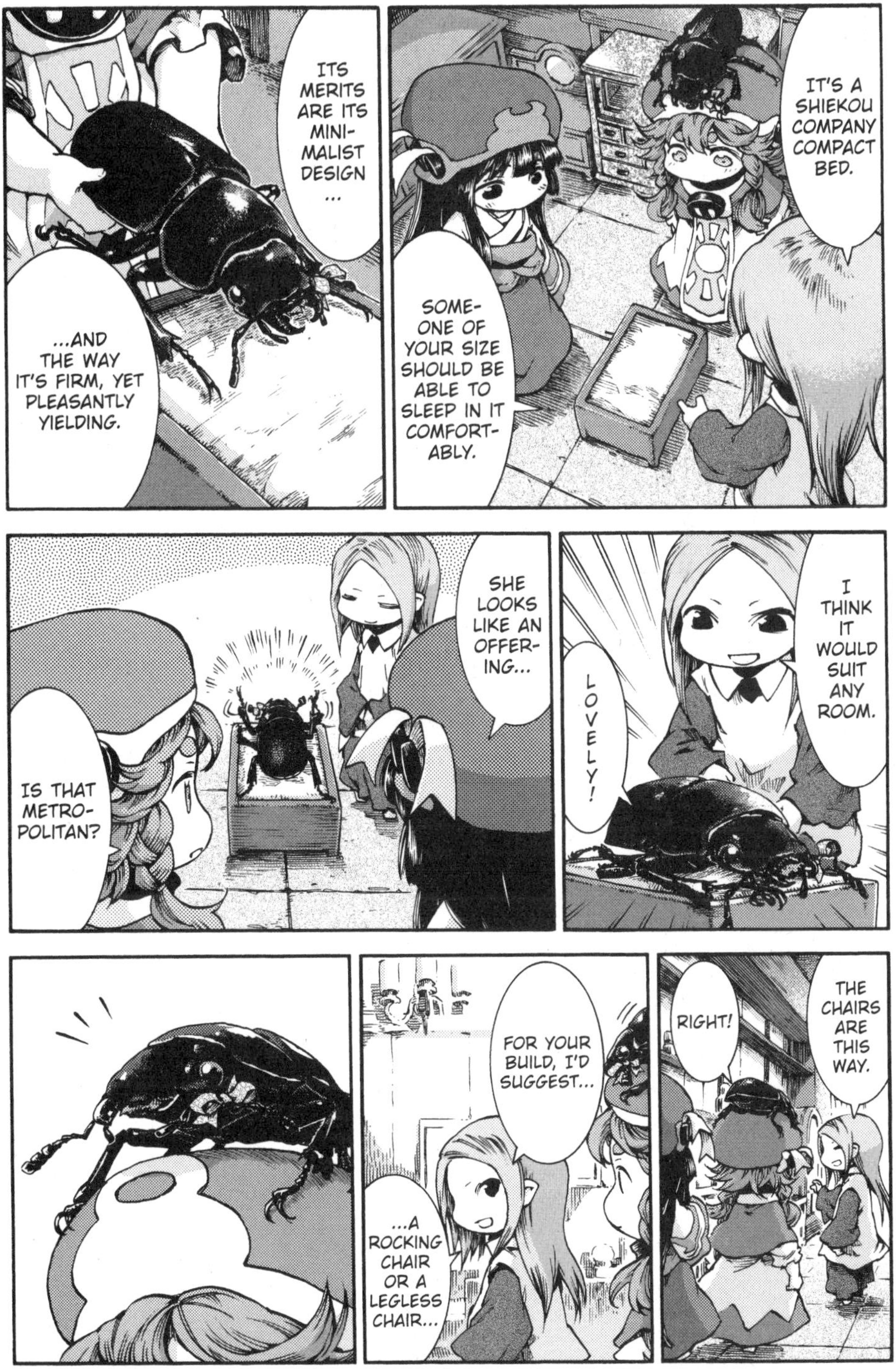
IT'S A SHIEKOU COMPANY COMPACT BED.
SOME-ONE OF YOUR SIZE SHOULD BE ABLE TO SLEEP IN IT COMFORT-ABLY.
ITS MERITS ARE ITS MINI-MALIST DESIGN ...
...AND THE WAY IT'S FIRM, YET PLEASANTLY YIELDING.
I THINK IT WOULD SUIT ANY ROOM.
LOVELY!
SHE LOOKS LIKE AN OFFER-ING...
IS THAT METRO-POLITAN?
THE CHAIRS ARE THIS WAY.
RIGHT!
FOR YOUR BUILD, I'D SUGGEST...
...A ROCKING CHAIR OR A LEGLESS CHAIR...

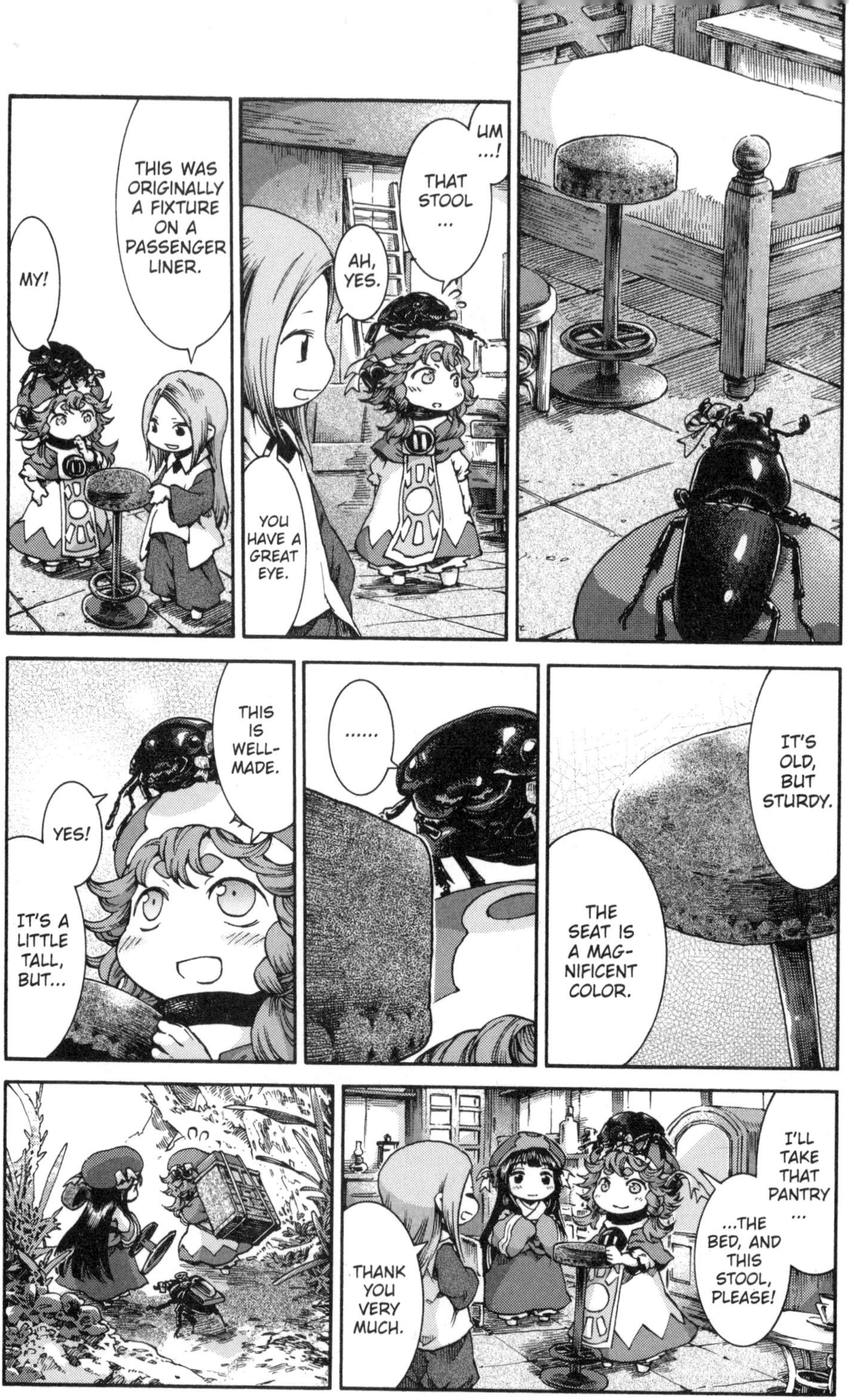
UM ...!
THAT STOOL ...
AH, YES.
YOU HAVE A GREAT EYE.
THIS WAS ORIGINALLY A FIXTURE ON A PASSENGER LINER.
MY!
IT'S OLD, BUT STURDY.
THE SEAT IS A MAG-NIFICENT COLOR.
......
THIS IS WELL-MADE.
YES!
IT'S A LITTLE TALL, BUT...
I'LL TAKE THAT PANTRY ...
...THE BED, AND THIS STOOL, PLEASE!
THANK YOU VERY MUCH.

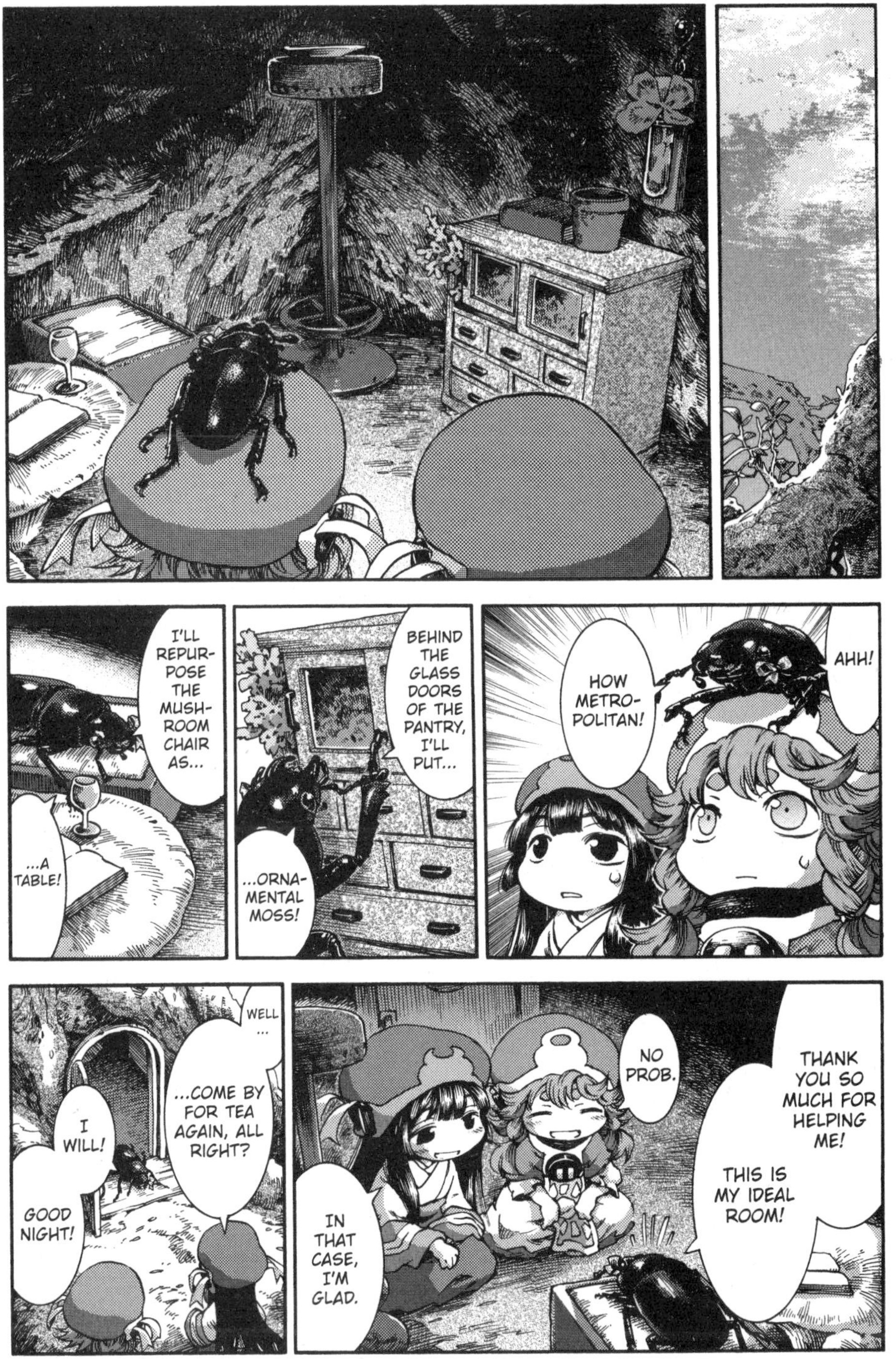
AHH!
HOW METRO-POLITAN!
BEHIND THE GLASS DOORS OF THE PANTRY, I'LL PUT...
...ORNA-MENTAL MOSS!
I'LL REPUR-POSE THE MUSH-ROOM CHAIR AS...
...A TABLE!
THANK YOU SO MUCH FOR HELPING ME!
THIS IS MY IDEAL ROOM!
NO PROB.
IN THAT CASE, I'M GLAD.
WELL ...
...COME BY FOR TEA AGAIN, ALL RIGHT?
I WILL!
GOOD NIGHT!

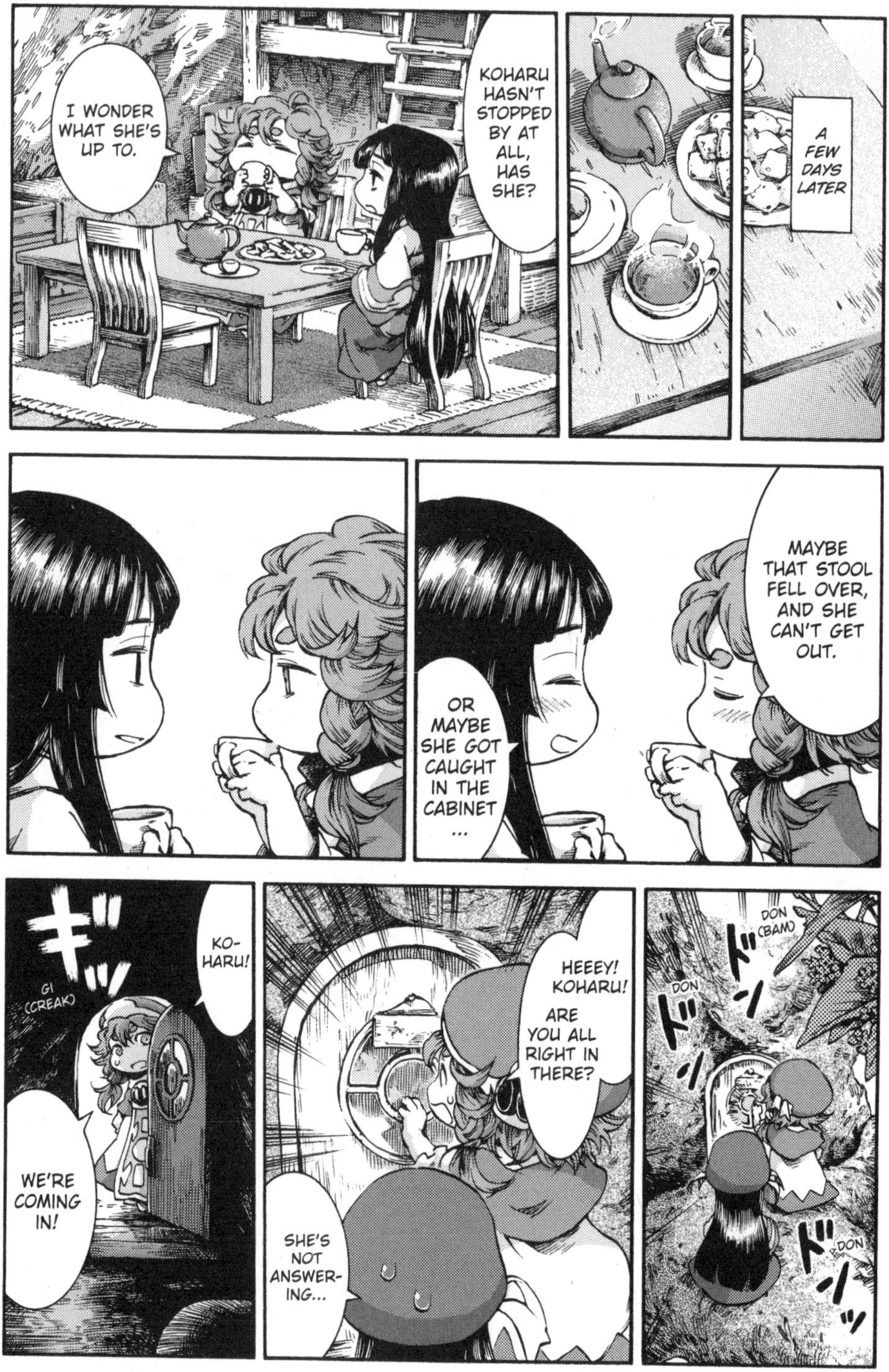
A FEW DAYS LATER
KOHARU HASN'T STOPPED BY AT ALL, HAS SHE?
I WONDER WHAT SHE'S UP TO.
MAYBE THAT STOOL FELL OVER, AND SHE CAN'T GET OUT.
OR MAYBE SHE GOT CAUGHT IN THE CABINET...
ドン DON (BAM)
ドン DON
ドンッ DON
HEEEY! KOHARU!
ARE YOU ALL RIGHT IN THERE?
SHE'S NOT ANSWERING...
ギッ GI (CREAK)
KO-HARU!
WE'RE COMING IN!

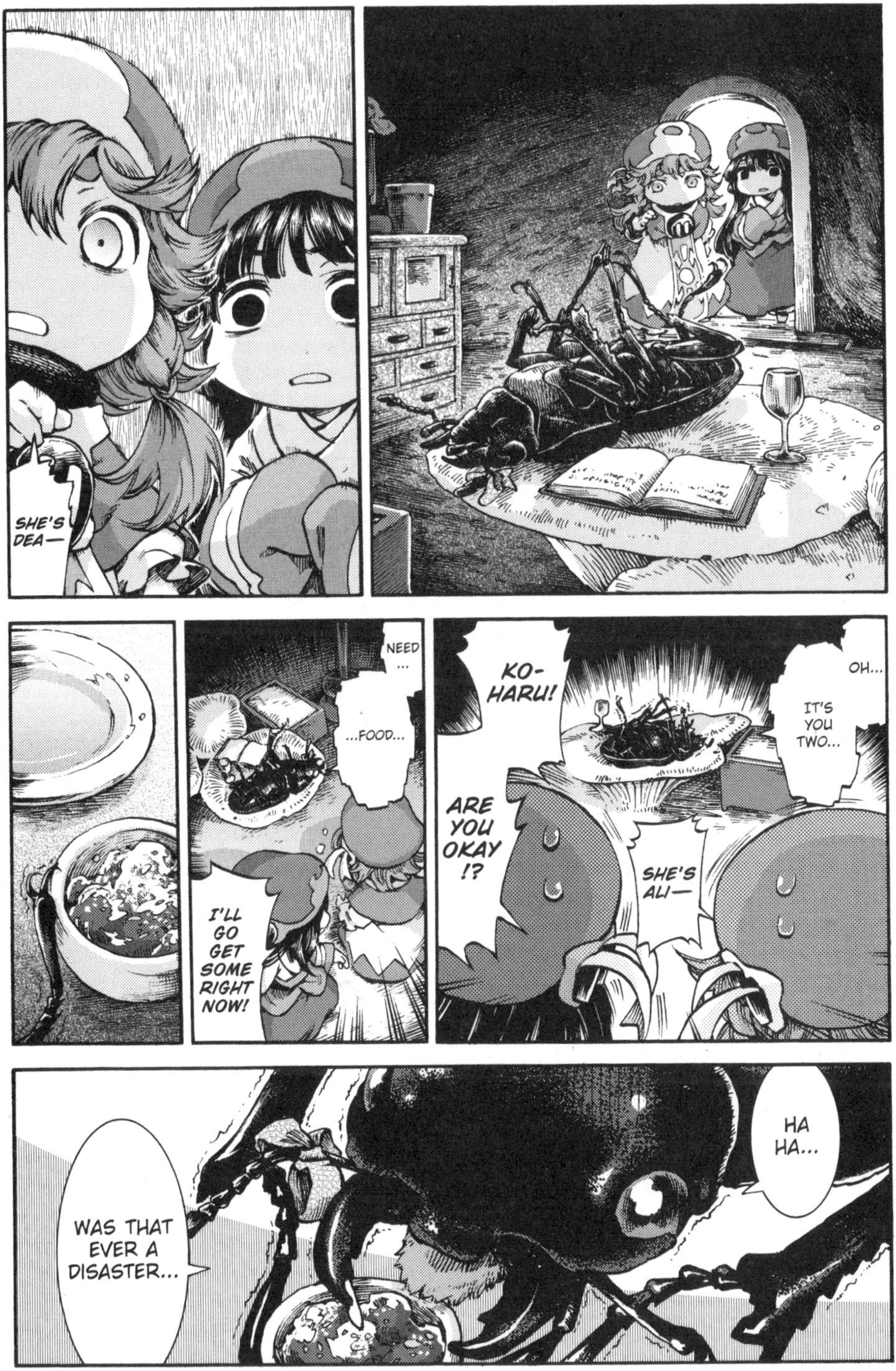
SHE'S DEA—
KO-HARU!
ARE YOU OKAY!?
SHE'S ALI—
OH... IT'S YOU TWO...
NEED... ...FOOD...
I'LL GO GET SOME RIGHT NOW!
HA HA...
WAS THAT EVER A DISASTER...

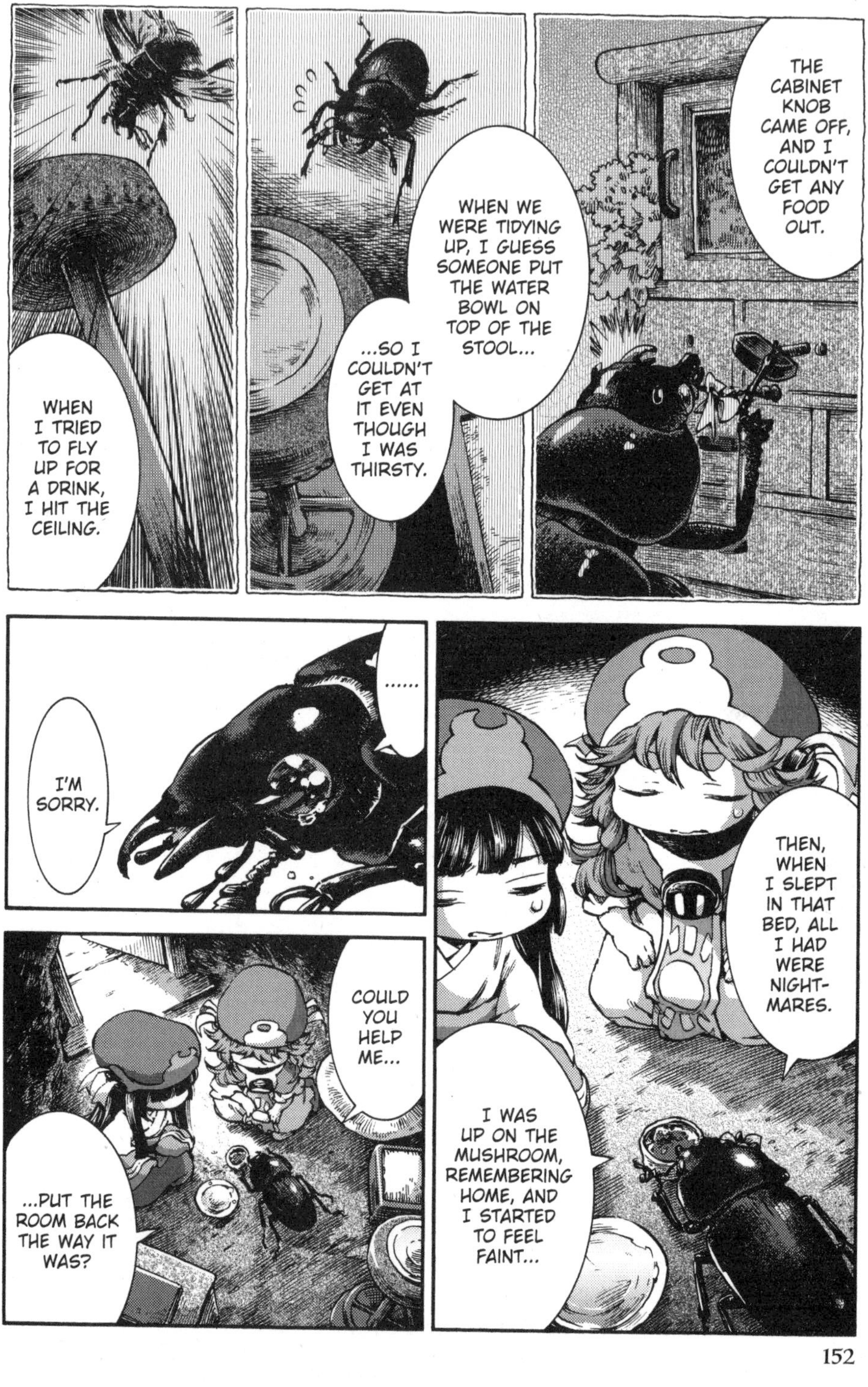
THE CABINET KNOB CAME OFF, AND I COULDN'T GET ANY FOOD OUT.
WHEN WE WERE TIDYING UP, I GUESS SOMEONE PUT THE WATER BOWL ON TOP OF THE STOOL...
...SO I COULDN'T GET AT IT EVEN THOUGH I WAS THIRSTY.
WHEN I TRIED TO FLY UP FOR A DRINK, I HIT THE CEILING.
THEN, WHEN I SLEPT IN THAT BED, ALL I HAD WERE NIGHT-MARES.
I WAS UP ON THE MUSHROOM, REMEMBERING HOME, AND I STARTED TO FEEL FAINT...
......
I'M SORRY.
COULD YOU HELP ME...
...PUT THE ROOM BACK THE WAY IT WAS?

......

WE'LL HELP.

UUNH!

UU!

ARE YOU SURE?

YOU SAID THIS WAS YOUR IDEAL...

HAKU-MEI.

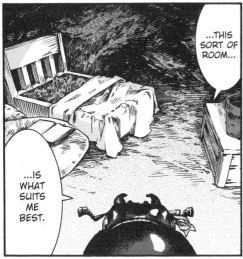

...THIS SORT OF ROOM...

...IS WHAT SUITS ME BEST.

HAAH...

I GUESS...

153

KO-HARU...

I'LL RETURN THE FURNI-TURE.

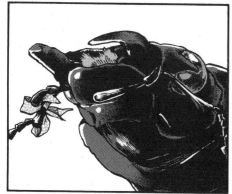

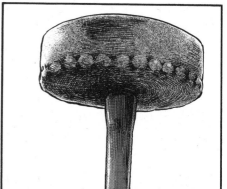

COULD I...

...ASK YOU FOR ONE MORE FAVOR?

HAKUMEI-SAN.

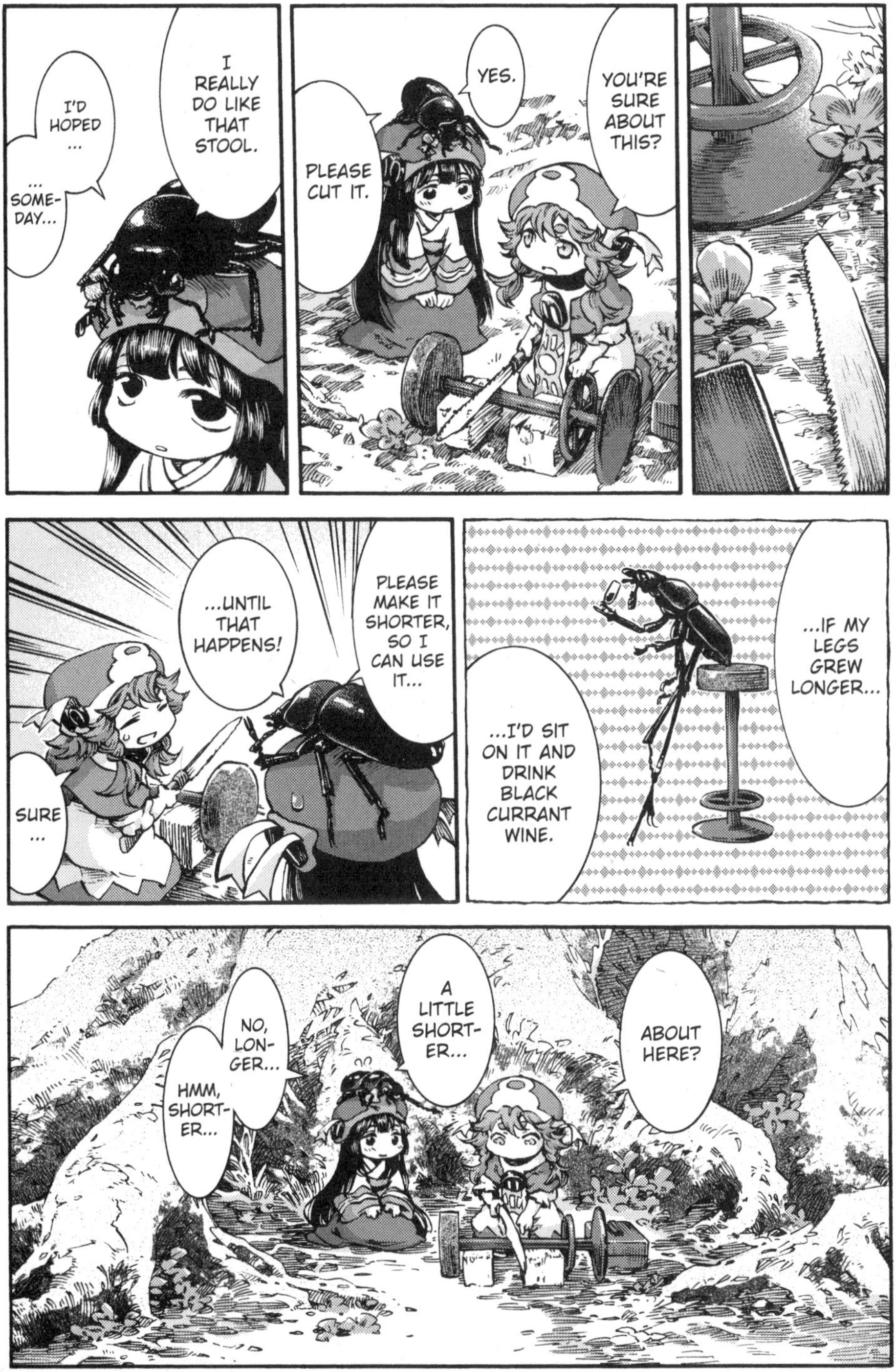
YOU'RE SURE ABOUT THIS?
YES.
PLEASE CUT IT.
I REALLY DO LIKE THAT STOOL.
I'D HOPED ...
... SOME-DAY...
...IF MY LEGS GREW LONGER...
...I'D SIT ON IT AND DRINK BLACK CURRANT WINE.
PLEASE MAKE IT SHORTER, SO I CAN USE IT...
...UNTIL THAT HAPPENS!
SURE ...
ABOUT HERE?
A LITTLE SHORT-ER...
NO, LON-GER...
HMM, SHORT-ER...

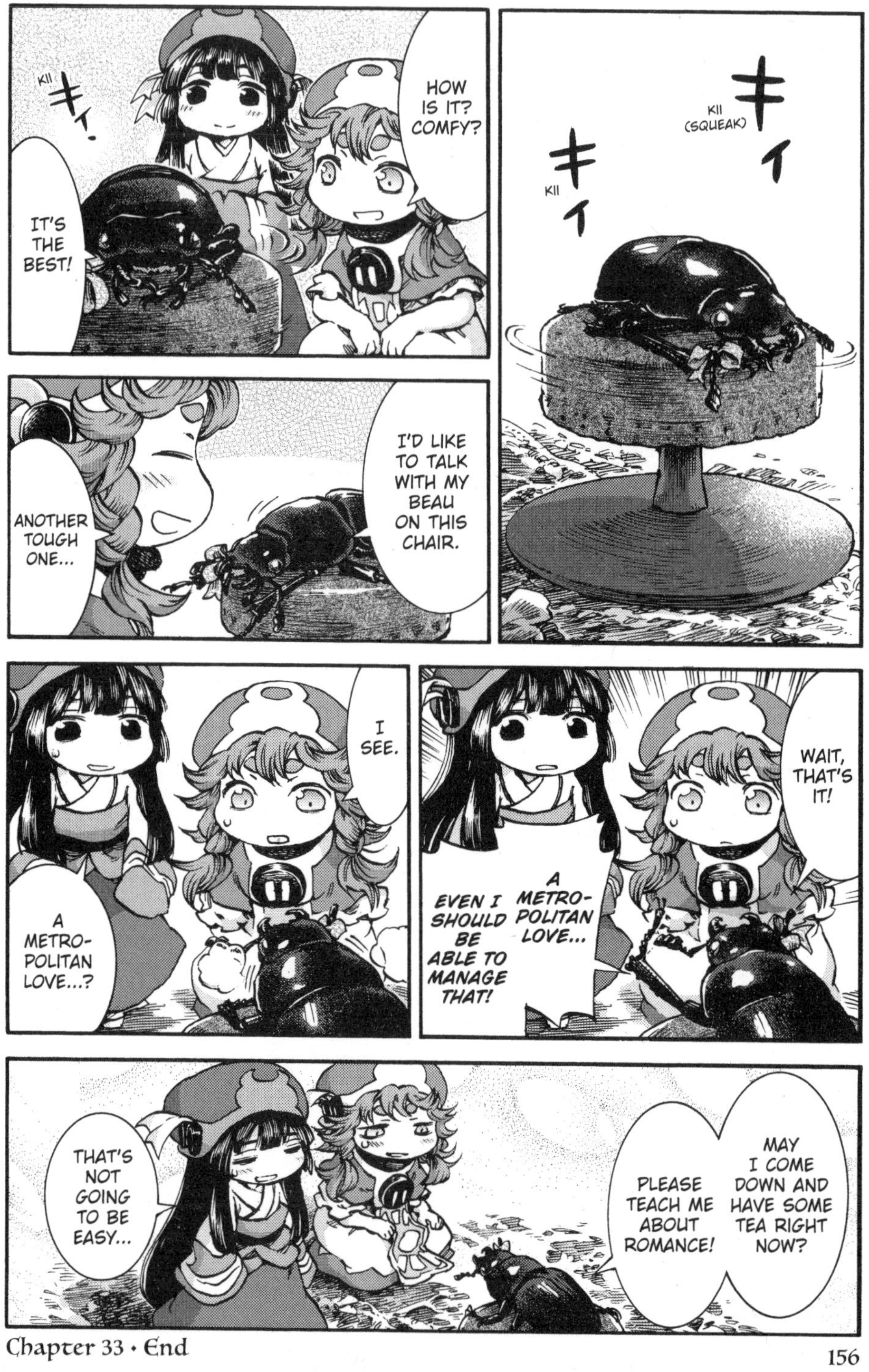
KII
キイ
HOW IS IT? COMFY?
IT'S THE BEST!
I'D LIKE TO TALK WITH MY BEAU ON THIS CHAIR.
ANOTHER TOUGH ONE...
KII (SQUEAK)
キイ
KII
キイ
I SEE.
A METRO-POLITAN LOVE...?
WAIT, THAT'S IT!
A METRO-POLITAN LOVE...
EVEN I SHOULD BE ABLE TO MANAGE THAT!
THAT'S NOT GOING TO BE EASY...
PLEASE TEACH ME ABOUT ROMANCE!
MAY I COME DOWN AND HAVE SOME TEA RIGHT NOW?

Chapter 33 • End

It's been four days since I left my hometown.

I'm still not used to traveling by ship yet, but I've finally found a place where I belong.

It's a very tall stool at the end of the bar.

It's in the very back, but the truth is, the orchestra's performances sound best there.

Besides, the seat right next to it is the singer's favorite spot once she's finished her songs.

We've gotten into the habit of drinking and talking until dawn, just the two of us.

Tomorrow, I think I'll tell her I'd like to stay together even after we disembark.

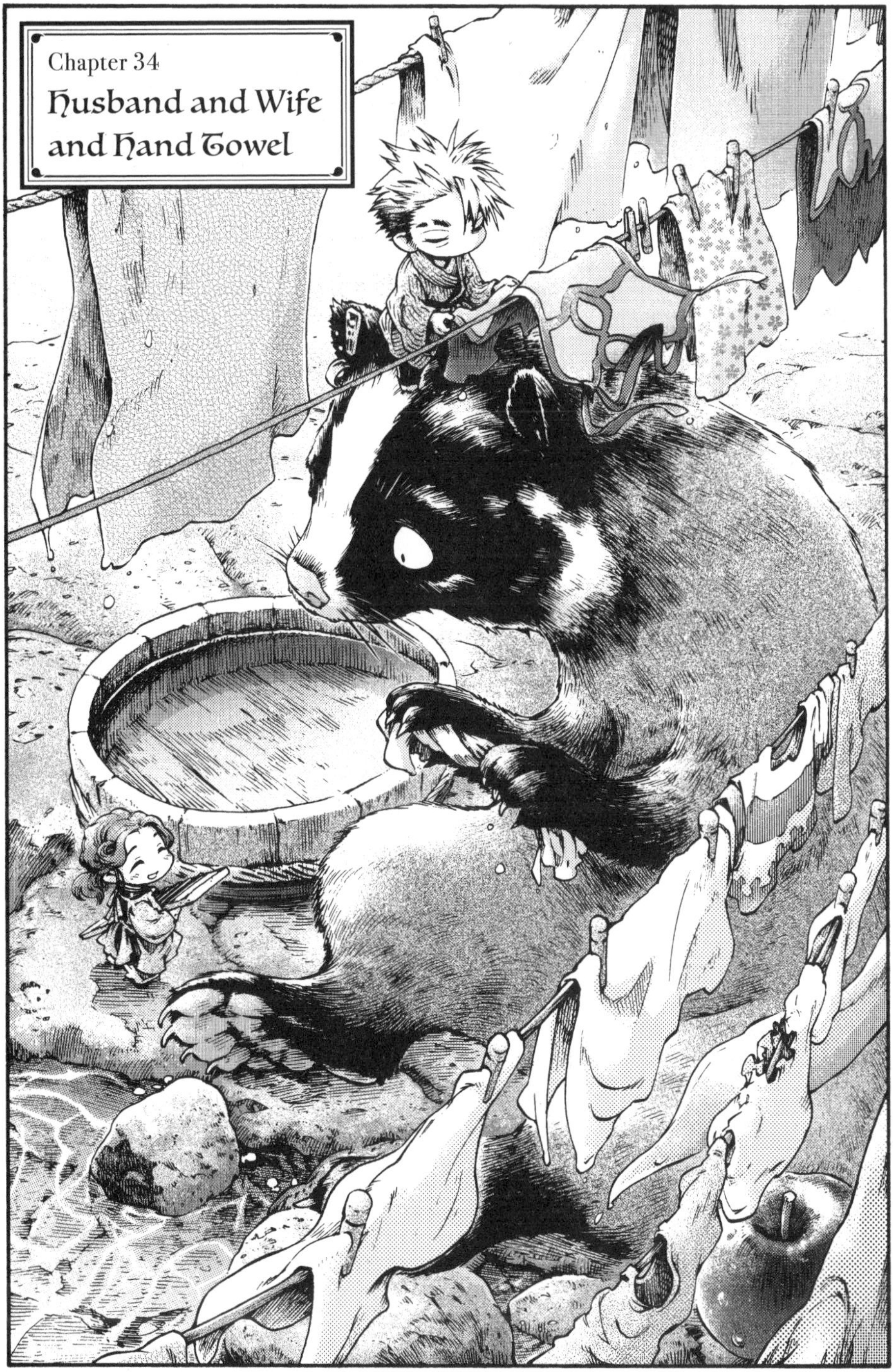
Chapter 34
Husband and Wife and Hand Towel

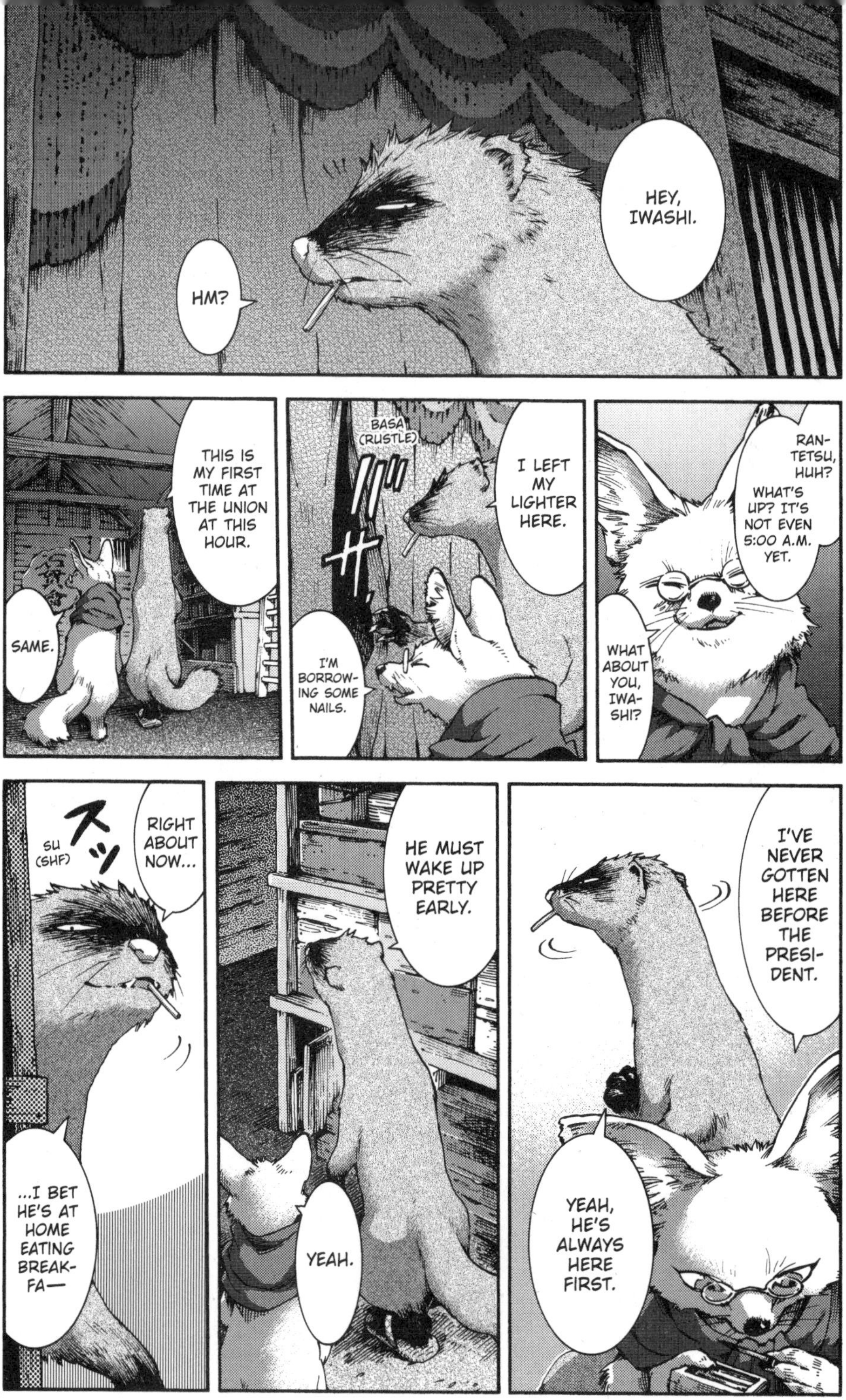
HEY, IWASHI.
HM?
RAN-TETSU, HUH? WHAT'S UP? IT'S NOT EVEN 5:00 A.M. YET.
WHAT ABOUT YOU, IWASHI?
BASA (RUSTLE)
I LEFT MY LIGHTER HERE.
I'M BORROWING SOME NAILS.
THIS IS MY FIRST TIME AT THE UNION AT THIS HOUR.
SAME.
I'VE NEVER GOTTEN HERE BEFORE THE PRESIDENT.
YEAH, HE'S ALWAYS HERE FIRST.
HE MUST WAKE UP PRETTY EARLY.
YEAH.
スッ
SU (SHF)
RIGHT ABOUT NOW...
...I BET HE'S AT HOME EATING BREAKFA—

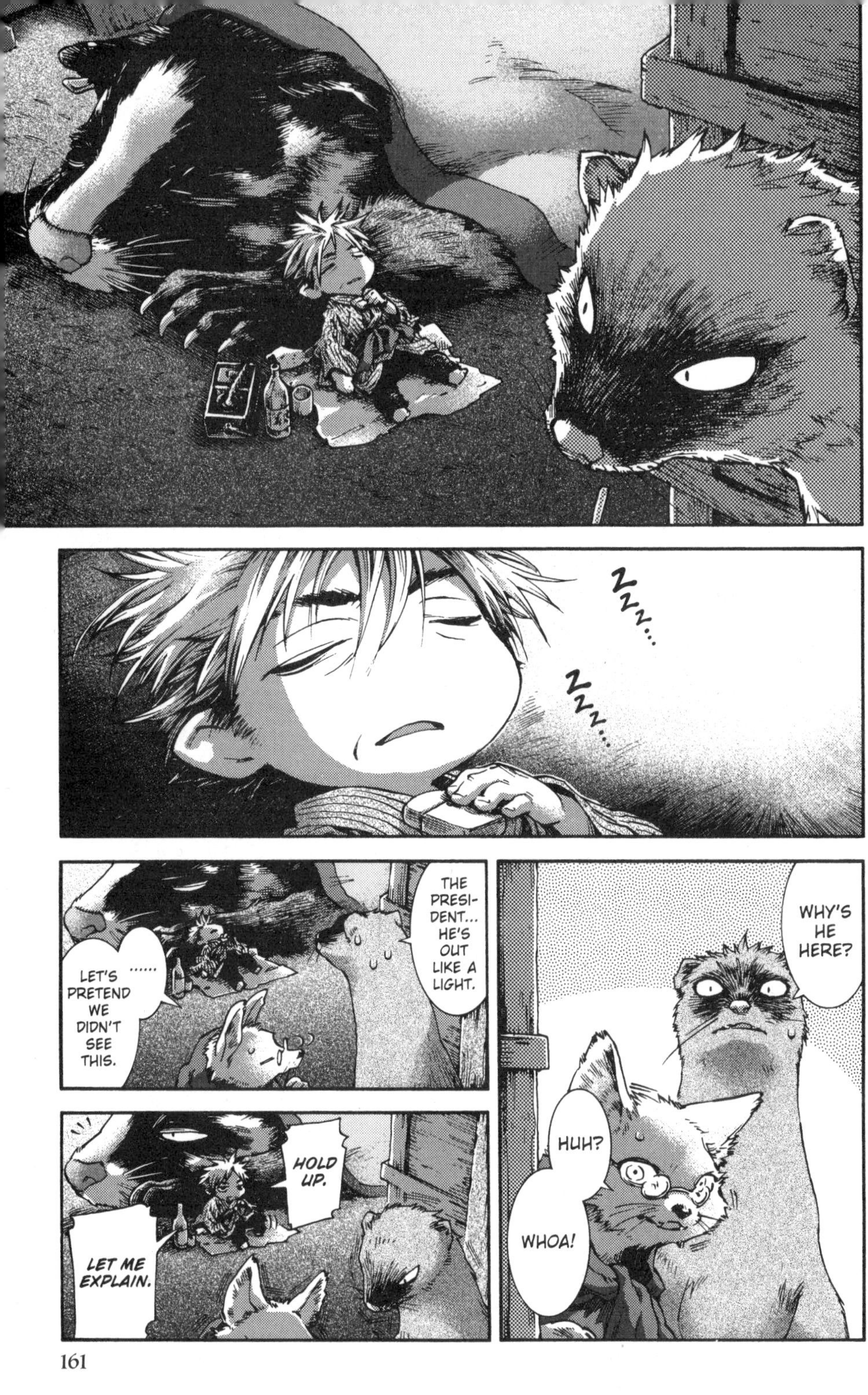
Zzz...
Zzz...
WHY'S HE HERE?
HUH?
WHOA!
THE PRESI-DENT... HE'S OUT LIKE A LIGHT.
......
LET'S PRETEND WE DIDN'T SEE THIS.
HOLD UP.
LET ME EXPLAIN.

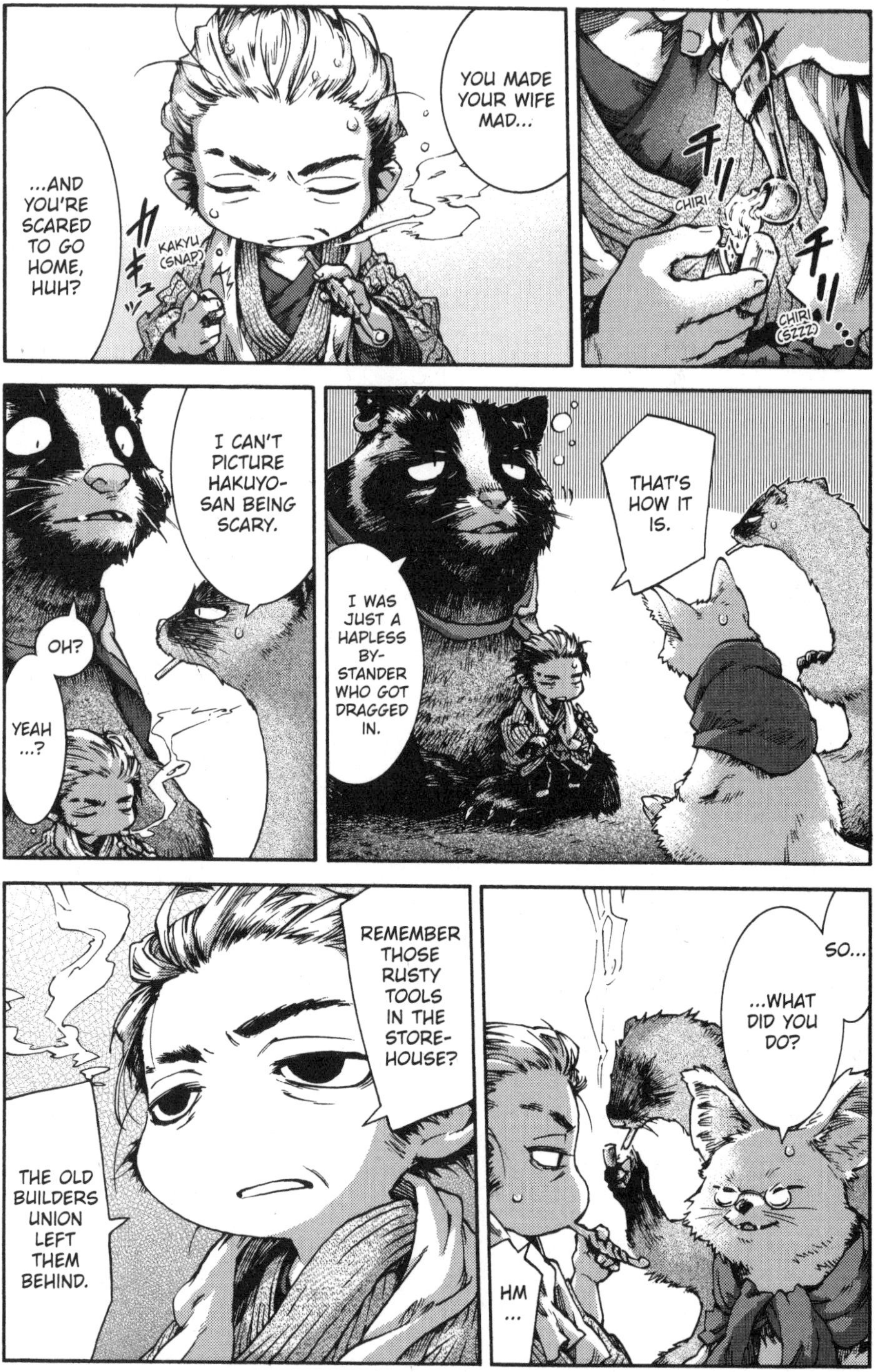
チリ
CHIRI
チリ…
CHIRI (SZZZ)
YOU MADE YOUR WIFE MAD...
...AND YOU'RE SCARED TO GO HOME, HUH?
カキュ
KAKYU (SNAP)
THAT'S HOW IT IS.
I WAS JUST A HAPLESS BY-STANDER WHO GOT DRAGGED IN.
I CAN'T PICTURE HAKUYO-SAN BEING SCARY.
OH?
YEAH ...?
SO...
...WHAT DID YOU DO?
HM ...
REMEMBER THOSE RUSTY TOOLS IN THE STORE-HOUSE?
THE OLD BUILDERS UNION LEFT THEM BEHIND.

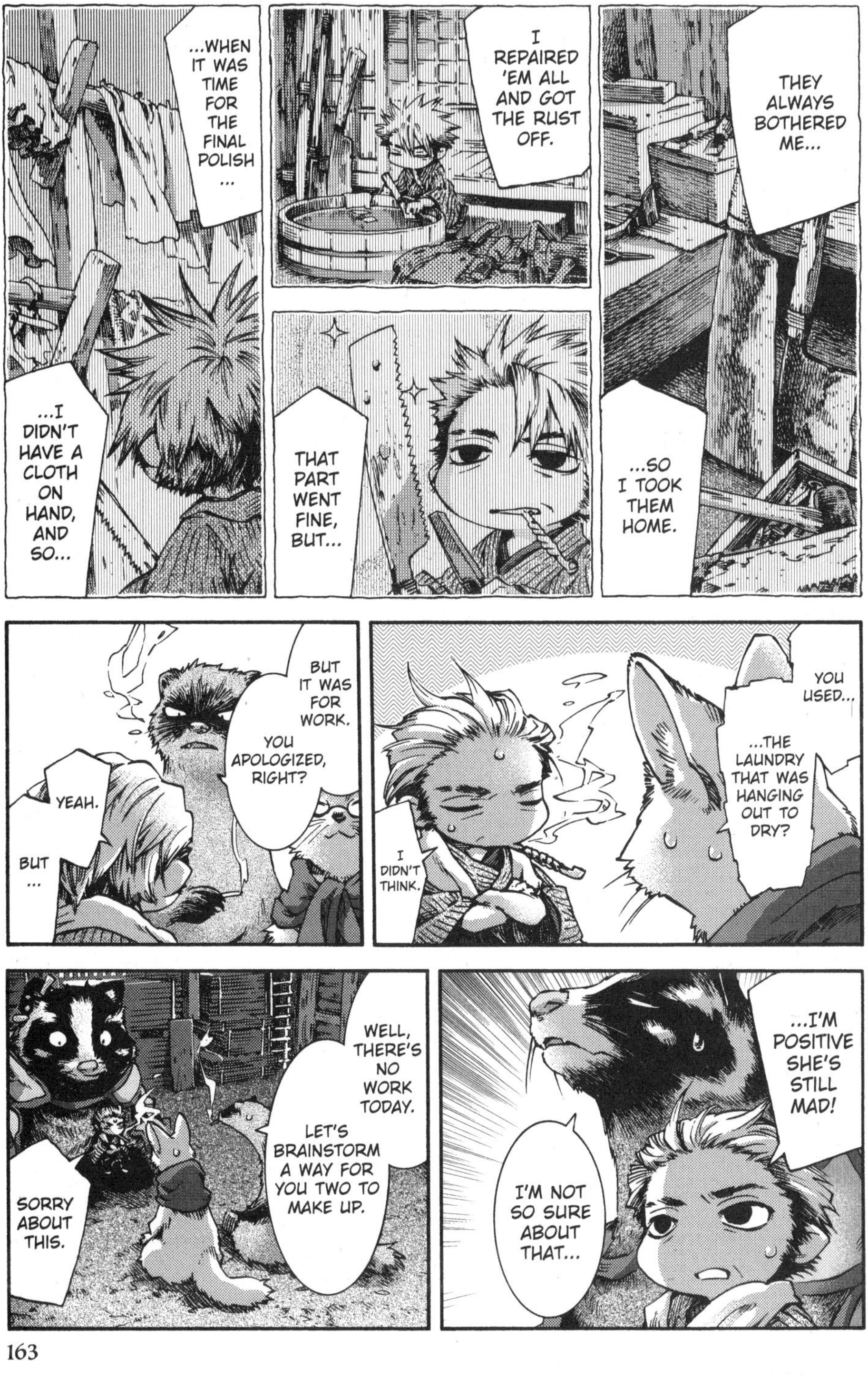
THEY ALWAYS BOTHERED ME...
...SO I TOOK THEM HOME.
I REPAIRED 'EM ALL AND GOT THE RUST OFF.
THAT PART WENT FINE, BUT...
...WHEN IT WAS TIME FOR THE FINAL POLISH...
...I DIDN'T HAVE A CLOTH ON HAND, AND SO...
YOU USED...
...THE LAUNDRY THAT WAS HANGING OUT TO DRY?
I DIDN'T THINK.
BUT IT WAS FOR WORK.
YOU APOLOGIZED, RIGHT?
YEAH.
BUT...
...I'M POSITIVE SHE'S STILL MAD!
I'M NOT SO SURE ABOUT THAT...
WELL, THERE'S NO WORK TODAY.
LET'S BRAINSTORM A WAY FOR YOU TWO TO MAKE UP.
SORRY ABOUT THIS.

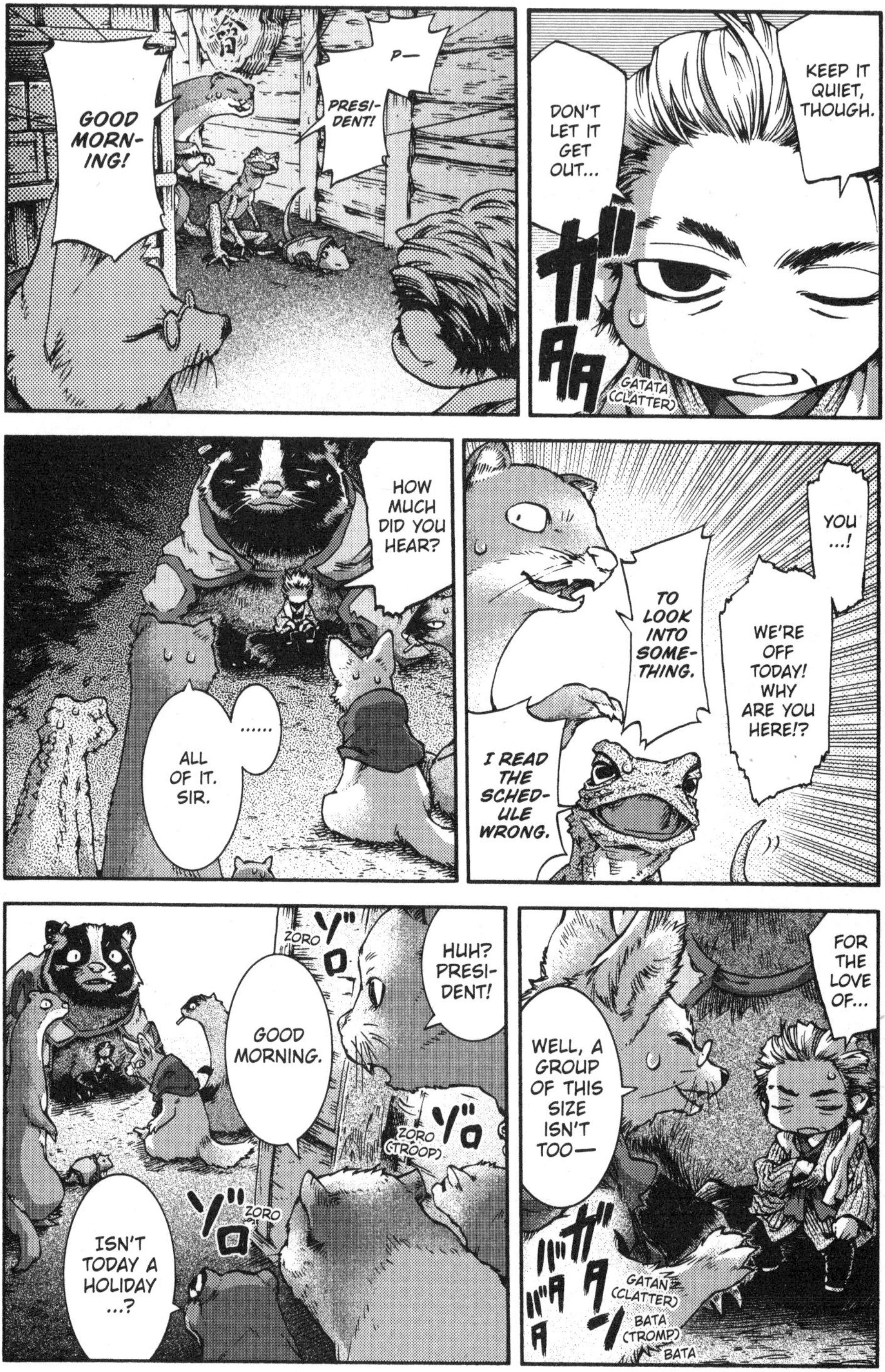
KEEP IT QUIET, THOUGH.
DON'T LET IT GET OUT...
GATATA (CLATTER)
P—
PRESIDENT!
GOOD MORNING!
YOU ...!
WE'RE OFF TODAY! WHY ARE YOU HERE!?
TO LOOK INTO SOMETHING.
I READ THE SCHEDULE WRONG.
HOW MUCH DID YOU HEAR?
......
ALL OF IT. SIR.
FOR THE LOVE OF...
WELL, A GROUP OF THIS SIZE ISN'T TOO—
GATAN (CLATTER)
BATA (TROMP) BATA
HUH? PRESIDENT!
ZORO
GOOD MORNING.
ZORO (TROOP)
ZORO
ISN'T TODAY A HOLIDAY ...?

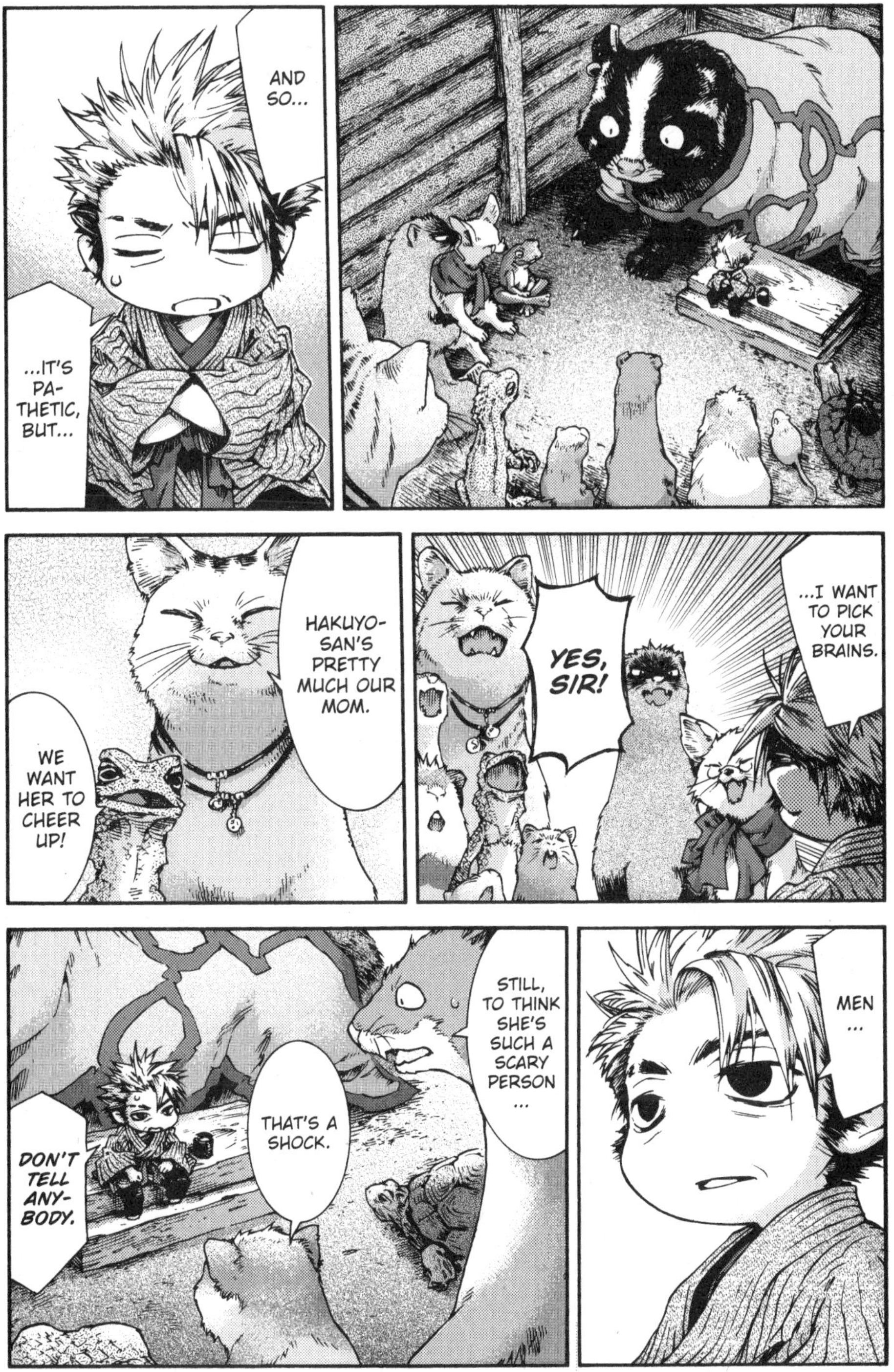
AND SO...
...IT'S PATHETIC, BUT...
...I WANT TO PICK YOUR BRAINS.
YES, SIR!
HAKUYO-SAN'S PRETTY MUCH OUR MOM.
WE WANT HER TO CHEER UP!
MEN ...
STILL, TO THINK SHE'S SUCH A SCARY PERSON ...
THAT'S A SHOCK.
DON'T TELL ANYBODY.

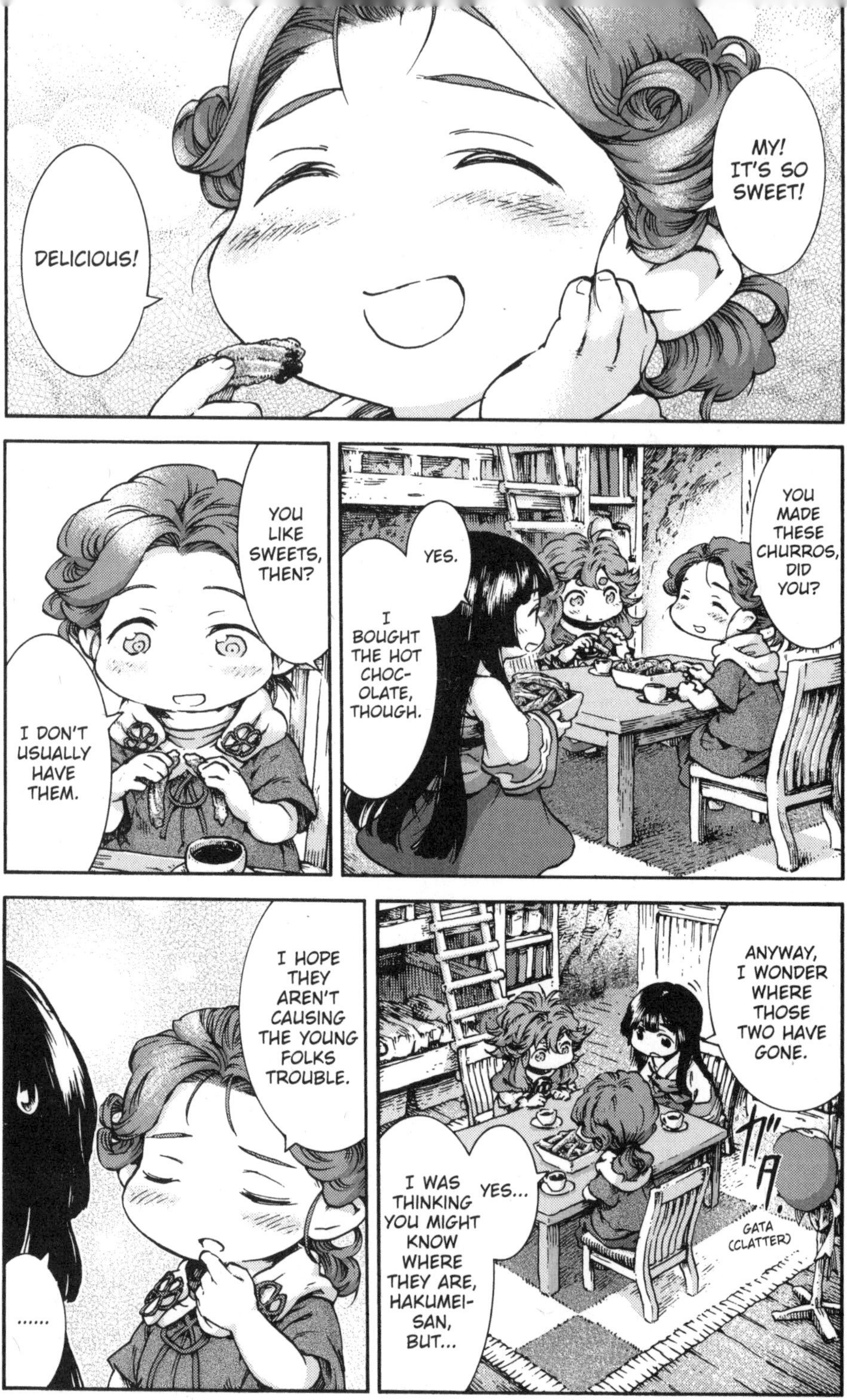
MY! IT'S SO SWEET!
DELICIOUS!
YOU MADE THESE CHURROS, DID YOU?
YES.
I BOUGHT THE HOT CHOC-OLATE, THOUGH.
YOU LIKE SWEETS, THEN?
I DON'T USUALLY HAVE THEM.
ANYWAY, I WONDER WHERE THOSE TWO HAVE GONE.
YES...
I WAS THINKING YOU MIGHT KNOW WHERE THEY ARE, HAKUMEI-SAN, BUT...
GATA (CLATTER)
I HOPE THEY AREN'T CAUSING THE YOUNG FOLKS TROUBLE.
......

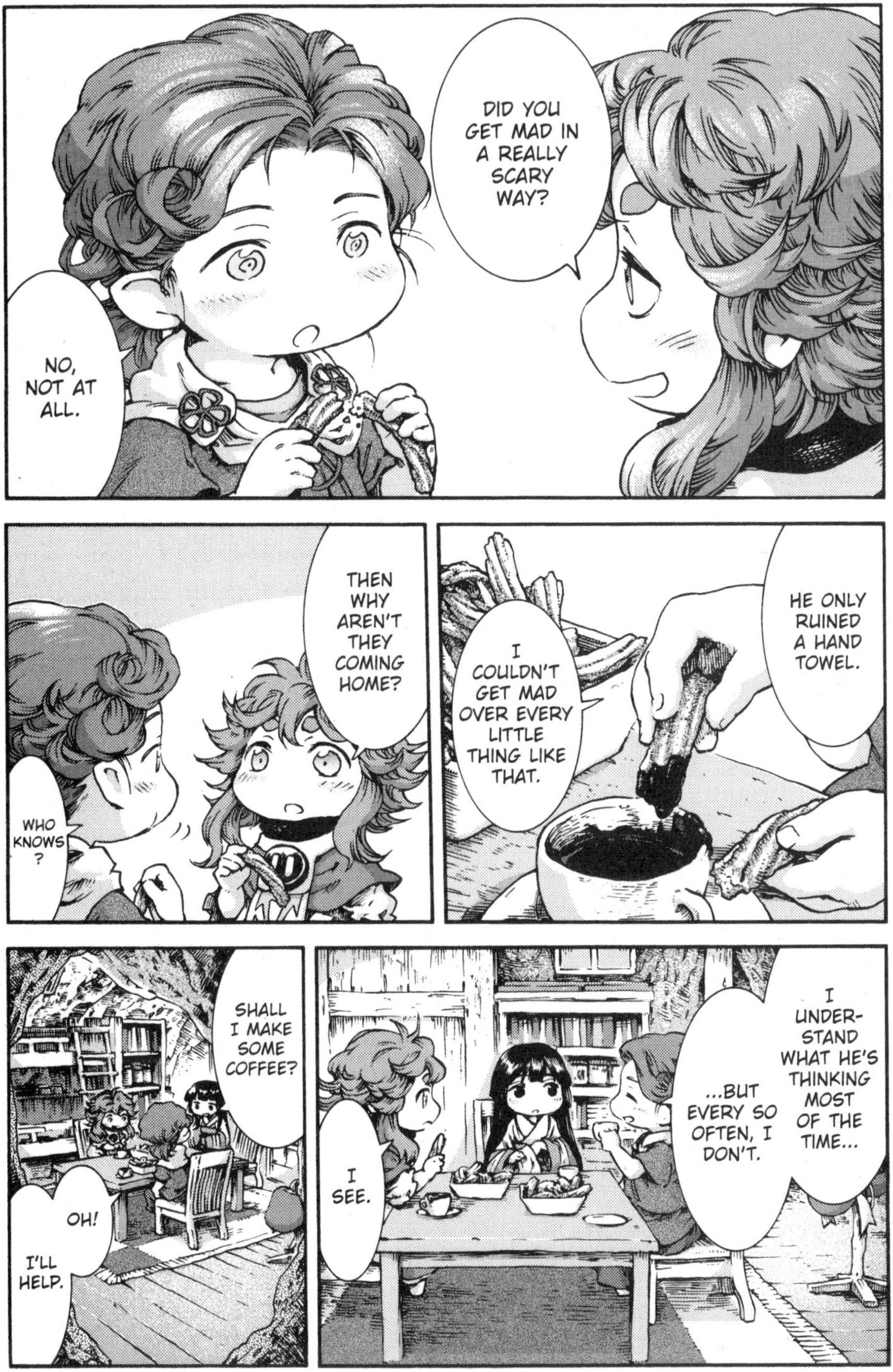
DID YOU GET MAD IN A REALLY SCARY WAY?
NO, NOT AT ALL.
HE ONLY RUINED A HAND TOWEL.
I COULDN'T GET MAD OVER EVERY LITTLE THING LIKE THAT.
THEN WHY AREN'T THEY COMING HOME?
WHO KNOWS?
I UNDER-STAND WHAT HE'S THINKING MOST OF THE TIME...
...BUT EVERY SO OFTEN, I DON'T.
I SEE.
SHALL I MAKE SOME COFFEE?
OH!
I'LL HELP.

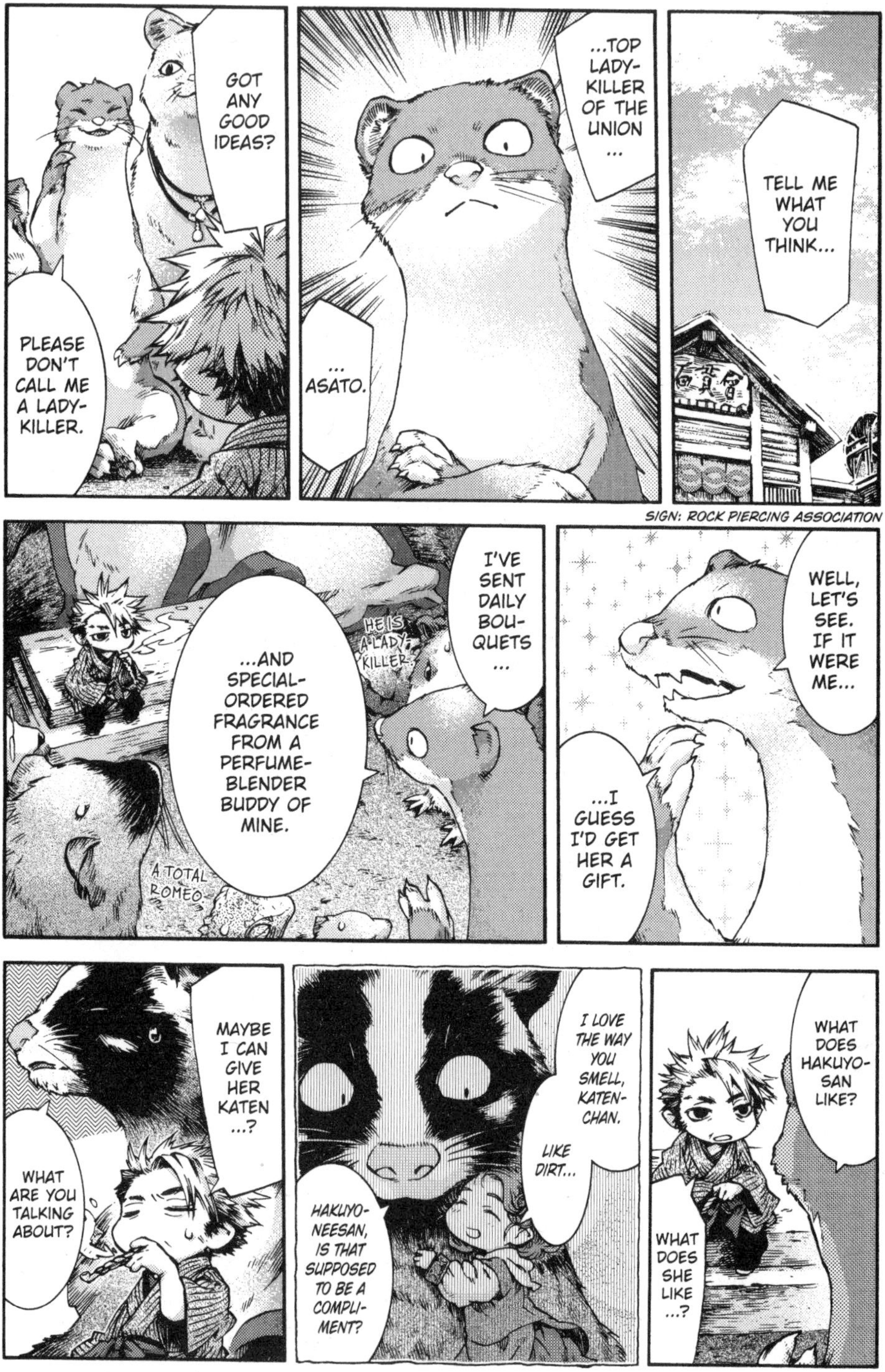
TELL ME WHAT YOU THINK...
...TOP LADY-KILLER OF THE UNION...
...ASATO.
GOT ANY GOOD IDEAS?
PLEASE DON'T CALL ME A LADY-KILLER.
SIGN: ROCK PIERCING ASSOCIATION
WELL, LET'S SEE. IF IT WERE ME...
...I GUESS I'D GET HER A GIFT.
I'VE SENT DAILY BOUQUETS...
...AND SPECIAL-ORDERED FRAGRANCE FROM A PERFUME-BLENDER BUDDY OF MINE.
HE IS A LADY-KILLER.
A TOTAL ROMEO.
WHAT DOES HAKUYO-SAN LIKE?
WHAT DOES SHE LIKE...?
I LOVE THE WAY YOU SMELL, KATEN-CHAN.
LIKE DIRT...
HAKUYO-NEESAN, IS THAT SUPPOSED TO BE A COMPLIMENT?
MAYBE I CAN GIVE HER KATEN...?
WHAT ARE YOU TALKING ABOUT?

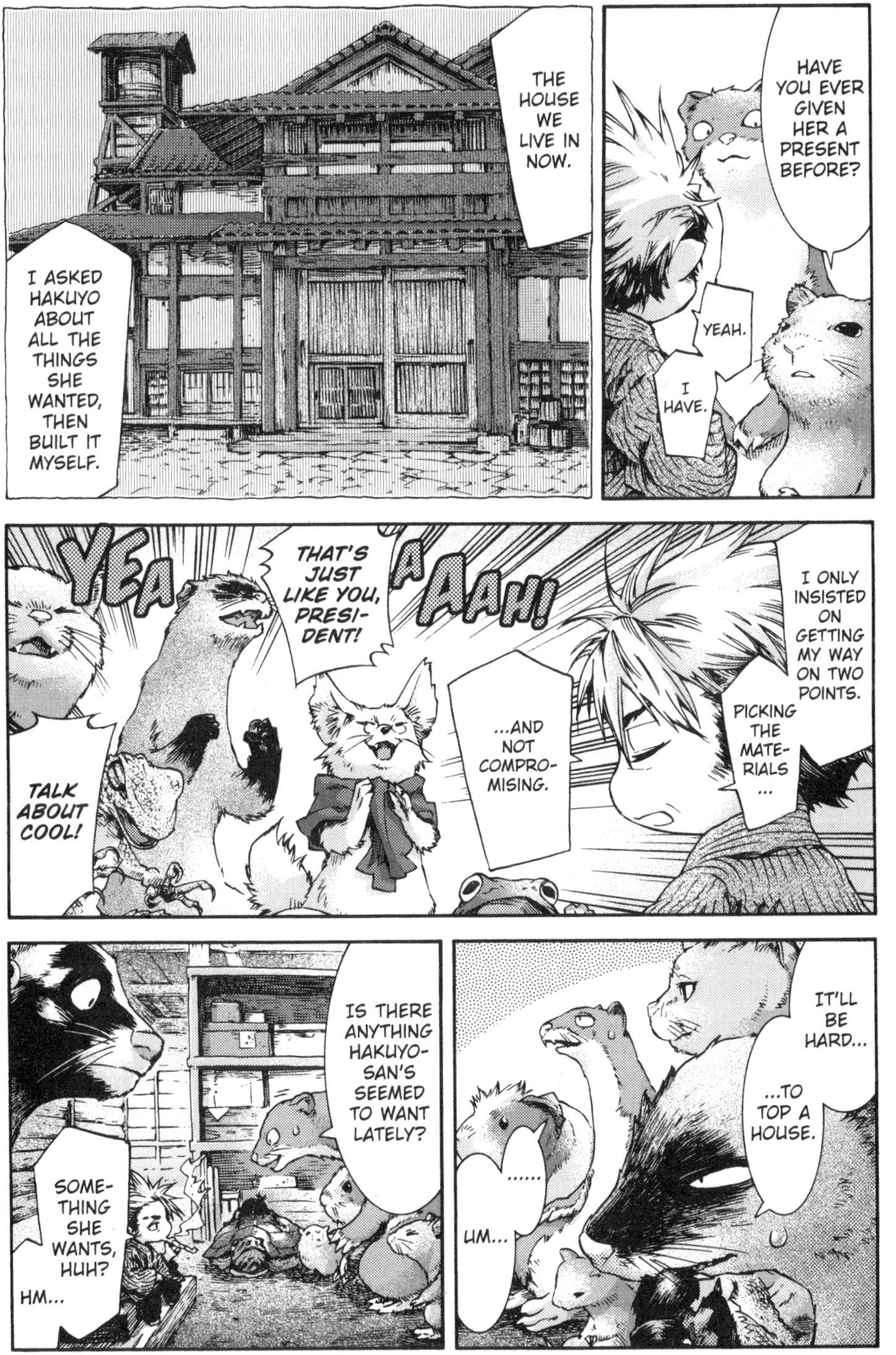
HAVE YOU EVER GIVEN HER A PRESENT BEFORE?
YEAH.
I HAVE.
THE HOUSE WE LIVE IN NOW.
I ASKED HAKUYO ABOUT ALL THE THINGS SHE WANTED, THEN BUILT IT MYSELF.
I ONLY INSISTED ON GETTING MY WAY ON TWO POINTS.
PICKING THE MATE-RIALS...
...AND NOT COMPRO-MISING.
YEA AAAH!
THAT'S JUST LIKE YOU, PRESI-DENT!
TALK ABOUT COOL!
IT'LL BE HARD...
...TO TOP A HOUSE.
......
UM...
IS THERE ANYTHING HAKUYO-SAN'S SEEMED TO WANT LATELY?
SOME-THING SHE WANTS, HUH?
HM...

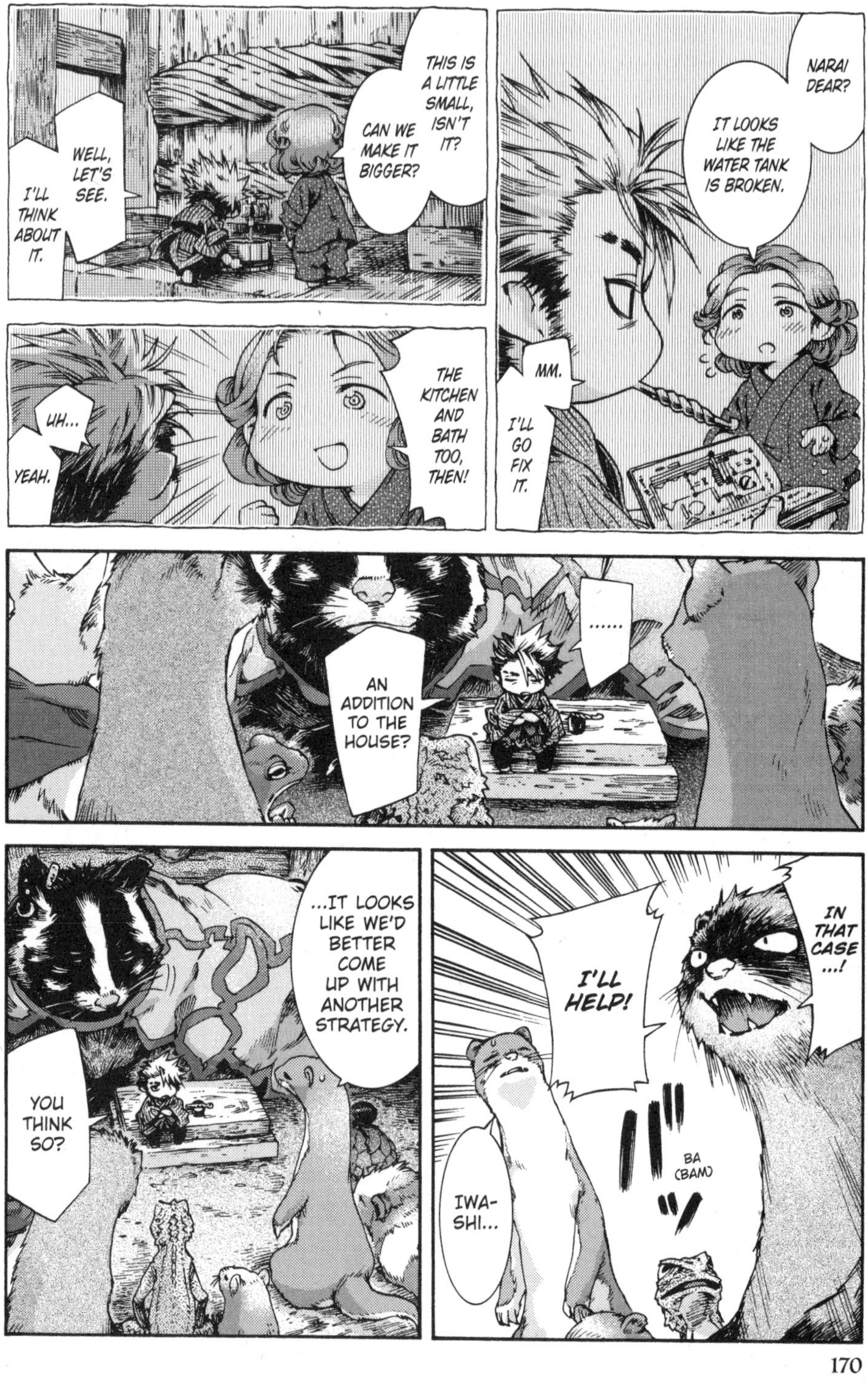
THIS IS A LITTLE SMALL, ISN'T IT?
CAN WE MAKE IT BIGGER?
WELL, LET'S SEE.
I'LL THINK ABOUT IT.
THE KITCHEN AND BATH TOO, THEN!
UH...
YEAH.
NARAI DEAR?
IT LOOKS LIKE THE WATER TANK IS BROKEN.
MM.
I'LL GO FIX IT.
AN ADDITION TO THE HOUSE?
......
...IT LOOKS LIKE WE'D BETTER COME UP WITH ANOTHER STRATEGY.
YOU THINK SO?
IN THAT CASE...!
I'LL HELP!
BA (BAM)
IWASHI...

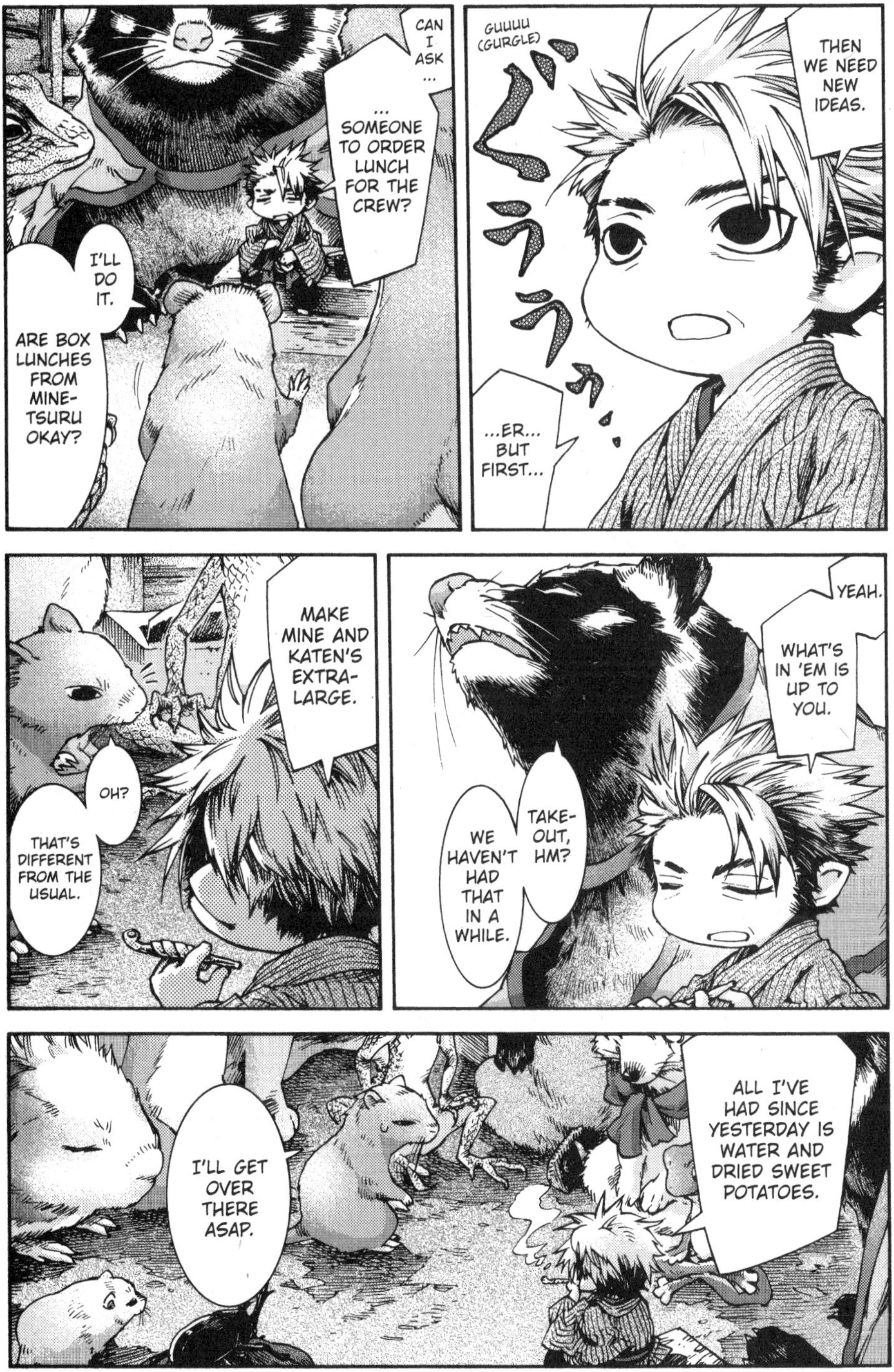
GUUUU (GURGLE)
THEN WE NEED NEW IDEAS.
...ER... BUT FIRST...
CAN I ASK ...
... SOMEONE TO ORDER LUNCH FOR THE CREW?
I'LL DO IT.
ARE BOX LUNCHES FROM MINE-TSURU OKAY?
YEAH.
WHAT'S IN 'EM IS UP TO YOU.
TAKE-OUT, HM?
WE HAVEN'T HAD THAT IN A WHILE.
MAKE MINE AND KATEN'S EXTRA-LARGE.
OH?
THAT'S DIFFERENT FROM THE USUAL.
ALL I'VE HAD SINCE YESTERDAY IS WATER AND DRIED SWEET POTATOES.
I'LL GET OVER THERE ASAP.

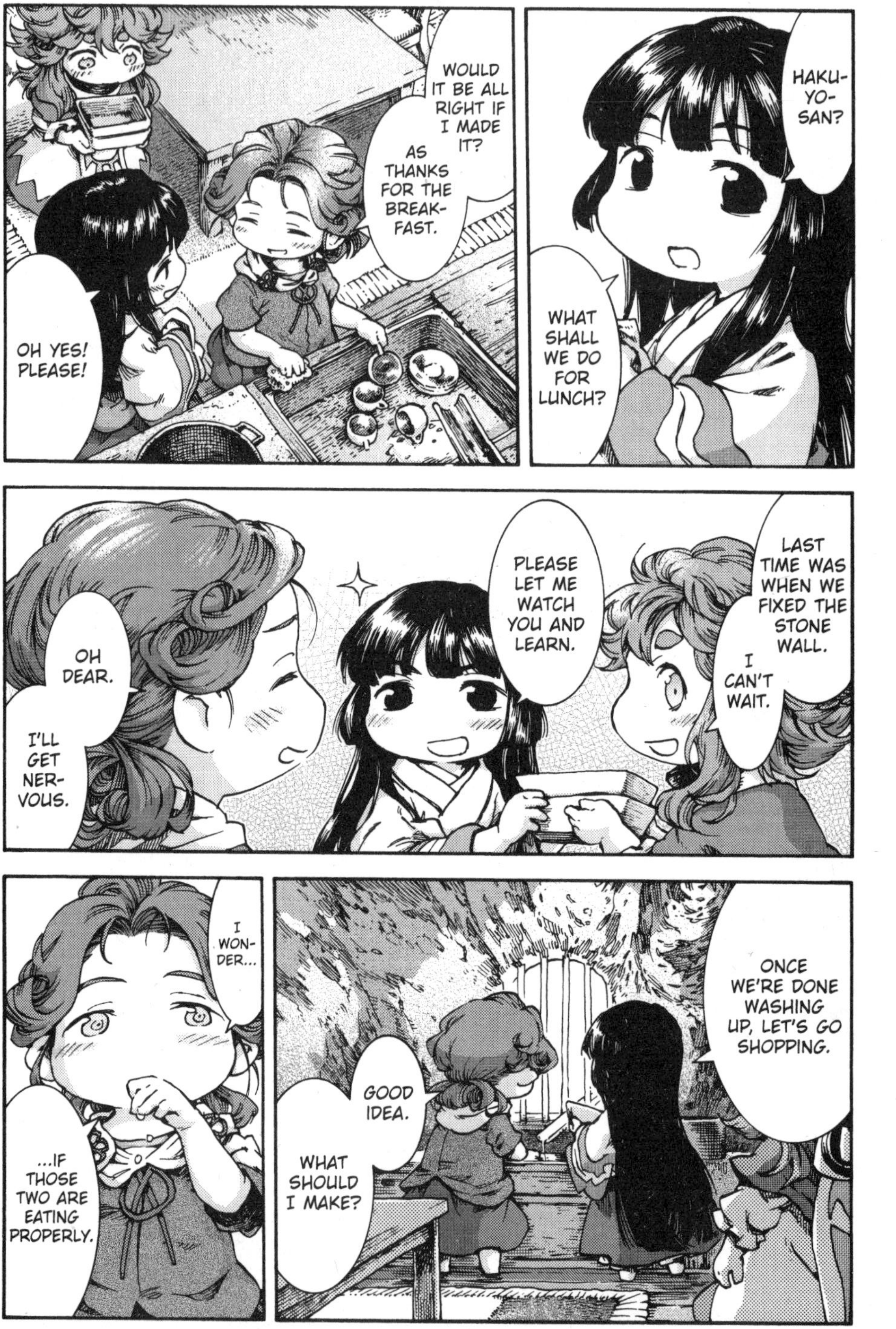
HAKU-YO-SAN?
WHAT SHALL WE DO FOR LUNCH?
WOULD IT BE ALL RIGHT IF I MADE IT?
AS THANKS FOR THE BREAK-FAST.
OH YES! PLEASE!
LAST TIME WAS WHEN WE FIXED THE STONE WALL.
I CAN'T WAIT.
PLEASE LET ME WATCH YOU AND LEARN.
OH DEAR.
I'LL GET NER-VOUS.
ONCE WE'RE DONE WASHING UP, LET'S GO SHOPPING.
GOOD IDEA.
WHAT SHOULD I MAKE?
I WON-DER...
...IF THOSE TWO ARE EATING PROPERLY.

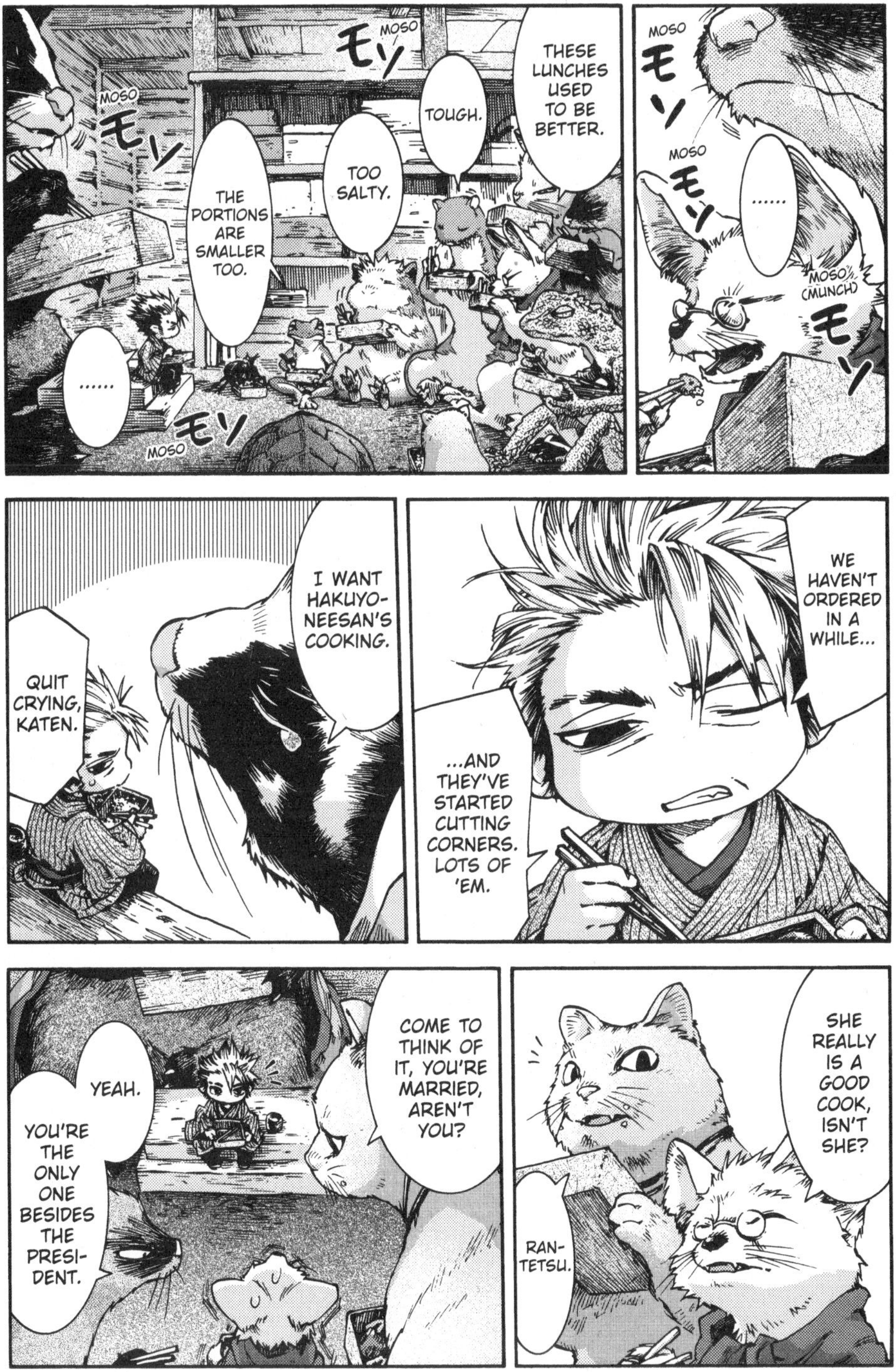
MOSO
モソ
MOSO
モソ
......
MOSO (MUNCH)
モソ
THESE LUNCHES USED TO BE BETTER.
TOUGH.
MOSO
モソ
TOO SALTY.
MOSO
モソ
THE PORTIONS ARE SMALLER TOO.
......
MOSO
モソ
WE HAVEN'T ORDERED IN A WHILE...
...AND THEY'VE STARTED CUTTING CORNERS. LOTS OF 'EM.
I WANT HAKUYO-NEESAN'S COOKING.
QUIT CRYING, KATEN.
SHE REALLY IS A GOOD COOK, ISN'T SHE?
RAN-TETSU.
COME TO THINK OF IT, YOU'RE MARRIED, AREN'T YOU?
YEAH.
YOU'RE THE ONLY ONE BESIDES THE PRESIDENT.

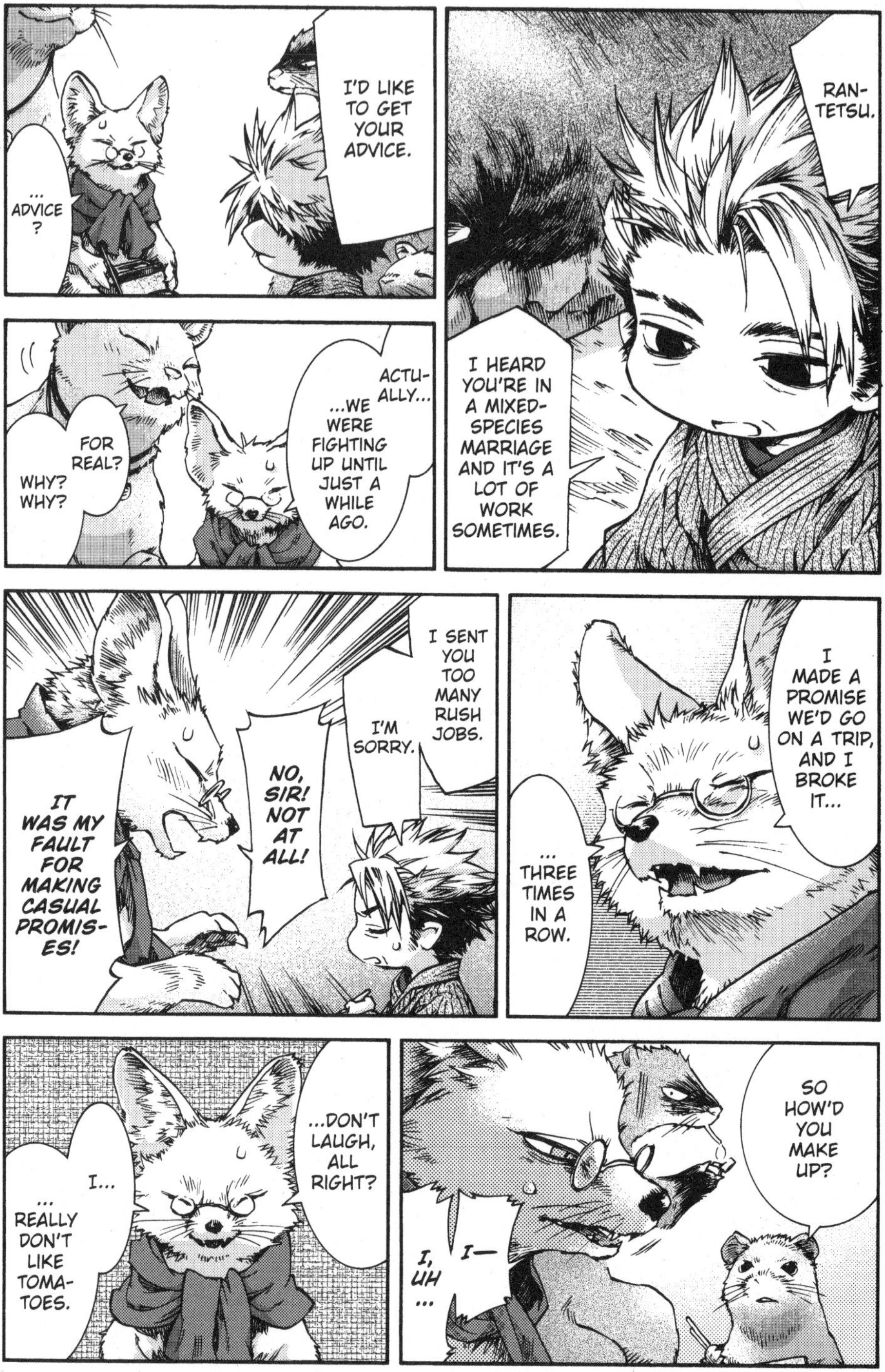
RAN-TETSU.
I HEARD YOU'RE IN A MIXED-SPECIES MARRIAGE AND IT'S A LOT OF WORK SOMETIMES.
I'D LIKE TO GET YOUR ADVICE.
...ADVICE?
ACTU-ALLY...
...WE WERE FIGHTING UP UNTIL JUST A WHILE AGO.
FOR REAL?
WHY? WHY?
I MADE A PROMISE WE'D GO ON A TRIP, AND I BROKE IT...
...THREE TIMES IN A ROW.
I SENT YOU TOO MANY RUSH JOBS.
I'M SORRY.
NO, SIR! NOT AT ALL!
IT WAS MY FAULT FOR MAKING CASUAL PROMIS-ES!
SO HOW'D YOU MAKE UP?
I—
I, UH...
...DON'T LAUGH, ALL RIGHT?
I...
...REALLY DON'T LIKE TOMA-TOES.

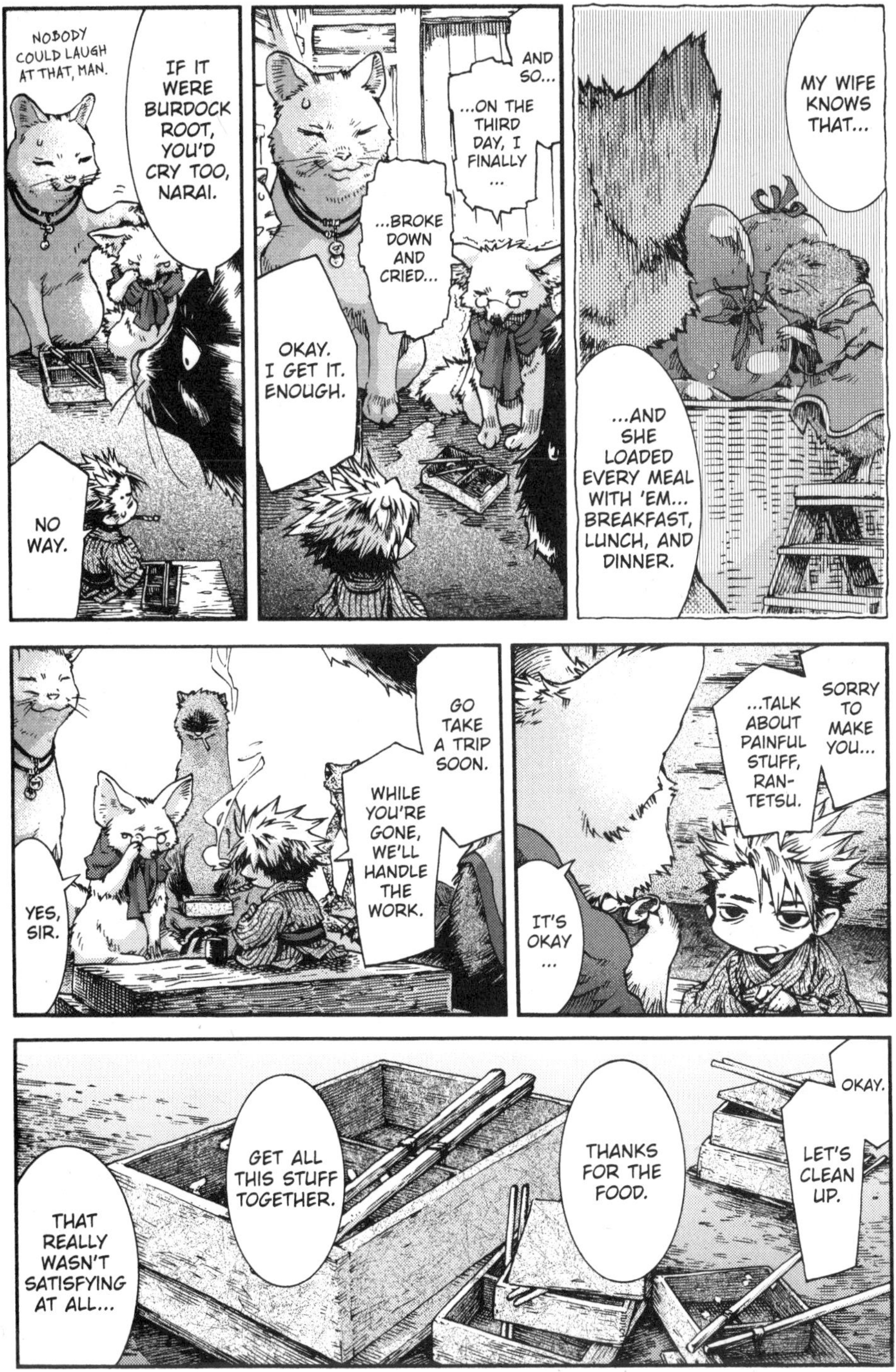
MY WIFE KNOWS THAT...
...AND SHE LOADED EVERY MEAL WITH 'EM... BREAKFAST, LUNCH, AND DINNER.
AND SO...
...ON THE THIRD DAY, I FINALLY...
...BROKE DOWN AND CRIED...
OKAY. I GET IT. ENOUGH.
IF IT WERE BURDOCK ROOT, YOU'D CRY TOO, NARAI.
NOBODY COULD LAUGH AT THAT, MAN.
NO WAY.
SORRY TO MAKE YOU...
...TALK ABOUT PAINFUL STUFF, RAN-TETSU.
IT'S OKAY...
GO TAKE A TRIP SOON.
WHILE YOU'RE GONE, WE'LL HANDLE THE WORK.
YES, SIR.
OKAY.
LET'S CLEAN UP.
THANKS FOR THE FOOD.
GET ALL THIS STUFF TOGETHER.
THAT REALLY WASN'T SATISFYING AT ALL...

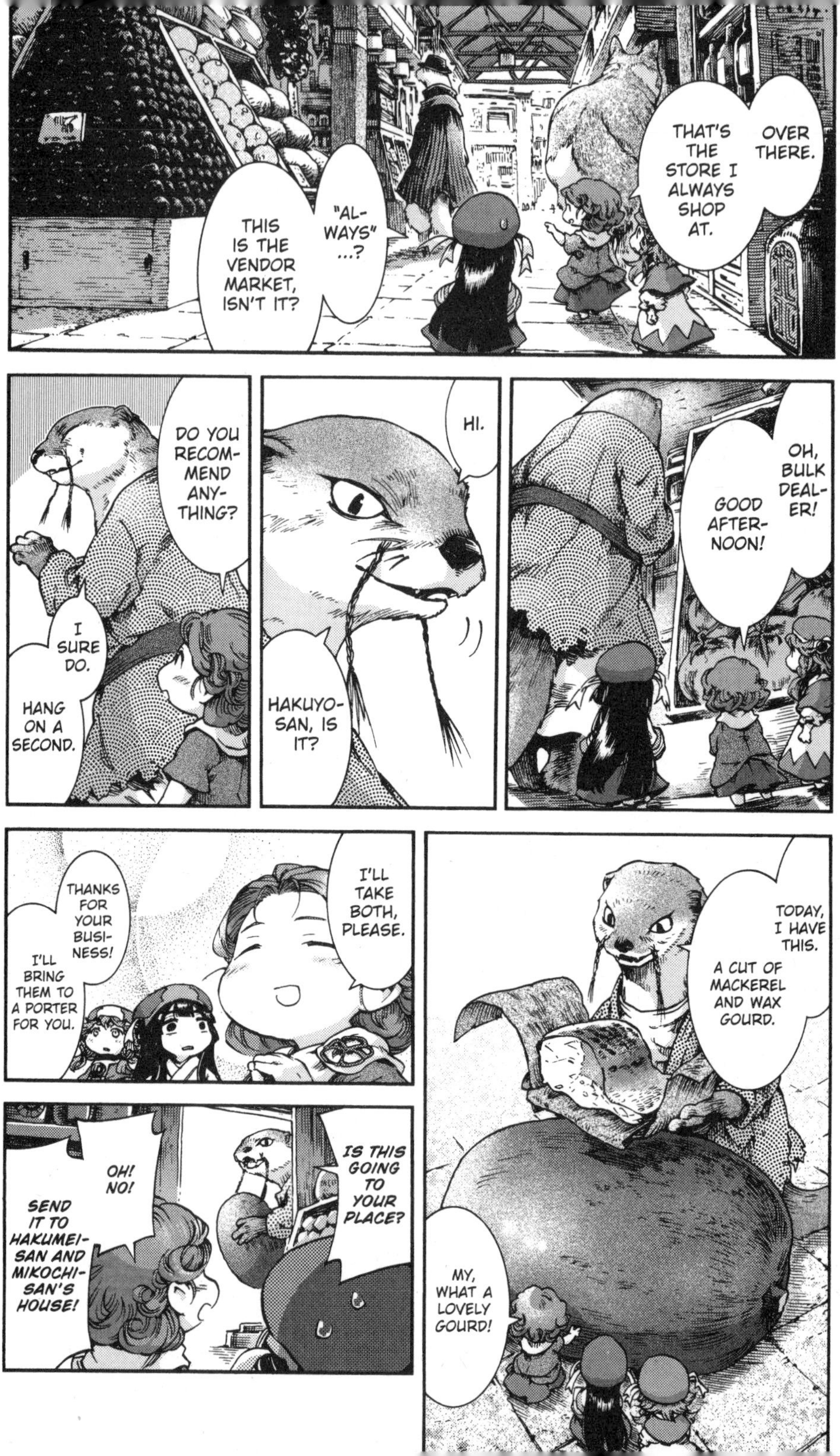
OVER THERE.
THAT'S THE STORE I ALWAYS SHOP AT.
"AL-WAYS"...?
THIS IS THE VENDOR MARKET, ISN'T IT?
OH, BULK DEALER!
GOOD AFTERNOON!
HI.
HAKUYO-SAN, IS IT?
DO YOU RECOMMEND ANYTHING?
I SURE DO.
HANG ON A SECOND.
TODAY, I HAVE THIS.
A CUT OF MACKEREL AND WAX GOURD.
MY, WHAT A LOVELY GOURD!
I'LL TAKE BOTH, PLEASE.
THANKS FOR YOUR BUSINESS!
I'LL BRING THEM TO A PORTER FOR YOU.
IS THIS GOING TO YOUR PLACE?
OH! NO!
SEND IT TO HAKUMEI-SAN AND MIKOCHI-SAN'S HOUSE!

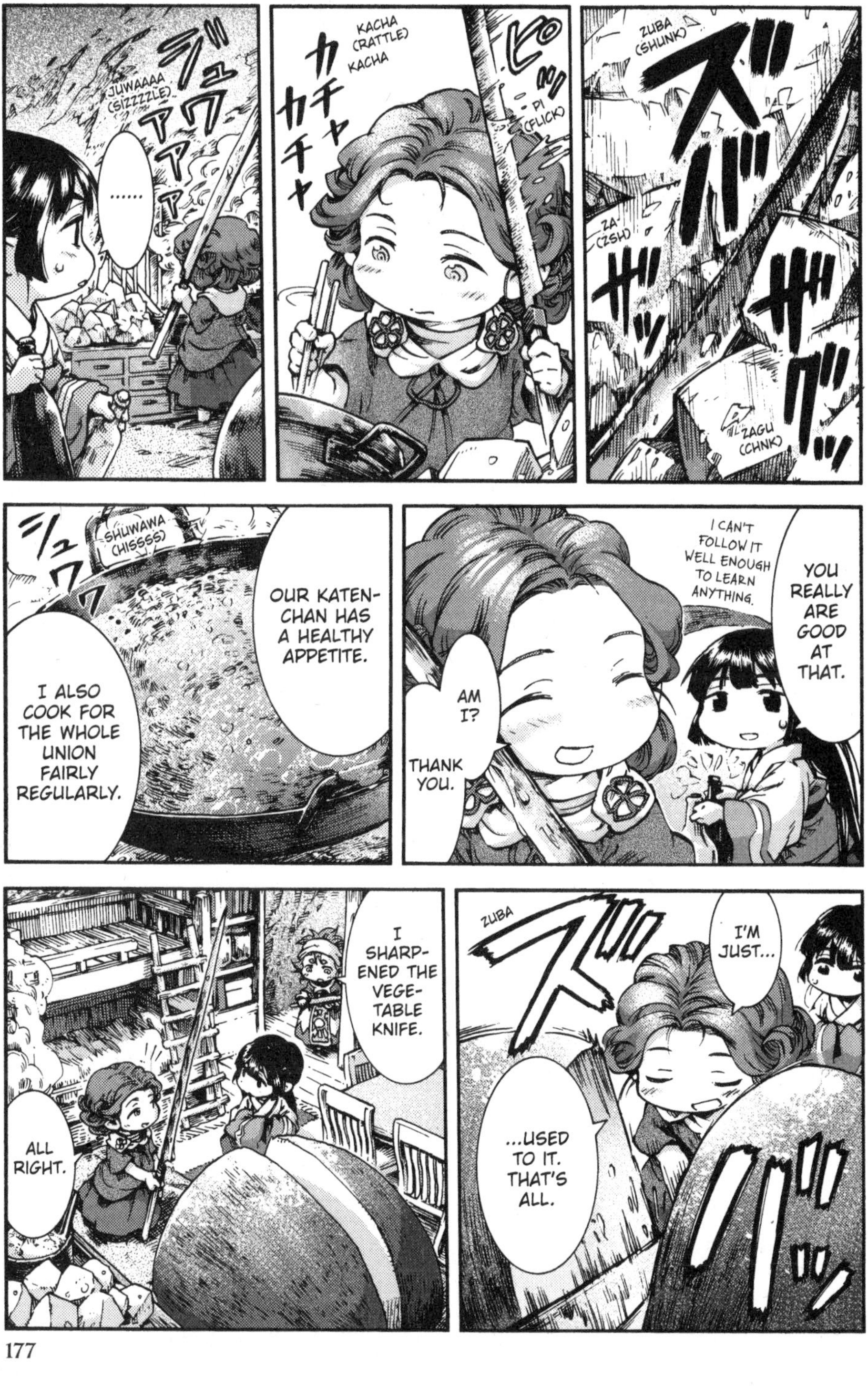
ZUBA (SHUNK)
ズバ
ZA (ZSH)
ザッ
ザグッ
ZAGU (CHNK)
KACHA (RATTLE) KACHA
カチャカチャ
ピッ
PI (FLICK)
ジュワアアア
JUWAAAA (SIZZZZLE)
......
YOU REALLY ARE GOOD AT THAT.
I CAN'T FOLLOW IT WELL ENOUGH TO LEARN ANYTHING.
AM I?
THANK YOU.
シュワワ
SHUWAWA (HISSSSS)
OUR KATEN-CHAN HAS A HEALTHY APPETITE.
I ALSO COOK FOR THE WHOLE UNION FAIRLY REGULARLY.
ZUBA
I'M JUST...
...USED TO IT. THAT'S ALL.
I SHARPENED THE VEGETABLE KNIFE.
ALL RIGHT.

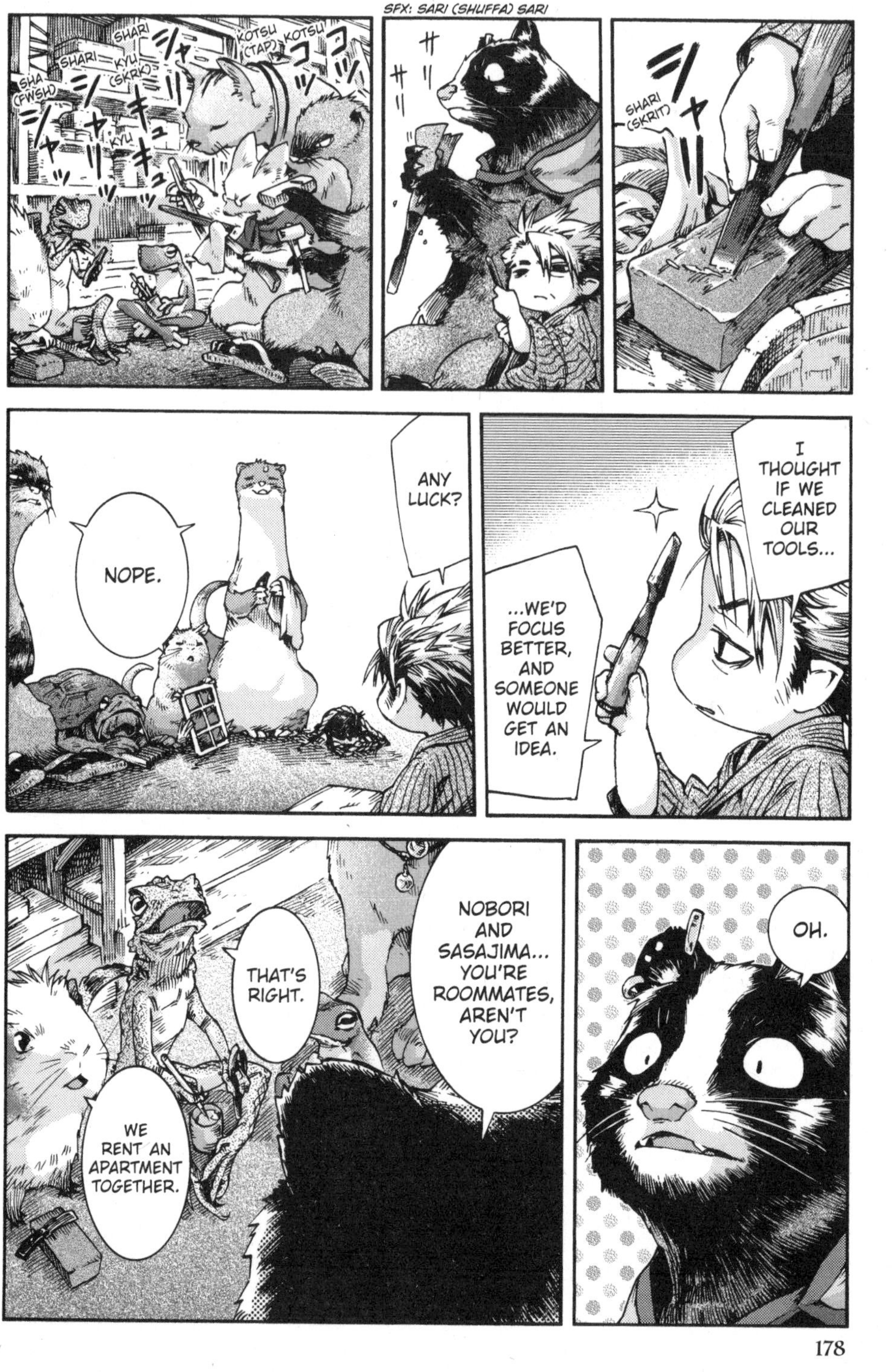
SHARI (SKRIT)
SFX: SARI (SHUFFA) SARI
KOTSU (TAP) KOTSU
SHARI
SHARI
KYU (SKRK)
KYU
SHA (FWSH)
I THOUGHT IF WE CLEANED OUR TOOLS...
...WE'D FOCUS BETTER, AND SOMEONE WOULD GET AN IDEA.
ANY LUCK?
NOPE.
OH.
NOBORI AND SASAJIMA... YOU'RE ROOMMATES, AREN'T YOU?
THAT'S RIGHT.
WE RENT AN APARTMENT TOGETHER.

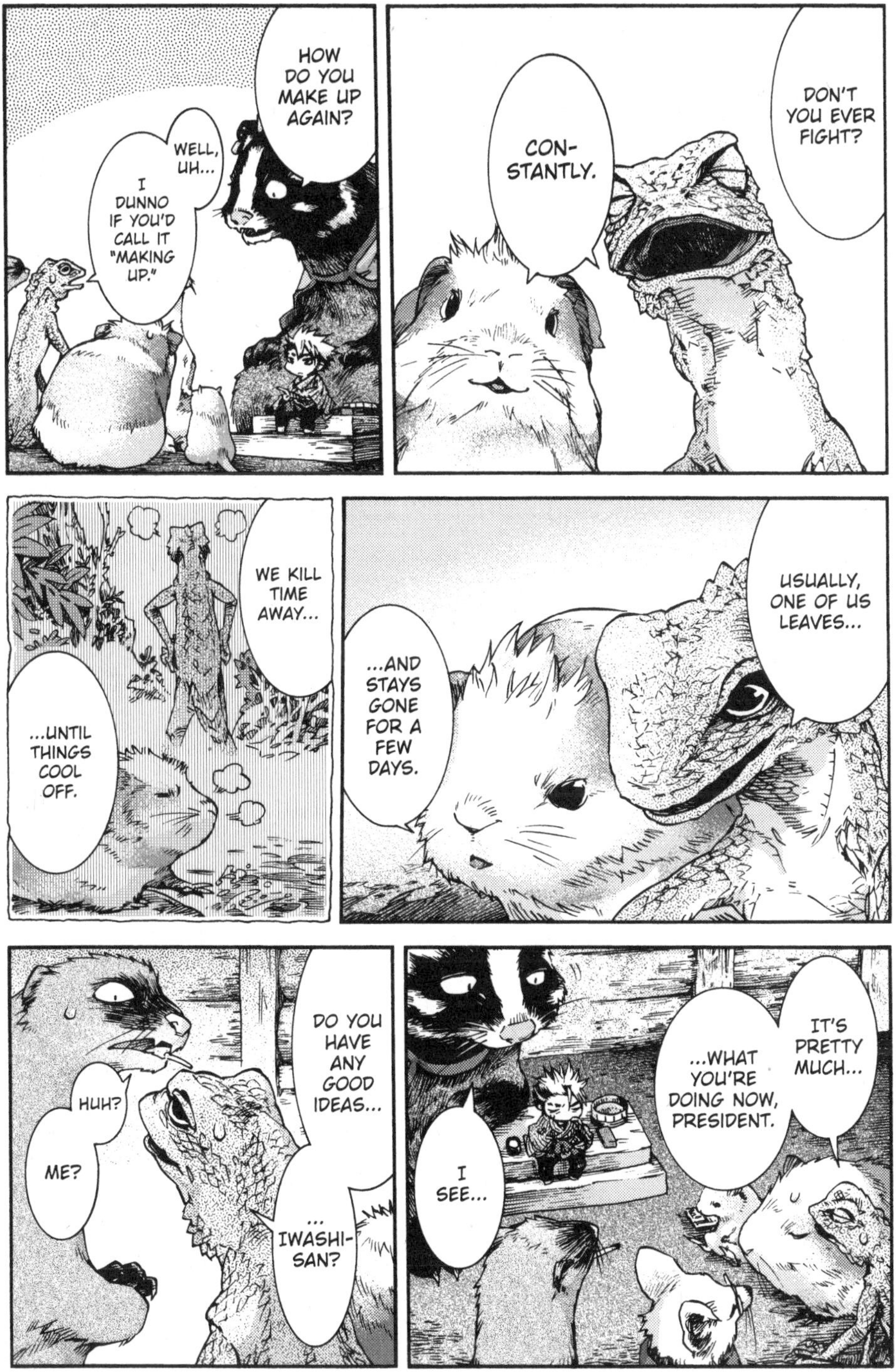
DON'T YOU EVER FIGHT?
CON-STANTLY.
HOW DO YOU MAKE UP AGAIN?
WELL, UH...
I DUNNO IF YOU'D CALL IT "MAKING UP."
USUALLY, ONE OF US LEAVES...
...AND STAYS GONE FOR A FEW DAYS.
WE KILL TIME AWAY...
...UNTIL THINGS COOL OFF.
IT'S PRETTY MUCH...
...WHAT YOU'RE DOING NOW, PRESIDENT.
I SEE...
DO YOU HAVE ANY GOOD IDEAS...
...IWASHI-SAN?
HUH?
ME?

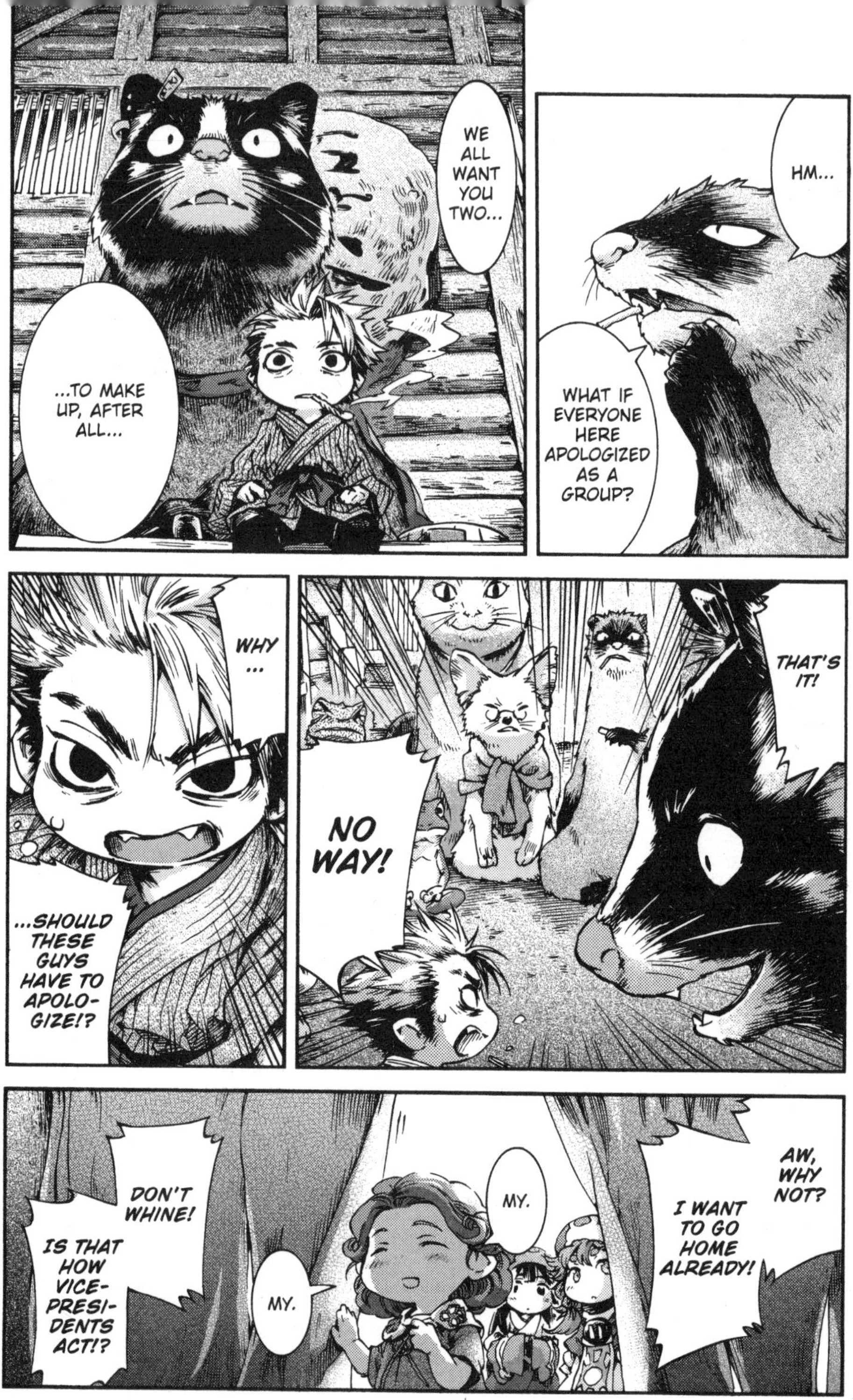
HM...
WHAT IF EVERYONE HERE APOLOGIZED AS A GROUP?
WE ALL WANT YOU TWO...
...TO MAKE UP, AFTER ALL...
THAT'S IT!
NO WAY!
WHY...
...SHOULD THESE GUYS HAVE TO APOLOGIZE!?
AW, WHY NOT?
I WANT TO GO HOME ALREADY!
MY.
MY.
DON'T WHINE!
IS THAT HOW VICE-PRESIDENTS ACT!?

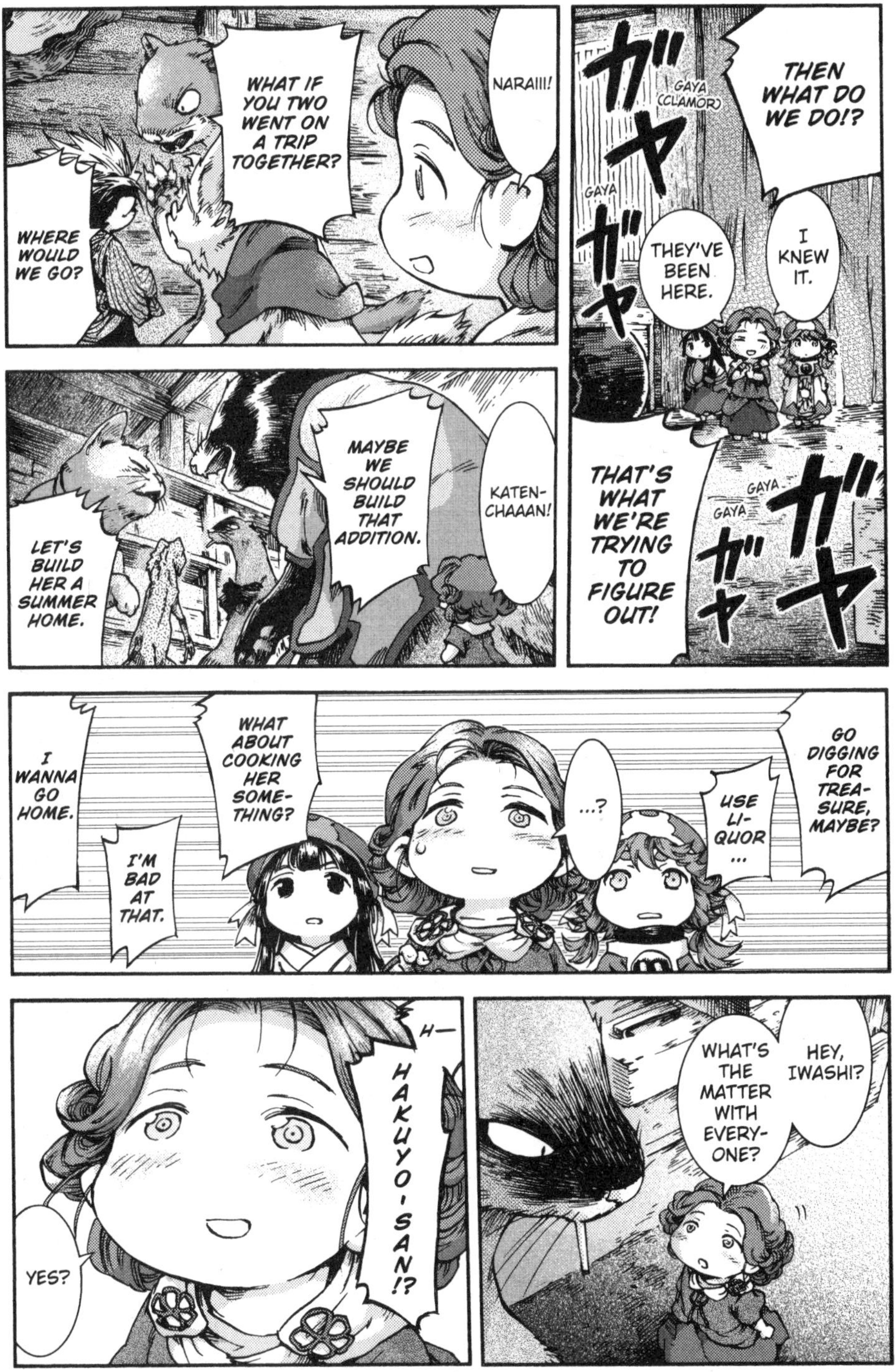
THEN WHAT DO WE DO!?
GAYA (CLAMOR)
GAYA
I KNEW IT.
THEY'VE BEEN HERE.
THAT'S WHAT WE'RE TRYING TO FIGURE OUT!
GAYA
GAYA
NARAIII!
WHAT IF YOU TWO WENT ON A TRIP TOGETHER?
WHERE WOULD WE GO?
KATEN-CHAAAN!
MAYBE WE SHOULD BUILD THAT ADDITION.
LET'S BUILD HER A SUMMER HOME.
GO DIGGING FOR TREASURE, MAYBE?
USE LIQUOR...
...?
WHAT ABOUT COOKING HER SOMETHING?
I'M BAD AT THAT.
I WANNA GO HOME.
HEY, IWASHI?
WHAT'S THE MATTER WITH EVERYONE?
H— HAKUYO-SAN!?
YES?

SFX: ZAWA (MURMUR) ZAWA

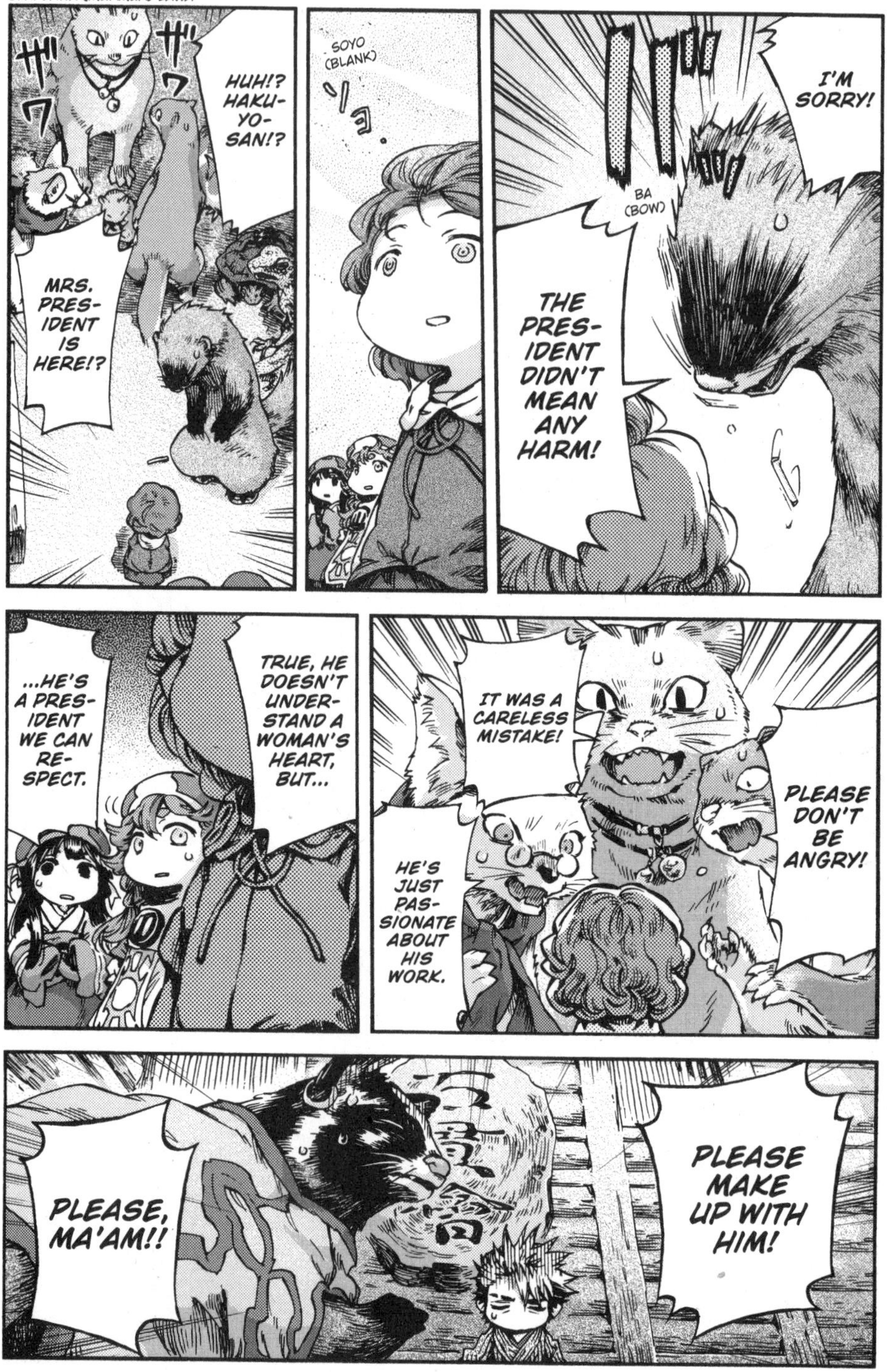
I'M SORRY!
BA (BOW)
THE PRESIDENT DIDN'T MEAN ANY HARM!
SOYO (BLANK)
HUH!? HAKUYO-SAN!?
MRS. PRESIDENT IS HERE!?
IT WAS A CARELESS MISTAKE!
PLEASE DON'T BE ANGRY!
HE'S JUST PASSIONATE ABOUT HIS WORK.
TRUE, HE DOESN'T UNDERSTAND A WOMAN'S HEART, BUT...
...HE'S A PRESIDENT WE CAN RESPECT.
PLEASE MAKE UP WITH HIM!
PLEASE, MA'AM!!

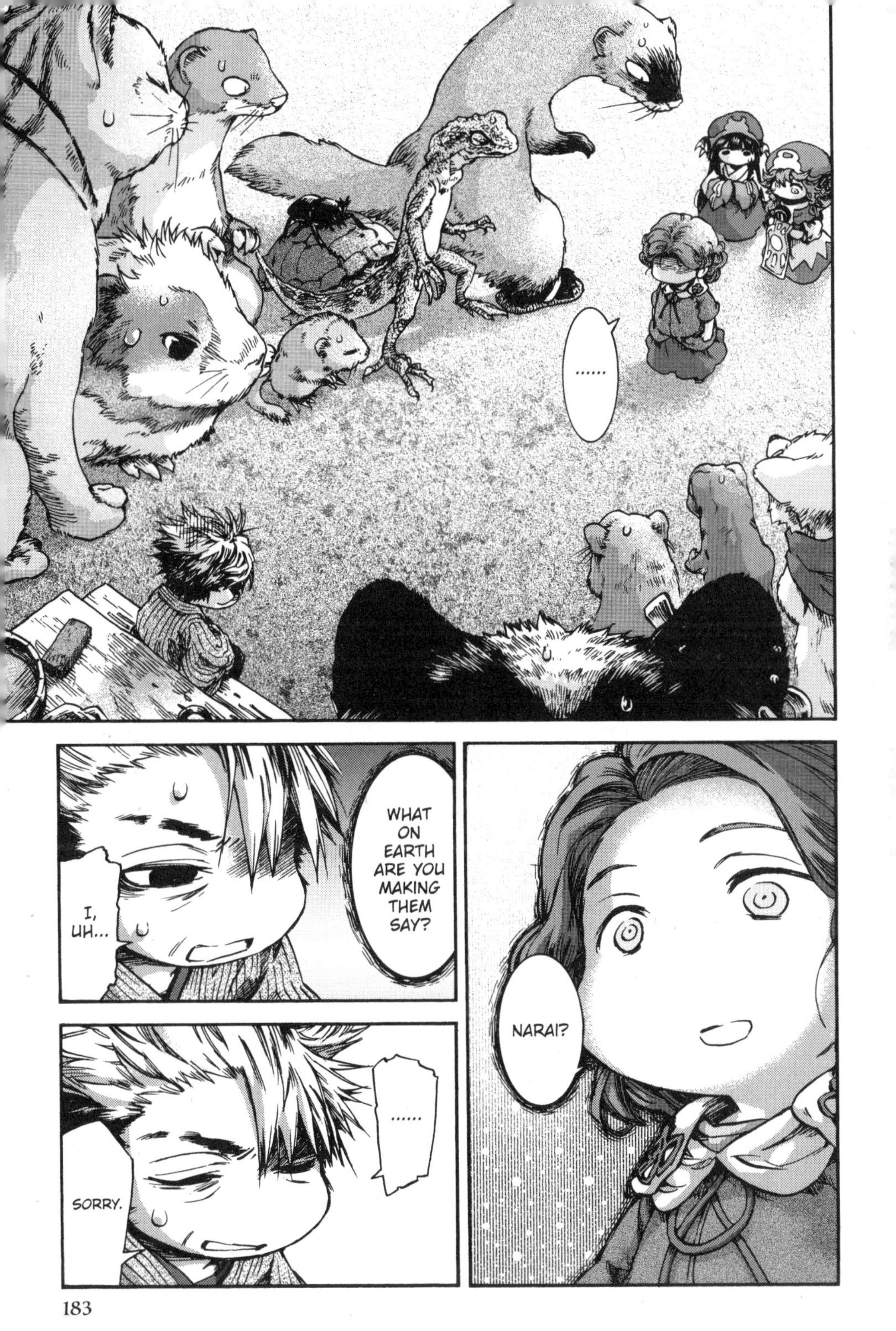
......
NARAI?
WHAT ON EARTH ARE YOU MAKING THEM SAY?
I, UH...
......
SORRY.

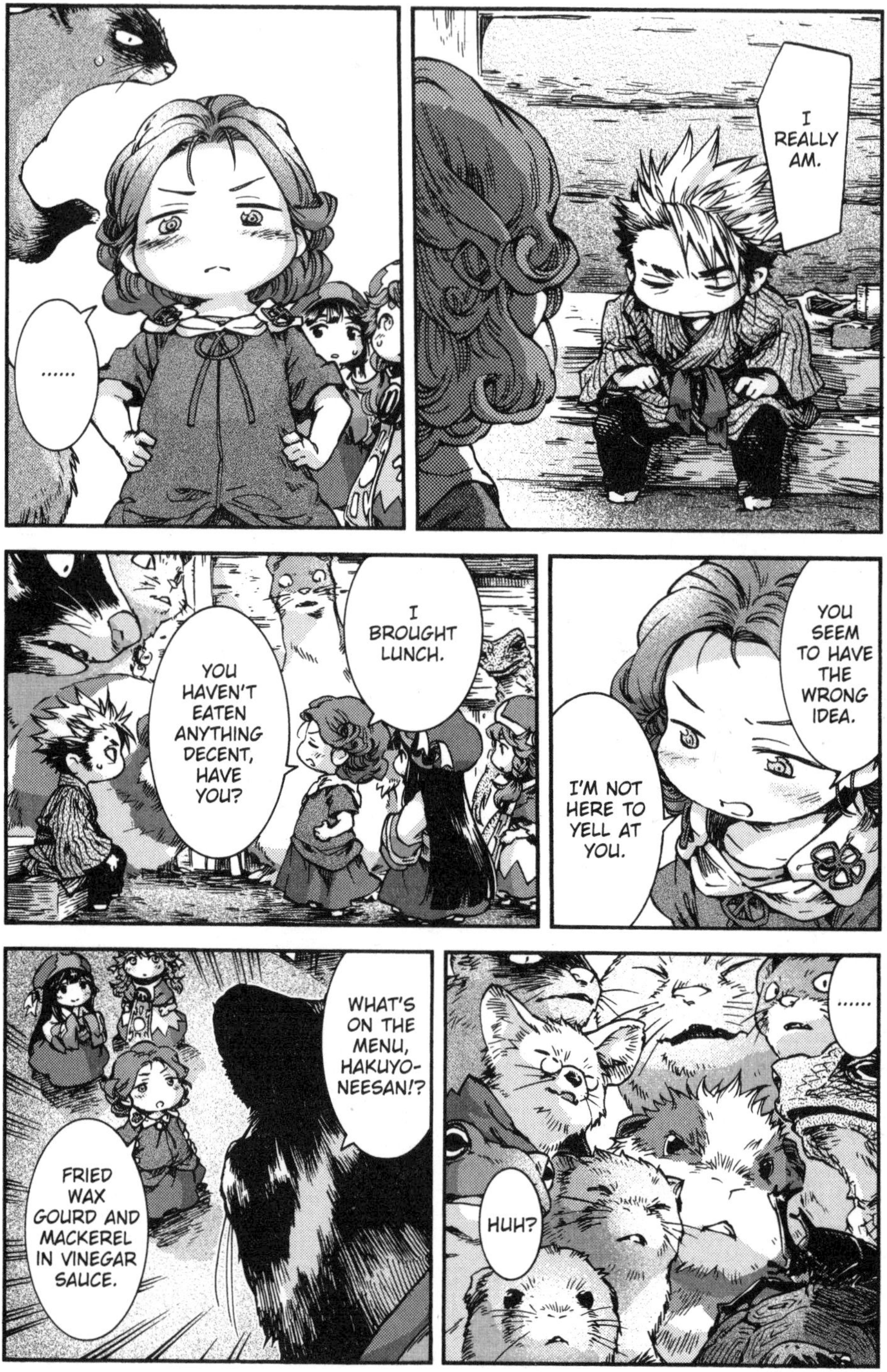
I REALLY AM.
......
YOU SEEM TO HAVE THE WRONG IDEA.
I'M NOT HERE TO YELL AT YOU.
I BROUGHT LUNCH.
YOU HAVEN'T EATEN ANYTHING DECENT, HAVE YOU?
......
HUH?
WHAT'S ON THE MENU, HAKUYO-NEESAN!?
FRIED WAX GOURD AND MACKEREL IN VINEGAR SAUCE.

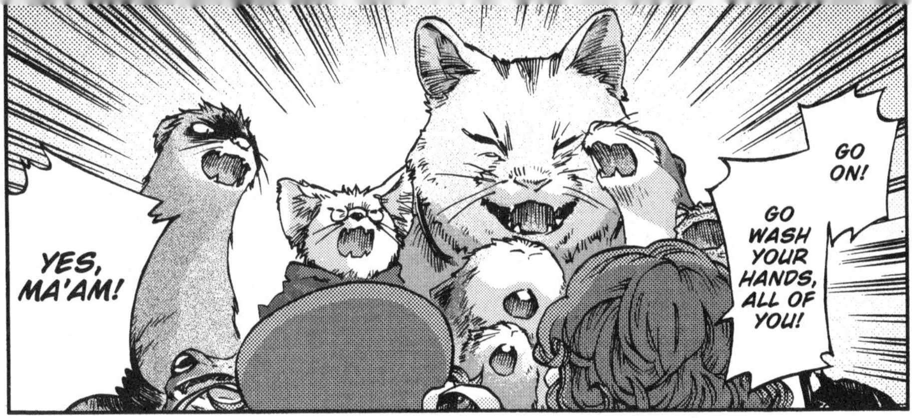
GO ON!
GO WASH YOUR HANDS, ALL OF YOU!
YES, MA'AM!

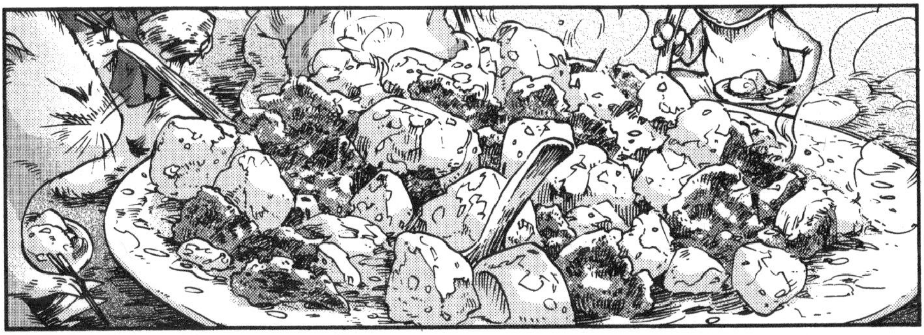

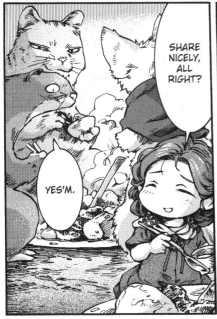

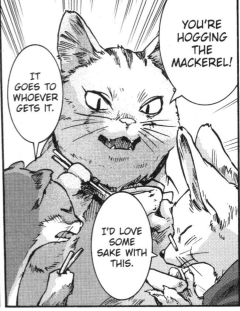

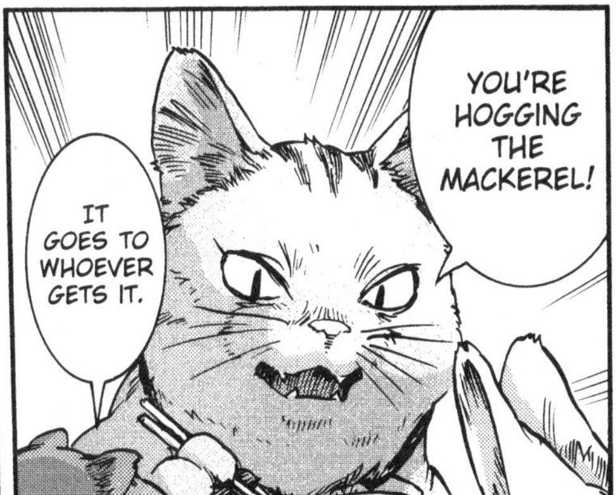
YOU'RE HOGGING THE MACKEREL!
IT GOES TO WHOEVER GETS IT.
I'D LOVE SOME SAKE WITH THIS.

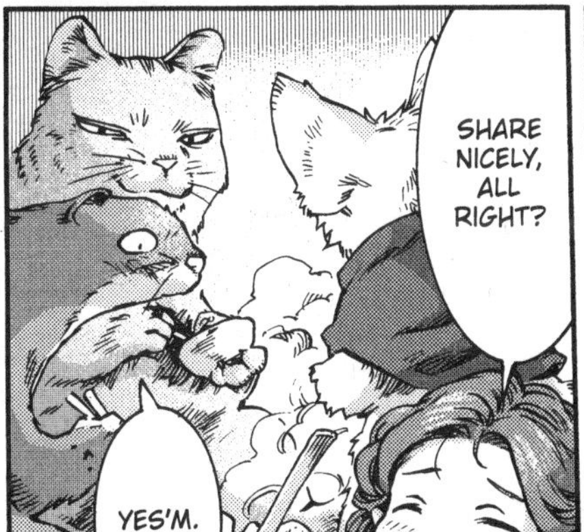
SHARE NICELY, ALL RIGHT?
YES'M.

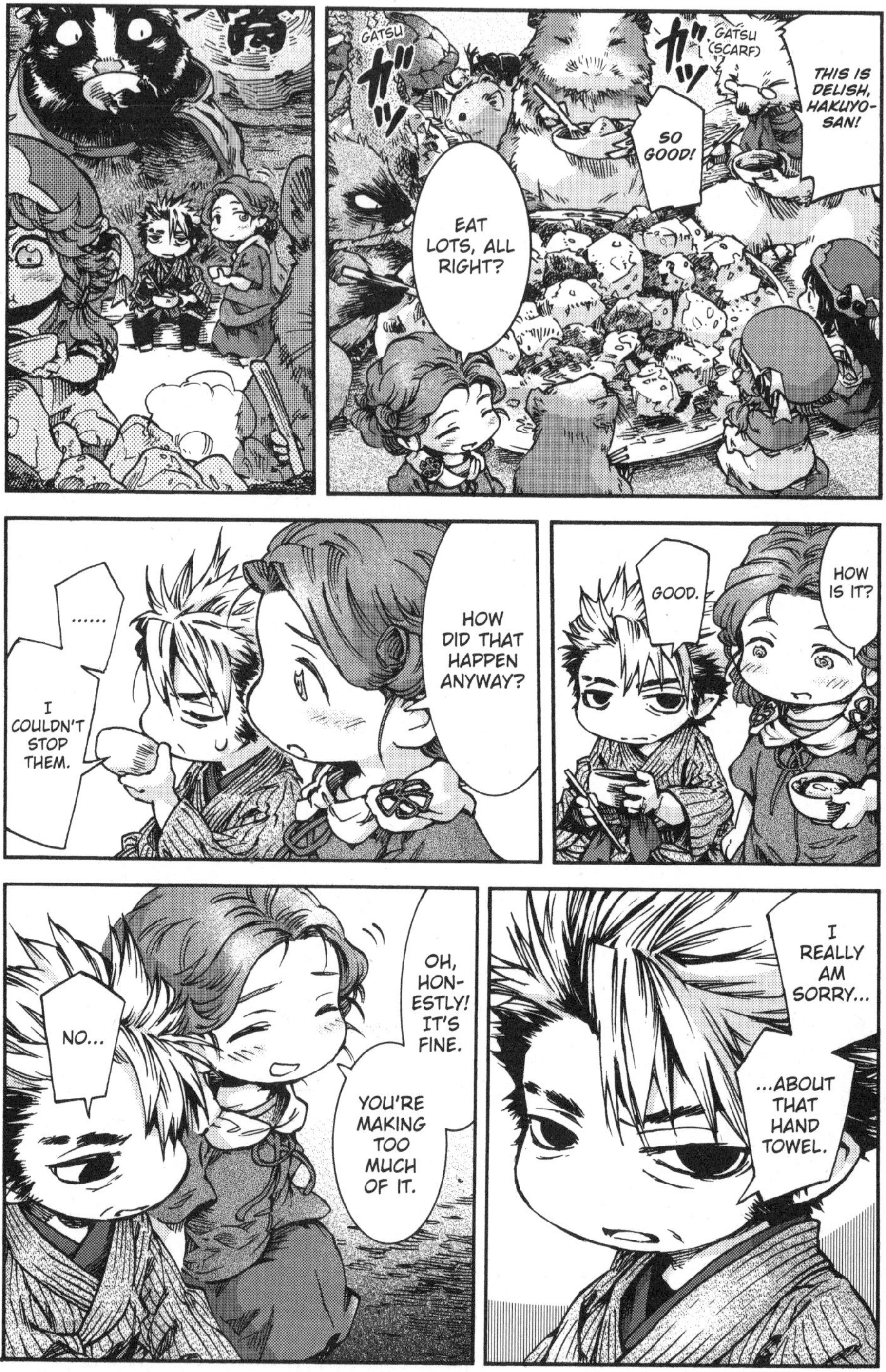
THIS IS DELISH, HAKUYO-SAN!
GATSU (SCARF)
SO GOOD!
GATSU
EAT LOTS, ALL RIGHT?
HOW IS IT?
GOOD.
HOW DID THAT HAPPEN ANYWAY?
......
I COULDN'T STOP THEM.
I REALLY AM SORRY...
...ABOUT THAT HAND TOWEL.
OH, HONESTLY! IT'S FINE.
YOU'RE MAKING TOO MUCH OF IT.
NO...

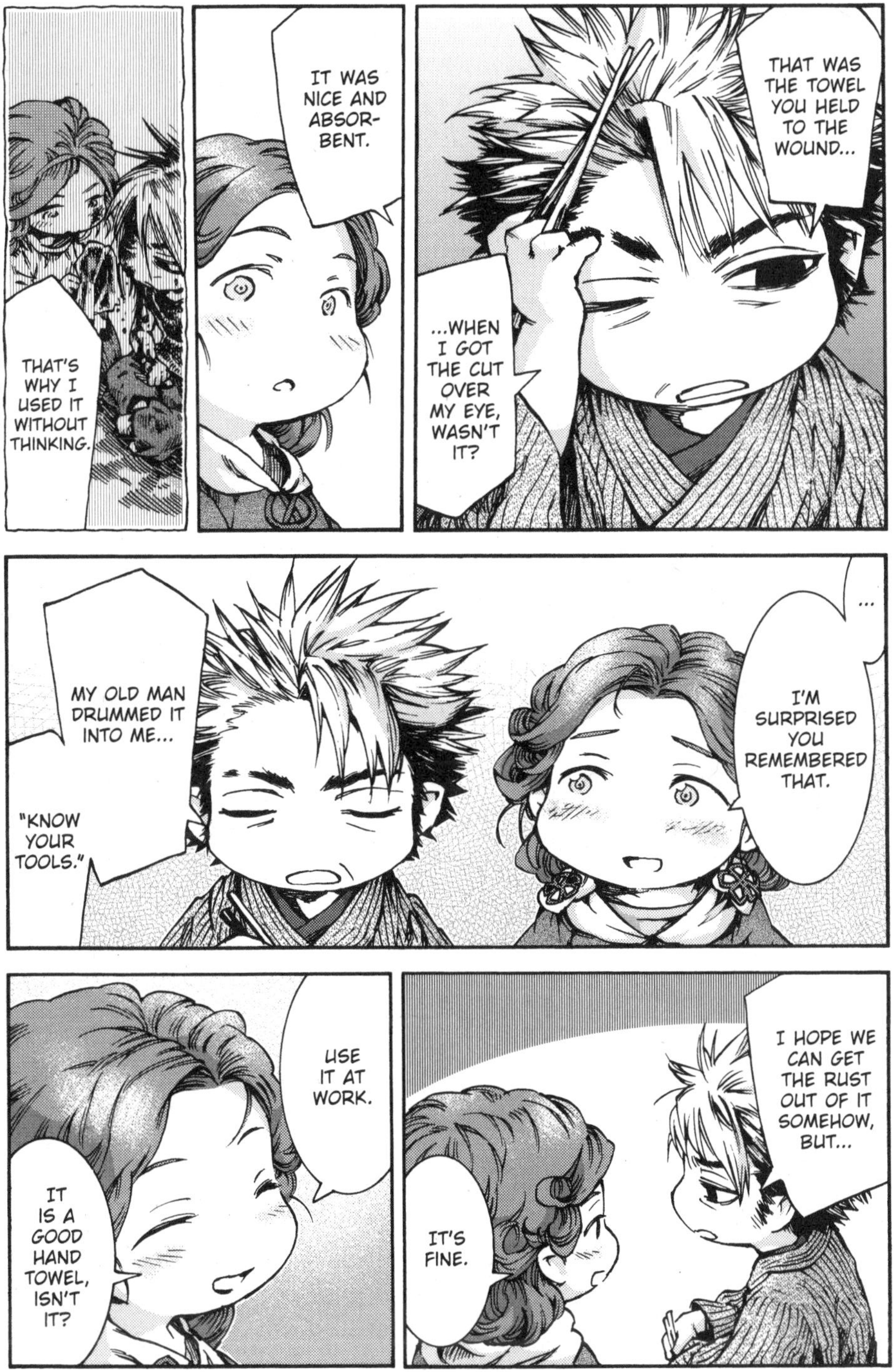
THAT WAS THE TOWEL YOU HELD TO THE WOUND...
...WHEN I GOT THE CUT OVER MY EYE, WASN'T IT?
IT WAS NICE AND ABSOR-BENT.
THAT'S WHY I USED IT WITHOUT THINKING.
...
I'M SURPRISED YOU REMEMBERED THAT.
MY OLD MAN DRUMMED IT INTO ME...
"KNOW YOUR TOOLS."
I HOPE WE CAN GET THE RUST OUT OF IT SOMEHOW, BUT...
IT'S FINE.
USE IT AT WORK.
IT IS A GOOD HAND TOWEL, ISN'T IT?

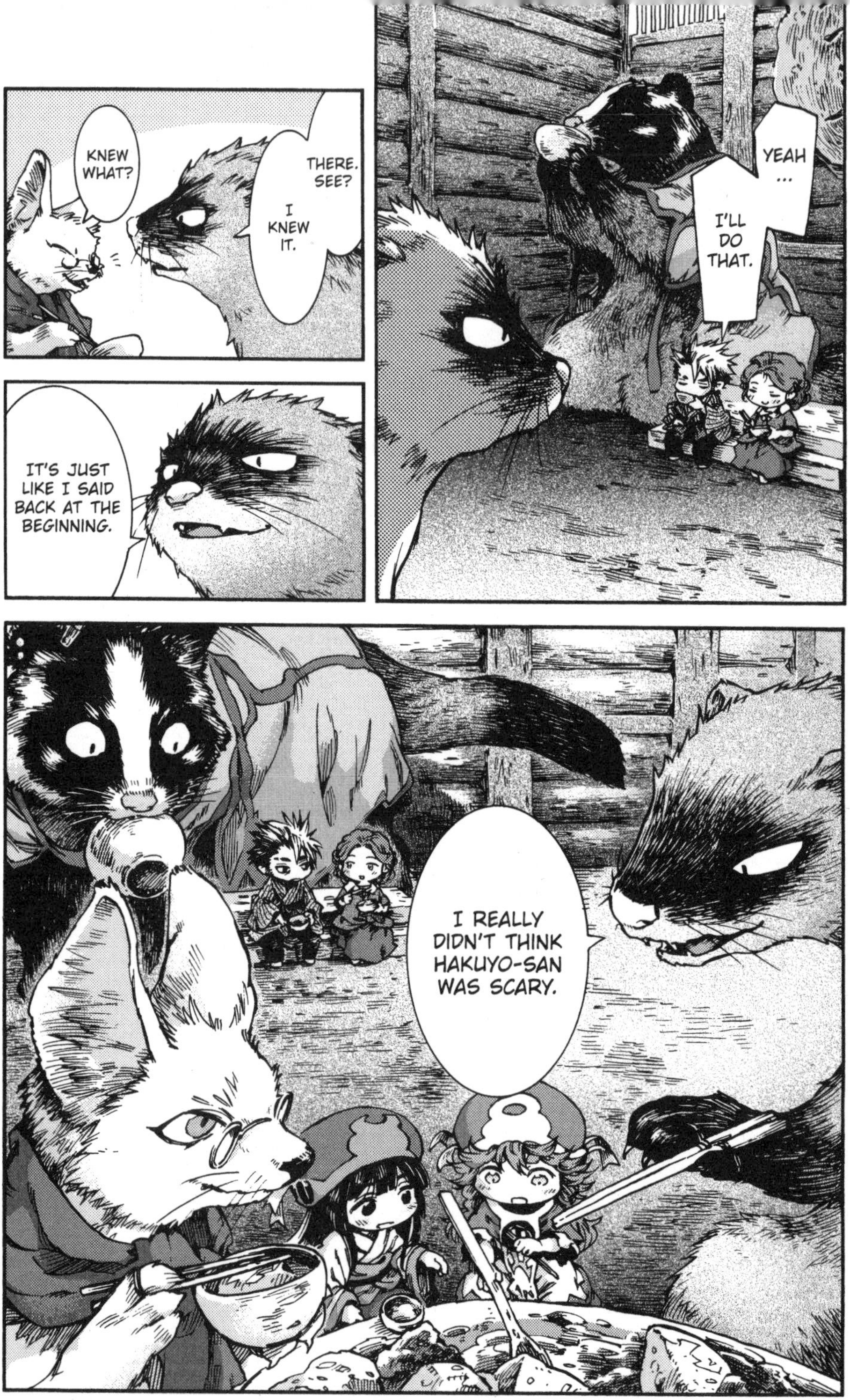
YEAH ...
I'LL DO THAT.
THERE. SEE?
I KNEW IT.
KNEW WHAT?
IT'S JUST LIKE I SAID BACK AT THE BEGINNING.
I REALLY DIDN'T THINK HAKUYO-SAN WAS SCARY.

Chapter 34 • End

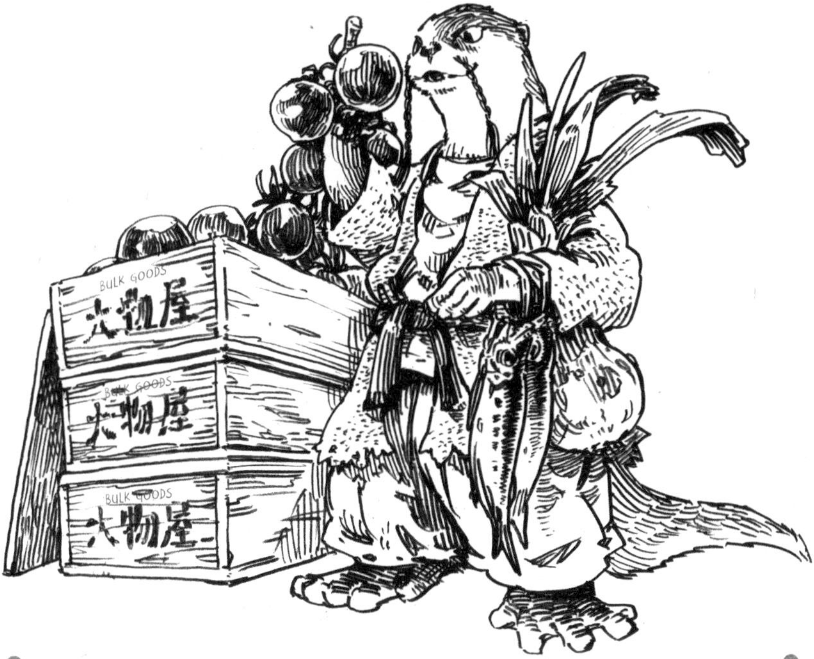
BULK GOODS
大物屋
BULK GOODS
大物屋
BULK GOODS
大物屋

A venerable old grocer in Makinata's East Wholesale Market. As the shop's name indicates, it sells whole vegetables, cuts of large fish, liquor, and seasonings by the barrel. Its clientele primarily consists of restaurant proprietors, large animals, and big families.

Its current owner is Mozukumaru, an Asian small-clawed otter. He says he was born in Port Town Arabi but left it for Makinata because he couldn't stand the sea wind. The previous owner took him in, and when they died, he took over for them. Since then, he's developed his own unique trade route, importing marine products from Arabi and exporting land products from Makinata.

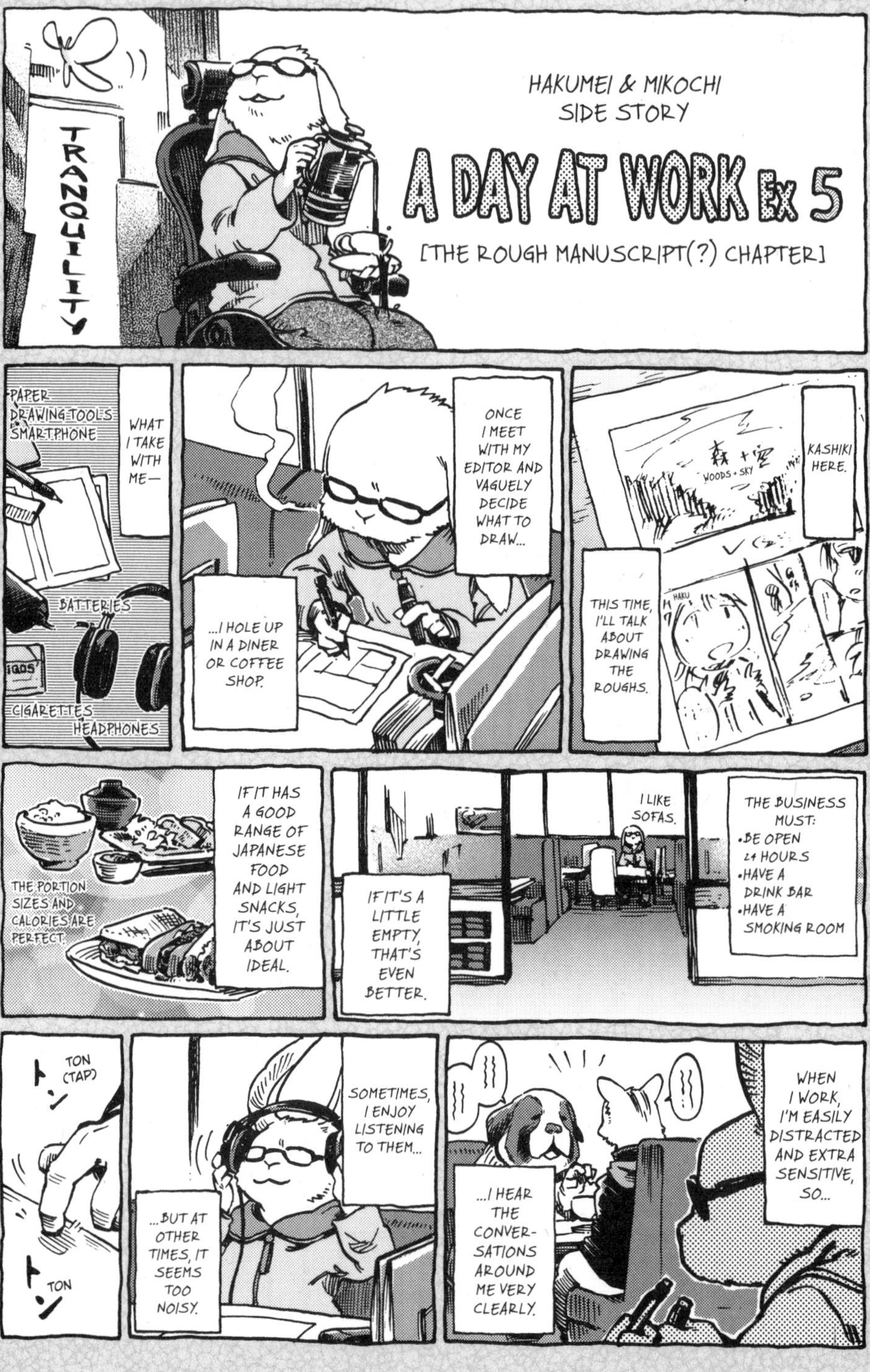
HAKUMEI & MIKOCHI SIDE STORY
A DAY AT WORK Ex 5
[THE ROUGH MANUSCRIPT(?) CHAPTER]
TRANQUILITY
KASHIKI HERE.
WOODS + SKY
THIS TIME, I'LL TALK ABOUT DRAWING THE ROUGHS.
ONCE I MEET WITH MY EDITOR AND VAGUELY DECIDE WHAT TO DRAW...
...I HOLE UP IN A DINER OR COFFEE SHOP.
WHAT I TAKE WITH ME—
PAPER
DRAWING TOOLS
SMARTPHONE
BATTERIES
CIGARETTES
HEADPHONES
I LIKE SOFAS.
THE BUSINESS MUST:
•BE OPEN 24 HOURS
•HAVE A DRINK BAR
•HAVE A SMOKING ROOM
IF IT'S A LITTLE EMPTY, THAT'S EVEN BETTER.
IF IT HAS A GOOD RANGE OF JAPANESE FOOD AND LIGHT SNACKS, IT'S JUST ABOUT IDEAL.
THE PORTION SIZES AND CALORIES ARE PERFECT.
WHEN I WORK, I'M EASILY DISTRACTED AND EXTRA SENSITIVE, SO...
...I HEAR THE CONVERSATIONS AROUND ME VERY CLEARLY.
SOMETIMES, I ENJOY LISTENING TO THEM...
...BUT AT OTHER TIMES, IT SEEMS TOO NOISY.
トン TON (TAP)
トン TON